RED SEA–BLACK RUSSIA

Prolegomena to the History of North Central Eurasia in
Antiquity and the Middle Ages

by

Jacques BAČIĆ

East European Monographs
Distributed by Columbia University Press, New York

1995

EAST EUROPEAN MONOGRAPHS, NO. CDXXI

To Sharifah Munirah ALATAS

Contents

ACKNOWLEDGEMENTS

Many people have helped me in a variety of ways with the conception, the shaping, and the production of this book. In the early stages Syed Hussein Alatas, Robert Austerlitz, Robert Belknap, Tibor Halasi-Kun, Stephen Fischer-Galati, and Rado Lencek gave me moral support and advice to start and continue. Jeffrey Barr, Lucy Bulliet, Alan Cameron, Robert Horn, and Ihor Ševčenko read kindly and critically an early version, giving me valuable advice. I have greatly profited from the vast knowledge and experience of Peter Martinez, Ronald Wixman, and others.

Eve Halasi-Kun is thanked for the countless hours and days which she spent preparing the manuscript for the public appearance by eliminating stylistic and factual inconsistencies.

Eugenie Bietry's editorial inverventions were numerous, most of them incorporated, and all are greatly appreciated. She also did the graphic design and typsetting.

ABBREVIATIONS

BGA	*Bibliotheca Geographorum Arabicorum*, ed. M.J. de Goeje (Lugduni Batavorum, 1870–94)
BzN	*Beiträge zur Namenforschung*
CAH	*Cambridge Ancient History*
CMH	*Cambridge Medieval History*
DAI	Constantine Porphyrogenitus, *De Administrando Imperio*, Greek text ed. Gy. Moravcsik, English transl. R.J.H. Jenkins (Budapest, 1949); Vol. II: *Commentary*, various authors, ed. R.J. Jenkins (London, 1962)
EI	*Encyclopaedia of Islam* (Leiden, 1913–42), new ed. (Leiden, 1960–)
EIr	*Encyclopaedia Iranica* (London, 1985–)
EJ	*Encyclopaedia Judaica*
MGH	*Monumenta Germaniae Historica*, ed. G.H. Pertz, et al. (Hannover, 1826–)
-- SS	Scriptores
-- SRGUS	Scriptores rerum Germanicarum ad usum scholarum
PG	*Patrologiae cursus completus*, ed. J. Migne: *Patrologia Graeca*, (Paris, 1844–66)
PVL	*Povest' vremennyx let* (Laurentian), transl. S.H. Cross and O.P. Sherbowitz–Wetzor (Cambridge, Mass., 1953)
PWRE	*Pauly-Wissova Real Encyclopaedie der classischen Altertumswissenschaften*, new ed. G. Wissowa, et al. (Stuttgart, 1893–)
REW	M. Vasmer, *Russisches Etymologisches Wörterbuch* (Heidelberg, 1950–58), transl. into Russian by O.N. Trubačev, 2nd ed., 4 vols. (Moscow, 1986–88)
SSS	*Słownik starożytności słowiańskich*, I– (Wrocław–Warsaw–Cracow, 1961–)
ŹADS	T. Lewicki, *Źródła arabskie do dziejów słowiańszczyzny*, vols. 1–2 (Wrocław, 1956–1977)

PROLOGUE

BLACK BEAVER–WHITE STONES

The urge to understand the origin and meaning of words, to
know their etymologies, is ancient, modern, and universal.
Isidore of Seville (570–636 AD) explains the purpose of
etymology:

> Etymology is the derivation of words, when the force of a verb or
> a noun is ascertained through interpretation. This Aristotle called
> *symbolon*, and Cicero, *adnotatio*, because it explains the names of
> things; as, for example, *flumen* is so called from *fluere*, because
> it arose from flowing. A knowledge of etymology is often
> necessary in interpretation, for, when you see whence a name has
> come, you grasp its force more quickly. For every consideration
> of a thing is clearer when its etymology is known.[1]

Some of Isidore's etymologies have been rejected and even
derided as simple-minded or wrong, but many have not been replaced by better substitutes. The following passage shows
Isidore's awareness of difficulties and traps one may face and
fall into while laboring in this field:

> [T]he etymologies of some names are not found, since certain
> things have received their names not according to the quality in
> which they originated, but according to man's arbitrary choice. ...
> Certain words also were formed by derivation from other words.
> ... Certain also from cries. ... Certain also have sprung from a
> Greek origin, and have changed over into the Latin. ... Other
> things have derived their names from the names of places, cities,

---

[1] *Etymologiae*, I.xxix; the English is from E. Brehaut, *An Encyclopedist
of the Dark Ages: Isidore of Seville* (New York, 1912), pp. 99–100.

or rivers. Many also are drawn from the languages of foreign peoples; whence their derivation is perceived with difficulty; for there are many barbarous words unknown to the Greeks and Latins.[2]

In the course of the past two centuries, linguists have established certain guidelines for those wishing to investigate the origin of words and names. By following these, one is expected to produce scientific and avoid folk etymologies. But, despite rapid advancement in the pertinent fields only a few who set out to explain proper names return with roses or pearls of knowledge. Often, an etymology offered by one scholar as the most accurate is readily rejected by others enthusiastically presenting "better" ones.

Like others, I have on many occasions succumbed to the urge to analyze words and proper names. Among these is a toponym that has been on my mind since early childhood—Crni Dabar, the name of a village in the county of Gospić, situated in the region called Lika in southwestern Croatia. The birthplace of my paternal grandmother, this village is a part of a larger agglomeration of hamlets named *Crni Dabar, Ravni Dabar*, and *Došen Dabar. Dabar* means "beaver" in Croatian, *ravni* is "plain or flat," *Došen* is a family name derived from the verb *doći* "to come," and *crni* means "black." Thus, the name *Crni Dabar* means "Black Beaver." Why black? What is the function of the color in this name?

Years ago I tried to answer this question by searching through written documents, but was unable to discover the reason why one of the three hamlets of Dabar was called black. Having obtained no answer to my query from the disciplines of history, linguistics, and lexicography, I turned to the simple folk as givers and users of the name, as well as the repository of oral wisdom. I went around asking the people of the county of Gospić, "Why is Black Beaver called 'black'?" The majority of my informants considered the question trivial or irrelevant and gave me such answers as: "Why do you care?," "What is it to you?," or "Who can tell?," all in the style of Balkan peasants who like to answer questions with questions of their own. How-

[2] *Ibid.*

ever, a garrulous minority offered to enlighten me. Some of their explanations of the function of the color attribute in the name Black Beaver were:

Explanation 1: A long time ago a woman of Black Beaver went to Gospić to buy red dye to color her family's woolens. The merchant had no red dye in stock, and sold her black dye instead. She discovered the merchant's deceit only after she had poured some of the dye into the vat. Seeing the dye was black, she did not know what to do. Also, she was stupid and believed the woolens would somehow come out red as they always had before, for the people of her village used to wear only red-colored woolens. So, she poured the remainder of the dye into the vat, and, of course, all her family's new stockings, socks, gloves, pullovers, and caps were colored black instead of the traditional red. The neighbors laughed at the appearance of the unfortunate woman's family, while the people from the neighboring hamlets began to call them *Crni Dabrani* "Black Beaverites." Little by little the whole hamlet came to be known as Black Beaver, though the villagers have continously worn red, not black, woolens.

Explanation 2: There was a time when every goat in Beaver was either white or mottled. There were no black goats. Then came a man from afar with five she goats and a billy goat. The billy goat was as black as could be. The newcomer settled in Beaver, and for seven years, the lifetime of the billy goat, the she goats of Beaver gave birth only to black kids. So, that section of Beaver where the man with the black billy goat had settled was named Black Beaver after the black billy goat and his offspring.

Explanation 3: In Turkish times a man from Gospić, which was then under Ottoman rule, went to a village on the Christian side of the border to buy a pig. As he was returning home, the Turkish border patrol, suspecting him of carrying dynamite to blow up the fortress of Medak (near Gospić), stopped and searched him and his wagon. The pig got loose, ran away, and hid someplace in the bushes near Beaver. The man went after the pig but could not find it. So, he cursed both the pig and the people of Beaver, for he thought they had stolen his pig. He said: "May you be black, accursed, and enslaved by the giaours!" Some years later the Christians of the Military Frontier captured Beaver from the Turks, who then named a section of the village Black Beaver, because the stolen pig owner's curse had come true.

Explanation 4: The Turks had conquered Croatia as far as Beaver. Then they stopped. Refugees from Beaver settled a short distance from the Turkish border. They began to call their abandoned village Black Beaver, because the Turks imposed heavy taxes on those who had stayed behind. This made their life black and miserable.

Explanation 5: During the Turkish rule all the Christian heroes of Lika perished in battles with Muslim Croats. Only one man survived. As he rode toward sunset, a black raven followed him from the field of the last battle. When the sun set behind the mountains the raven perched in a tree, while the hero, pitching his tent under that tree, decided to end his journey there. His descendants then renamed that section of the village Black Beaver, after the black raven that led their ancestor to the place.

Unfortunately, the folk wisdom regarding the origin of the attribute "black" in the name Black Beaver could not be verified. Since the obtained explanations were all equally plausible, or equally farfetched, I continued the search for the meaning of the color in the toponym Black Beaver hoping to find a satisfying answer. When I visited Lika several years ago there were very few people in and around Black Beaver. The herds of goats and sheep that used to fill the hills and valleys of that region of Croatia were also fewer in number. The depopulation of the countryside has been progressing through the Mediterranean countries since the Second World War, and Croatia is no exception. I drove along the dirt road used now mostly by lumber trucks. About a kilometer west of the village I had to pull off the one-lane road to let a truck with a Bosnian registration pass. The driver's radio was playing a well-known pseudo-folk song which starts:

> *Rujna zora sa istoka rudi,*
> *Siv' se soko' pod šatorom budi!*

(As the ruddy Dawn shows her redness from the east,
  A grey falcon awakens under his tent!)

This simple couplet struck me as an expression of some ancient truth, and I understood why. It is a Croatian adaptation of a celebrated verse from the *Iliad* and the *Odyssey*, which appears in many places of both epics, with the following couplet as a typical example:

De ēmos ērigeneia rhododaktylos Ēos phanē,
kai tote epeita anagonto meta euryn straton Achaiōn.

(But when the young Dawn showed again with her rosy fingers,
they put forth to sea toward the wide camp of the Achaians.)[3]

That the east is red, rosy, golden, or yellow has been known to people in the temperate zone of the earth since time immemorial. In the 1960s, this notion was carried through the airwaves and printing presses as both the title of a Chinese song and that of a popular book *The East Is Red,*[4] with the red representing the color of the flag, star, and other symbols of communism, as summed up by the following Croatian marching song:

Od Jadrana do Kitaja
Crveni se barjak vije!

(From the Adriatic to Cathay
Red flags fly!)

We see that the east is universally represented by red, ruddy, yellow, or golden colors. Therefore, one might ask if the other cardinal points of the compass are also symbolized by appropriate colors.

I drove past Black Beaver toward sunset and a beech forest, looking for a place the natives call *Bile stine* "white stones." Years earlier a fire had destroyed a large tract of fir and beech forest around White Stones, and I wanted to see how the trees had grown back after the devastation. I arrived just before sunset to an area covered with younger trees, and started to look for the white stones, which I imagined as weather-bleached cliffs. Though there were no cliffs in sight, the place was unmistakably the site of the White Stones fire. I got out of the car and started to walk toward a shed and an old man who appeared to be at home there. A native of Black Beaver, he turned out to be my relative (his mother and my great-grandmother were sisters). Having exchanged obligatory civilities and reestablished kinship,

---

[3] *Iliad,* I.477–8; the English is from R. Lattimore's translation (Chicago, 1951).
[4] M. Williams, *The East Is Red* (New York, 1967), pp. 30–37, where the song is described and some lyrics quoted.

he explained that his job was to repair the road after heavy rains by filling the potholes with earth and pebbles. I asked him if the place was really White Stones, and, if so, where were the stones? At first he was puzzled by my question, then said: "The stones you are looking for are not of the type that people call 'cliffs,' but the stuff you see over there. Those must be the stones you want to see." He was pointing to remains of house walls, ramparts, and other physical evidence of human habitation abandoned long ago.

Suddenly I realized that there once was a village called White Stones. Situated west of Beaver, the attribute white signified its western geographical location. This realization convinced me that the black color attribute in my grandmother's native village reflected that place's geographical location, the north.

As the sun "went to bed" into the Adriatic, to borrow an expression for sunset from the natives of that part of Croatia, the original meaning of the attributes of color in the toponyms Black Beaver and White Stones appeared to me in all its primeval beauty and simplicity. The ancient Croats of Lika did not add the adjective "black" to one of the three hamlets of the village of Beaver because it had *appeared* black to them, nor did the village of White Stones obtain its name because of its white appearance, but because they were *located* in specific directions in relation to the people who first named them. Indeed, the village of Black Beaver was called "black" because it was to the north, the village called White Stones was named "white" because it was west of the namegiver.

This method of differentiation may go back to an ancient tradition of designating the east, as the abode of the sun, with bright colors, the west with absence of color, that is, white or dark, and the north, as the domain of darkness, with color black. For example, this notion was current in Homeric Greek, as seen by the way Odysseus described the location of his native Ithaca. This was an island, he told King Alcinous, lying "toward darkness" in relation to the neighboring islands which were "toward sunrise." By "darkness" Homer means the north.[5]

---

[5] "*pros zophon, hai de t' aneuthe pros ēō t' ēelion te,*" *Odyssey*, IX.26; Strabo, 1.2.28, interprets *pros zophon* as "toward the north"; R. Fitzgerald, *The Odyssey* (New York, 1961), as "northwest." (Unless otherwise indicated

Alcinous' Kingdom was on Scheria Island which the ancients identified with Corcyra (Corfu), originally occupied by Liburni.[6] In historical times the Liburni held another island also named Corcyra. It was north of the first-named Corcyra, that is, in the "direction of darkness," from the perspective of Greeks and Romans who, for this reason, called it *Korkyra melaina, Corcyra nigra* "Black Corcyra." Medieval Croats called their island Krkar without any attribute, while their descendants today use the name Korčula, the Venetians Curzola.

While the village of White Stones no longer exists, and its color attribute had lost its relevance, the color attribute in the name Black Beaver is still functional, differentiating today this hamlet from Ravni Beaver and Došen Beaver. When asked to explain the name Black Beaver, the common people imaginatively produce answers which show that they believe the color reflects the village's physical, moral, or emotional qualities. Scholars who argue that *all* places (and even peoples!) named after colors look like the colors reflected in their names are often as far from the truth as are the common people with their colorful folk etymologies.

QUALITAS CORPORIS *OR* POSITIO LOCI?

In the tenth century, Bishop Liudprand of Cremona wrote:

> *Gens quaedam est sub aquilonis parte constituta, quam a qualitate corporis Greci vocant* Ρο υ σ ι ο ς, *Rusios, nos vero a positione loci nominamus Nordmannos. Lingua quippe Teutonum nord aquilo, man autem dicitur homo; unde et Nordmannos aquilonares homines dicere possumus.*

(There is a certain northern people whom the Greeks call Rusii, "*les roux*" from the colour of their skins, while we from the position of their country call them Nordmanni, "northmen." In the

---

all English versions of the Greek and Latin classical writers are from the Loeb Classical Library editions.)

  [6] *Odyssey*, VI.1–11; Strabo, 6.2.4; 7.3.6.

Teuton language "nord" means "north," and "man" means "human being," so that Nordmanni is equivalent to "men of the north.")[7]

Liudprand had heard the name *Rusii* in Constantinople. It reminded him of the color adjective *rhousios* "red." The only "red" thing he could see about this people was their ruddy complexion, so he concluded that the name must be descriptive, referring to the people's *qualitas corporis*. The Latinized form Rusii derives from a colloquial form of that people's name, while educated Rhomaeans preferred to refer to the same people as *hoi Rhōs, Skythai, Boreoi Skythai, Tauroskythai, Hyperboreoi, Hellēnes, Dromitai, Achilleiodromitai*, etc. Since the Rusii he had met at Constantinople had come from the north, Liudprand identified them also as *Nordmanni* "men of the north."

The globe abounds in names of villages, towns, cities, regions, countries, rivers, lakes, islands, seas, mountains, and peoples which derive from words designating color, while countless names are further defined with attributes of color. Ever since antiquity people have been trying to explain such names. For example, the explanations of the functions of the attributes "red" in the name Red Sea, "white" in the name White Russia, and "black" in the name Black Russia offered by scholars over the centuries are as unverifiable, implausible, and contradictory as are those I collected from the common folk of Lika concerning the origin of the attribute "black" in Black Beaver. The profusion of popular and scholarly explanations of color attributes in geographical names and in names of peoples is an indication that there is no consensus on their function.

Indeed, in analyzing names that derive from words designating colors and those that are limited by color attributes we are treading on a very shaky ground.

First, unless a name is explainable from a known language, it is very difficult to establish its etymology. It is the same with color names. The question becomes insoluble when unrecorded extinct languages are involved. Thus, for example, appellations such as Olympus, Corinth, Danube are still not satisfactorily

---

[7] *Antapodosis*, V.15 [= *MGH SS*. III (36). ed. G.H. Pertz (Hannover, 1839)]. The English is from *The Works of Liudprand of Cremona*, transl. by F.A. Wright (New York, 1930), p. 185.

explained, while no serious difficulties exist with designations such as Kara Dağ, Belgrade, Bistrica, whose meaning is clear in the languages of the peoples who coined them.

Second, it is rarely possible to establish whether a color designation stands for the named object's physical appearance or for its geographical location. To isolate those natural features and settlements which were given their color attributes according to their relative geographical position is a rather complex matter.

For example, we know that in the name of the Black Sea the color attribute is a fixed epithet, for, in most living languages it stands for the color black. Yet, the same sea was called *Pontos Euxinos* "hospitable sea" by the ancients. A team of scholars labored a long time to establish, though only tentatively, that the Greek term *euxinos* is an antonym of *axenos* "inhospitable," which, in turn, is allegedly a folk rendering of that sea's unattested Old Iranian designation *axšaena* "black." Assuming that the ancient Iranians had called the Black Sea "black," we are still far from understanding what could have prompted the designation. Did the sea look black to them, or did they name it so for another reason?[8]

The designation Pacific Ocean is the modern name of the Eastern Sea of the ancients. But the section of this great body of water, where the Mediterranean peoples imagined the "ultimate" east, we call the Yellow Sea and believe that the name derives from its supposedly yellow color, which is also the color of the Yellow River that empties into it, and of the "yellow" people settled on its shores. However, this same sea was called *al-Baḥr al-akhḍar* "green sea" by medieval Arabs. The Arabic designation, attested relatively late, may be a translation of a name given to that sea by some ancient people who used attributes of color unrelated to the physical appearance of the named objects. The fact that this sea is called yellow by some, green by others, seems to indicate that the colors refer to the sea's location rather than to its appearance.

Further, to those familiar with the Slavic languages it is clear that the name *Belgrade* signifies "white city." But why is this

---

[8] In the Middle Ages, the Black Sea was often called Russian Sea by foreigners and Holy Sea by Russians.

particular city distinguished with the attribute "white"? The city's earlier name, *Singidunum*, is readily recognized as Celtic because of the element *-dunum* "town," attested in names of numerous settlements in the Celtic realms. But what is the meaning of the word *singi*? Since it also appears in the name of the Dacian town *Singidava* (*dava* "town"), some believe it is the name of a people, but no one really knows.

Third, the difficulty in finding correct explanations for color attributes in geographical names is compounded by the fact that there is no generally known systematical study of the use of colors to indicate the directions of the horizon.

In conclusion, though Liudprand was correct regarding the meaning of the ethnonym Rusii, he erred in explaining the function of the color red as reflecting the *qualitas corporis* of the designated people. He did not know that the ethnonym was coined by people who used colors to indicate the geographical location of the named objects, their *positio loci*. The Black Beaver–White Stones pair is a clear example that color attributes in such names may more readily be understood by people who use colors both to describe the physical appearance of objects and also their relative spatial positions. Indeed, several Native American peoples use sets of four or five colors in this sense. It appears certain that the Croats who named Black Beaver and White Stones applied at least two colors for this purpose. The present work will show that various other peoples, such as those who coined the names Red Sea, Rusii, White Russia, Red Russia, and Black Russia have also used colors to represent the directions of the horizon.

Sixteen years ago, O.N. Trubačëv wrote: "It is desirable that a special study be devoted to vestiges of color symbolism in designating the cardinal points among the Slavs."[9] May my effort be accepted as a partial fulfillment of this scholar's desideratum.

---

[9] Quoted in V.A. Nikonov, "Naimenovanija stran sveta," *Ètimologija* (1984), p. 164.

INTRODUCTION

RUSSIA AS THE OTHER

In 1988, Belarus, Russia, and Ukraine marked, with muted pomp, the completion of their first millennium as Christian nations. The peoples who profess Islam, Hinduism, Buddhism, and other religions ignored the event, while some in the West tried to cast it against the significance they see in the end of the second millennium of the Christian era. These East Slavic nations (known traditionally as White, Great, and Little Russians), whose country has generally been known abroad as Russia since the Middle Ages, occupy a remarkably unique place in the imaginative and scholarly writings of the peoples of Western Europe and North America. There, the sight and sound of the name "Russia" frequently evokes emotional responses in a great many people, such as irrational fear, violent hatred, complacent dismissal, contempt, and, last but not least, tender love. Some Westerners see Russia and the Russians as the embodiment of evil, while others hold that they stand for everything good in humankind. In the minds of the Western elites and the common people, Russia is engraved as *the other* portion of the planet. Many among the Westerners still insist on a bi-polar division of humanity and perceive the Russians as *them*. The reason for this lies in Russia's aspiration to the status of a great power over the past three centuries.

Russian history used to be divided into two periods: pre-1917 and post-1917. Between the French and the Russian February and October revolutions, when the dominant form of government in the West were constitutional monarchies and parliamentary democracies, with Christian religion and divine-grace monarchs considered in growing measures as quaint survivals of the past,

1

Russia was hated and feared for its stubborn adherence to autocracy and Christian Orthodoxy. Because Russia was regarded as the principal defender of the *status quo*, the enemy and suppressor of various "progressive" movements sweeping through Europe between the Congress of Vienna and World War I, the Russians were generally portrayed as awe-inspiring "Asiatics" who had no right to live in "civilized" Europe. Russia's participation in the partitions of Poland, its contribution to the destruction of Napoleon's empire, its role as an ally of "reactionary" Austria and Croatia in the putting down of the Hungarian uprising of 1848, Russia's victories in the wars of "liberation" with Sweden, Persia, and Ottoman Turkey, are reasons why pre-1917 Russia was so much demonized by its rivals and enemies.

After the February and October revolutions had destroyed tsarist autocracy and Christian Orthodoxy in Russia, new Russia began to be viewed by some as a model to be imitated and even as a utopia. At the same time, Russia's desire to maintain its rank as a great power rekindled old hatreds. Its victory over the Third Reich, as well as its nuclear capabilities, became the source of new anxieties for Russia's rivals and enemies.

The earliest enemies of communist Russia accused its new leaders of engaging in and propagating free love and building a godless society. Paradoxically, as secularism, atheism, pornography, sexual licentiousness, and consumerism came to characterize Western culture, Soviet Russia once again became an object of hatred, "provoked" now by the alleged prudishness and a quasi-religious devotion of its people and elites to the established state ideology.

Due to these facts, the ethnonym "Russi" has a complex semasiology in the Western world. On the one hand, during the past two centuries the Russians have been portrayed as a bellicose nation. Soviet Russia's "seriousness" has even inspired some imaginative exegesists of Old and New Testament prophets to identify Russia as the leading nation in the Gog and Magog federation of peoples at Armageddon.[1] It is clear that their past

---

[1] A representative example of this genre is H. Lindsey's *The Late Great Planet Earth* (Grand Rapids, Mich., 1970), especially Chapter 5, "Russia Is a Gog," pp. 48–60. Serious scholars dismiss this type of literature as low brow pulp. Nevertheless, a copy of this "best-seller of the decade" made an

victories over many peoples and states, their supposedly warlike character, and their alleged severity and moral purity are the reasons why the Russians occupy a place of doubtful honor at Armageddon. On the other hand, they are perceived by many in a diametrically opposite light, as a peace-loving people who would do anything, even allow others to enslave them, to avoid war. They have earned the latter reputation solely because they *are Slavs.* Indeed, the Slavs, and especially the Russians, who are often declared to be the "quintessential" Slavs, have for the past two hundred years been described as a peaceful people by many Western writers. While this idealized Slavic ethnic trait continues to be admired by some people, the erroneous belief that the Slavs are peaceful and even slave-like by nature is frequently adduced as argument that they could not have played an active role in the shaping of the destiny of humankind, including their own.

Currently, Russia and its rivals appear to be making efforts to accept each other as equal members of the world community and to coexist in the spirit of interdependence. It is too early to tell whether the West will put an end to a bi-polar division of the world and stop seeing Russia as *the other.* But, even if Russia were no longer perceived as *the other* its place may be taken by another nation or nations in the imagination of those in the Western world who need an enemy.[2]

In modern history, the Great, White, and Little Russians, dominated demographically, economically, culturally, and politically a colossus of a state that spanned most of North Eurasia and Central Asia. In the recently dissolved Union of Soviet Socialist Republics they numbered about 215 million souls out of the population of 290 million, or 75% of its total. Though Belarus and Ukraine figured independently among the founding members of the United Nations in addition to the Soviet Union representing Russia proper as well as the other republics, the whole Soviet Union was almost universally called Russia. This is because Russia, known officially after July 10, 1918, as the

---

impact on Ronald Reagan, inspiring his speech writer to declare the Soviet Union the "evil empire."

   [2] Ukraine, known historically as Little Russia, and the Muslim peoples may eventually fill this need.

Russian Soviet Federated Republic, played the leading role on December 30, 1922, when the Soviet Union was established as a federation comprising Russia, Belarus, Ukraine, and Transcaucasia. The Russian Soviet Federated Republic, itself, had succeeded to the Russian Republic which was proclaimed on March 16, 1917, when the Grand Duke Michael refused the throne of the Russian Empire offered to him after his brother Tsar Nicholas II had abdicated on his and his son's, Alexis, behalf.

Since Peter the Great's reign the titles of tsars of Russia included the Latin term *imperator*, in addition to the traditional Russian honorifics tsar, *velikij knjaz* "grand duke," and *samoderžec* "autocrat." The same emperor introduced the name *Rossija* as a designation for the Empire. Ignoring the fact that a fair portion of North Central Eurasia had been known abroad as Russia since the ninth century AD, Russophobe publicists and even some careless scholars claim that Russia was an "invention" of Tsar Peter. In fact, Peter merely replaced at home the native, traditional name *Rus'* with a more "elegant," Latinate, or international name *Rossija*. Nevertheless, Russia continues to be colloquially and poetically known by its people as Rus', evidenced by the Soviet national anthem which begins as follows:

> *Sojuz nerušimyj respublik svobodnyx*
> *Naveki splotila mogučaja Rus'!*
> (This eternal, indestructible union of free republics
> Was created by mighty Rus'.)

THEORIES OF RUSSIA'S ORIGIN

Normanists

Concerning the origin and early history of Russia two schools of historiography are dominant today: the Normanist and the Anti-Normanist. Though generally *tertium non datur*, scholars who cannot be pigeonholed into one of these two categories are described as Eurasianists. The Normanist school was founded on September 6, 1749, by G.F. Müller (1705–1783) when he was asked by the Russian Imperial Academy to deliver his lecture entitled "On the Origin of the Russian People and Their Name"

(*De origine gentis et nominis Russorum*). The lecture was the result of Müller's research into Russia's past initiated by G.S. Bayer (1694–1738). Russian patriots interrupted the scholar because he intended to prove that the name and the founder of the dynasty which ruled Russia until the end of the sixteenth century, as well as the first state organization among the East Slavs, were of Scandinavian origin. The brave warriors who allegedly accomplished these deeds were variously called Vikings, Varangians, and Normans.

Although over the past three centuries some details have been added to the theory on Russia's origins as formulated by Müller, its Normanist structure has remained basically unchanged. While tidbits culled from writings of medieval Muslims have also been added to the primary sources, scholarly exegeses of this corpus have not brought us closer to a solution, and neither archaeology nor linguistics, as *ancillae historiae*, have advanced our knowledge of Russian origins sufficiently to cause us either to accept or reject the Normanist theory.

The cornerstone of the Normanist theory, the belief that Russian history began in 862 with a band of Russi, led by three brothers, coming to Russia, rests on medieval tales, misunderstood by modern scholars. In our opinion, those who hold that the name "Russi" was imported in 862 to northern Russia from "overseas" do so at the expense of common sense and recorded facts. First, they are unable to identify positively a region in Eurasia outside of Russia where the Russi supposedly originated. Some maintain that the east coast of Sweden, known as Roslagen, was their *Urheimat*, others claim it was Denmark, and still others believe the Russi came from Frisia. The island of Rügen is also frequently indicated as the homeland of the mysterious Russi, and Roussillon in southern France has often been suggested as their cradle. These hypotheses cannot be corroborated by trustworthy sources and thus remain mere speculations. Second, this fundamental Normanist tenet must also be rejected for reasons of chronology. While Normanist scholars maintain that the name Russi was brought by "Russian" immigrants to North Russia in 862 and gradually expanded to the Pontic basin, there is evidence that a Russian kaganate had existed in the area that is present-day Ukraine (Little Russia) prior to 839. We reject both dates as the birthdates of Russia because we shall show that ancestral namesakes of the Russi were settled along the shores of the Black Sea in the fourth century and in the Derbent Gate area in the mid-seventh century. Regarding the ethnicity of the first Russians, the Normanist school insists they belonged to the Germanic branch of the white race. Although some of the early Russians had Germanic-sounding names and many more might have spoken or understood one or several Germanic languages, this is not sufficient to support the claim that the Russians were a Germanic people. This Normanist tenet rests on the belief that the Slavs are a peaceful people, and, since the medieval Russians were warlike, they could not be Slavs but Germans. The father of this error is Johann Gottfried von Herder (1744—1803) who portrayed the Slavs as a musical, peaceful people unwilling and unable to make war.[3] During the past two centuries the scholars cultivating the field of Slavic studies have walked bent under a load of sweeping pronouncements about the nature of the Slavs made not only by Herder but also by some later writers whose ignorant, mean-spirited, and racist opinions permeate even scholarly interpretations of the primary sources on the Slavs. As an example of such opinions, we cite Hegel, as the most popular and enduring "authority" on the nature of the Slavs:

> We find, moreover, in the East of Europe, the great Slavonic nation, whose settlements extended west of the Elbe to the Danube. The Magyars (Hungarians) settled in between them. In Moldavia, Wallachia and northern Greece appear the Bulgarians, Servians, and Albanians, likewise of Asiatic origin—left behind as broken barbarian remains in the shocks and counter-shocks of the advancing hordes. These people did, indeed, found kingdoms and sustain spirited conflicts with the various nations that came across their path. Sometimes, as an advanced guard—an intermediate nationality—they took part in the struggle between Christian Europe and unchristian Asia. The Poles even liberated beleaguered Vienna from the Turks; and the Sclaves have to some extent been drawn within the sphere of Occidental Reason. Yet this entire body of peoples remains excluded from our consideration, because hitherto it has not appeared as an

---

[3] J. Bačić, *The Emergence of the Sklabenoi (Slavs)* (Ann Arbor, Mich., 1983), pp. 18—20.

independent element in the series of phases that Reason has assumed in the World.[4]

Hegel's followers, not caring to waste too many words on such "ahistorical" people, simply dismissed most or all Slav as: "ethnic trash" (Karl Marx, referring to Slovaks, Slovenes, Croats, and Serbs), or "Untermenschen" (Adolf Hitler, speaking of all Slavs and Slavic Jews and Romi [Gypsies]).

Though Herder might be excused for his distortion of the true nature of the Slavs because he was insufficiently familiar with the primary sources on the early history of that people, the same generosity should not be extended to this great scholar's later disciples who should know better. The Herderians cling so stubbornly to their dated views on the Slavs that, when they are shown passages from writers of late antiquity and the Middle Ages proving that the Slavs made as much war as music, they hasten to argue that the people whom the contemporary witnesses had called Slavs could not have been Slavs, who, according to Herder, were a peaceful people, but rather warlike Germans or Turks. A good example of a Herderian interpretation of the sources on Russian origins is Ernst Kunik's *Die Berufung der schwedischen Rodsen durch die Finnen und Slawen* (St. Petersburg, 1844). Kunik continues to have many epigones.

In sum, as Herder's followers, the Normanists view the Slavs as a peaceful and an un-warlike people playing a minor part in the shaping of Russia. The Normanist school of Russian historiography continues to flourish upon the embedded belief that the destiny of North Central Eurasia was shaped by the nomadic and wandering Iranian, Germanic, and Turkic tribes, while the native and generally settled Baltic, Finno-Ugric, Slavic, and other *Untermenschen* were mere ethnographic material in the able hands of these foreign *Uebermenschen*.

---

[4] Georg Wilhelm Friedrich Hegel, *The Philosophy of History*, transl. by J. Sibree (Dover Publ., New York, 1956), p. 350.

Anti-Normanists

Beginning with Lomonosov, many scholars have tried to disprove the Normanist theory. The body of writing produced as a reaction against it is labeled Anti-Normanist.[5] Because they assail a theory based on racist opinions that irritate them, some Anti-Normanist scholars have produced works that are rather polemical. Exaggerations found in the antitheses of the Anti-Normanists, though unacceptable, are understandable reactions to the assault on the common sense and Slavic national dignity propagated in the theses of the Normanist school. Nevertheless, it is unfair to dismiss all Anti-Normanists as over-enthusiastic Russophiles, for, if it could be proven beyond reasonable doubt that the founders of Russia belonged to a Germanic tribe, Byelorussian, Ukrainian, and Russian historians would accept this and would find a way to teach their people how to live with that fact. After all, the Scandinavian Rurik would not have been the only foreigner ever on the throne of Russia. One of the greatest Russian monarchs, Catherine the Great, was a German, Lenin was of mixed stock, Jakov Sverdlov, the first president of the Russian Soviet Federated Republic, was a Jew, and Stalin was a Georgian, to name only some of the more prominent "Russians."

Eurasianists

The Normanist theory of Russian origins, though still popular, can no longer satisfy objective historians. Today, only those unfamiliar with the primary sources on early Russia, or those who accept *a priori* the superiority of the Germanic race may be comfortable with it. At the same time, the Anti-Normanist corpus is too antithetical to serve as a synthesis. Seeking a way

---

[5] The best survey of the Normanist—Anti-Normanist controversy is A. Mošin's "Varjago-russkij vopros," *Slavia*, X (Prague, 1931), pp. 109–36, 343–79, 501–53. For a more recent discussion, *see*, G. Schramm, "Die Herkunft des Namens Rus': Kritik des Forschungstandes," *Forschungen zur osteuropäischen Geschichte*, XXX (1982), pp. 7–49.

out of the impasse, some historians have produced studies which may be classified as Eurasianist.

Among the attempts to bridge the chasm which separates the Normanists from the Anti-Normanists a notable place belongs to the works of George Vernadsky. In his search for Russia's origins he refused to be bogged down on the shore of one lake or to the valley of one river. He let his imagination range across the vast expanse of North Central Eurasia, from sunrise to sunset, from the Black Sea to the White Sea. Neither was he bound by chronological strictures imposed by the reductionists who begin Russia's history with the year 862 or 839 AD. Instead, Vernadsky studied the whole multi-lingual corpus of primary sources on Russia and correctly concluded that Russians had lived in southern Russia many centuries before the mythical Rurik and his equally mythical brothers allegedly came to northern Russia from overseas.[6] A scholar who wrote so much is bound to say things which cannot be accepted by all, and some of Vernadsky's conclusions have justly been criticized and rejected. However, we must be grateful to this worshipper of the Muse Clio for summoning her to govern again those who seek Russia's origins. Since the eighteenth century, Clio has been forced to share the field of early Russian history with the Erinyes.

The search goes on, for some basic questions of Russia's past have not yet been satisfactorily answered. From among the recent studies of Russian origin, written neither from the Normanist nor from the Anti-Normanist point of view, but rather in the spirit of the wholeness of Eurasia, mention should be made of the first volume of a planned multi-volume treatise of Omeljan Pritsak. This work is reminiscent of an old Ukrainian theory which connects the Ruthenians (as the Little Russians have been known by their western neighbors) with the Ruteni of southern France.[7] Pritsak's thesis on the origin of Rus' may be

---

[6] *Opyt istorii Evrazii: s poloviny vi veka do nastojaščego vremeni* (Berlin, 1934); *Ancient Russia* (New Haven, 1943); *Kievan Russia* (New Haven, 1948); *The Origin of Russia* (Oxford, 1959).

[7] S. Šeluxin, *Zvidkilja pohodit' Rus': Teorija kel'ts'kog poxoždennja Rusi z Franciji* (Prague, 1929); O. Pritsak, *The Origin of Rus'*, I (Cambridge, Mass, 1981).

represented by the following statement: The founders of the first
East Slavic state with a seat at Kiev were an amalgam of
warriors and merchants who were agents of an international
Eurasian slave-trading company (like a contemporary multinational business) dominated by Jewish merchants from southern
France, the Rādāniya from the Rhône Valley and the Ruteni
from Roussillon. In Slavia, the chief "business" of the company
was to capture or purchase young men and women. Some of the
poor wretches were castrated and sold as eunuchs, others were
shipped unmutilated to the slave markets throughout Christendom and the Domain of Islam. The scholarly community has
rejected Pritsak's interpretation of the origin of Russia.[8] We
believe it is an example of unbridled Herderianism. Some of
Pritsak's and other scholars' views on the role of Jews in
medieval Eurasia have been expanded and woven into fantastic
tales by undisciplined scholars and mean-spirited publicists.[9]

Clearly, those guided by Herder's romantic opinions of the
early Slavs while interpreting the sources on Russia's origin
cannot offer solutions acceptable in our unromantic age. Further,
those who rely almost exclusively on late native tales and even
later and derivative Western European sources, while glossing
over or even wholly ignoring the earlier evidence, can not be expected to tell the whole story.

OUR APPROACH TO THE STUDY OF RUSSIA'S ORIGINS

We may define Russia as a vast North Eurasian landmass occupied now and in the past by Russians. Taking an eastern point
of reference, one may look at it from the Russian River in California and the Russian Fort on Hawaii, which once marked the
eastern limits of the Russian Empire. To the native peoples of
North America and East Asia whose past observations and
opinions have not come down to us Russia was, naturally, a
western land. From the point of geographical and cultural

---

[8] *See*, review by Je. Melnikova, *Byzantinoslavica*, XL/2 (1985), pp.
199–203.
[9] *See*, as an example, L.N. Gumilëv, *Drevnjaja Rus' i Velikaja step'*
(Moscow, 1989).

references of the ancient and medieval Chinese, Russia was ensconced in the unknown and barbarous West extending from their Wall, across the deserts of Eastern Turkestan and Dzungaria, through the Dzungarian Gate, and over the Tien Shan ranges. Their knowledge of Central Asia and Northwest Eurasia, as transmitted to us, was scant and secondhand, obtained from the various Mongol and Turkic peoples and long-distance merchants who came to the frontiers of China to buy silk.

From the north, the Finns and other peoples, whose domain extends from Estonia, Finland, and Lapland to Kamchatka, have always had contacts with the peoples of Russia. However, until the coming of Christianity to their regions, in the Late Middle Ages, they had no writing, and thus were unable to transmit to us their early observations.

From the west, Russia was observed by Slavic, Baltic, Germanic, Celtic, and other peoples living in Northern and Western Europe in prehistory, antiquity, and the Middle Ages. To them Russia was an eastern land, though, again, since they did not write, we do not know what they thought of it. It was only in the Middle Ages that the peoples of continental Western Europe and those of the British Isles, having accepted Christianity and acquired the art of writing, began to record their observations on Russia. Under the influence of Christian literature, they saw it as a region in the fabulously rich and mysterious East.[10] Modern West European and North American scholars generally follow medieval observers and treat Russia as a region of the eastern quarter, its people as East Slavs, frequently unloading on them the West's age-old fears of and admiration for the East.

The peoples of ancient Russia have always communicated with those living in the central belt of the earth where settled life and civilization originated. Over the millennia, North–South contacts and conflicts took place chiefly in the interface of the two macroregions, a broad swath which ran from the Wall of China to the Roman *limes* on the Danube and the Rhine, but especially in Upper Asia, in the former Soviet and Russian Transcaucasia, Anatolia, and the Balkans. The oldest civilized

---

[10] Helmold in his *Chronica Slavorum*, Book I [F.J. Tschan's English translation (New York, 1935), p. 46], says: "By the Danes, Russia is also called Ostrogard because, situated in the east, it abounds in all good things."

peoples of South Asia, Southwest Asia, and North Africa imagined the "extreme" north in Central Asia, Upper Asia, and Transcaucasia, where they had their first encounters and intense contacts with the peoples who came from the "more extreme" north, from Russia. From their mythology, folklore, and belle-lettres we learn that this region had captivated their imagination. At the same time, various scholarly disciplines teach that numerous peoples came to the central belt from the north, beginning with the Sumerians and the so-called Dynastic race of Egypt, whose original homelands some authorities locate in the former Russian Empire. These were followed by the Asianic Gutians, Kassites, and Hurrians, and these, in turn, by a number of Indo-European peoples, such as the Indo-Aryans, Medes, Persians, Hittites, Cimmerians, Scythians, Sarmatians, Goths, and others. Most modern scholars indicate Ukraine and Russia as the Indo-European original homeland, even though, with the exception of the Goths who traversed Russia on their way from Scandinavia to Romania, none of the many Indo-European peoples who originated from Russia made record of the fact, that is, none that has come down to us. Paradoxically, the early Russians, themselves, traced their own roots to Mesopotamia.

For these reasons, Russia's image among its southern neighbors combines myth and reality. To illustrate, the Aryans of the Indian Subcontinent are believed to have originated from Russia though they appear not to have cared to commemorate this. While in their mythology the north, where Russia lay, was the domain of the mythical Uttara Kuru people, in reality the region was occupied by the Sacae and other nomads who followed the Aryans and each other across the Hindu Kush on their way to India.

The ancient Iranians saw Russia and Ukraine as part of a vast steppe country extending from the Tien Shan, Pamir, Hindu Kush, and Kopet Dagh ranges in the east to the Carpathians and the Balkans in the west. They believed that it was dominated by one nomadic people whom they generally called Sacae, referring to those of Russia and Ukraine as *Saka paradraya* "overseas Sacae." They comprehended Russia as part of Aniran, the opposite of Iran, their own domain. The Persian king Darius the Great led a multi-ethnic army of invasion into Russia but was forced to retreat. Neither the Persians nor any of their Iranian cousins managed to record their own observations of Russia and transmit them down to us.

The Sumerians might have originated from Russia, but after they settled in their new homeland they believed they were natives of the soil. Their field of vision reached only as far as the southern boundaries of Russia, defined by the steppes of Central Asia, Upper Asia, and the Caucasus.[11]

The field of vision of the Babylonians and Assyrians was wider, and it may have included southern Russia. The ancient Mesopotamians believed Ziusudra/Utnapishtim (a predecessor of the Hebrew Noah) had escaped from the Great Flood to the Mountain of Salvation (Mount Ararat of the Hebrew Bible). They had to cross it on their imaginary journeys to Russia.

The ancient Egyptians, whose earliest dynasties appear to have been founded by immigrants from Transcaucasia, believed the world ended in Upper Asia where they imagined the Pillars of Heaven. The belief, based on Herodotus, that the Egyptians campaigned and even conquered a portion of Ukraine and Russia has been rejected by modern scholars. It has recently reemerged in polemical contexts with scholarly pretensions.[12]

The Greeks placed in the Caucasus the cliff where Prometheus was chained, while imagining Russia occupied by an array of such mythical peoples as the Abii, whom Homer called "men most just," Amazons, Hyperboreans, One-eyed folks of the Arimaspians, Canibals, Black-Cloaks, etc., as well as by the real and awesome Tauri and the invincible Scythians.

The Macedonians, bent on bringing the whole world under their sway and within their ken, tried to conquer Russia and organized scientific expeditions to survey it. They entertained themselves and their Greek and Afroasian subjects with tales of Alexander's exploits which included the discovery of the Breasts of the North and the building of an iron gate between them to enclose the peoples of ancient Russia and to prevent them from invading the Macedonian Empire.[13] The states that succeeded to

---

[11] S.N. Kramer, *The Sumerians* (Chicago, 1963), p. 284.

[12] *See*, M. Bernal, *Black Athena*, I–II (New Brunswick, N.J., 1987–91), II, pp. 226–35.

[13] A.R. Anderson, *Alexander's Gate, Gog and Magog, and the Inclosed Nations* (Cambridge, Mass., 1932).

Alexander's empire communicated with Russia through real passes and gates, and most specifically through the Scythian Gate, the Daryal Pass, and the Derbent Gate.

The Roman conquerors of the Macedonian Empire took possession of the literary sources on Russia and its peoples recorded originally by the ancient societies of Southwest Asia and North Africa and later collected and preserved by the Macedonians. Using chiefly Greek and Latin, Roman subjects selectively copied and transmitted down to us mere fragments of this material, the bulk of it perishing through wanton destruction or neglect. These spotty sources form the basis of our knowledge of ancient and medieval Russia. Generally, the Romans placed Russia in relation to the Danube, the Black Sea, and the Caucasus.

Using a literary genre with roots in the more ancient traditions of Mesopotamia, Hebrew eschatologists imagined Yahweh summoning Gog and Magog and other savage but uncorrupted peoples of the North to swoop through Upper Asia to Lower Asia to punish the sinners there. Their Christian and Muslim heirs, merging several ancient traditions with Macedonian legends, feared the day when Gog and Magog, among whom some included the Russians, would burst through the Iron Gate built by Alexander/Iskander, as a prelude to the Day of Judgment.

In the Early Middle Ages, the Rhomaeans (Byzantines), Persians, Arabs, and Latin Christians who had contacts and conflicts with the Russians saw them either as one people, or as a variety of peoples identical or related to the Slavs and confused with the Men of the North, with *Majūs* "fire-worshippers, pagans," and with Gog and Magog.

Since, for lack of written sources, we cannot look at ancient and medieval Russia from the east and the north, and while admitting that an exclusively western approach may be partly justified only for the late medieval and modern periods of Russian history, we suggest that it is more profitable to seek this nation's beginnings in the records of its southern observers, that is, in the available works of ancient Afroasian, Balkan, and Roman writers, as well as in those of their medieval Rhomaean, Muslim, Jewish, and Western Christian successors and cultural heirs. To them Russia was a region of the awesome and inscrutable North separated from the civilized South by the formidable *Catena mundi,* a range of real and imaginary mountains running east—west through the middle of the earth. Nevertheless, it was in these mountains that the ancestors of the Russians had friendly and hostile encounters with the Muslims and the Rhomaeans. For example, in the Caucasus where Christians and Muslims faced pagan Russians in the seventh century AD, and in the Rhodope and Balkan mountains, where the Russians traded with everyone, schemed with the Rhomaeans against the Bulgars and Slavs, and battled the Rhomaeans, telling them even on one occasion to go back to Asia where they came from. To these peoples Russia was a northern land and as such it occupied a special place in their imagination. The written records of ancient Afroasian societies and their cultural heirs in the Balkans are permeated by hatred, awe, fear, and admiration for the peoples of the northern quarter, reflecting millennia of complex relationships between the civilized South and the underdeveloped North. Naming these irrational feelings *boreophobia* "fear of the North," we hasten to add that they were thrown at the Russians the moment they appeared in the field of vision of their literate southern neighbors.

Conclusions reached by examining this, the southern corpus of written sources on ancient and medieval Russia, must be taken into account when evaluating the much younger northern corpus, that is, the observations on Russia provided by its first native writers (for example, those who wrote the *Russian Primary Chronicle*) and their Baltic, Finnic, and Germanic neighbors. It cannot be stressed enough that the northerners who produced the corpus of sources upon which most investigators of Russia's origin rely belonged to the peoples who acquired the art of writing long after Russia had become well known through the works of ancient and medieval Mediterranean writers. These earliest sources on Russia must be evaluated before a serious attempt can be made to draw conclusions from later writings in and around that land.

Even though the ancient peoples of South Asia, Southwest Asia, North Africa, and the Balkan Peninsula, with the exception of the Persians whose opinions have trickled down to us through Ionian filters, and the Macedonians whose knowledge was selectively transmitted to us by their Roman conquerors, appear to have recorded only vague notions of the peoples of Russia, they nevertheless had opinions of the northern quarter where the Russians emerged in late antiquity and the Early Middle Ages. The data they provided and the names of places and peoples they recorded, though generously interspersed with mythical beings and events, are the primary basis for our knowledge of ancient and medieval Russia. Their mythology, folklore, belles-lettres, and historical records were adopted and further developed by Jews, Muslims, and Christians, who used this material as a basis to formulate their own perceptions of the North in general and of Russia in particular.

The earliest positively dated form of the Russian national name is *Rhos,* recorded in a Western Christian chronicle under the year 839. It is a Latin transcription of the Greek form *Rhōs,* which, in turn, comes from the Book of Ezekiel of the Septuagint, a translation of the Hebrew Bible into the *koine,* the *lingua franca* of the Macedonian Empire. In Hebrew the name was written *rš* and vocalized as Roš. Although modern scholars see no connection between the Rhōs of the Septuagint and the Russians, they admit that literate Rhomaeans patterned both the national name and character of their northern neighbors and enemies after the awesome Rhōs who would command Gog and Magog at the end of time. We shall suggest that long before 839 AD the Russians had been observed through the Derbent Gate, called "the Gate of Gates" by Muslims.

Consequently, we have decided to seek the origin of the ethnonym Russi in the written records of the peoples who lived in the southern quarter of the *oikoumene* in relation to Russia, the ancient civilized peoples of Southwest Asia and North Africa and their cultural heirs in the Balkans. This approach is justified even without accepting the belief of the medieval Russians that their ancestors, originating on the Plain of Shinar in Mesopotamia, migrated voluntarily to the Balkans and the Danube Basin where they lived for many years until they were forced by Vlachs (either Celts or Romans) to move to Russia.

Clearly, while the primary sources on ancient and medieval Russia are scarce, ambiguous, and inconclusive, the immense literature offers a wide variety of opinions regarding the beginnings of Russia, the origin and meaning of its name, and the ethnicity of the founders of the Russian state. All possible answers to the old question: *Otkudu est' pošla ruskaja zemlja?* "Whence comes the Russian land?", asked and answered in the mid-eleventh century by a Kievan chronicler, have been offered and repeatedly criticized, defended, and elaborated during the past three centuries. At the same time, efforts to locate the earliest Russians and Russia on the map of Eurasia have brought no lasting results, and the beginnings of Russia are still hidden behind a veil which generations of diligent scholars have been unable to lift. The literature shows that three questions essential for an understanding of the origin of Russia have not been answered. They are:

1) *What is the origin and meaning of the name Russi?*
2) *When and where did the name first appear?*
3) *What was the ethnicity of the early Russians?*

We hope the reader will find the answers in the present work. An attempt is made here to explain the name Russi, to place the earliest Russians as precisely as possible in space and time, and to indicate the ethno-linguistic groups that bore this appellation from its first appearance in works of foreign observers to the middle of the eleventh century when it became a self-designation of a Slavic people.

The following sketch of Russia's natural setting is intended as a guide through the written sources on that land in antiquity and the Middle Ages.

THE NATURAL SETTING

The geographical stage where Russia was established as a Christian Kingdom a millennium ago had, in antiquity, been known to Greek and Latin writers as Scythia or Great Scythia. In late antiquity the region was renamed and divided into Sarmatia Europaea and Sarmatia Asiatica. In the middle of the first Christian millennium the name changed to Antia, then to Slavia, and finally toward the end of that millennium to Russia. Scythia has been described by Herodotus, Sarmatia's geographical co-ordinates were given by Ptolemy, but Slavia and Antia must be defined because modern scholars avoid the names, although writers who lived at the time when Russia was about to be born used them quite freely and profusely.

Medieval Christians, Muslims, and Jews understood by the name *Slavia* that geographical area of Eurasia where Slavs were politically the dominant people, where Slavic was spoken, and where Slavs were the majority of the population. Taking the Derbent Gate as a reference point and the year 22 AH/642 AD, a perceptive Muslim might define its borders as follows:

On the northwest, Slavia reached the banks of the Salava/-Saale and the lower Laba/Elbe rivers in Germany. Slavs occupied all of the former East Germany, except parts of Thuringia, through the Middle Ages, some surviving till this day.[14]

On the north, Slavs held the Baltic coast from the bays of Kiel and Lübeck to the mouth of the Vistula. The island of Rügen remained Slavic well into the High Middle Ages. The rest of the Baltic coast was held by Prussians, Lithuanians, Latvians, Estonians, Finns, Swedes, and Danes.[15] The Slavs were separated from the eastern Baltic coast by the Balts who inhabited a somewhat larger area in the Middle Ages than their descendants do in modern times. Slavia extended along the Volkhov River to the southern shore of Lake Ladoga. It was cut off from the Neva River Valley by the Finno-Ugric Vod people. Slavs were settled in the Upper Volga basin down to the point where the Oka, having gathered to itself the waters of the Ugra, Moskva, and the Kljazma rivers, meets "the Russian river," as the Volga is affectionately called. Speakers of Finno-Ugric languages still live among Slavs in this region, an indication that in the Middle Ages their ancestors had occupied a larger territory. It is

---

[14]   Many German cities which grew on the Great North European Plain and along the Baltic coast were founded and named by Slavs, as the history and their present names clearly indicate. Lübeck, Rostock, Leipzig, Dresden, Chemnitz, and other famous and less well-known cities, towns, and villages in what is today Germany were founded and named by Slavs. Their current names are German adaptations of Slavic toponyms. *See*, generally, J. Herrmann, *Die Slawen in Deutschland: Geschichte und Kultur der slawischen Stämme westlich von Oder und Neisse vom 6. bis 12. Jahrhundert* (Berlin, 1970).

[15]   *See*, a map in F.J. Tschan's English translation of Helmold's *Chronica Slavorum*, p. 2.

generally held that Slavs began to settle north of the line Polotsk–Vitebsk–Smolensk–Kaluga in the Early Middle Ages.[16] Although no precise eastern boundary of early medieval Slavia can be established for lack of information, it is certain that the Russian domain reached the Don, the Caucasus, and the Derbent Gate, where it bordered on the realm of the King of Derbent who, in 642, told the Muslims the Russians were "enemies of the whole world." The Great Eurasian Steppe was also home to various nomadic peoples. The Crimean Peninsula offered refuge for the Goths who had survived the Hunnic invasions, and boasted the cosmopolitan city of Cherson, a Rhomaean outpost in that region of Russia.

Medieval Slavia comprised all of modern Austria as far west as the Aniža/Enns River and the source of the Drava River. The ethnolinguistic boundary between Slavs and the Germanic Lombards and their Romance-speaking subjects in northern Italy ran along the Tilment/Tagliamento River. Today, the dividers are the Soča/Isonzo and the Nadiža/Natisone rivers, but islands of Slavic speakers still exist deep in the province of Friuli–Venezia Giulia.

From the conflux of the Danube and the Aniža to the Delta, the Danube Basin was the heartland of medieval Slavia. However, the steppes in modern Hungary, Bačka, the Banat of Timişoara, Oltenia, Walachia, the Dobrudja, and Moldavia, though settled on the fringes and culturally and politically dominated by Slavs, were also home to a succession of nomadic peoples. Nevertheless, the whole continued to be correctly called Slavia well into the modern age because the chancellery, liturgical, and literary language in the Rumanian principalities was Slavic until recently, while the Kingdom of Saint Stephen was as much Slavic as it was Magyar.

The situation in the Balkan Peninsula was more complex. Although Slavic armies and navies made frequent incursions into

---

[16] Early medieval boundaries between Slavs on the one hand and Balts and Finno-Ugrians on the other have been drawn on the basis of historical, archaeological, and linguistic evidence. *See*, *PVL*, maps; M. Gimbutas, *The Balts* (New York, 1963); *eadem*, *The Slavs* (New York, 1971); and M. Vasmer, *Die alten Bevölkerungsverhältnisse Russlands im Lichte der Sprachforschung* (Berlin, 1941).

Italy, the Aegean Islands, and Asia Minor, several coastal areas were not under Slavic control. Chief among these were Constantinople, Salonica, Athens, Patras, Durrës, as well as the islands in the Aegean and some in the Ionian seas. This medieval Slavia was brought to life by conquest and expansion originating from a smaller area which we may call the "pristine or old" Slavia. Numerous medieval and early modern writers knew well the location of the original homeland of the Slavs. That is, they knew where to look for Old Slavia. The evidence on this issue indicates that the historically attested first Slavia was on the banks of the Danube. We have demonstrated that the currently popular theories that the Slavs originated from the banks of the Odra, Vistula, and the Dnieper, from the Pripyat Marshes, or from the Western Sea are based on error and fable. Our examination of the sources led us to agree with the traditional writers who stated: *Pannonia est mater et origo omnium Slavonicarum nationum.* We have suggested that Pannonia and the adjacent areas along the Danube be designated *Slavia Antiqua* and that the ethnonym *Slav* derives from the hydronym Sala(va), designating a feeder of Lake Balaton.[17]

Slavia Antiqua, known by a variety of names, the most common ones being *Donauraum, Donaubecken,* Danubian Europe, and the Middle and Lower Danube Basin,[18] is today an ethnic mosaic of Slavs (Ukrainians, Slovaks, Bulgarians, Serbs, Bosnians, Croats, and Slovenes), Germans (Austrians, Transylvanian Saxons, and Banat Swabians), Hungarians, Rumanians, Romi, and Jews. Only the Slavs among these peoples can trace their roots in this region through the Middle Ages and the *Pax Romana* into prehistory.[19]

In the course of the sixth century, the Slavs took from the Romans a portion of their empire and annexed it to Slavia Antiqua. We call this area *Slavia Nova.* Many names were used in

---

[17] Bačić, *op. cit.*, p. 183; *idem,* "Slav: The Origin and Meaning of the Ethnonym," in *Lubi Slovenci: A Festschrift to Honor R.L. Lencek, Slovene Studies,* IX/1–2 (1987), pp. 33–41.

[18] Bačić, *The Emergence of the Slavs,* pp. 24–40.

[19] Of course, we are not claiming that all today's Hungarians and Rumanians are descendants of immigrants, only that the languages they speak were brought to the banks of the Danube from those of the Volga and the Tiber.

antiquity and the Middle Ages to designate this region of North Central Eurasia. In modern times, the term Balkan Peninsula is applied synonymously with the expression Südosteuropa.[20]

Expanding from Slavia Antiqua, some Slavs settled in and brought under their control the Czecho–Moravian plateau, known today as Czechia and Moravia. Although closely linked with the Middle Danube Basin or Slavia Antiqua, this region is populated by Slavs whose language belongs to the West Slavic branch, and it may be treated as a separate geomorphological and cultural area.

The majority of West Slavs settled on the Great North European Plain, which extended eastward into the domain of East Slavs and westward into that of the Germans and other peoples. The Slavs of Germany and Poland were called the Venedae, those of Belarus, Ukraine, and Russia, the Antae.

Therefore, early medieval Slavia may be divided into three parts: Slavia, consisting of Slavia Antiqua and Slavia Nova, Venedia, and Antia. Czechia and Moravia may be treated either as part of Slavia or Venedia.

Antia

In the Early Middle Ages, the domain of the Antae extended from the Danube to the Don and from the eastern foothills of the Carpathians to the northern slopes of the Caucasus. We call this region Antia, with the understanding that the name covered roughly the same area which in antiquity had been known as Scythia or Great Scythia, in late antiquity as Sarmatia Europaea and Asiatica, and since the seventh century as Slavia or Russia.

The region where the Russian state emerged was separated from Slavia Antiqua by the Carpathian Mountain ranges. The division was not sharp and the Carpathians were not a major obstacle to the passage of people, goods, and ideas. Medieval Russia was demarcated by the Danube from Slavia Nova and braced to it by the steppe country which extended across the river toward the Balkan Mountains, called the Haemus by the learned, Stara Planina by the region's common folk. The Danube

---

[20] Bačić, *The Emergence of the Slavs*, pp. 40–58.

is a convenient natural boundary between states that choose to regard it as such, but throughout history it has facilitated communication among peoples.

The medieval Russians believed their first European homeland was in Slavia Antiqua. The first peculiarly Slavic script, the Glagolitic, and the oldest Slavic literary language, Old Church Slavonic, were created and used in Slavia Nova and Slavia Antiqua. They were diffused from there to Russia and other Slavic lands. In Russia, the Glagolitic was later replaced by the Cyrillic, fashioned in Slavia Nova.

Antia or Russia cannot readily be separated from Venedia because they impinge upon each other through the connecting terrain, and both regions are part of the Great North European Plain, a flat, glaciated, forested, country which stretches from the Paris Basin to the Urals. On the south, the Plain extends to the northern foothills of the Alps, the Sudeten, and the Carpathians in Germany, Czechia, Slovakia, Poland, and Ukraine. In antiquity, most of the Plain was covered by deciduous forests. Among the many swampy regions still barely suitable for human occupation are the Pripyat Marshes in Ukraine and Belarus.[21] However, most of the Plain has, over the centuries, been cleared of forests, drained and turned into agricultural land and pastures of fair quality.

Throughout antiquity that portion of the Plain which extended eastward from the Elbe lay beyond the field of vision of Mediterranean writers. They imagined it occupied by countless tribes of savages about whom they knew little and rarely wanted to learn more. At the beginning of the Christian era, the southerners divided the Great North European Plain along the Vistula into Magna Germania and Sarmatia Europaea. The section occupied by Slavs, at least since the sixth century AD, stretched from the Elbe and Saale rivers in the west to the Upper Volga and the Don in the east.

While medieval Russian chroniclers believed that all Slavs, including the Venedae, whom they called *Čexy* and *Ljaxy*, originated from Slavia Antiqua, they stressed a closer kinship between the Russians and the Venedae. First, they claimed that

---

[21]   The majority of modern scholars eliminate the ancient Slavs from the stage of history by assigning this region as their *Urheimat*.

the Russian Radimiči and Vjatiči were founded by two Ljax brothers, Radim and Vjatko. Second, ethnogonic myths which appeared among the West and East Slavs in the Middle Ages derive their people's origin from the brothers Čech, Lech, and Mech (or Rus). Born in Slavia Antiqua, called Pannonia by writers using Latin, Croatia by those writing in the vernacular, they migrated north to found Czechia, Poland (Lechia), and Muscovy–Russia. A close relationship and interconnectedness between Antia and Venedia is also reflected in the name Venäjä, from Venedae, applied by the Finns to Russia.

The Ecological Zones of Russia

To explicate properly the sources on Russia's origins, it is necessary to distinguish the land's main ecological zones. Since Russian presence beyond the Urals was not remarkable in antiquity and the Early Middle Ages, we focus here on that portion of Eurasia called European Russia. Though the northern regions of Russia remained for a long time *terra incognita,* this did not stop the southerners from "settling" along the coasts of the imaginary northern or Scythian/Sarmatian Ocean the happiest of humankind, the Hyperboreans, and a multitude of other wholly fabled peoples. Among the many names by which the southerners knew the Russians the Hyperborean "ethnonym" figures prominently.

Starting from the north, in the abode of the Hyperboreans, European Russia is mostly flat with occasional old and eroded low hills. The land is poorly drained and swamps abound during the short summers, frozen ground the rest of the year. From the coast of the Arctic Ocean down as far as the Arctic Circle, the vegetation, known as the *tundra* (a Russian word of Finno-Ugric or Lapp origin), consists of stunted trees, grasses, and lichens. Hunting and fishing have been the main source of livelihood for the peoples who have made this country their habitat. Dogs and reindeer are their principal domestic animals. From remote antiquity to this day the tundra zone has been inhabited by Lapps, Nency, Samoyeds, and other groups whose racial characteristics and way of life resemble those of the Eskimos of North America. Although individual Slavs had visited this region in ancient times, their systematic settlement here began only in the High Middle Ages.

South of the tundra extends a broad forest zone consisting mostly of coniferous trees, spruce and fir, known as the *taiga* (a Russian word borrowed from some native Siberian language). Wildlife, especially fur animals, abounds in this zone. The taiga extends as far south as the line Tallinn–Novgorod–Nižnij Novgorod–Kazan–Ufa. Slavs began to settle at the southern rim of the taiga in the seventh century AD.

Next is the zone of deciduous mixed forests which covers all of Estonia, Latvia, Lithuania, and Belarus, as well as parts of Russia, and Ukraine as far south as the line Kiev–Tambov–Saratov–Samara.

The next ecological zone, as we move toward the Black Sea, is the forest–steppe country, known in Russian as *lesostep'*. As the name indicates, this belt forms a transition between the true forest and the true steppe. At Kiev, the two zones come together. North of the Ukrainian capital, and covering the upper valley of the Dnieper and those of its tributaries, is the forest zone. Then comes the forest–steppe country which extends from the right bank of the Dnieper in a northwesterly direction toward Podolia. There is an island of the forest belt that stretches from the right bank of the Dnieper toward the eastern foothills of the Carpathians. In the ninth century this was the domain of the *Drevljane* "forest-dwellers." East and southeast from Kiev, and between the left bank of the Dnieper and the Carpathian Mountains, stretches the forest–steppe zone, which, with occasional intrusions from the forest belt, runs uninterruptedly eastward into Asia. The *Poljane* "field-dwellers" settled in the steppe–forest zone in and around Kiev and downstream as far as the Ros River and east as far as the Psël. North and east of them but still in the forest–steppe ecological belt lived the *Severjane* "northern folks."

The bulk of the remainder of Ukrainian and Russian territory consists of the Great Eurasian Steppe. This belt begins roughly at the confluence of the Ros and the Dnieper rivers. In fact, the Great Eurasian Steppe extends from the Carpathians across the lower valleys of the Dnieper, Donec, Don, and Volga over the Ural Mountains to the Pacific Ocean. The steppe remained a domain of pastoral nomads until it was incorporated into the Russian Empire and largely transformed into agricultural land.

Of course, the steppe zone is not an ecological monolith, so that long and, in places, broad strips of land along the rivers have always supported agricultural populations. The upper and middle valley of the Donec, a region of Ukraine known as the Donec Coal Basin, is a hilly plateau which had been suitable for agricultural occupation long before the whole steppe was conquered by plowmen. In the past, large tracts of forest country intruded into the steppe at the boundary between the domain of nomads and that of farmers. One was *Hylaea* "woodland," described by Herodotus in his Scythian logos.[22] The name of another woodland entered the epic poetry of the Germanic peoples at the beginning of the Middle Ages under the linguistically intelligible but geographically vague name *Myrkwiðr* "murky forest." Its location and even its very existence in the real world have been the subject of a scholarly controversy.[23] In the High Middle Ages, when the Polovcians were forced to relinquish mastery of the steppe and seek the security of forests, two large tracts of wooded terrain along the Dnieper received them. These were *Černyj les* "black forest," covering both banks of the Dnieper from the modern city of Dniepropetrovsk to the conflux of the Dnieper with its left tributary, the Orël, and *Goluboj les* "blue forest," extending along the left bank of the Dnieper up the valley of the Volčja River.

Slightly south of Volgograd the steppe begins to give way to sand dunes. In Asia, the grassy steppe often becomes a sandy desert. The mixed steppe–desert terrain extends along the banks of the Volga and across its delta toward the Caspian Sea. The northern and eastern shores of the Caspian and a good portion of the country between that sea and the foothills of the Kopet Dagh, Hindu Kush, Pamir, Tien Shan, and Altai mountains is a desert with numerous oases and river valleys suitable for agriculture. This region of Central Asia, which is today shared among Russians, various Turkic peoples, and the Iranian-speaking Tajiks, was in antiquity occupied chiefly by nomads of

---

[22] IV.76 and *passim.*
[23] For a witty solution to the problem of location of Myrkwiðr, *see*, O.J. Maenchen–Helfen, *The World of the Huns* (Berkeley, 1973), p. 154.

Indo-European parentage. Russian presence there dates from the Early Middle Ages, while Russian conquest, settlement, and rule belong to more recent history.

On the south, the steppe continues toward the northern foothills of the Caucasus Mountain ranges where it gradually gives way to the domain of settled agriculturalists. But the Kuban and the Terek river valleys had been a domain of nomads since antiquity until the latter were replaced by Cossacks whose life-style resembled that of the former denizens of the Great Eurasian Steppe.

The last ecological belt of Russia is the coastal and mountainous zone of the Crimean Peninsula. The Tauric Mountains, covering about a third of the Crimea, have supported people who lived off the land and sea. The healthy climate, the abundance of Mediterranean-type vegetation, and the open sea with numerous natural harbors contributed to the development of a Mediterranean culture in this corner of Russia. The native Tauri engaged in piracy before they understood that trade was more profitable. Although they disappeared without leaving evidence of their language, their name resurfaced in the tenth century as one of the names foreigners used to designate Russians. The first Tauric ruler was the mythical King Thoas who appeared in Euripides' *Iphigenia in Tauris*, followed, after a long interval, by Svjatoslav, the Tauroscythian and father of St. Vladimir, and finally, by Catherine the Great who reconquered the Crimea and annexed it to the Russian Empire in 1783. Today, the Crimea belongs to Ukraine.

From around the beginning of the seventh century BC until well into the twentieth century, numerous cities thrived along the Ukrainian and Russian Black Sea coasts. They and the small tracts of land in their vicinity on which the city folks grew the essential produce formed the thinnest ecological belt in this region. Archaeologists have established that most of such cities were founded by native people. Around the middle of the second millennium BC, some of these small and perhaps ethnically homogeneous settlements began to attract, as permanent residents, foreign merchants, craftsmen, and adventurers. The earliest foreigners were Carians, followed by other Aegean peoples and Phoenicians. Prevented from settling in the Levant by the Assyrians, in North Africa, Spain, Sardinia, and Sicily by the Phoenicians, and forced by regularly recurring famines to flee their native land, large numbers of Ionian and other Greeks began arriving into the established and thriving coastal cities of ancient Ukraine and Russia after ca. 700 BC.

The settlers, occasionally supported by their metropolises, tried unsuccessfully to use these cities to turn Russia into a colony. Several ancient writers have noted the precarious position of Greek and other immigrants along the coasts whose hinterlands they did not control. In an often quoted passage, Plato likened them to so many "ants or frogs at the side of a swampy pool." Cicero wrote that these same Greek cities resembled "a hem stitched on the broad cloths of the barbarian fields." At the opening of the Middle Ages, the Gothic historian Jordanes remarked that the Greeks had established colonies on the northern shores of the Black Sea, with the permission of the Scythians, implying that the latter could cancel the permission at will. Nevertheless, the coastal cities played an important role in the transmission of elements of Afroasian civilizations to Scythia and Russia.

The Caucasus and Transcaucasia

In the past, the Russian Empire and until recently the Soviet Union ruled the whole of the Caucasus and Transcaucasia. We include them in this sketch because of their special place in the real and mythical history of the Black Sea basin, Scythia, and Russia. The ancients treated the Caucasus as a boundary between Europe and Asia. Though the Scythians lived primarily in Europe, when they first appeared on the horizon of their literate neighbors they were settled in Transcaucasia. The Russians, too, were first observed by those who recorded the fact as a people living in the vicinity of the Derbent Gate, the most frequented North–South passageway between Russia and Southwest Asia.

The country which extends from the crest of the Caucasus and the middle valley of the Terek River to the Caspian Sea is known as *Dagestan* "mountain country." In antiquity, the name Albania was applied both to Dagestan and to the eastward tilting Azerbaijan. The fertile valleys of the Terek, Samun, Kura, and Aras rivers were a sure source of livelihood for any agricultural population that cared to till them, while the hills and mountain slopes supported herds of livestock. A number of tribes and nations who could not survive the pressure from stronger groups in the steppes and other lowland areas found security in ancient Albania. Due to their linguistic heterogeneity and small numbers, the peoples of Dagestan, Azerbaijan, and other Caucasian and Transcaucasian regions are attractive subjects for ethnographic studies. It is here that scholars have discovered some numerically humble descendants of the once mighty and populous denizens of the steppe.

By its geographical location and its role in history, Georgia, the heiress of ancient Colchis and Iberia, deserves attention in any attempt to understand the past of the Pontic region. The ancients believed that both Iberia and Colchis were part of Scythia. Natural and man-made routes led from Georgia in several directions. Access to Scythia proper was possible along the Black Sea coast and through the Scythian Gate, by way of the central Caucasus and the Daryal Pass, or along the Kura and Aras river valleys to the Caspian Sea and northward through the Derbent Gate. The Kura and Aras valleys are the chief avenues of communication with Iran. Colchis, Iberia, Albania, and Armenia have always had close contacts with Scythia. Ancient trade routes from Russia to Tbilisi and Erevan were transformed into motor roads and railroads by Imperial and Soviet Russia.

Although the Pontic Alps drop, in places, quite abruptly to the coast of the Black Sea, history shows that there was steady intercourse between northern Anatolia and Russia by way of Colchis. In antiquity and in the Middle Ages, the Laz people straddled today's border between Turkey and Georgia. While negotiating steep mountain slopes and watching for hostile tribesmen, ancient voyagers could reach Scythia proper and the Bosporan Kingdom along the coast of the Black Sea. This is the route taken by Mithridates, king of Pontus, fleeing from his Roman pursuers. As late as the Russian Civil War the journey could still be arduous, due to the danger caused by nature and people. During the brief *Pax Sovietica*, millions of vacationers made this trip every year by railroad from Moscow and other "Hyperborean" regions to Armavir. From there one line went along the Terek Valley and through the Derbent Gate to Azerbaijan, the other by way of Majkop, Tuapse, Sochi, and

Sukhumi to Poti and Batumi in Georgia. The seaward slopes of the Caucasus between the Ingur River and the border of the Russian Federation, with Sukhumi as the center, are inhabited by the Abkhazian people who are now trying to preserve their autonomy within Georgia. In antiquity their country was the domain of the Achaeans, often called Scythian Achaeans to be distinguished from their namesakes in the southern Balkans.

The stretch of land from Sochi to Novorossijsk belongs to the domain of settled agriculturalists, fishermen, traders, and mountain pastoralists. The steppe ends at the line running from Novorossijsk to Armavir. Many tribes of settled agriculturalists have lived there since the region had entered history as the homeland of the Sindi people.

Waterways, Passes, Gates

The ancients believed that both the Caspian and the Black seas communicated with the Circumambient Ocean by a channel that was used by the Argonauts to sail from Colchis to the Red Sea and by Odysseus to reach the Western Ocean. Based on their understanding of geography, medieval Arabs affirmed that the Russians of their day were the only people who navigated through a mysterious northern channel connecting the Black Sea, known to the Arabs as the Russian Sea, with the Western Ocean. Some thought that the Black and the Caspian seas were also linked.

In Russia, rivers have served as chief natural avenues of communication from antiquity until this day. With the help of powerful icebreakers, even the Arctic Ocean is now navigable for a short time in summer. Before St. Petersburg was built, and when the Baltic Sea was controlled by powers hostile to Russia, the city of Arkhangelsk, built at the estuary of the Northern Dvina in the White Sea, served as the chief port of the land. The Northern Dvina has in the past been the principal, and, at times, the only connection by water between the Moscow region and Western Europe. In other epochs, other waterways played the role of avenues of communication with the outside world.

The Northern Bug, the Neman, and the Western Dvina have their sources close to those of the Dniester and the Dnieper

rivers, which facilitates communication by water between the
Baltic and the Black seas. In antiquity, amber was exported
along the Bug and the Neman to the Dniester and the Dnieper
systems and onward to the Black Sea coast. In the Middle Ages,
when Scandinavian peoples increased their contacts with centers
of civilization in the south, they availed themselves of two at the
time well-established principal entries into Russia from
Scandinavia. One went through the Gulf of Riga and along the
Western Dvina to Smolensk. From there, those wishing to reach
the coasts of the Black Sea and Constantinople took the Dnieper
route. If Baghdad and other Muslim centers in Southwest Asia
and Central Asia were their destination, the road, by portages,
led to the Volga's tributaries and on to the Caspian sea. The
second entry was through the Gulf of Finland into the Neva
River, and then along the Volkhov and Lovat rivers, by the
cities of Staraja Ladoga, Novgorod, and Staraja Russa, either to
the Volga system or to that of the Dnieper.[24] The Dnieper route
was a well-travelled international waterway which entered
written history from the East Slavic point of view as *Put' iz
Varjag v Greki* "road from the Varangians to the Greeks." Since
there were gaps between the waterways, boats and goods had to
be pulled or carried by people and animals across stretches of
dry land. The process had to be repeated to bypass the Dnieper
rapids, some of which have been made famous by Constantine
Porphyrogenitus who recorded their Slavic and "Russian" names.

Countless individuals, tribes, and nations have journeyed from
Great Scythia to Southwest Asia ever since the invasion of the
Cimmerians and their Scythian pursuers described by Herodotus.
Although many routes are possible, two points have seen most
of the traffic: the Derbent Gate and the Daryal Pass. The
Derbent is actually a narrow defile, a strip of sandy terrain at a
point where the foothills of the Caucasus come abruptly to the
sea. The Georgians call it *Zghvis kari* "sea gate," whereas to the
Arabs it is the *Bāb al-abwāb* "gate of gates." The second main
route from Scythia to Southwest Asia is the Georgian Military

---

[24] Novgorod was built at the point where the Volkhov comes out of
Lake Ilmen, Staraja Ladoga where it flows into Lake Ladoga, Staraja Russa
south of Lake Ilmen, and St. Petersburg was built at the coast of the Gulf of
Finland and on the banks of the Neva River which drains Lake Ladoga.

Road built by Imperial Russia across the Caucasus. The road follows the valley of the Strungda River, a tributary of the Terek, high into the mountains, where the city called *Vladikavkaz* "ruler of the Caucasus," known as Ordzhonikidze in the Soviet era, was built to ensure and symbolize the mastery of the mountains by Russia. High in the mountains is the Daryal Pass (Krestovyj pereval) 2379 m. Its relatively recent name is owed to the Alans, the powerful steppe nomads who appeared there in antiquity. The name *Daryal* is a simplification of the Persian name *Dār-i Alān* "gate of the Alans." The Alans are known today as the Ossetians, and their language is believed to be descended from an idiom related to the languages spoken in antiquity by the Alans, Scythians, and Sarmatians. Today, the Ossetian country is divided by the crest of the Caucasus into Northern Ossetia, an autonomous republic in the Russian Federation, and Southern Ossetia, a region struggling to preserve its autonomy within Georgia.

Among the many true and legendary exploits of Alexander the Great, the belief that he built an iron barrier at the Daryal Pass and/or at the Derbent Gate to keep the "savage hordes" out has, since the Macedonian era, been entrenched in the minds of the peoples of Southwest Asia. Writers of late antiquity and the Early Middle Ages called the hordes Gog and Magog or Yājūj wa Mājūj. We shall see that in the seventh century, the gate keeper, the king of Derbent, called his Russian neighbors "enemies of the whole world" and that the people of Constantinople thought Gog and Magog were led by Russians. Centuries before Western Europe had established relations with the Russian Christian kingdom, Hellenic (*i.e.*, pagan) Russians had been passing regularly through the Gate of Gates as peaceful merchants going to the markets of Southwest Asia or as pagan warriors marching against the Christian Republic or the Domain of Islam. The first Russians who appeared in the field of vision of their literate southern neighbors were those who lived beyond the Derbent Gate.

The Daryal Pass and the Derbent Gate are the principal passageways used by many nations originating in North Central Eurasia in their invasions of states and empires of the civilized southerners. Alexander the Great built his iron gate to keep out the unclean savage peoples of the north centuries after Gilgamesh, a semi-divine king of Uruk in Iraq, and his companion, Enkidu, had pulled down the gate into the "Country of the Living," opening the less developed northern quarter for trade, colonization, and conquest by the more advanced peoples of the south. An eternal watchman at the gate could describe for us the march of civilization from the place of its origin in Lower Mesopotamia, through the various gates leading into Russia and on to the Arctic Ocean, while keeping a list of peoples coming out of Russia and passing between the Breasts of the North and through the Iron Gate on their way to exchange goods, ideas, insults, and blows with their Asian neighbors. Derbent was captured and annexed to Russia by Peter the Great. Today, the Russian Federation keeps the Derbent Gate, the Daryal Pass, and the Scythian Gate, which connect Europe with Asia in this region.

****

In concluding this sketch of the geographical setting of Russia, it must be pointed out that well into the Middle Ages those who reported on Russia used coastal cities as their points of observation. Because of this thalassic point of view, their descriptions of the hinterland are inaccurate. Some who lacked information on Russia admitted their ignorance, while others offered fables in order to "complete" their descriptions of the *oikoumene*. An example of confusion arising from the mixing of mythological conventions with real geography is the function of the Don in geographical descriptions of Russia. Most classical writers considered this river as a divider between Europe and Asia. Not knowing its sources some claimed it issued out of the Caucasus, others that it drained the fabled Rhipaean Mountains. In Ptolemy's *Geography*, the Volga is shown to originate from the Hyperborean Mountains, an imaginary natural feature introduced to accommodate an unreal people. The Hyperboreans, the Rhipaean Mountains, and other mythical peoples and places remained part of Russia's landscape until 1517, when Maciej z Miechowa updated, by personal observations, the classical and medieval knowledge and ethnographic terminology of Russia.[25]

---

[25]   *Tractatus de duabus Sarmatiis, Asiana et Europiana, et de contentis in eis* (Cracow, 1517).

THE NAMES FOR AND THE DIVISIONS OF RUSSIA

The name *Russi*, at the root of which we propose is a word for the color red, became, in the course of history, a self-designation for a variety of peoples inhabiting an enormous land. It replaced numerous ethnonyms which either disappeared or acquired new meanings. Some of these were color words, for the Russian land has also been associated with colors other than red. We shall show that the Red Sea was called "red" only by people who looked at it from the north, "green" by those who approached it from the west. Likewise, we shall suggest here that the red color attribute was given to Russia by observers standing at a particular angle to it, possibly west or north. We should treat the red angle as merely one out of four color angles of looking at Russia and allow for the possibility that namers viewing that land from the other three angles attributed different colors to the land and its people. In fact they did, as will be shown in this work.

The people who entered the medieval history of Eurasia as Russians had earlier been known by other names. In the Middle Ages, we find a variety of ethnonyms that were used synonymously with the name Russi. Before this appellation became common, the "Russians" were known by other names, just as the Franks, Alemanni, Bavarians, Slavs, and other peoples whose ethnonyms first appeared in late antiquity had earlier been known by other designations. Even when they were known as Russians, the people of Kievan Russia still used their particular names, some being known as *Kriviči*, others as *Poljane* "field-dwellers," others as *Drevljane* "forest-dwellers," and still others as *Severjane* "northern folks." Some of this ethnonymy survives to this day.

Rhomaean, Muslim, and Western Christian writers used many ethnonyms to designate the people we call Russians. For instance, among the Rhomaeans it was customary to call the Russians by the following names: Barbarians, Antae, Hellenes (*i.e.*, pagans), Scythians, Northern Scythians, Tauroscythians, Hyperboreans, Slavs, *hoi Rhōs*, and *Rhousioi*. In Muslim sources the Russians were called Slavs, *al-Majūs*, and *al-Rūs*. Some Western Christian writers, who were familiar with the Normans and their activities along the shores of the Western Sea, occasionally applied the designation *Nordmanni* to the Russians because they lived in the north and were as "savage" as were the Normans. A more common name for the Russians in Scandinavia was *Austr-Winðar* "Eastern Wends."

Though today the Russians are called Russians by most of their neighbors, there are two notable exceptions, the Finnic and the Baltic peoples. The Finns call Russia *Venäjä*. The name derives from the ethnonym *Venedae*, which is related to the Eneti of Paphlagonia, mentioned by Homer in the *Iliad*. We shall suggest that the name Venedae derives from a word for the color white. The Latvians use the name *Krijevija* for Russia (from the name of the Kriviči) and further distinguish Russia into *Krijevija* proper and *Baltkrijevija*, or Russia and White Russia.[26] For Belarus the Lithuanians use the name *Gudija* (the ethnonym is Gudas), which derives either from the name Getae, or from a Baltic word signifying forest-dwellers.

In tenth-century Constantinople, a section of Russia was called Outer Russia, presupposing the existence of an Inner Russia as well. The dividing and renaming of Russia continued through the Middle Ages, resulting in such pairs as Little and Great Russia and Upper and Lower Land. At the dawn of the modern era there appeared Red, White, and Black Russias. Today, a region of Russia, Belarus or White Russia, is differentiated from Russia proper by the attribute *belyj* "white." Clearly, the people who distinguished the different regions of Russia by colors used the colors as symbols of the directions of the horizon. In order to understand the rationale for such divisions, we offer a survey of various universal methods of differentiation in geographical nomenclature, including the most common method of dividing the earth into four quarters and named after the four cardinal points of the compass.

This effort is intended as an introduction to the study of North Central Eurasia where Russia originated. By offering here findings from some of the older written records on the Byelorussian, Ukrainian, and Russian lands and people made by

---

[26]   Had the Russophobes among Byelorussian nationalists prevailed and replaced their national name with the name Kriviči, they would have deprived their Latvian neighbors of differentiating them from the Russians.

foreign observers we hope to have come closer to understanding those native Russian writers who, in the mid-eleventh century, began to record the history of their country in their native language. We hope to have dispelled some darkness from the land which since the ninth century has been called *Rus'* and *Rossija* by its native sons and daughters, Russia by some foreigners, *Venäjä* by others, and *Krijevija* by still others.[27]

******

Chapter One is about global divisions of the earth according to the four cardinal points of the compass, leading to a discussion of some geographical names created in accordance with such divisions. Chapter Two deals with various methods of differentiating identical names aimed at explaining the paired attributes great−little, outer−inner, upper−lower, and others which over the centuries have accompanied the name Russia. Chapter Three shows that colors have universally been used as symbols of the directions of the horizon. Chapter Four lists and discusses some names of natural features, settlements, and countries where colors may symbolize the named objects' positions in space rather than their physical appearance. The discussion of such names as Red, Green, Black, and White seas, and other color names of natural features is intended to help us understand the name Russi, as well as White, Red, and Black Russias. Chapter Five deals with colors in ethnonymy generally and treats in detail some names of peoples from Anatolia to the Baltic Sea that are significant for an understanding of ancient and medieval Slavic and Russian ethnonymy. In Chapter Six are discussed the origin and meaning of the name Russi. In Chapter Seven are quoted and discussed some Rhomaean sources on the Russi and Russia. Chapter Eight concludes the work with an analysis of some pertinent Muslim sources on medieval Russia.

---

[27] In English Russia has been the preferred form since the High Middle Ages after the form *Russe* (attested in Chaucer) went out of usage.

CHAPTER I

CARDINAL POINTS OF THE COMPASS

THE GLOBAL VIEW

Today, we know that the earth's surface consists of dry land and sea, and we use five (or seven) names to label the continents, four to divide the sea into oceans. Using scientific instruments, we can readily establish the exact location for any place by calculating its latitude and longitude, that is, distances in degrees from the equator and from the 0 degree which, cartographers agree, runs from the North Pole to the South Pole through the English town of Greenwich. Our ancestors made do with less precision. While placing their own domain within the world they knew, some imagined and transmitted to us their views of the whole earth.

The oldest, simplest, and the most common image of the earth is that of an island in a vast sea.[1] Traces of this belief are found in folklore, literature, and figurative arts in many parts of the world. The ancient Mesopotamians imagined the earth surrounded by a body of water. A Babylonian *mappa mundi* shows Mesopotamia and neighboring lands encircled by a river whose Old Babylonian designation is rendered by modern scholars as the "great circle of the salt sea."[2] According to a Babylonian myth, an ordered world was created by the god Marduk who overwhelmed a monster which personified this sea and other

---

[1] F. Gisinger, "Geographie," *PWRE*, Suppl. IV (1924), cols. 521–685, especially section Der alte Orient, cols. 527–38.
[2] *See,* a reproduction in J. Oates, *Babylon* (London, 1979), figure 16, p. 34.

waters in the universe. The monster is known as Tiamat in Babylonian, Lotan in Canaanitish, and Leviathan in Hebrew.[3] Basically the same idea was expressed by the Germanic artists and craftsmen who made figurative representations of their own creation myths. A well-known example of such art are figures depicting the warrior-god Thor slaying a monster, the Midgard Serpent, who lay in the ocean surrounding the Miðgarð "middle earth."[4]

Returning to the Mediterranean world, we note that the ancient Egyptians believed the earth was an island washed by five seas, one of which they called the Great Circle. The Phoenicians named the same encircling sea *Baḥr mā'uk* "circular sea."[5] Like other Mediterranean peoples, the Greeks, too, believed the earth was surrounded by sea, which they named *Okeanos*, after the Titan Okeanos. Homer calls this sea *Okeanos potamos* "river ocean," imagining it as a river running around the earth personified by his wife Tethys, a Titaness.[6] The Arab polyhistor, al-Mas'ūdī, summed up medieval Muslim views of the Great Circle of the Salt Sea:

> No one sails upon it; there is no cultivated land there and no people. Neither its size nor its boundaries are known. And it is called the Sea of Darkness, Green Sea or Circumambient Sea (*al-Baḥr al-ẓulumāt, al-Baḥr al-akhḍar,* and *al Baḥr al-muḥīt*.[7]

---

[3] S.H. Hooke, *Middle Eastern Mythology* (Harmonsdworth, Middlesex, 1963), pp. 41, 82.

[4] D.M. Wilson, ed., *The Northern World* (New York, 1980), pp. 20, 32.

[5] V. Burr, *Nostrum Mare* (Stuttgart, 1932), pp. 80–3, 96.

[6] *Iliad*, XIV.201; *see* also, Hesiod, *Theogony, passim*. The name *Okeanos* (early form *ōgēnos*) seems to have been borrowed by Greeks from the Afroasian peoples. *See*, F. Gisinger, "Okeanos," *PWRE*, XVII.2 (1937), cols. 2309–10.

[7] *Murūj al-dhahab* (The Golden Meadows), transl. by B. de Meynard and P. de Courteille (Paris, 1861–1877; revised and corrected C. Pellat, Paris, 1962), I, ¶ 273, p. 106; the Arabic text ed. by Y.A. Dāghir (Beirut, 1965–6).

The Chinese[8] and the Aryans of India,[9] on the other hand, imagined the world as islands surrounded by seas, and the whole archipelago washed by one great circumambient ocean. The ancient Iranians, whose cosmology is reflected in the Avesta, described the world as seven circular continents separated from one another by seas and mountains. Only the central continent, "the splendid region of *Khvaniratha*," was inhabited. The whole was surrounded by *Vourukaša*, the Iranian equivalent of the Circumambient Ocean.[10]

Though a variety of images of the earth is found among tribes and nations throughout the world, the ancient civilized societies of Eurasia and North Africa generally believed that the earth was an island washed by a great uncharted sea, which, as we saw, was usually given the name Great Circle. The Greeks and Romans used several names for this body of water, such as Ocean River, Great Sea, Outward or External Sea, etc. The logic behind these designations is obvious. The first name reflects the sea's function as imagined by the ancients: flowing around dry land. The name Great Sea signifies not only the size, but also that this sea was both farther away, as if in the area of "the great unknown," as well as actually greater than its implied counterpart. Its often quoted Latin appellation *Mare tenebrosum* is identical to the Arabic *al-Baḥr al-ẓulumāt*. The Great Sea was called "outward" and "external" in contradistinction to the Mediterranean or Internal Sea, which remained without a common name until it became known by the Romans as *Nostrum mare* and universally as the Mediterranean Sea.[11]

Okeanos potamos was also called the Atlantic Ocean and the Arctic Ocean. The name Atlantic was associated with the Titan Atlas, the Atlas Mountains, and Atlantis. The term Arctic comes from the Greek word *arktos* "bear," applied to the constellation

---

[8] J. Needham, *Science and Civilization in China*, II (Chicago, 1954), p. 232.

[9] W. Kirfel, *Die Kosmographie der Inder nach den Quellen dargestellt* (Bonn–Leipzig, 1920), pp. 18–19.

[10] G. Gnoli, "Avestan Geography," *EIr*, III (1989), pp. 44–7.

[11] Burr, *op. cit., passim;* H. Stürenburg, *Relative Ortsbezeichnung* (Leipzig–Berlin, 1932), pp. 5–6.

which the Romans called *Ursa major*, the English Great Bear.[12] The directional opposite of *arktos* was called *notos*, the god of the south wind. *Notia thalassa* was the name given by ancient Greeks to that section of the Circumambient Ocean that encompassed the earth from the south. That portion of this same ocean, where the dawn and sun rose, was called *Eōos ōkeanos, Eous oceanus* "ocean of dawn." It was perceived as the directional counterpart of the Atlantic Ocean *stricte*, which frequently was called *Dytikos ōkeanos, Occidentalis oceanus* "western ocean."[13]

Ancient Mediterranean geographers named portions of the Circumambient Ocean after peoples who lived, or were presumed to live, on its shores. Thus, the Ocean of Dawn frequently bore the names of the Seri and the Sinae, the most easterly peoples known to Mediterranean observers.[14] The Arctic Ocean was invariably named after the Scythian and Sarmatian peoples, whose domain verged on the northern shores of the Black Sea in reality, reaching the Arctic Circle only in the imagination of Afroasian and Roman writers.[15] The North Atlantic Sea appears in Ptolemy's *Geography* as *Oceanus Hyperboreus, Hibernicus, Britannicus, Germanicus,* and *Duecaledonius.*[16] The Caspian Sea, which the ancients, except Herodotus, thought communicated with the Circumambient Ocean, has also been known by the names of the peoples who succeeded the original Caspii and each others on its shores.[17]

Clearly, the ancients of the Mediterranean basin named the water surface of the earth in a bino-quinary manner. The binary

[12] Another Greek name for this constellation is *Boōtes* "ploughman." The Latin equivalent, *Septemtriones*, "seven-plough-oxen" gave the word *septemtrionalis* "northern."
[13] A. Ronconi, "Per l'onomastica antica dei mari," *Studi Italiani di Filologia Classica*, N.S., ed. G. Pasquali, IX (1935?), pp. 193–242, 257–331.
[14] Our names East China Sea, South China Sea, Sea of Japan, Sea of the Philippines continue that ancient practice of naming seas after peoples.
[15] We shall show that the name Russi, which first appeared at the Derbent Gate and along the shores of the Caspian and Black seas, was occasionally extended northward and westward beyond the original Russian domain in the imagination of medieval writers and regularly in that of their modern commentators.
[16] Tabula Europae I.
[17] Herodotus, I.203; VII.67, 86.

set consisted of a center and the periphery. In the center was the well-known Internal Sea or Our Sea, while at the periphery loomed the uncharted Circumambient Ocean, named also the Great Circle, Great Sea, External Sea, Sea of Darkness, and Green Sea. The quinary set consisted of a center, designated as the Internal Sea, and four sections of the peripheral sea, named after the stars or planets associated with the four cardinal points of the compass. Thus, the Eastern Sea was defined by Eos (the morning star) and sunrise; the Western Sea was governed by Hesper (the evening star) and sunset; and the Northern Sea was ruled by Arktos (the Great Bear) and night. No single star presided over the southern segment of the Great Ocean whose Greek name, *Notia thalassa*, comes from the name for the south wind, and its Latin equivalent, *Oceanus australe*, from *auster* "south wind."

The ancient writers who communicated in Greek and Latin were aware of three continents: Asia, Europe, and Libya. (The Romans used the name Africa for the continent which the Greeks called Libya.) They believed that the world's western limits lay beyond the Pillars of Heracles (modern Gibraltar), the eastern at the Phasis River in Colchis (the Rioni in Georgia). The southern quarter was traversed by the Nile, which some authorities designated as the boundary between Asia and Africa.[18] The river's name often stood for the south generally, while the estuary of the Don symbolized the north. The Don served as a conventional border between Asia and Europe.

In poetry, light, day, life, and youth had their daily births east of Colchis. Preceded by the morning star, Helios rose out of Ocean to begin his journey across the sky, first bathing with his golden rays his beloved Colchians who kept the Golden Fleece until it was taken away by Jason the Argonaut. Beyond the Pillars of Heracles, in the Western Ocean, the ancients imagined an island, where the *Hesperides* "daughters of night" resided, guarding the golden apples. This region was associated with evening and sweet old age.

---

[18] Cf., Pliny, *n.h.*, V.47–8, and Ptolemy, *Geography*, II. Prologue, ed. C. Müllerus, 2 vols. (Paris, 1883); the English text in E.L. Stevenson's translation, introd. by J. Fischer (New York, 1932; Dover Publ. 1991), p. 47.

In schematic representations Europe usually occupies the northern quarter, Asia and Libya (Africa) taking up the eastern and southern quarters.[19] However, in more common arrangements Asia is assigned the eastern quarter, Europe the northern, and Libya the southern. This tripartite division of the *oikoumene* survived through the Middle Ages, when the more common image of the earth was shown by the so-called T–O maps. The "O" represents the Circumambient Ocean and the "T" drawn within divides it into three segments or continents. The stem of the "T" is the Mediterranean Sea. It receives the Nile and the Don which together form the crossbar. Asia is at the top representing the East, Europe takes up the left or the North segment, Libya the right or the South.[20] The peoples of the Old World had no positive knowledge of a continent in their back, the West, until Columbus' discovery of America became universally known.

Only fragments of cosmographic ideas of extinct Mediterranean civilizations have come down to us through Greek and Latin filters, making it often impossible to identify original contributions of peoples whose thoughts have not survived in their own languages. Thus, we are better informed about cosmographic beliefs of the literate Afroasian peoples, such as Egyptians and Mesopotamians, than about those held by Scythians, Colchians, Pelasgians, Thracians, Macedonians, Illyrians, and other nations whose literary monuments have not survived.

EAST, WEST, NORTH, SOUTH

When journeying beyond their fixed abodes people use the sun, the stars, vegetation, natural features, and man-made objects to orient themselves and to find their way back home. The Greeks whose world view is reflected in Homer followed mainly dawn and evening (Eos and Hesper) or sunrise and sunset, treating the

---

[19]   E.H. Bunbury, *A History of Ancient Geography*, 2nd ed., 2 vols. (London, 1883; Dover ed., New York, 1959), I, map facing p. 148.
[20]   J.K. Wright, *The Geographical Lore of the Time of the Crusades* (New York, 1925; reprinted 1965), pp. 66–7.

south, usually, as an extension of sunrise,[21] while they comprehended the north either as a separate sphere of darkness or attached it to sunset. When unable to place themselves in relation to these two cardinal points, as were for instance Odysseus and his crew after they had landed on Circe's Island, they felt totally lost, and their captain spoke:

> 'Shipmates, companions in disastrous time,
> O my dear friends, where Dawn lies, and the West,
> and where the great Sun, light of men, may go
> under the earth by night, and where he rises—
> of these things we know nothing. Do we know
> any least thing to serve us now? I wonder.'[22]

Some tribes still remain at the level of these Homeric heroes and orient themselves in relation to the two cardinal points. Like Odysseus, the peoples of the Northern Hemisphere have, during most of their recorded history, viewed the world divided politically and culturally in a bi-polar manner, according to two cardinal points: East and West, represented in this century by Imperial and Soviet Russia and a succession of its Western rivals.[23]

At the same time, others have always held a quadri-polar view of the world. Polybius, a second-century BC historian, wrote:

> Now the primary and most general conception and one common to all mankind is the division and ordering of the heavens by which all of us, even those of the meanest capacity, distinguish East, West, South, and North.[24]

---

[21]   Generally, the south is equated with midday, as shown by the names for that quarter in Greek (*mesembria*), Latin (*meridies*), German (*Mittag*), Polish (*południe*), and so on.

[22]   *Odyssey*, X.191–6. (R. Lattimore's translation.)

[23]   Now that hostilities between them appear to be subsiding and the twain are meeting in the recently "discovered" spirit of interdependence across the Northern Hemisphere extending from Big Diomede to Little Diomede and from Vladivostok to San Diego, the ancient North–South cleavage is coming into focus again.

[24]   III.36.

Such division was imagined by the Sumerians who distinguished "four *ubda's*, that is, four regions or districts, which seem to cor, respond roughly to the four points of the compass."[25]

A complete set of names of the cardinal points was used by Yahweh in a promise to Abram. We adduce the passage to show how these terms were translated into some languages. In the most popular English version, the deity spoke:

> Lift up now thine eyes, and look from where thou art *northward*, and *southward*, and *eastward*, and *westward*: for all the land which thou seest, to thee will I give it, and to thy seed for ever.[26]

"Translated out of the original tongues," the King James version agrees with St. Jerome's translation into Vulgar Latin, which reads:

> leva oculos tuos et vide a loco in quo nunc es
> *ad aquilonem* et *ad meridiem ad orientem* et *ad occidentem*
> omnem terram quam conspicis tibi dabo et semini tuo usque in
> sempiternum.

The directions of the horizon in the Septuagint are: *pros borran kai liba kai anatolas kai thalassan* "toward the Borea (northern wind) and toward the (moist) southern wind and toward the rising sun and toward the sea." In Hebrew the terms employed are: *tzifonah* "toward the cold" (from *tzafon* "cold"), *v'negbah* "toward dry country" (from the root *ngb* "to be dessicated"), *v'kedmah* "in front," and *v'yamah* "toward the sea."[27] Generally, in biblical Hebrew the

> geographical regions correspond to the division of the horizon into four equal sections, which are the cardinal points. In the designations of these directions there can be discerned three different systems of names, each resting on a separate principle. The first system is based upon the functional relation between the position of the observer facing one direction (i.e., east); the determination of the other three is related to the direction toward east. The direc-

[25] Kramer, *op. cit.*, p. 284.
[26] Gen. 13:14–15.
[27] *Biblia Hebraica*, ed. by R. Kittel, and P. Kahle, 13th ed. (Stuttgart, 1962).

tions are defined in relation to him facing *qdm* "that which is before," which corresponds to the east. ... The opposite of *qdm* is *'ḥwr* or *'ḥrwn* "behind," corresponding to the west. ... The direction to the north is defined in relation to the left-hand side of the observer facing east. The word *šm'l* "what is on the left side" occurs in the expression *mšm'l ldmšq* which may plausibly be translated "what lies north of Damascus" (Gen.14:15). Similarly *ymyn* "the right hand, lying to the right" (the favorable side), and *tymn* "what is on the right-hand side" denote the south. ... The second system of names used to designate the four cardinal points is associated with the sun's daily course. ... The third system, which takes into account the topographical features of Palestine, indicated directions by means of descriptive terms corresponding to local panorama.[28]

We see that the system used in Gen. 13:14−15 is syncretic. Since Abram was facing the rising sun as he heard the promise, the east was before him, and the word for this cardinal point belongs to the first system. The words for the remaining cardinal points, being determined by the meteorology and topography of Palestine, belong to the third system available to the ancient Hebrews.

The peoples of Eurasia created names for the cardinal points, generally: in accordance with their position at prayer; from the names for the heavenly bodies and their movement across the skies; from some characteristic winds; and occasionally from natural features, man-made objects, and even from imaginary features.

The ancient Egyptians, as if turning their back to the Mediterranean Sea while seeking the source of the Nile, established their conception of the four cardinal points by facing the south. The expressions "going up the Nile" meant also "southward," "down the Nile" could be interpreted as "northward." Using the human body as an analogy, the south was associated with the

---

[28] L.I.J. Stadelmann, *The Hebrew Conception of the World: A Philological and Literary Study* (Rome, 1970) (=*Analecta Biblica*, 39), pp. 131−3.

head, the north with the back, the east with the left hand, and the west with the right.[29]

Since the ancient Semites prayed facing the rising sun, in biblical Hebrew the word *qdm* "east," means literally "that which is in front," *'ḥwr* or *'ḥrwn* "west" and "behind." In Arabic "the rising of the sun" is the meaning of *šrq*, *mašriq* "east, the East," while the root *ghrb* "behind, sunset," yields *maghrib* "the West." To an Arab the words for north and south literally mean "that which is on the left side" and "that which is on the right side," respectively.

It appears that some Indo-Europeans also arrived at their expressions for the cardinal points while facing or praying to the rising sun. We infer this from the English words "north" and "south," which derive from terms meaning "left" and "right," respectively, presupposing an eastern orientation.[30]

The English word "east" derives from the Indo-European **aues* "leuchten," source also of the Greek *Eos* "the morning star." The word "west," as well as the Greek *Hesper* "the evening star," has been traced to the Indo-European **uesperos (uekeros)* "Abend, Dunkel."[31] Verbs denoting sunrise serve to build the terms for "east" in Greek, Latin, and Russian, while verbs or nouns describing sunset in these languages are used to render the meaning of "west."

The north is equated with cold—as well as cold northerly winds—in Hebrew, Greek, Latin, and perhaps Russian. The names for the rain-bringing southerly winds are the source for the word for "south" in Greek and Russian.

The expression "toward the sea" was readily understood to mean "westward" by the ancient Hebrews while they lived in Palestine, a country bounded by the Mediterranean Sea on the west. But for the Greeks, *e.g.*, who lived on numerous peninsulas and islands it must have seemed confusing. Saint Jerome

---

[29]   G. Posener, "Sur l'orientation et l'ordre des points cardinaux chez les Égyptiens," *Göttinger Vorträge* (1965), pp. 69–78 (=*Nachrichten v. d. Akad. d. Wiss. zu Göttingen, Phil.-hist. Kl.*); D. Kessler, "Himmelsrichtungen," *Lexikon der Ägyptologie*, II (1977), cols. 1211–13.

[30]   F. Kluge, *Etymologisches Wörterbuch der deutschen Sprache*, W. Mitzka, ed. (Berlin, 1963), 19th ed., s.v. "Nord" and "Süd."

[31]   J. Pokorny, *Indogermanisches etymologisches Wörterbuch* (Bern––Munich, 1949–1959), I, pp. 86, 1173.

seized the meaning accurately when he rendered the Hebrew
v'yamah as "ad occidentem."

Some languages have two sets of words for the cardinal
points: the scientific or standardized, and the poetic or imaginative. The scientific set, used on maps, in scholarly prose, and in
official documents, is a closed system with no synonyms or
alternates. The poetic set is an open one, for its sources are
dialects, popular imagination, and other languages. An example
of this duality is found in modern German, where the first set
consists of the words *Ost, West, Nord,* and *Süd,* the second of
Morgen, Abend, Mitternacht, and *Mittag.*[32] In the western
Romance languages, the scientific set consists of four words
derived from the Germanic nomenclature, while the poetic set
draws upon Vulgar Latin. Thus, in French, for example, the
scientific set is Germanic in origin—*est, ouest, nord,* and
sud—whereas the poetic one—*orient, occident, septentrion,* and
midi—comes from Vulgar Latin.

We see that the universal and ancient "division and ordering"
of heaven and earth did not become the intellectual property of
all humanity at the same time, as Polybius thought. Rather,
different peoples acquired the ideas in stages, often borrowing
concepts or words from their neighbors. Written documents
show only how literate folks oriented themselves in the past.[33]
Since we are in the dark regarding the customs of ancient tribes
and nations who had no written language, we may arrive at
tentative answers by studying their homeland's toponymic and
ethnonymic material recorded in ancient writings of their literate
neighbors.

CARDINAL POINTS AND DIVINE LAND GRANTS

The notion of the four cardinal points is reflected in numerous
ways in many cultures and civilizations. In Mesopotamia, it was
incorporated not only into Sumerian cosmography but also into

---

[32]   In translating the Bible into German Martin Luther used the poetic set
for the directions of the horizon.
[33]   C.D. Buck, *A Dictionary of Selected Synonyms in the Principal Indo-
European Languages* (Chicago, 1939), pp. 870f; *see* also, Nikonov, *op. cit.*

their architecture and politics and into those of their neighbors, political successors, and cultural heirs. For example, in Assyria, at Tepe Gawra, near Nineveh, archaeologists have unearthed three painted temples: Central, Northern, and Eastern. The colors applied were red, black, ochre, and vermillion. Later, other structures were built on the ruins of the temples, among them the White Room—so called because of its whitewashed walls—whose corners were oriented toward the cardinal points of the compass.[34] In Elam the cardinal points had a specific meaning. In the kingdom's capital, Susa, there was a ziggurrat-type temple on the acropolis, surrounded by a sacred wall, with one of its towers functioning as *nūr kibrāti* "light of the (four) regions (of the world)."[35]

Numerous fortresses, palaces, temples, and cities across Eurasia, from China to Britain, show that their planners were guided by the same notion, while soldiers, princes, priests, and politicians residing in them often claimed their power extended in the four directions to the very end of the earth.

In early societies, political powerholders legitimized their right to rule by connecting it with the supreme deity in the imagination of those they governed. The deity, presiding over the four quarters of heaven, ruled through his or her vicars over the four quarters of the earth.[36]

In China, the emperor, as the Son of Heaven, was divine. From the center of the earth he presided over the whole "civilized" world extending in the four directions. Beyond his realm was the domain of barbarians, and it was his mandate to "civilize" them.

Egyptian pharaohs were gods ruling in Egypt, the only portion of the world which the Egyptians acknowledged as civilized. Their rule over the totality of the world was assured by their gods' positioning themselves at the world's extremities and the god Amon's turning toward the cardinal points at the

---

[34]   M.E.L. Mallowan, "The Development of Cities from Al-`Ubaid to the End of Uruk 5," *CAH*, I.1³ (1970), p. 382.

[35]   R. Labat, "Elam c. 1600–1200 B.C.," *CAH*, II.2³ (1975), p. 391.

[36]   Today, with the exception of those who claim to be gods themselves, supreme rulers of lands and peoples hold their office either by the grace of some god or by the will of the people, which is the will of the prevailing deity, as shown by the saying: *vox populi, vox dei.*

accession of a new pharaoh.[37] Some pharaohs and their subjects may have, in fact, believed they ruled the whole world as shown, for example, by the title *Nb r-dt* "lord of the universe" assumed by Senwosre I.[38]

In ancient Mesopotamia, the idea and the symbols of kingship originated from Anu, the sky-god, who caused the pertinent insignia to descend into the antediluvian city of Eridu.[39] Even though they did not generally stress their divine origin, kings who ruled from Kish and other Mesopotamian cities after the Great Flood claimed for themselves and on behalf of the gods of their imagination a broad and vague territorial jurisdiction.

The earliest known ruler claiming the whole world was the Sumerian king Lugalzaggisi (ca. 2371–47 BC) who stated that his god, Enlil, had removed his opponents "from the Lower Sea by the Tigris and Euphrates unto the Upper Sea. ... [and] from the rising sun unto the setting." He was defeated by Sargon of Agade (ca. 2371–16 BC), whose "hand reached over the four regions of the world." Sargon's grandson, Naram-Sin (2291–55), was the first monarch who assumed the title "king of the four regions."[40] Naram-Sin's realm was overwhelmed by the Gutians whose kings did not claim to rule over the whole world. Following the expulsion of the Gutians by Ur-Nammu (2113–2096) and the establishment of the Third Dynasty of Ur, the title "king of the four regions" was reintroduced in Sumer and Akkad.[41]

Sumer's neighbors to the east, the Elamites, claimed their own particular connection with the gods, for they called their land

---

[37]   Posener, *op. cit.*, pp. 74–5.

[38]   J. Vercoutter, *L'Égypte et le monde égéen préhéllenique: Étude critique des sources égyptiennes (du début de la XVIIIe à la fin de la XIXe Dynastie)* (Cairo, 1956), pp. 132–3, doc. 34. *See*, an inspired interpretation of this title in Bernal, *op. cit.*, II, p. 255.

[39]   C.J. Gadd, "The Cities of Babylonia," *CAH*, I.2³ (1971), p. 102. Later, Enlil and Marduk became the sources of royal power in Mesopotamia, Ashur in Assyria, Yahweh in Palestine, Zeus in Hellas, etc.

[40]   C.J. Gadd, "The Dynasty of Agade and the Gutian Invasion," *CAH*, I.2³ (1971), pp. 421, 424–5, 448.

[41]   *Idem*, "Babylonia c. 2120–1800 B.C.," *CAH*, I.2³ (1971), p. 598.

Halamti or Hatamti, an equivalent of "god's land."[42] Following the turmoil in Mesopotamia caused by the Gutian invasion, Elam's king Kutik-In-Shushinak grew in power and declared himself "king of the four regions,"[43] saying in an inscription that Elam's god, In-Shushinak, gave him "the four quarters of the earth."[44]

People succeeded people, gods replaced gods, monarchs and dynasties rose and fell, but the custom of claiming titles from the gods to a piece of land or to the four quarters survived throughout ancient Southwest Asia and North Africa. To name only some of the most outstanding examples, when Babylon rose from the seat of a modest Amorite dynasty to that of the preeminent center of supreme power in Mesopotamia, its king, Hammurabi (1792−50 BC), proclaimed himself not only "king of Sumer and Akkad" but also "king of the four quarters."[45] As the prestige of Babylon grew, the city's own god, Marduk, replaced Enlil and ultimately took over his function of dispenser of land grants to mortals. After the Kassites conquered Babylon their kings claimed they ruled by the grace of the Babylonian god Marduk from his city over Sumer and Akkad, as well as "the whole world."[46] Nabonidus (555−39 BC), a Chaldaean ruler of Babylon, enjoyed the favor of Marduk in his city and in "the whole world" until the god "offered his hand" to the Persian king Cyrus the Great (550−29 BC) and made him the legitimate king of Babylon. A Hebrew writer "saw" Yahweh, a deity of his own people, hold Cyrus' right hand and make him his christ or messiah.[47] But Cyrus was an elect of Ahura Mazda, his people's god, who granted him the title "king of kings," an equivalent of the four quarters of other potentates. After annexing the Fertile Crescent to his empire, Cyrus assumed the titles *Šar Bābili* "king of Babylon" and *Šar matāti* "king of lands."

In Assyria, beginning with Shamshi-Adad I (1813−1781 BC), kings ruled by the grace of their national god, Ashur, who gave

---

42   W. Hinz, "Persia c. 2400−1800 B.C.," *CAH*, I.2³ (1971), p. 644. In Sumerian, Elam's name, written with the sign NIN, signifies "highland."
43   Gadd, "The Dynasty of Agade," p. 455.
44   Hinz, *op. cit.*, pp. 653−4.
45   Oates, *op. cit.*, pp. 65−7.
46   M.S. Drower, "Syria c. 1550−1400 B.C.," *CAH*, II.1³ (1973), p. 441.
47   Isaiah 45:1.

them not only his city but "the totality of the countries," an equivalent of the four regions.[48]

Hittite rulers used the title "great kings." Tudkhaliash IV (*regn.* ca. 1250 BC), the last great king, assumed the title *Šar kiššati* "king of the world," in imitation of his Assyrian rivals.[49]

As we saw, the ancient Hebrews, heirs of the civilizations of Southwest Asia and Egypt, believed their particular deity had promised to make their founder Abram (called Abraham soon thereafter) master over the four regions. Though undated, the promise appears to be a relatively late Hebrew version of an ancient tradition. The deed to the "promised land" is styled in accordance with the well-established Southwest Asian custom of defining divine land grants in terms of the four regions.

The early Greeks believed that in mythical times the gods took part in siring rulers, giving them land, taking it back, and helping them against their earthly and heavenly foes. Divine land grants in Hellas were circumscribed by the existing boundaries of the city-states. Thus, the Spartan poet Tyrtaeus (*fl.* 685–68 BC) says:

> For Cronus' Son Himself, Zeus the husband of fair-crowned Hera, hath given this city [Sparta] to the children of Heracles, with whom we came into the wide isle of Pelops from windy Erineus.[50]

The Macedonian king Philip II, though a "descendant" of the semi-divine Heracles, who conquered Greece by force of arms and had himself appointed "Commander of the Greeks," did not insist on his divine origin or heavenly mandate. His son, Alexander the Great, conquered Egypt, Southwest Asia, and parts of Central and South Asia. Although all could see that a force of rough Macedonian, Thracian, Illyrian, and Greek peasants and shepherds had accomplished this feat, Alexander was greeted as a god in Egypt. He crowned himself "king of Asia" in Babylon and insisted on being worshipped as a god. In legends recorded after his death, Alexander is depicted as a conqueror of three

---

[48]   H. Lewy, "Assyria c. 2600–1816 B.C.," *CAH*, I.2³ (1971), pp. 735–6.
[49]   A. Goetze, "The Hittites and Syria (1300–1200 B.C.)," *CAH*, II.2³ (1975), p. 262.
[50]   Tyrtaeus, fragment 2.

quarters, that is, west, east, and south. He was also believed to have built an iron gate to keep out the savage and unconquerable peoples of the northern quarter.

Though the Roman emperors ruled over a good portion of the known world, they did not explicitly claim mastery of the four regions. However, the Emperor Diocletian and his three associates in office, all Illyrians, symbolically assumed this title, as can be implied from a sculptural ensemble located in Venice, which shows their "divine" figures presiding over the four cardinal points of the compass. Some of Rome's ancient universalist pretensions have been appropriated by the city's Christian bishops who use the ancient pagan title of *Pontifex maximus* "supreme bridgebuilder [to the other world]," while addressing their pronouncements *Urbi and orbi.*

After Jesus of Nazareth was proclaimed messiah or christ, John the Divine, one of his followers, steeped in Levantine rhetoric, envisioned his teacher with the title "king of kings and lord of lords" written on his vesture and tattooed on his thigh.[51] The teacher himself is often quoted as saying: "All power is given unto me in heaven and in earth."[52] His early followers invested Jesus with the lofty title *christos pantokrator* "the anointed ruler of all" and understood this as their obligation to spread his teachings to the four quarters of the earth.

Andrew, one of the twelve apostles of Jesus, went to Scythia. The contemporary sources do not specify whether he went to Little or Great Scythia.[53] Though it is almost certain that, in either case the apostle hugged the coast, medieval Russian Christians, living in the land then still called Scythia and eager to establish the divine origin of the Kiev bishopric and to sanctify the secular authority established there, made Andrew journey into the interior up the Dnieper to Kiev. They imagined him planting a cross on the site of the future city to serve as "proof" that Russian Christianity had been established by the first follower of Christ.[54] Having been visited and sanctified by

[51] Rev. 19:16.
[52] Mat. 28:18.
[53] Eusebius, *The Ecclesiastical History*, III.1. *See* below, pp. 81ff. for the two Scythias.
[54] *PVL*, pp. 53–4.

Andrew, Kiev, "the mother or Russian cities," had obtained the right to claim equal status with New Rome (Constantinople) which claimed to possess the relics of this man, and feel superior to Old Rome where the bones of his brother Peter were housed and displayed as "proof" that the seat of the dead pagan empire had become the head of its Christian successor and that the universal pretensions of the first had been transferred to the second by the *christos pantokrator*.[55]

In the second half of the eleventh century, on the Day of the Red Disc, either on the banks of the Amur River or at Kara-korum, the Mongol warrior Temudžin was proclaimed "Genghis Khan." The title was conferred by the chief deity of the Mongols through a shaman. Those who claim the title derives from a Turkic word for "ocean" interpret it as "universal khan or ruler of the whole world."[56]

The peoples who built the civilizations, states, and empires in the New World also endowed those they obeyed with divine attributes. To name just a more remarkable example, the Incas of Peru. The first Inca, Manco Copac, was a son of the Sun. He built the city of Cuzco with a sun temple in the center, established civilization, government, laws, and engendered a line of semi-divine rulers and nobles, who, through the succeeding generations, partook of his solar divinity. The empire founded by Manco Copac was called *Tawantinsuyu* "kingdom of the four quarters," that is, the four regions which extended north, east, south, and west from Cuzco.

As we see, Eurasia, Egypt, and the Americas have seen a long parade of monarchs who claimed they were chosen by a god or gods to rule over a piece of land. Since the divine domain is limitless, the territories leased by gods to mortals are also normally inclusive of the whole known world. Some of the more ambitious potentates affirmed that the deity of their imagination had appointed them to rule over "the four regions" or "the whole world." And, while no ruler has yet virtually ruled the whole world, some thought they came close to it. For instance, at the

[55] F. Dvornik, *The Idea of Apostolicity in Byzantium and the Legend of the Apostle Andrew* (Cambridge, Mass., 1958).

[56] P. Brent, *Genghis Khan: The Rise, Authority and Decline of Mongol Power* (New York, 1976), pp. 11–25.

dawn of the modern age, Charles I of Spain (1516–56)—V of the Holy Roman Empire (1519–56)—ruled a realm on which the sun never set. When Great Britain was a naval power, the British boasted that the sun never set on their empire. Russia's emperors might have once thought they also were masters of the four quarters, for theirs was the largest contiguous state in world history, stretching across three continents. Before the sun would set on western Russia it would already be rising over its eastern marches.

CARDINAL POINTS AND GEOGRAPHICAL AND ETHNIC NAMES: *Severjane, Nordmanni, Austr-Winðar*

In studying geographical names, we normally assume that some of them may derive from words designating the cardinal points of the compass. Thus, it is well known that the names *Ausonia*[57] (a poetical name for Italy), *Anatolia*,[58] *Khorāsān* (a province of northeastern Iran)[59], *Korea*, and *Japan* originated from words designating the east or the rising sun in the relevant languages. The names *Hesperia* (another poetical name for Italy)[60] and *Maghrib*[61] derive from the words for the west in Greek and Arabic, respectively. *Australia* obtained its name from the Latin word *auster* "south wind."[62]

The world's ethnonymy shows that peoples, too, may be perceived and named according to the cardinal points. Thus, seen from Sumer, the nomads of the Syrian Desert were collectively called *Martu* or *Amorites*. The name Martu was also the name of the god of the western quarter seen from Mesopotamia. The "westerners" appeared in later sources divided into many groupings, chief among them being *Benē Šim'āl* "sons of the north"

---

[57] C. Hülsen, "Ausones," "Ausonia," "Ausonium mare," *PWRE*, II.2 (1896), cols. 2561–2.

[58] On the origin of the name, *see*, *EI²*, I (1960), s.v. "Anadolu," pp. 461–2.

[59] *See*, *EI*, II (1927), s.v. "Khorāsān," pp. 966–7, where the name is explained as "the country of the rising sun."

[60] J. Weiss, "Hesperia," *PWRE*, VIII (1913), col. 1243.

[61] For the origin of the term *see*, *EI²*, V (1985), pp. 1183–4.

[62] G.R. Stewart, *Names on the Globe* (New York, 1975), pp. 348ff.

and *Benē Iamina* "sons of the south."[63] The name *Bene Qedem* "children of the east" was a collective designation for the nomads living east of Palestine.[64] The ethnonym *Saraceni*, which in the Middle Ages was applied to Muslims in general, derives from the root *šrq* "east" with the meaning of "easterners."[65]

A few more commonly known examples from the Germanic languages may be adduced. On their way from Scandinavia to Romania, via Russia, the Goths separated into *Ostrogoths* and *Visigoths* "Eastern Goths" and "Western Goths."[66]

After they had conquered parts of Roman Britain, the Anglo-Saxons established a heptarchy which included the kingdoms of Essex, Sussex, and Wessex, that is, East, South, and West Saxons, respectively. However, there was no "Nossex," for the Saxons' northern neighbors were the Angles of the kingdoms of Mercia and Anglia. But, the word "north" appeared in the name *Northumbria*, the northernmost member of the heptarchy, which stretched beyond the Humber River. Its inhabitants were known as "northern people," as were those who lived in northern East Anglia, in the modern county of Norfolk. The latter were named as directional counterparts of "the southern folk" of East Anglia, after whom the modern county of Suffolk is named.[67]

The realm of the Franks was divided into Austrasia and Neustria. Although in Latin they were called *Francia orientalis* and *Francia occidentalis*, some scholars believe that the name Neustria means "new land" across the Rhine, which the Franks had annexed to their old country in Germany. But, an identical divi-

---

[63]   J.–R. Kupper, "Northern Mesopotamia and Syria," *CAH*, II.1³ (1973), pp. 24–6.

[64]   *See* below, pp. 64ff.

[65]   P.K. Hitti, *History of the Arabs*, 6th ed. (London, 1958), p. 43. For a recent analysis of the sources and a critique of the traditional etymologies, *see*, I. Shahīd, *Rome and the Arabs* (Washington, D.C., 1984), pp. 123–41.

[66]   On the Goths in general, *see*, the best scholarly edition of Jordanes' *Getica* by E.Č. Skržinskaja (Moscow, 1960). *See* also, H. Wolfram, *History of the Goths*, transl. by T.J. Dunlap, new and rev. ed. from 2nd German ed. (Berkeley, 1988), pp. 25–6. The more recent Western literature is discussed in P.J. Heather's *Goths and Romans 332–489* (Oxford, 1991).

[67]   E. Ekwall, *The Concise Oxford Dictionary of English Place-Names*, 4th ed. (Oxford, 1960), s.v. "Norfolk, Northumbria, and Suffolk." *See* also, a fold-out map in the Loeb Classical Library edition of Bede's *Opera Historica*.

sion of the Lombard Kingdom in Italy into Austria and Neustria, both new lands, shows that the Latin translation of *Neustria* as "western land," that of *Austrasia* as "eastern land," is accurate.[68] This contention is especially confirmed by the case of *Austria*, *Oesterreich* "eastern Reich," which grew out of the *Marca orientalis* founded by Charlemagne at the extreme east of ninth-century Germandom.

There is a set of seas in northwestern Europe named after the words designating the cardinal points in the Germanic languages. Looking from Denmark, the sea wherefrom the sun rises is called *Østersø*, and the one into which it sets is called *Vesterhav*. The North Sea is divided into *Noordzee* and *Zuidzee* by the Dutch. Designations of this nature are also used on land. For example, the entrance into the Oslo Fjord is flanked by the *Vestfold* and the *Östfold*. The same North Germanic peoples who coined these names also designated the routes leading out of the central regions of their homeland by using their words for the cardinal points. Thus, the route leading north was named *Norðvegr* (from which we derive the name Norway), that going west was called *Vestrvegr*, the road to the continent and Rome was called *Suðrvegr*, and the one into Russia was named *Austrvegr*.[69]

One of the states of the Federal Republic of Germany is called North Rhine-Westphalia. While Westphalia has no directional counterpart today, in the Middle Ages it had it, when Saxony was divided threefold into Westphalia, Eastphalia, and Angria.

The domain of the Goths in Sweden is partitioned into *Östergötland* and *Västergötland*, while the east-central province of Sweden is divided into *Västermanland* and *Södermanland*, and the northern or upper country is called *Uppland*. The coastal region of Uppland is known as *Roslagen*, a name of debatable origin. Its similarity to *Ruotsi*, the Finnish name for Sweden, and their resemblance to the name Russi are, in our opinion, the

---

[68]   P. Kretschmer, "Austria und Neustria," *Glotta*, XXVI (1938), pp. 207–40; *see* further, *Encyclopaedia Britannica*, XVI (1972), p. 302, s.v. "Neustria."

[69]   A. Holtsmark, "Himmelstrøk og -retninger," *Kulturhistorisk Leksikon for nordisk middelalder*, VI (Copenhagen, 1961), pp. 566–7.

principal reasons why some scholars believe that the Russians originated from Roslagen.

Today, the Slavs are divided into East, West, and South Slavs. In the Middle Ages, a northern branch of the South Slavs who settled in Thrace was called *Severoi* by the Rhomaeans, while some Slavs in Ukraine and Russia were given the appellation *Severjane* by other Slavs. At the root of these ethnonyms is the Old Church Slavic word *sěver"* "north," so that both names mean "northern folks."[70] Their counterparts were not marked at that time. The name "Jugoslavs," from *jugo*, "south," was coined in the nineteenth century. Occasionally, the Russians and other Slavs were called *Nordmanni* "men of the north" by Western Christian writers, who were most likely translating the Slavic *Severjane* or its equivalent Rhomaean terms *Hyperboreoi* and *Boreoi Skythai*.

The Scandinavian peoples had their own names for Russia, which, from their point of reference stretched through the domain of the morning star. The road to the fabled east was called *Austrvegr*. It was in Russia, known to them as *Austrríki*, that pagan Scandinavians placed the abode of their gods and Christian Scandinavians imagined paradise. The Slavs were generally called Wends by the Germanic peoples, while those of Russia were appropriately distinguished as *Austr-Winðar* "Eastern Wends." Austrvegr, Austrríki, and Austr-Winðar, names prefixed with the Germanic *austr-* "east," are semantically related to the names which in other languages are defined by "anti." We shall see that the Austr-Winðar and Austrríki had appeared also as Antae and Antia in Roman and Rhomaean sources. Moreover, we intend to prove that the same people were known as *Russi* "reds" by their western Slavic neighbors who used colors to express the directions of the horizon.[71] It will be shown here that the ancient Slavs identified the east or southeast with the color

---

[70]   Vasmer, *REW*, III, pp. 588–9, s.v. "sever."

[71]   In Latin the name *Russi* was used for all three branches of the East Slavs. The form *Rutheni*, once a common Latin name for the Russians, was often used restrictively for the nearest branch of the Russian people, the Little Russians or Ukrainians. In Polish the Ukrainians are called *Rusiny* and the Russians *Rosjanie*. The Croats know the Ukrainians as *Rusini*, the Russians as *Rusi*.

red, just as the ancient and modern Germanic peoples assigned to the same quarter words that derive from the Indo-European *aues, reflected in Latin Aurora, Greek Eos. Though one does not readily associate the color red in the Germanic words that derive from *aues, the expression *Morgenröte*, as a poetical synonym for the east, renders such connotation.

To conclude, since the beginning of written history in Eurasia words for the directions of the horizon have often served to differentiate geographical names and names of peoples. The Germanic nations appear to have always preferred to name peoples and places with words known in their modern English forms as "east, west, north, and south." Thus, appellations which can be traced to recognizable words for the cardinal points are readily understood because they signify a named object's spatial position. The function of such differentiating words is relative, not descriptive. To illustrate, since we know that at the beginning of the Christian era words which derived from *aues symbolized the east, the Wends (Slavs) who were differentiated from other Wends with the word *austr* (from *aues) were merely Eastern Wends rather than "shiny, rosy, or ruddy Wends." The name *Austr-Winðar* was coined by observers situated closer to the unmarked or Western *Winðar*. While many Germanists interpret the element *austr-* in the name Ostrogoths as "the Goths glorified by the rising sun," none have suggested extending this significance to the Austr-Winðar, a people more permanently glorified by the rising sun of North Central Eurasia than had been the Goths who merely halted there on their way from the gloom of Scandinavia to the sun-drenched Romania.[72]

Names that derive from the Germanic words for the cardinal points are readily explained because we use them knowing full well their meaning. Thus, Liudprand of Cremona's explanation of the name *Nordmanni* as *aquilonari homines* "men of the north," is accepted. At the same time, modern scholars dismiss as a folk etymology the same author's explanation of the name *Rusii* as "reds," because neither the bishop nor the interpreters of his text understood the function of colors in geographical names. They failed to see that colors stood not only for the

[72] Wolfram, *op. cit.*, p. 25.

physical appearance of objects named but might also symbolize their relative positions in space.

Although many geographical names and names of peoples derive from words for the directions of the horizon in different languages, we cannot state that the system of four cardinal points is reflected with equal completeness and from the same antiquity among all peoples of the Old World.[73] Other ways of seeing and naming the environment are as common and as ancient. Before we discuss the use of colors in geographical names and in ethnonymy we shall survey some of these other ways of differentiation. In our search for the etymology and semasiology of the name Russi we must take into account the name Antae. The ethnonyms Austr-Winðar, Severjane, Antae, and Russi refer to one and the same people. No one has seriously challenged the fact that the name Austr-Winðar means "Eastern Wends" or "Eastern Slavs," since the word *austr* means "eastern" in Old Norse and the name *Winðar* is the Nordic form of the name *Venedae*, which in ancient and medieval Latin and Germanic sources was applied to the Slavs generally and to the West Slavs in particular. At the same time, there is a veritable library of scholarly efforts to explicate the names Antae and Russi. We reject these because they fail to take into account the fact that these names are mere synonyms of the name Austr-Winðar. We shall also show that the ethnonym Winðar (from Venedae) derives from a word for the color white.

The next chapter offers a basis for an explanation of the name Antae, as well as some binary divisions of Russia.

[73] Novikov, *op. cit.*

CHAPTER II

DIFFERENTIATING IDENTICAL NAMES

Along with the custom of distinguishing geographical names and ethnonyms according to the cardinal points, other methods to achieve differentiation have also been used since recorded history. This chapter surveys some of them.

When people first see a natural feature or come in contact with another people, they may simply name them "mountain, lake, river, people," etc. When the need arises to name additional objects of the same type, to avoid confusion, they might resort to the use of synonyms. Even then, two or more objects of the same nature might occasionally end up with identical names. In order to distinguish such objects, people add qualifying words.

The aim pursued here is to discuss some more common categories of qualifying words added to primary geographical names and names of peoples in order to understand why and how Russia was divided into Great and Little, Upper and Lower, Inner and Outer, why the same medieval Russians who were called *Austr-Winðar* "Eastern Wends" or *Severjane* "northerners" were also known as *Antae*, and why some Russians were called *Poljane* "field-dwellers," others *Drevljane* "forest-dwellers." The chapter concludes with the name *Dromitae* "people of (Achilles') racecourse," which Rhomaean writers used for the Russians.

WORDS OF DISTANCE: Antia, Ukraine, Outer Russia

Anti

The word *anti* and its cognates in Indo-European languages are readily recognized in Old World toponymy and ethnonymy. Using this word differentiation is achieved by marking the more distant objects, while the closer objects remain unmodified.[1]

Cities: Rhion–Antirhion are names of two capes and towns at the entrance to the Gulf of Corinth.[2] In ancient Hellas two towns bore the name Anticyra, as counterparts of Cirrha. One was located on the Spercheius River, in the Maliac Gulf, and is known today as Glypha. The other one was in the Corinthian Gulf, in Phocis, and was called Phocian for distinction. Its name today is *Aspra Spitia* "white houses."[3] There were Cinolis––Anticinolis in Paphlagonia.[4] In ancient Lycia, the city of Phellos had its counterpart in Antiphellos.[5] In Gaul, we surmise that Nicaea (modern Nice) was seen as the *polis*, because a neighboring Greek settlement was called Antipolis (modern Antibes). Bari's opposite in Red Croatia was named Antibari. The Croats ignore the preposition *anti* added by others to the name of their city and persist in calling it Bar; the Albanians of the region, however, use the name Tivari, which is a derivative of Antibari.

Islands: Kythera–Antikythera (called Cerigo–Cerigotto by the Venetians), Milos–Antimilos, Paros–Antiparos, Paxos–Antipaxos (called also Propaxos in the Middle Ages), Psara–Antipsara, and Lesbos (once called Issa)–Antissa[6] are well-known pairs of islands in the Aegean Sea. Rhodes had its spatial counterpart (and commercial rival) in Antirrhodos, an island off

---

[1] *See*, Kluge, *op. cit.*, s.v. *"ant-, Ende,* and *ent-"*; A. Holder, Alt-celtischer Saprachschatz, 3 vols. (Leipzig, 1896–1907), I, col. 139, s.v. "ande-," where the word is defined as "praefix der bewegung hin und her, intensiv und augmentativ, 'gegen'."

[2] Strabo, 8.2.3; Antirhion was also known as Molycrian Rhion.

[3] Strabo, 9.3.3.

[4] *Ibid.*, 12.3.10.

[5] *Ibid.*, 14.3.7.

[6] *Ibid.*, 1.3.9.

the harbor of Alexandria in Egypt.[7] Andros, the most northerly
island of the Cyclades, may have been given this name by those
who saw it either "in front, at end" or "at the border." While
Andros has no named insular counterpart, the city of Antandros
in Mysia, in Asia Minor, may have been viewed as "the city
opposite Andros" and named accordingly.[8] Finally, in the
Azanian Sea (the Indian Ocean) Pliny mentions the islands of
Bachia and Antibachia.[9]

Mountains: Casius–Anticasius in Syria, Cragus–Anticragus
in Lycia, Libanus–Antilibanus in Syria, Taurus–Antitaurus in
Syria and Turkey, Chasia–Antichasia in Greece, and Atlas–An-
tiatlas Mountains in the Maghrib are pairs of oronyms differentiated by the preposition anti. Occasionally, the mountains in
Tuscany, which are situated south of the main Apennine ranges
between the rivers Tiber and Arno, are called the Anti-Apen-
nines.

Miscellanea: The continent of Antarctica, named in contradistinction to the Arctic Ocean, and a good portion of the Southern Hemisphere were *terra incognita* in antiquity and in the
Middle Ages. It was believed that *antipodes* "people with feet
opposite," also called *antoikoi* and *antichthones*, dwelt in those
regions. Some writers named the unknown land *Antichthon* in
opposition to *Chthon*, which was the name of the world they
knew.[10]

In Italy, in Sabine country, at the conflux of the Anio and the
Tiber, stood the town of *Antemnae* "front water." In Latium
there was *Antium*, modern Anzio. Since the town was at the end
of the Latin domain, its name may signify "border town." This
appears to be the case with *Anthedon*, a town and harbor in
Boeotia, mentioned by Homer who calls it "Anthedon, on the
uttermost borders."[11]

We should note that it is not always possible to know with
certainty whether a given name that appears to be built on this

[7] *Ibid.*, 17.1.9.
[8] *Ibid.*, 13.1.5.
[9] *n.h.*, VI.173.
[10] Aristotle, *De Caelo*, II.XIII; *see* further, the fold-out map of Pomponius Mela's description of the world in Bunbury, *op. cit.*, II, facing p. 368.
[11] *Iliad*, II.508.

preposition means "in front" or "at the end." Also, names which derive from the preposition *anti* may easily be confused with those which contain the Greek noun *anthos* "a flower." For instance, there was an Arcadian town by the name of Andania, situated between Messene and Megalopolis. Its modern successor is called Andorossa.[12] Homer mentions Peloponnesian *Antheia* with the epithet "deep-meadowed," an indication that the name probably derives from *anthos*.[13] But the island of Samos, also known as *Anthemis*, may be seen either as "front" or "flower" island.[14]

Without intending to offer an anthology of names that are modified with the preposition *anti*, below some personal names are given that may be pertinent to our purpose of explicating the ethnonym Antae.

Antaeus, a Libyan giant, derived his force from his mother, the Earth. Heracles overpowered him by lifting him up and holding him in the air so that he could not renew his strength. Appropriately, the anthroponym derives from the word *anthos* "blossom." Though, the ancients believed Antaeus was the founder of Antium in Latium, the city's name appears to signify "border town" and is unrelated to Antaeus.

Antenor was a Trojan who led the Eneti from Paphlagonia to the Po Valley, where he founded Patavium (modern Padua). His name is composed from the preposition *anti* and the noun *anēr* "man," signifying "front man."

Antigone was a daughter of Oedipus and a great-granddaughter of Cadmus. Several towns were named Antigonea or Antigonia, the best known among them being those in Epirus and Macedonia. The masculine form, *Antigonus*, was especially popular in Macedonia and was borne by several successors to Alexander the Great. The name signifies "first born" (from *anti* "front" and *gonē* "offspring").

It seems that the anthroponym *Antipatros* derives from *Antipatria*, a town in Illyria, meaning "the border of patria." The name was popular in Macedonia, and several prominent

---

12   Strabo, 8.3.6.
13   *Iliad*, XI.151.
14   Strabo, 14.1.15.

Macedonians were called Antipater, including Alexander the Great's successor General Antipater (397–19 BC).

Antiochus, a Macedonian name, was popular among the Seleucid kings of Syria. The element *ochos* means "a carriage, *vehiculum*." Thus the name signifies "front carriage." In the form of Antiochia or Antiocheia it was spread far and wide as the name of cities, the most famous of which was Antiochia in Syria (today, Turkey).

A diligent investigator would find a large number of names differentiated by the preposition *anti* and its cognates. To name just one, in the Greek name *Propontis* the preposition *pro* "before" renders the same meaning conveyed by *anti*. The Propontis extends between the Bosporus and the Dardanelles and is known today as the Sea of Marmara. The ancient name describes the sea's location in relation to the Pontus Euxinus. The meaning of the preposition *pro* here is "in front, before," though the designation Propontis does not show whether the contrast was to the Aegean or the Black Sea.[15]

Ancient Palestine was seen by its inhabitants as a land bounded by two seas, the Dead Sea and the Mediterranean. Because the Palestinians followed an eastern orientation, they called the Dead Sea "the front sea," the Mediterranean "the back sea."[16]

Peoples, too, may be paired and named so that one group is designated with the preposition *anti*, or with a noun which means the "front." Though our information on ancient Mediterranean names comes chiefly through Greek and Latin filters, it appears that other peoples also used their equivalents of this preposition to divide humanity into the "ones here" versus "those over there," *i.e.*, "anti." An example from the eastern Mediterranean illustrates that this method was popular among the Semites. Cadmus, a mythical immigrant from the east, founded the city of Lychnidus in Macedonia at the point where the Black Drin River issues from Lake Ohrid.[17] In Greece, Cadmus

---

[15]   Burr, *op. cit.*, pp. 19–21.

[16]   *Ibid.*, p. 89.

[17]   Apollodorus, *The Library*, III.v.4; *see* also, N.G.L. Hammond, *A History of Macedonia*, I (Oxford, 1972), p. 93, n.1.

founded Thebes, called Cadmeia after him.[18] In Great Phrygia, a mountain called Cadmus is the source of the Lycus and Cadmus rivers which join the Meander.[19] Cadmus and his wife Harmonia were buried in Boka Kotorska in Red Croatia where their descendants ruled over the native Encheleii.[20] The name *Cadmus* is related to *Qedem* or *Bene Qedem*, a people living "in front" of the ancient Hebrews, as their name shows. In the Bible they are called *Cadmonites*, from the adjectival form *qadmoni*. Some translators refer to these people as "Easterners" or "Children of the East."[21]

The name Cadmus in the sense of "in front" occurs in the form Antani, an ancient Illyrian people living near Lake Ohrid. Centuries later a city by the name of Antania was also mentioned. We consider the Eneti settled in the vicinity as the positional counterparts of the Antani.[22] In antiquity, the same or other "front people" were attested in Slavonia as Andiantes, in the Po Valley obliquely as Andes, in Gaul as Andes, and in Scythia as Anthi. Also, in the Early Middle Ages, in the same general area of North Central Eurasia where the names Severoi, Severjane, and Russi were attested lived a people called Antae. The examples adduced ought to suffice to place the ethnonym Antae within the context of a Eurasian custom of attaching words signifying distance to more distant objects. The pair Antae—Venedae of North Central Eurasia clearly resembles the pairs Antenor—Eneti of Paphlagonia, Antani—Eneti of Macedonia, Andiantes—Veneti of Slavonia and northern Italy, the hypothesized pair *Antes (from Antenor)—Veneti of northern Italy, and the pair Andes—Veneti of Gaul. These names are discussed further in Chapter V, together with other ethnonyms applied to the Russians by their neighbors. We shall demonstrate that the *Antae* were so named because they settled "in front" of peoples who were given the name Venedae.

[18]   Strabo, 9.2.3, 32.

[19]   *Idem*, 12.8.16.

[20]   *Idem*, 7.7.8

[21]   "Kedemites or Easterners," *EJ*, X (1971), p. 865.

[22]   *See*, Hammond, *op. cit.*, pp. 76–7, on the Antani; Constantine Porphyrogenitus, *De thematibus*, 2.35, on Antania; and Appian, *The Mithridatic Wars*, 55, on the Eneti.

Contra

Names modified by *anti* are common among the Celts, Greeks, and eastern Mediterranean peoples. While the Romans appeared not to have availed themselves of the Latin preposition *ante*, they distinguished numerous paired names as follows: (0)-*contra*, *cis-trans*, *citerior-ulterior*. Naturally, many such pairs appeared at what used to be the changing frontiers of the Roman state.

When Rome was still limited to the hills and valleys along the left bank of the Tiber its citizens coined the name *Transtiberini* for the people living on the river's right bank, opposite Rome proper. Later, the settlement of the Transtiberini, called today Trastevere, became a part of the Eternal City. Similarly, a section of New Rome/Istanbul was named *Pera*, meaning "trans" in Greek. Moscow, which once claimed to be the Third Rome, rose on the left bank of the river of the same name. As the city expanded to the river's right bank, the name *Zamoskovje* "beyond the Moskva" was coined.

The Celtic domain in Italy entered history divided bi-polarly along the Po/Padus River. From the Roman point of view, the portion of Gallia closer to Rome was named *Gallia Cispadana*, that across the river *Gallia Transpadana*. Later, the Romans divided Gallia into *Gallia Cisalpina* and *Gallia Transalpina*.[23] After they had planted their standards along the Rhine, the Romans divided the peoples in its valley into *Cisrhenani* and *Transrhenani*. In the Middle Ages, after Rome's Frankish successors in Gallia and Germania had extended their rule to the Laba/Elbe River, the land beyond and north of the Laba, occupied then by Slavs and Saxons, obtained the designations *Transalbingia* and *Nordalbingia*.[24] Until recently, the Elbe was used in part as a demarcation line between two Germanies. Colloquially, the people of West Germany refer to the land east of the Elbe as *drüben* "over there" and to its inhabitants as *Ossies* "easterners."

---

[23]   In 1797, Napoleon Buonaparte established a state in northern Italy under the name of Cisalpine Republic.
[24]   Helmold, *Chronica Slavorum*, I.8.

Classical writers divided Asia along the Taurus Mountains into two sections: Cis-Tauran and Trans-Tauran (*entos/ektos tou Taurou*).[25] They consistently perceived India bi-polarly, with the Ganges River as the demarcation line between the two parts. Thus, geographical maps made after Ptolemy's *Geography* and before scientific cartography show two Indias: *India cis* (or *intra*) *Gangem* and *India trans* (or *extra*) *Gangem*. The appellations *India Citerior* and *India Exterior* were also used.[26] Occasionally, Abyssinia was called Middle India.[27] Scythia was the name given by late classical and early medieval geographers to the Eurasian steppe-land which extended from the Volga River to the Chinese frontier. It was divided along the Imaus Mountains into *Scythia intra Imaum* and *Scythia extra Imaum*. The name "Imaus" is a version of the name "Himalaya," which derives from the root word for winter, attested in Greek as *cheima*, in Russian as *zima*. The Imaus Mountains which "divided" the Scythians were, in fact, the mountains we know as the Pamirs.[28] The divisions of India and Scythia by Mediterranean geographers were learned conventions of outsiders, which neither the Indians nor the Scythians appear to have followed.

Hispania was divided by its Roman conquerors into *Hispania Citerior* "hither" and *Hispania Ulterior* "farther." Although the boundary between the two parts changed through time, the bipolar division of Iberia remained after the demise of Roman rule.[29]

Modern cartographers use the designations Hither and Farther India, Nearer and Farther China, Near, Middle, and Far East, etc.

During the first centuries of the Christian era the Romans extended their state to the Danube, which served as a demarcation line between Romania and Barbaricum and in part as a border between the domain of tillers of the soil and that of

---

[25]   Strabo, 2.5.31. The Halys River (the modern Kizil Irmak) also served as an acknowledged natural divider of Asia Minor; *see*, Herodotus, I.6, 28, and Strabo, 12.1.3.
[26]   S. Gale, *Early Maps of India* (New York, 1976).
[27]   Marco Polo, *Travels*, ch. 8 (p. 303 of the Penguin ed.).
[28]   Ptolemy, *Geography*, VI.xiv–xv, Tabulae VII–VIII, Asiae.
[29]   Isidore of Seville, *Etymologiae*, XIV.iv.30; *see* also, Strabo, 3.4.19.

pastoral nomads. Settlements situated across the Roman border and the Danube, in Barbaricum, were differentiated by the prepositions *trans* and *contra* from their counterparts in Romania. Thus, the Romans distinguished their own Aquincum (modern Buda) from Contra Aquincum (modern Pest) and Trans Aquincum in Barbaricum.[30]

Centuries later, the Magyars, living in the nomadic terrain across the Danube, where, in Roman times, the "trans" and "contra" settlements had been located, reversed the naming and designated as *Dunántúl* "Transdanubia" the land which stretched from the river's right bank towards the Eastern Alps. In the nineteenth century, the Habsburgs divided their possessions along the small Leithe River in Pannonia into *Cisleithania* and *Transleithania*. Since the division was made in Vienna, that part of the monarchy in which the imperial city was located and where the monarch resided was honored with the preposition *cis*.

In the Germanic language area a well-known pair are the *Vorder Rhein* and *Hinter Rhein*, two streams which meet at Chur in Switzerland to form the Rhine River.

The southern coast of the Baltic Sea and a portion of northern Germany, an area that runs from around Hamburg and Lübeck to Gdańsk, was in the Middle Ages inhabited by Slavs. The coastal region east of the Odra River was occupied by the Pomerani and called *Pomorze* "littoral." The German conquerors who eventually named themselves Prussians changed the Slavic name into *Pommern*, while the English and other foreigners kept the Latinized native form *Pomerania*. Under Prussian rule the name Pommern was extended westward into Mecklenburg, and Pomerania was divided along the Odra River into *Vorder Pommern* and *Hinter Pommern*. The part of Pomerania which was closer to the areas whence the German conquest had originated, that is, the land west of the Odra River, received the designation *vorder*. The Poles use the terms *Pomorze Gdańskie* "Gdańsk littoral" and *Pomorze Zachodnie* "western littoral" to designate former Prussian Hinter Pommern, which now belongs to Poland. Under the German Democratic Republic the name Pommern did not function as an official territorial designation.

---

[30] *Tabula Imperii Romani 1:1,000,000, L34* (Budapest, 1968).

It has recently been restored as the second name of the federal state Mecklenburg—Vorpommern.[31]

Slavia abounds in toponyms which derive from, or are accompanied by, prepositions such as *preko* "across" in Croatian and *za* "beyond, trans" in all Slavic languages. We have already mentioned Zamoskovje. The town of *Preko*, on the Island of Ugljan off the city and harbor of Zadar, obtained its name from the mainlanders, for whom it was across the channel that separated it from the mainland. The capital of Croatia, *Zagreb*, owes this name to its original location: *za* "beyond" *greb* "row." A region across the Mura River in Slovenia is known as *Prekmurje*. The Serbs refer to the Banat of Timişoara, Bačka, Srijem, Bosnia, and their inhabitants as *Preko* and *Prečani*, respectively, because the latter are across the Danube, Sava, and Drina, the rivers which serve as the borders of Serbia.

From among the many places called *Zagorje* and *Zagora* "beyond the mountain" in Slavia, we mention here a region of Bulgaria called *Zagora* and often used synonymously for the whole country in the Middle Ages, Croatian *Zagorje* (the country beyond Mount Medvednica), looking from Zagreb, the region of *Zagora* in southern Croatia situated beyond Mount Kozjak looking from Split, the canton of *Zagorië* in the Vijosë River Valley in Albania, the district of *Zagori* beyond the mountains looking from the Epirote city of Ioannina, the cities of *Stara Zagora* and *Nova Zagora* in Bulgaria, the village of *Zagora* on the Island of Andros, the town of *Zagora* in Thessaly, beyond Mount Pelion, and the *Zagoritikos* River which flows through the district of *Zagori* and joins the Arachthus River in Epirus. Similar Slavic toponyms and hydronyms are found throughout Albania, Epirus, and Greece, the lands which the native Balkan peoples reconquered from the Roman Empire in the sixth century AD.[32]

A region of Russia, situated beyond the forest zone, looking from the south, is called *Zalesje* "land beyond the forest." Several cities founded there and named after their southern namesakes were distinguished by the epithet *zaleskij* "transylvan." Slavic

---

[31]   The preposition *vor* is superfluous now that the former Hinter Pommern is Polish territory.
[32]   M. Vasmer, *Die Slaven in Griechenland* (Berlin, 1941), *passim*.

settlers had established their demographic, economic, and political domination of the forest belt before Russia became a Christian nation. Huge tracts of forest were cleared and turned to agricultural use. The location of the cities named Perejaslavl' and Vladimir, for instance, may be used as corroborating evidence that Slavs expanded northward into Russia from the Danube in antiquity and the Middle Ages, not southward to the Danube from Russia, as most modern scholars believe. The earliest known settlement named Perejaslavl' (Preslav in South Slavic) was Great Preslav, the center of the Bulgar state in Scythia Minor (the Dobrudja). North of it, on the Danube, stood another city by the same name, distinguished from its old namesake by the diminutive suffix *-ec*, resulting in Perejaslavec. In 969 AD, it was the preferred residence of the Russian ruler Svjatoslav.[33] Later, another Preslav, called Perejaslavl', was built by Russian Slavs south of Kiev near the left bank of the Dnieper and the city of Rodna. Still later, two more cities named Perejaslavl' were founded, one near Rjazan, the other near Moscow. To distinguish between these cities of the same name, the one near the Dnieper came to be known as *Južnij* "southern" or *Russkij* Perejaslavl', the one near Rjazan was called *Rjazanskij*, and the farthest Perejaslavl', located in the vicinity of Moscow, was called Perejaslavl' *Zalesskij*. The latter city was correctly seen as situated *za* "beyond" *lesom* "forest," for it was built at the point where the forest belt ended, in the region known as *Zalesie* "transylvania." Among the several cities named Vladimir, the one located in Zalesie is called *Vladimir Zalesskij*.

Names differentiated by the Russian preposition *za* are very common throughout northern Eurasia. It suffices to list some of the better known ones. *Zakavkazje* "Transcaucasia," a region of Imperial and Soviet Russia, situated south of the Caucasus, was named by people who approached it from the north.[34] Looking downstream, a region beyond the Dnieper cataracts is called *Zaporožje* (from *porog* "cataract"). Finally, viewed from Kiev, a province of Ukraine in the Middle Danube Basin is called

---

[33]   *PVL*, pp. 84ff.
[34]   Zakavkazje is still known by this name, though the people who live there prefer to be called Russians, Ukrainians, Ossetians, Abkhazians, Georgians, Armenians, Azeris, Kurds, and so on.

Zakarpatskaja Ukraina. The same land is also known as *Podkar-patskaja Rus'* "Subcarpathian Russia" by those who look at it from Hungary.

The Don River once separated Russia from its eastern Muslim neighbors. The expressions *zadonskoe carstvo* "kingdom beyond the Don" and *zadonskij saltan* "sultan from beyond the Don" were used in folklore both to designate Russia's eastern neighbors as well as some mythical "overseas" land and ruler.[35]

The best known "land beyond the forest" is called *Erdely* in Hungarian and Croatian, Transylvania in English and other languages which borrowed the name from Latin.

Additional examples presented here may serve as evidence of the universality of the application of this method of differentiating ethnonyms and geographical names. The ancient Persians knew several Sacae peoples, naming those who occupied the steppes of Russia *Saka paradraya* "Sacae beyond the sea." Having conquered Mesopotamia, the Persian king Cyrus added to his titles those "King of Babylon" and "King of the Land Beyond the River," that is, of the land west of the Euphrates, for he came from the east. After they had conquered the land between the Euphrates and the Mediterranean Sea, comprising Syria, Phoenicia, Jordan, and Palestine, the Persians annexed the whole as a territorial unit under the name of the satrapy *Abarnahara* "beyond the river."[36] *Transjordania*, however, obtained its name from those who approached it from the right, or west, bank of the Jordan River. In antiquity, a portion of Transjordania went by the Greek name *Peraea* "across." (Today, Transjordania is known as the Hashemite Kingdom of Jordan.) An area of Central Asia beyond (looking from the west) the Amu Darya (the ancient Oxus) is called *Transoxiana* by Europeans, *Mā warā' al-nahr* "that which [lies] beyond the river" by native people. Extremadura, a region of Spain, was so named because it was beyond the Duero River to those viewing it from northern Spain (*extrema Durii ora* "the other bank of the Duero"). In the thirteenth century, a strip of the Crimea, having

[35]   A story called *Zadonščina* is about a victory won by the Russian prince Dmitrij Donskoj over the Muslims at the Kulikovo field, September 8, 1380.

[36]   Ezra 6:6.

become subject to the Empire of Trebizond, was named *Perateia* "overseas." The state established by European settlers beyond the Vaal River in South Africa is called *Transvaal*, while in the same region the Kei River was used as a reference in naming two native states, *Ciskei* and *Transkei*. The terms Near East, Middle East, and Far East show that they were coined by Europeans, just as the term Midwest originated among the inhabitants of the eastern seaboard of the United States of America. If the naming had been done in California, Chicago would not be a midwestern but a mideastern city.

Middle and Periphery

Any people may believe that their village, city, or country is situated in the center of the world. Among examples which reflect such belief is the traditional self-designation of China as "middle kingdom." This Chinese belief, however, is not subscribed to by other peoples. While the Chinese assert that their country is in the middle of the world, the Europeans, for example, think of it as a part of the Far East.

The European point of view has prevailed in the name of the Mediterranean Sea, for throughout much of the world that sea is today called and regarded as "the sea in the middle of the earth." This designation is relatively recent. In Homer the sea had no common name. Until around 500 BC the Greeks called the Mediterranean "the great sea." As they learned more about it, they contrasted it with the Circumambient Ocean. This led to the coining of the expressions *hēde hē thalassa* "this sea," *hē entos Hērakleiōn stēlōn thalassa* "the sea this side of the Pillars of Heracles," etc.[37]

The use of the notion of the middle versus the periphery in differentiating geographical names and ethnonyms is ancient and well attested. A few examples will suffice. Cleisthenes, a sixth-century Athenian statesman, replaced the ancient tribal principle of political division with a new territorial method of organizing the land and people of Attica by dividing the country into three

---

[37] Burr, *op. cit.*, pp. 95–135.

zones: *Asty* "the city," *Paralia* "the coast," and *Mesogeia* "midland."

The Romans made copious use of the Latin equivalent of the Greek adjective *mesogaios* in dividing their provinces. Roman Noricum and Dacia Aureliana were both divided into two parts. That section of Noricum situated along the Danube was called *Noricum Ripense*, while the inland part was designated *Noricum Mediterraneum.*[38] Dacia along the Danube was called *Dacia Ripensis*, its inland portion received the appellation *Dacia Mediterranea*.

The administrative center of Roman Dacia Mediterranea was at Serdica. The city's name derives from the ethnonym Serdi, which may be explained from the Common Slavic word **serda* "center, middle."[39] Among the neighbors of the Serdi were the Medi or Maedi. It is possible that the Serdi and the Maedi were one people with two synonymous names, both meaning "middle people." Since they occupied the central region of the Balkan Peninsula, this explanation seems logical.[40]

In late antiquity Pannonia was divided into four provinces, one of which, perhaps Pannonia Savia, was called *Media provincia* "middle province."[41]

The Medes, whose name resembles that of the Balkan Medi, may have been called so because of their central or "middle" location in relation to other Iranian peoples. We support this suggestion by indicating the following directional counterparts of the Medes: 1) the Persians of the province of Phars south of Media; 2) the people of the province of Parsua, situated around Lake Urmia northwest of Media; 3) the Parthians who settled east of Media in a region called Parthia; and 4) the Persiani, one of the several peoples settled north of Media. According to

---

[38]   This Roman division continues as the autochthonous Slavic designation *Notranjsko* (in German *Binnen Oesterreich*), which covers roughly the same area as ancient Noricum Mediterraneum.

[39]   Vasmer, *REW*, III, p. 607, s.v. "sereda." Serdica's name changed to Srĕdec in the Middle Ages. Later, it was replaced by the name of the Church of St. Sofia. The city, now known as Sofia, is the capital of Bulgaria.

[40]   Strabo, 7.5.7; 7.5.12; *see* also, G. Mihailov, "Thrace before the Persian Entry into Europe," *CAH*, III.2² (1991), pp. 600–1.

[41]   N.M. Fluss, "Media provincia," *PWRE*, Suppl. VI (1935), cols. ⁀89–91.

Iranists, these ethnonyms derive from the word **parsa* "frontier, end, periphery."[42]

The Old Indian adjective *madhyas* "middle" appeared in the name *Madhyadēsha* "midland" in antiquity and today in the name *Madhya Pradesh* "middle state," one of the states of modern India. As its name indicates, Madhya Pradesh is situated in the geographical center of the Indian Subcontinent. *Uttar Pradesh* "upper or northern state" may be considered its directional counterpart.

The name *Cymmry*, the Welsh' name for themselves, derives from the reconstructed form **Cambroges*, whose meaning is clarified when contrasted to the *Allobroges* "outsiders" (from **cam* "middle," *allo* "out," and *broges* "people").[43]

The Germanic nation of the *Marcomanni*, who emerged and vanished in Czechia, Moravia, and Slovakia, were given this name by their conationals because they occupied a *marca* "borderland" of ancient Germania.[44]

The Germanic conquerors of Britannia used the opposition middle versus periphery in naming political subdivisions of the island. Several territorial entities of medieval Britain reflect this point of view. Thus, the name of the kingdom of *Middlesex* came from its central location, while that of the kingdom of *Mercia* (from *marca*) indicated it was at the periphery. Today, the central area of England is called *Midlands*.

When tribes and nations think of themselves and their lands as the center of civilization, they might relegate mentally the rest of humanity to the periphery and beyond. For instance, the early Christians, who saw themselves as a chosen people, called non-Christians simply *hoi exō* "those outside."

Throughout history, states and empires whose people accepted this belief were forced to protect their frontiers from those beyond. Thus, the Sumerians defended themselves from the nomadic Martu by a wall, the oldest known structure of this nature.[45] Chinese emperors built the Great Wall to defend their

---

[42]   I.M. Djakonov, *Istorija Midii* (Moscow–Leningrad, 1956), p. 69; *cf.*, *ibid.*, p. 149.

[43]   Holder, *op. cit.*, I, cols. 96–8, 1072.

[44]   A. Franke, "Marcomanni," *PWRE*, XIV.2 (1930), cols. 1609–37.

[45]   Gadd, "Babylonia c. 2100–1800 B.C.," pp. 609–10.

sedentary populations from the nomads. The Romans also believed they needed to secure their borders, so they built an
elaborate system of defenses called the *limes*.

The territorial and ideological successors of the Romans, the
Rhomaeans and the Carolingian Franks, continued the tradition
of seeing their states as centers of civilization and, consequently,
had to defend themselves from their neighbors. The Rhomaeans
met the challenge by building defensive walls around
Constantinople—which then acquired the epithet "God-protected
city" in Byzantine propaganda—and by establishing frontier
provinces called *themata* to defend the empire from those
beyond its borders. The Franks' response to the challenge of
their neighbors was to create a series of *marcae* "marches," a
Latin word borrowed from the Germanic languages. The
marches were situated in those regions of Europe where the
Frankish empire and its successor states bordered on free peoples. For instance, an area of southern France marching with
unconquered Spain was called the Spanish march, while that
section of Francia which served as a launching ground for
attacks on free Bretons was called the Breton march. In the
Middle Danube Basin, the Franks established a march called
Marca Avarorum or *Marca orientalis* with the purpose of exter-
minating the nomadic Avars and subjugating the free settled
Slavs of modern Austria, Slovenia, Hungary, and Croatia. The
Avars vanished and the province became known as *Oesterreich*
or *Austria* "Eastern Reich." A province of Italy called Marche
grew out of the March of Ancona and some neighboring districts
in the Middle Ages when this region of Italy was divided among
hostile powers.

The Slavic peoples also made use of the opposition center
versus periphery in geographical names and in ethnonymy. Some
regions which found themselves at the border of Slavdom or at
the edge of a Slavic state at the time when their names were
coined were designated as *kraj*, *krajina* or *ukraina* (from *kraj*
"end, border"). The oldest known Krajina was an area of Red
Croatia at Lake Skadar/Shkodër. The name appeared in the
eleventh century when Croatian territory faced the Rhomaean
theme of Dyrrhachium/Durrës. At the western limits of medieval
Croatia a region called *Bela Krajina* "white march" designated
White Croatian territory bordering on the province of Carniola,

which, then, belonged to the Holy Roman Empire. Bela Krajina belongs today to Slovenia.

The Croats were "frontiersmen" through most of their history. In antiquity, their ancestors stood guard on the Danube *limes* and fought the enemies of the Roman state not only along the Danube and in the Balkans, where they were known as the *limitanei*, but also wherever Romans battled non-Romans. In the Middle Ages, with the Roman Empire dead, and pressed by its illegitimate (from the Croatian point of view) successors, both vaingloriously claiming its ancient glory and universalist pretensions, the Danubian and Balkan Croat states responded by establishing defensive territorial units called *banati* or *banovine* (from *ban* "duke, viceroy"). Like the Rhomaean *themata* and the Carolingian *marcae*, the Croatian *banati* were military frontier provinces in which the civilian and military authority was held by bans appointed by and accountable to the Croatian king. After Croatia entered a personal union with Hungary, the banate system was preserved, and several new banates were established in areas of Catholic Croatia which bordered on the Christian Orthodox regions of the Balkans. The number of banates increased with the coming of Muslim Turks to Europe. Remnants of this medieval Croatian nomenclature are Banija, a region of central Croatia, and the Banat of Timişoara. In modern times, the Croats who defended the *Dār al-Islām* "Domain of Islam" were called the *Serhatli* by the Ottoman Turks, *Krajišnici* by Croats, both terms meaning "frontiersmen." Their conationals but religious foes on the Christian side were called the *Graničari* and also the *Krajišnici*, and their land was known as *Krajina, Confinium,* and *Militärgrenze*. Some Muslim Croats, who prefer to be called Bosnians, believe their fellow Muslims of Southeastern Europe, Southwest Asia, and North Africa should be grateful to them for having stood guard at the *Serhat* "frontier" against the giaours. At the same time some Catholic Croats like to remind the West Europeans of Catholic Croatia's historical role as the *Antemurale Christianitatis* "the rampart of Christendom."

In old Russia, a frontier province was called *ukraina*. The earliest among such appellations was *Ukraina galič"skaja*, a region of the Volhynian principality facing Catholic Poland, first mentioned in 1189. In the sixteenth century, a southwestern re-

gion of the Muscovite state was called *Ukraina*.[46] In the nineteenth and the twentieth centuries, the people who until then had
been known as Rusini, Rutheni, and Little Russians decided to
call themselves Ukrainians, believing it was more dignified to
be known as "frontiersmen" than as Little Russians.

In medieval Arab sources the more distant Bulgars, those
living in the middle Volga Valley, were named Outer Bulgars,
while their conatinals who occupied their original Pontic homeland, and thus were closer to the Arabs, were called Inner
Bulgars.[47] The same principle was applied to Armenia in that its
regions that were more distant from the Muslims were called
Outer Armenia in contrast to the rest of the country which was
named Inner Armenia.[48]

The Bashkir people were also once divided into Inner
Bashkirs, who lived in Europe between the Volga and the Ural
Mountains, and Outer Bashkirs, who settled east of the Urals in
Asia.[49]

The names Inner and Outer Hebrides originated from the west
coast of Scotland. The division of Mongolia into Inner and
Outer is another example of this method of differentiation. The
Outer Mongolians justly rejected the "honor" after they became
a sovereign state, asking that their country be simply called
Mongolia. This method of differentiating identical names is
attested in Hungary, too, where the county Somogy is divided
into Belsősomogy (inner) and Külsősomogy (outer).

Finally, *Exō Rōsia* "Outer Russia" has aroused controversy and
its counterpart is yet to be discovered. We shall show that, seen
from tenth-century Constantinople, there were two Russias. The
one nearer to the observer, though unmarked, may be called
Inner Russia. Its existence is implied by those who named the
more distant regions Outer Russia.[50]

---

[46]   Vasmer, *REW*, IV, pp. 156–7, s.v. "Ukraina."
[47]   V. Beševliev, *Die protobulgarische Periode der bulgarischen
Geschichte* (Amsterdam, 1981), pp. 154–5.
[48]   Ibn Ḥawqal, *Kitāb ṣūrat al-arḍ*, BGA, 2nd ed. J.H. Kramers (Leiden,
1938–9), p. 343; transl. as *Configuration de la terre*, J.H. Kramers and G.
Wiet, I–II (Beirut–Paris, 1964).
[49]   C.A. Macartney, *The Magyars in the Ninth Century* (Cambridge,
1930), map at end.
[50]   *See* below, pp. 312ff.

ATTRIBUTES OF SIZE: *Little Russia–Great Russia*

Any natural feature, settlement, or people may be perceived as big, great, etc., without necessarily being named in contrast to a little opposite. We use names such as the Great Lakes with the understanding that they are truly large. In Native American languages the name Michigan means "great lake," Massachusetts "great mountain place," Alaska "great land," Arizona "little spring," and so on. The Rio Grande is truly a great river. The Lago Maggiore is so called because it is one of the larger lakes in northern Italy. Every independent state is a power and some are informally called great powers, but only Britain is officially named great.

Since this method of differentiation has been applied from remote antiquity by common folks, geographers, and administrators to a wide variety of objects, there is a profusion of names which are distinguished by attributes of size. Here to follow are briefly mentioned some paired names so distinguished, which may help us understand the generally misunderstood meaning of the modifiers "great" and "little" added to the names Russia and Russians.

Seas

The oldest known geographical names distinguished by attributes of size are the Great Water of the Sumerians and the Great Circle of the Egyptians, both designating the Circumambient Ocean. It seems that at first the Sumerians were not aware of seas other than the Persian Gulf, so the appellation "great water" may have been their way of saying "the sea" in opposition to other, lesser bodies of water. The Egyptians knew several seas, and the one they called "the great circle" was truly larger than those more familiar to them. They knew that the Great Circle was out there, but they had not sailed it, and were ignorant of its measurements. It was truly a great unknown, the uncharted sea.[51]

Other peoples also used the attribute great to describe the seas of which they were ignorant and afraid. Thus, the sea which the

---

[51] Burr, *op. cit.*, pp. 80–95.

ancient Greeks first so designated was *mega laitma thalassēs*
"the great depth." The expression appears in the *Odyssey*, where
it stands for a section of the Mediterranean Sea south of Crete
and other islands known to the Greeks at the time the epic was
composed. It is usually translated as "the great south sea."[52]
Later, the Greeks called the Mediterranean generally "the great
sea" when they wished to differentiate it from some sea or bay
closer to Greece. Gradually, as they came to know the entire
sea, from the Pillars of Heracles to the Phasis River, other more
distant seas became "great." Now the Indian Ocean, now the
Atlantic were called "the great sea" by Greeks and their Roman
pupils in geography.[53]

The ancients did not call the Black Sea "great," although
some, like Ovid, feared it greatly. After the leadership in Mediterranean maritime commerce was assumed by the Italian merchant republics, this sea, though relatively well known to their
mariners, became designated as "the great sea." The attribute of
size was added to distinguish this particular sea from the Mediterranean. There is no evidence that the medieval Italians attached the word "great" to the ancient Pontus Euxinus because
they believed it was larger than the Mediterranean. Rather, it
loomed large in their imagination, because they knew less about
it and because it was more distant from them. Medieval and
early modern writers who used Latin called the Black Sea *Mare
maius* or *Mare magnum*. In vernacular Italian, the term was
Mare maggiore, in French *Mer majour*, while Marco Polo used
the expression *Mar maior*.[54] At this same period of history, the
Russians, who called the Black Sea "Russian," "black" or "holy,"
referred to the Mediterranean as "the great sea."[55]

[52]   *See*, R. Fitzgerald's translation of the *Odyssey* for the expression
"Great South Sea," *passim*.
[53]   Burr, *op. cit.*, p. 95.
[54]   X. de Planhol, "Kara Deniz," *EI*, IV, pp. 575–6.
[55]   *PVL*, 7 (p. 53); Vasmer, *REW*, III, p. 740, s.v. "Sredizemnoe more";
IV, p. 345, s.v. "Černoe more."

Rivers

During Roman rule, the valley of the Timok (Timachus) River in Moesia Superior (Serbia) was settled by a people called Timochi after their river. We know that they used attributes of size in differentiating homonymous natural features and settlements because one settlement was designated Timacum *Maius*, another one Timacum *Minus*, so named after the streams—also differentiated by the attributes of size—that met at Zaječar to form the Timok River.[56] In western Serbia, the Little and Great Rzavs come together at the town of Arilje and flow into the Moravica, a tributary of the Western Morava. In Friuli–Venezia Giulia, the Tilment/Tagliamento is formed from two streams which in antiquity were differentiated by the adjectives *maius* and *minus*.[57] In the Bukovina the Siret River is formed from the *Velikij* ("great") Siret and *Malij* ("little") Siret. In Transylvania there are Tîrnava *mare* and Tîrnava *mică/Nagy* Kükülő and *Kis* Kükülő (*mare/nagy* "great," *mica/kis* "little"). In the same region the Someş River is formed from Someşul *mare* and Someşul *mic*. In Siberia, at the town of Nižne-Kolymsk, the estuary of the Kolyma River receives the Great Anyuv and the Little Anyuv rivers. In Kurdistan, a tributary of the Tigris is called the Lesser Zab, another the Greater Zab. In Brazil, the Araguaia River receives the Braço *Maior* and Braço *Menor* streams.

There are numerous instances where only one of the homonymous rivers is modified with the attribute of size. Such pairs are the *Boljšaja* ("great") Kama and the Kama in Russia; *Malki* ("little") Iskăr and the Iskăr in Bulgaria; *Malý* ("little") Dunaj, a smaller branch of the Danube in Slovakia, and *Kis* ("little") Duna, a smaller branch of the same river in Hungary (so distinguished from the main branch of the Danube, which is unattributed). Further, there are also the *Grosse* Mühl and *Grosse* Kamp and the Mühl and the Kamp in Upper Austria, the *Grosse* Soelk and the Soelk in Styria, and the *Mała* ("little") Panew and the Panew in Silesia, the Little Bighorn and the Bighorn in

---

[56] *Tabula Imperii Romani K34* (Ljubljana, 1976), s.v. "Timacum Maius," and "Timacus flumen." Today, these streams are called Black Timok and White Timok.

[57] Pliny, *n.h.*, III.126.

Wyoming and Montana, the Little Colorado and the Colorado, the Little Missouri and the Missouri, etc.

Differentiation of rivers into great and small may also be expressed by diminutive and augmentative suffixes. The following pairs belong to this category: Struma—Strumica (*-ica* is a diminutive suffix) in Macedonia; Morava (called also Great Morava)—Moravica and the trio Resava—Resavica and Resavčina (*-čina* is an augmentative suffix, and this river joins the Great Morava) in Serbia; Sana—Sanica in Bosnia; Neretva— Neretvica in Herzegovina; Glina—Glinica in Croatia; Suceava— Suceaviţa, Moldova—Moldaviţa, Bistriţa—Bistricioara (*-iţa* is a diminutive, *ara* an augmentative marker) in Moldavia; Don— Donec and Dvina—Dvinica in Russia; Nitra—Nitrica in Slovakia; Wisła—Wisłoka and the Wisłok (*-ok* is a diminutive suffix), a tributary of the San, in Little Poland; Mur—Mürz/Mura—Murica in Styria; Gurk—Goertschitz/Krka—Krkica and Zilja—Ziljica in Carinthia, Rabnitz/Rábca—Raab/Rába in Styria and Hungary, etc.

Some unconnected but homonymous rivers are differentiated by the attributes small and great or by diminutive suffixes attached to one member of the pairs. For instance, in Anatolia flow the *Büyük* ("great") Menderes and *Küçük* ("little") Menderes. A river called Lepenac flows south from Kosova to join the Vardar, while its feminine equivalent, Lepenica, gushes northward into the Morava. An area of Slovenia and Croatia is drained by the Reka and Rečina rivers (the latter has an augmentative suffix in Croatian). The Morava River in Slovakia and Czechia may be paired with the Moravica, a tributary of the Opava River. A region of Ukraine is drained by the Ingul and the Ingulec. In Polish Galicia there is the San and the Sanok pair. Finally, the Dunajec in Poland may have been named as a replica of the mighty Danube, which the Poles call Dunaj.

Lands

Differentiation by attributes denoting size of lands is very common in choronymy. Some known examples are: Scythia Minor—Scythia Magna, Germania—Magna Germania, Little Britain (Bretagne)—Great Britain, Great Poland—Little Poland, and Little Russia—Great Russia. Under Roman rule Armenia was divided into Armenia Minor and Armenia Major. After the Persians took control of a portion of Armenia, the Romans introduced the name Persarmenia to distinguish that land from Roman Armenia.[58] The coastal region of Cappadocia was designated by the Roman conquerors of Anatolia as Cappadocia Pontica, while the interior part was named Cappadocia Magna.[59] An area of Anatolia inhabited by Phrygians was called Phrygia Magna and distinguished from the northwesterly province of the same name which was designated variously as Phrygia Hellespontica, Parva, or Epictetus.[60] After the Macedonian conquest, Media became divided into two parts: Media Magna and Media Atropatene.[61]

This method of differentiation continued to be applied in the Middle Ages. For example, the first known Bulgarian homeland, in the Kuban steppes, was named Great Bulgaria.[62] The East Roman Emperor Constantine Porphyrogenitus speaks of Great Croatia and Croatia, as well as of Moravia and Great Moravia.[63] Since the Middle Ages, Poland has been divided into Great Poland (Wielkopolska), with its ecclesiastical center at Gniezno, and Little Poland (Małopolska), with the Archbishop of Cracow as that region's highest ecclesiastical authority. Russia, with Kiev as the traditional political and spiritual metropolis, has until recently been known as Little Russia (Malaja Rus') in contradistinction to the more distant homonymous land governed

---

[58]   Strabo, 11.12.3; and Procopius, *Libri de Bellis* (*De bello Persico*), *passim*. The division of Armenia into Lesser and Greater persisted until the High Middle Ages. For instance, Marco Polo in his *Travels* devotes a chapter to each Armenia, chapters I and II.

[59]   Strabo, 12.1.4.

[60]   *Ibid.*, 12.4.1. The adjective *epictetus* "newly acquired" reflects the fact that Phrygians were believed to have expanded into this region from their original homeland in Phrygia Magna.

[61]   Strabo, 11.13.1. Media Atropatene was named in honor of the satrap Atropates who ruled this portion of the Persian Empire at the time of the Macedonian invasion. Atropatene is known today as Azerbaijan, which is divided into a sovereign Republic and an Iranian province.

[62]   Theophanes the Confessor, *Chronographia*, ed. C. de Boor, I (Leipzig, 1883), p. 357.

[63]   J. Bačić, "Some Notes on the Early History of the Serbs," *Serbian Studies*, II/2–3 (1983), pp. 19–40.

from Moscow and named symmetrically Great Russia (Velikaja Rus').[64]

At the beginning of the Middle Ages, refugees from Roman Britannia settled in the peninsula of Armorica and named it Brittany (Bretagne) after their old country, which became known as Great Britain, Grande Bretagne.[65]

From among the better known lands distinguished with attributes of size we mention Little Kabylia–Great Kabylia in Algeria, Kiskunság–Nagykunság (Cumania Minor–Cumania Magna) in Hungary, and Great Kabarda–Little Kabarda in Russia.

The cited examples show that attributes of size may reflect not only size but also distance. Thus, in antiquity the Danube demarcated the Roman province of Scythia Minor from the rest of the Eurasian steppe-land called simply Scythia or Great Scythia. The Rhine served the purpose of separating Roman Germania from the rest of Europe stretching between the Rhine and the Vistula and occupied, or presumed to be occupied, by free Germans.[66] Clearly, Magna Germania, Great Scythia, and other lands distinguished with the attribute great, were, in fact, both greater in size and farther away than their counterparts.

Even though some regions designated as "great" appear to be both greater in size and farther away than their counterparts, most attributes of size seem to reflect primarily the relative distance of the designated lands from the namer, rather than their actual size. Thus, for example, while in the case of the Brittany–Great Britain pair the attribute clearly indicates size, in other instances this may not be the case. There is no evidence that the "partitioners" of Croatia, Moravia, Poland, and Russia actually knew the boundaries of both the lesser and the greater portions of these lands. In this respect, the pairs Bulgaria–Great

[64] E. Borščak, "Rus', Mala Rosija, Ukraina," *Revue des Etudes slaves*, XXIV (1948), pp. 171–6.

[65] The name Great Britain became official for the whole Island of Albion with the Act of Unification of Scotland and England in 1604. However, since both Brittany and Britain are called *Bretagne* by the French, to distinguish one from the other, they appear to have used the adjective *grande* before 1604. On the other hand, Armorica was called Little Britain in Geoffrey of Monmouth's *History of the Kings of Britain*, VI.4 (p. 149 in the Penguin, 1966 ed.).

[66] Tacitus, *Germania*; Ptolemy, *Geography*, II.xi, Tabula IV, Europae.

Bulgaria and Hungaria—Magna Hungaria are instructive of how relative all this is. We saw that, viewed from the Balkans, where new Bulgaria appeared in the seventh century, the earlier Bulgarian homeland was named great (as well as old and black) while the new land remained unmarked. However, in some later Muslim sources this new Bulgaria was named great for no other reason than that it was more distant from the observer and namer.[67] When the medieval Hungarians discovered their old country in the Volga Valley, from which centuries earlier their ancestors had migrated to the Middle Danube Basin, they named it Magna Hungaria.[68] This does not mean that Hungary on the Volga was larger than Hungary on the Danube, but rather that the discoverers used the attribute great in the sense of "farther removed in space and time from us," just as grandparents are removed in time from their grandchildren.

As the pairs Germania—Magna Germania and Scythia Minor—Scythia show, the aim of differentiation may be achieved by limiting only one member with the attribute of size. This is also true of the Asia Minor—Asia pair. After a portion of Asia came to be known as Asia Minor there was no need to label the rest of the continent.[69] Some modern geographers use the expression *Africa Minor* for a portion of North Africa which others vaguely call the Maghrib or Barbary. The remainder of the continent is not normally accompanied by an attribute of size. In French the term *Afrique Noire* is used to distinguish the domain of the black race from Arab and Berber Africa. Until recently, West European cartographers applied the term Great Tartary to Russia

[67] Ibn Ḥawqal, *Kitāb ṣūrat al-arḍ*, BGA, p. 398; *see* also, *Hudūd al-ʿĀlam*, ed. V. Minorsky, 2nd ed. (London, 1970), pp. 438–40.

[68] Ricardus, *De facto Ungarie Magne a fratre Ricardo invento*; Macartney, *op. cit.*, pp. 156–73; the question of location is reexamined and the literature is given in V.P. Šušarin *et al.*, *Istorija Vengrii*, 3 vols. (Moscow, 1971), I, pp. 89–90.

[69] The term Asia Minor was introduced and popularized by Orosius in his *Historia adversus Paganos*, I.2.26. For definition, *see*, Isidore of Seville, *Etymologiae*, XIV.iii.38. The name Asia Maior (Ptolemy, *Geography*, V) is used today as the title of a scholarly journal. *See* additionally, L. Bürchner, "Asia-Kleinasien," *PWRE*, II (1896), col. 1538; and D.J. Georgacas, "The Name Asia for the Continent: Its History and Origin," *Names*, XVII (1969), pp. 1–90.

stretching between the Ural Mountains and the Sea of Okhotsk, while designating as Little Tartary the steppes of southern Russia and the Crimean Peninsula.

A large area of South Asia is frequently divided by West Eurasian cartographers into Greater India, comprising the Sub-continent of India proper, and Lesser India, covering Burma and Thailand.[70]

The eastern part of the great Arabian desert, al-Nafūd, is called Little Nafūd, the western Great Nafūd.

A section of southern Italy settled by Greek colonists was known as Magna Graecia. The attribute's function was to stress the fact that Italian Greece was faraway, rather than to claim that it was the original home of the Greeks, or that it was larger than Greece, for it was not. Pliny, however, believing the attribute to be a product of ethnic megalomania, said:

> The Greeks themselves, a people most prone to gushing self-praise, have pronounced sentence on the land by conferring on but a very small part of it the name of Great Greece.[71]

Like Pliny, some Ukrainians understand the attributes of size accompanying the name Russia as evidence that the Muscovites had named their own country Great Russia so that they could belittle Ukraine by calling it Little Russia. In fact, the Muscovites have nothing to do with this because the terms originated simultaneously in Galicia–Volhynia and in Constantinople.[72] At the same time, Pope John Paul II proudly calls his homeland Little Poland because he knows that the purpose of the attributes little and great attached to the name Poland is not to glorify one and belittle the other part of the nation but rather to tell one from the other.

---

[70] Marco Polo, *Travels*, map pp. 348–9 of the Penguin ed.
[71] *n.h.*, III.42.
[72] Borščak, *op. cit.*, p. 172 and note 4, p. 173 and note 1.

Peoples

Tribes and nations may also be divided into "great" and "little." The best known example is the pair Great Russians—Little Russians. If there is such a partition of both the land and the people, as is the case with Russia and the Russians, it is difficult to know which was divided first. Once Little Russia was established, anyone living there became a Little Russian. But who established Little Russia? Neither the Little nor the Great Russians but the Russians, for the distinction of Russians into Little versus Great appeared centuries after Russia had existed as a whole.

Surveyed here are some ethnic names differentiated by attributes of size. The Scordisci, an Illyrian people living in the Balkan Peninsula and the Middle Danube Basin at the dawn of the Christian era, were separated by the Sava River into the Little and Great Scordisci. The Little Scordisci occupied the land south of the river and were thus closer to those who recorded the names.[73] At approximately the same period, the Thracian Celaletae consisted of two groups: the Greater Celaletae, who lived at the foot of the Haemus (Balkan) ranges, and the Lesser Celaletae who settled in the Rhodope Mountains.[74] The Scordisci, the Celaletae, and other peoples in Southeastern Europe were eventually assimilated by their Slav neighbors, leaving us no information about their own method of differentiation. In Magna Germania Ptolemy and Pliny recorded two branches of the Chauci people, the lesser and the greater.[75]

In antiquity, a people called Getae lived in the Balkans, while an area of Central Asia was occupied by the Massagetae whose name appears to mean "the Great Getae."[76] A mighty Central Asian people known to the Chinese as the Yue-chi were also divided into the Little and the Great branches. A segment of the Yue-chi, called Kushānas, built an empire spanning regions of

---

[73] Strabo, 7.5.12; *see* also, Appian, *Illyrian Wars*, 1–3.
[74] Pliny, *n.h.*, IV.41.
[75] *Geography*, II.x; *n.h.* XVI.2; M. Ihm, "Chauci," *PWRE*, III.2 (1899), cols. 2201–2.
[76] Herodotus, I.201; IV.94; *see* also, A.I. Dovatur *et al.*, *Narody našej strany v "Istorii Gerodota"* (Moscow, 1982), pp. 181–3, n. 37.

Central Asia and India. Eventually, they, too, were divided into Little Kushānas and Great Kushānas.[77] The Venedae who settled on the Great North European Plain were called *ethnē megista* in Ptolemy's work. We follow those scholars who interpret the expression as "Greater Venedae," believing the Geographer intended to differentiate these Venedae from their namesakes living closer to or within the Roman Empire.[78]

Differentiation between homonymous groups of people may also be achieved by adding diminutive or augmentative suffixes to their primary name. Naturally, the method works even when only one member of a pair is marked. Pairs of this nature are numerous, some more easily recognizable than others. Thus, two pairs of Veneti were marked by suffixes denoting size: the unmarked Italic Veneti had their size counterparts in the Vindelici, who lived northeast of them in modern Austria, Switzerland, and Bavaria, the element *-elici* serving as a diminutive suffix; similarly, in Roman Gaul, north of the Veneti, lived their relatives, the Venelli, the suffix *-eli* making their name a diminutive.[79] Until recently the Vandals were considered to be Slavs for a variety of reasons, among which is the fact that their name, Vandali or Vindili, appears to be a diminutive form of the name Venedae, used by the Germanic peoples to designate Slavs. It is today believed that the Vandals were not Slavs, though the similarity of the names Vandali and Venedae is impressive. Since the original homeland of the Vandals was in Denmark, we suggest that those Vends, after whom the Vendsyssel in Denmark was named, may have been comprehended as the unmarked member of the postulated pair Vendi–Vandali.

Classical writers mention numerous peoples in Pannonia. Among these the Serapi and Serapili of modern Slavonia were differentiated by attribution of size, expressed by the diminutive suffix *-ili* in Serapili.

A close investigation would reveal a number of ethnonyms differentiated by diminutive suffixes in various languages. If the ending *-isci* serves as a diminutive formant in ethnonyms, we

---

[77]   B.N. Mukherjee, *The Rise and Fall of the Kushāṇa Empire* (Calcutta, 1988).

[78]   Ptolemy, *Geography*, III.v.

[79]   More on the Veneti, Vindelici, and the Venelli, below, Ch. V.

could compile a long list of peoples so divided. To mention only a few, there were the Boi and the Boisci, Eravi and Eravisci, Tauri and Taurisci, etc. The Scordisci themselves, who, as we saw, were divided into Great and Little, would then be a lesser division of the unattested *Scordi.

We suggest that the pair Great Russians–Little Russians corresponds to the native Danubian and Carpathian designation Rusi versus Rusini, where the suffix -ini may be understood as a diminutive.[80]

Differentiation by size may also be expressed by augmentative suffixes, such as -ones. To illustrate, we can cite in Britain the Picti, in Gaul the Pictones. (The name *Picti* means "painted ones.") The ethnonym Brittii also appeared with the augmentative -ones, Brittones.[81] The earliest recorded form of the Gothic name, Gutones, ends in an augmentative suffix. In the first century AD, the Gutones, living in the lower Vistula Valley, may have been seen as counterparts of the Swedish Gauti[82]. In passing we mention the pairs Suia–Suiones[83] and Burgundi–Burgundiones.[84] To this category of differentiation belong names of several pairs of lands fashioned after the pertinent ethnonyms, such as Francia and Franconia. The appellations Wenedonia, an area of the former Magna Germania occupied by Slavs,[85] Saxonia, Slavonia, Polonia, and others have no specifically indicated counterparts. We are not sure whether to include here the pair Lycia–Lycaonia of ancient Anatolia.

Throughout antiquity, the eastern Alps were occupied by many peoples, of whom the most numerous were those called Carni by their Celtic and Roman neighbors. In the Middle Ages, the Carni were divided into two main branches, called Carantanians and Carniolans. The name *Carantani* designated the more distant Carni, which fact was expressed by the augmentative suffix -antani, while the ethnonym *Carniolans*, clearly a

---

[80] *Cf.*, Vasmer, *REW*, III, p. 520, s.v. "rusin."

[81] Holder, *op. cit.*, I, col. 604.

[82] Wolfram, *History*, p. 20.

[83] H. Ståhl, "Svear," *Kulturhistorisk Leksikon for nordisk middelalder*, XVII (Copenhagen, 1972), pp. 479–83.

[84] M. Ihm, "Burgundiones," *PWRE*, V.1 (1897), cols. 1063–5.

[85] G. Labuda, "Wenedonia," *SSS*, VI (1977), pp. 372–3.

diminutive, attached to the Carni living closer to the people who gave them this name.[86]

Among the numerous peoples in Great Scythia were the Bastarnae and the Sciri, who were neighbors and perhaps related. The name *Bastarnae* means "bastards," while the name *Sciri* derives from a Germanic word meaning "clean or shiny ones." The Sciri would have preferred to be known by this name, but their neighbors called them *Soulones*, which Germanists explain from a word for "dirt," meaning that the Sciri who thought of themselves as a clean people were called "great dirty ones" by their neighbors, assuming the element *-ones* is an augmentative suffix. At the same time, a branch of the Sciri nation was called *Angisciri*. The adjective *angi* (German *eng*) means "narrow, small or little," so that we may pair the Angisciri with the unmarked Sciri.[87]

Miscellaneous Names

Settlements may also be marked by attributes of size for the purpose of differentiation. In England, three villages are distinguished as Greater, Middle, and Lesser Wallop.[88] The function of attributes of size attached to names of cities is mostly descriptive or glorifying. The original "great city," *Megalopolis* in the Peloponnese, obtained this name because of its size. When Slavs took control of this region of Hellas they changed the name to *Velegost*, from *velii* "big, great," and *gost'* "host."[89] Other medieval Slavs liked to think of some of their cities as megalopolises, as shown by the name *Velehrad* "great city" in Moravia,[90] by the name of the region of Mecklenburg, a German rendering of a Slavic name from the same area dominated by

---

[86]   In the Middle Ages, all Carni were called Horutane, a variant of the name Horvati (Croats). Since the eighteenth century, they prefer to be known as Slovenci (Slovenes).

[87]   F. Braun, *Razyskanija v oblasti goto-slavjanskix otnošenij*, Vol.I (St. Petersburg, 1899), p. 112, n. 2.

[88]   We owe this information to Alan Cameron of Columbia University.

[89]   Vasmer, *Die Slaven in Griechenland*, p. 150.

[90]   A. Wędzki, "Velehrad," *SSS*, VI (1977), pp. 358–9.

Veligrad,[91] as well as by the epithets *velikij* "great" regularly accompanying the name of the northern Russian city of Novgorod, Great Novgorod, of the center of the Volga Bulgar state, which in Russian was called Velikij Bolgar, and of the center of the land Perm′ called Velikaja Perm′. Today, we use the expression "Big Apple" for New York. The attributes of size in such names serve to glorify the cities whose names they accompany.

In medieval Slavia several cities were named Preslav. The one that stood on the Tundža River in Bulgaria was often called Great Preslav. We have already mentioned Preslavec/Perejaslavec on the Danube, its counterpart.[92] In addition to the Great Preslav–Perejaslavec pair, there were Kievec and Kiev, built by Kij on the Danube and on the Dnieper, respectively.[93] In today's Poland Lublin may be paired with Lubliniec; in Russia Rostov with Rostovec; in the Balkans, Belgrade on the Danube has a smaller namesake in a town downstream in Bulgaria called Belgradčik.

The mountain ranges in Slovakia, called the Little Carpathians, are truly smaller and lower than the main range of the Carpathians.

Frequently, islands, too, are differentiated into great and little. For instance, in the middle of the Bering Strait there are two small islands called Diomedes. The one, designated as Big Diomede, belongs to Russia, the other, called Little Diomede, to the United States of America. In the Mediterranean Sea, two major Balearic Islands are paired by size, the larger is called Mallorca, the lesser Minorca. In the past Sumatra was also known as Lesser Java in opposition to Java, even though the island designated as "lesser" is far larger in size than its unmarked counterpart, unless we assume that Kalimantan (Borneo) was actually comprehended as Greater Java.[94] In the Caribbean Sea, a chain of islands stretching from Cuba to Aruba is divided according to size into the Greater and Lesser Antilles. Several pairs of Caribbean islands are distinguished by attributes

---

[91]   The attested Latin name *Magnopolis* is a translation from the Slavic dialect of the Obodrite people. *See,* Herrmann, *op. cit.,* p. 188.

[92]   *See* above, p. 70. For location, *see,* Beševliev, *op. cit.,* map at end.

[93]   *PVL,* p. 55.

[94]   Marco Polo, *Travels, loc. cit.*

of size. Thus, among the Turk Islands the largest is called Grand
Turk. Here the attributes serve merely to differentiate between
the homonymous islands, without any additional meaning. The
members designated as great are truly larger in size.

This, as we saw, could not be the case with the attribute
"great" attached by west Mediterranean mariners to the Black
Sea, which was actually not greater but farther away and
dominated, as in Ovid's day, by fearsome peoples, especially
those ruled by the awesome monarch whom they called *le grand
Turc, il gran' Turco,* "the Great Turk."

We must not be confused by the application of the attributes
great and little in, for example, the sphere of modern nationalist
politics. The people who in the past advocated the *grossdeutsch*
solution of the German question envisaged the creation of a
truly large state that would include Austria, while the *klein-
deutsch* faction wanted a smaller German Reich without Austria.
Contemporary political language uses the attribute great attached
to ethnic names to reflect nationalist sentiments motivated by
territorial aggrandizement. Thus, greater Hans, Serbs, Albanians,
etc. are people who advocate their nation-state's territorial
expansion. Some Greek nationalists promote a policy called
Megale idea "the great idea," envisaging the conquest of
Istanbul and Asia Minor from the Turks, slaughter and expulsion
of Muslims, and the establishment of a greater Greek Christian
state in the "cleansed" land.

Today, since the Ukrainians refuse to be called *malorossy*
"Little Russians," believing that the term is belittling, the function of the attribute great when applied to their northeastern
neighbors is not always clear. In the Slavic languages, the term
velikorus "Great Russian" means primarily an ordinary Russian
wishing to distinguish himself from his White and Little Russian
brethren, and secondarily a Russian nationalist advocating the
creation of a greater Russia.[95]

[95] The (great) Russian people have traditionally been called *staršij brat*
"older brother," among the family of peoples who once made up the Soviet
Union. This should not be confused with the fictional Big Brother of George
Orwell's novel, *1984.*

TOPOGRAPHIC ATTRIBUTES: *Poljane—Drevljane*

The naming of regions and their inhabitants according to the landscape is a common phenomenon in human geography. In many parts of the world names of sections of seacoasts often derive from some word for the sea, water, mainland, and the like. Among the better known examples of this kind of appellations are *Aquitania* in Gaul, from *aqua* "water"; *Pomorze* in Poland, *Primorje* in Croatia and Russia, and similar names in other Slavic regions, from *po, pri* "at, along," and *more* "sea"; *Epirus* in the Balkans, from the Greek word *epeiros* "terra firma"; etc. Such names often survive ethno-linguistic changes. For example, the northern coast of the Peloponnese had in antiquity been known as Achaea, a name of elusive etymology. In the Middle Ages, the Slavic inhabitants of Hellas appear to have known that before the peninsula was named *Achaea* it had been called *Apia* "littoral" and applied their name *Morea* (from *more* "sea") to the whole of the Peloponnese, which was the central area of the Illyrican province of Achaea at the time of Slavic takeover.[96]

Many ethnonyms exist in pairs of opposites that describe a people's division according to the nature of the country they occupy. Thus, in parts of the world ethnic groups are sharply differentiated into highlanders and lowlanders, mainlanders and islanders, desert and oasis dwellers, covered-wagon or tent dwellers (nomads) and settled agriculturalists, forest-dwellers and field-dwellers, etc. Names of many extant and extinct peoples reflect this reality. For instance, it seems that the ethnonym *Arab* means "desert-dweller."[97] This name shows that at the time it originated the people it designated lived in a desert. Today, the settled Arabic-speaking peoples are distinguished from the nomadic desert-dwellers, the Bedouin, whose name derives from *badawi* "desert-dweller."

---

[96]   On the Morea, *see*, Vasmer, *Die Slaven in Griechenland*, p. 2, where Fallmerayer's Slavic etymology is rejected. On Achaea, *see*, H. Fisk, *Griechisches etymologisches Wörterbuch* (Heidelberg, 1960), s.v. "Achaioi." On the name *Apia*, *see*, M.B. Sakellariou, *Peuples préhelléniques d'origine indo-européenne* (Athens, 1977), p. 85.

[97]   R. Pietschmann, "Arabia," *PWRE*, II (1896), cols. 344—62.

Upper–Lower, Highlanders–Lowlanders

Before they knew other seas the Sumerians called the Persian Gulf "the great water," while their Babylonian successors used the expressions "the sea" and "the great circle of the salt sea." As the world view of these Mesopotamians, and especially that of the Assyrians, expanded, they became acquainted with other seas. The Nairi lakes, called today Lake Van and Lake Urmia, and, ultimately, the Mediterranean Sea were the "other sea," necessitating the introduction of differentiators. Thus, the Persian Gulf became the Lower Sea, the northern one the Upper Sea.[98]

Examples of regions, provinces, countries, and even a whole continent divided and designated according to altitude are ancient, numerous, and universal. The creators of the earliest civilization, the Sumerians, were lowlanders. Although they may have originally descended from mountains, they and their political and cultural heirs perceived humanity sharply as two irreconcilable camps: settled agriculturalist lowlanders, on the one hand, and transhumance highlanders and steppe nomads, on the other. The two groups have hated and despised each other ever since the farmer Enkimdu and the shepherd Dumuzi tried to seduce the goddess Inanna,[99] ever since Cain and Abel competed for the favors of Yahweh,[100] and ever since the lowlanders of Mesopotamia fashioned the term "slave girl" by depicting a woman and a mountain.[101]

The Sumerian city-kingdoms were divided into *Ki-Uri* and *Ki-en-gi*, or *Uri and Kengir*, signifying "upper land" and "lower land."[102]

North of Sumer and Akkad, and against the mountains, stretched the land called *Subir* or *Subartu* "steppe land."[103]

---

[98] Burr, *op. cit.*, pp. 80–8.
[99] Gadd, "The Cities of Babylonia," p. 100; Kramer, *The Sumerians*, p. 153.
[100] Gen. 4.
[101] I.J. Gelb, *A Study of Writing* (Chicago, 1952), pp. 65–6.
[102] Oates, *op. cit.*, p. 11.
[103] I.M. Diakonoff, *Hurrisch und urartisch*, transl. from the Russian by K. Sdrembek (Munich, 1971) (=*Münchener Studien zur Sprachwiss.*, N.F., VI), p. 6, n. 2.

Beyond Subartu, the mountain country from which the chief Mesopotamian rivers sprang was named *Urartu* "uplands." Urartu (Mount Ararat of the Hebrew scriptures)[104] and the neighboring lands were called *Hē anō Asia* "Upper Asia" by the Greeks and distinguished from the Fertile Crescent, which they called *Hē katō Asia* "Lower Asia." The Sumerians designated Elam with a sign rendering the idea of "highland."[105] Centuries later, when the Parthian state comprised the land between the Persian Gulf, the Indian Ocean, and the Caspian Sea, it was divided into eighteen provinces or kingdoms. Eleven of these verged on the Caspian and were called the Upper Kingdoms, the remaining seven inclined to the Red Sea and were called the Lower Kingdoms.[106] The final successors to the various civilizations of Mesopotamia, the Arabs, maintain the distinction of this region into highlands versus lowlands. Thus, the name ʿ*Irāq*, deriving from the Middle Persian *erāgh*, means "lowlands," while Iraq's highland counterpart, ancient Media, is called *al-Jabal* "mountain," by the Arabs.[107]

Other well known examples of differentiation according to altitude are Upper and Lower Egypt, Upper Land and Lower Land in the Hittite Empire, Upper and Lower Macedonia, Moesia, Austria, Germania, Britannia, Upper and Lower Georgia (Zemo Iveria and Kvemo Iveria), Upper Volta (now Burkina Faso), Upper Canada (Ontario) and Lower Canada (Quebec), Upstate New York, etc.[108] In most cases the logic of the division is clear from the lay of the land, especially when it is drained by mighty rivers such as the Nile, Rhine, Danube, Hudson, or the

---

[104]   *EJ*, III (1971), p. 290, s.v. "Ararat."
[105]   *See* above, Ch. I, n. 42.
[106]   Pliny, *n.h.*, VI.112.
[107]   Another name for ʿ*Irāq* is *Sawād* "black land," introduced to distinguish the cultivated land from the surrounding desert, which is of a reddish hue. *See*, Hitti, *op. cit.*, p. 155.
[108]   In Strabo's day, Germany was divided into two parts. The Romans hoped to establish their control as far as the Elbe (*Geography*, 1.2.1). Later, the Rhine, the Neckar, and the Danube became the border between Roman Germania and Magna Germania. *See,* the fold-out map in the Loeb Classical Library edition of Tacitus' *Germania* for location. On common people's difficulties with these terms, *see*, B.S. Phillips, "Upstate and Downstate in New York," *Names*, XXXI (1983), pp. 41–50.

Tigris and the Euphrates. Thus, Upper Egypt, Germania Superior, Moesia Superior, Upstate New York, and Upper Asia were truly experienced by their namers as areas that were higher in altitude than their lower counterparts. Likewise, when Isidore of Seville says: *"prima Europae regio Scythia inferior,"* we should assume that he understood its altitude counterpart to stretch "up" and beyond the Don and the Urals into Siberia.[109]

The Urartians, or highlanders, and their counterparts, the Subartians, or field-dwellers or lowlanders, are perhaps the oldest known pair of peoples whose names derive from the nature of the country they occupied.

The name *Macedones* seems to go back to the Greek adjective *makednos* "tall, taper."[110] According to the prevailing opinion, the Macedones were those of the northern neighbors of the Greeks whom the latter viewed as tall, slender, or long-faced barbarians. Since the original Macedones lived on high ground in relation to Greece and in relation to Emathia, a coastal area of Macedonia, our interpretation of the ethnonym as "highlanders" should be accepted. We further suggest that the Greek form of the ethnonym reflects the sense of some native name, perhaps Brygi, which coalesced with the form Mygdones (of disputed etymology) to render Macedones. The name Macedones resembles the tribal name *Magnetes*, designating a Greek people settled in Thessaly whose name also means "highlanders."[111] The Macedones came into their land from *Orestia*, a canton of the Macedonian Kingdom whose name signifies "highlands." The Macedones succeeded to the *Briges* or *Brygi*, whose name reflects the Old Slavic root *brĕg"* "hill."[112] The Macedonian Kingdom was itself divided into Lower and Upper Macedonia.[113]

The name *Croat* also derives from a word for "mountain-dweller." In antiquity, the peoples called *Carni* and *Carpi* lived in and around the Carnian Alps, the Karavanken Mountains, and

---

[109]   *Etymologiae*, XIV.iv.3.

[110]   M.B. Sakellariou, "Ancient Macedonia, the Early Years: The Inhabitants," in *Macedonia: 4000 Years of Greek History and Civilization*, ed. by M.B. Sakellariou (Athens, 1992), p. 63.

[111]   Sakellariou, *op. cit., loc. cit.*

[112]   J. Bačić, "Of Bryges and Macedones," *Macedonia, Curiosum Mundi*, I/3 (New York, 1993), p. 3.

[113]   F. Geyer, "Makedonia," *PWRE*, XIV (1928), cols. 638–81.

the Carpathian ranges. The same mountains have since the Middle Ages been home to the people called *Carniolans, Carantanians, Xorutane, and Hrvati*. These ethnonyms are variations of the names Carni and Carpi which are not only identical with the corresponding oronyms but appear to derive from the same Slavic or Celtic root for "mountain, height, or crest."[114] The name *Carni* appears to be a variant of the ethnonym *Carpi*. Both the Carni and the Carpi seem to be identical with the folks whom the Germans knew as *Harvada*, the Russians as *Xorutane*, the Rhomaeans as *Chrōbatoi*, and the Arabs as *Kharwāt*, the Western Christians using Latin as Croati.[115] The Pannonians and other peoples who settled in the lowlands of the Middle Danube Basin seem to have served as topographic counterparts of the Croats.[116]

The world's ethnonymy abounds in cases where names are not neatly paired, that is, lack marked counterparts. For example, the Kabyles of Algeria are highlanders. Their homeland, *Kabylia*, distinguished into Little Kabylia and Great Kabylia, is a mountainous land, its name deriving from a word for "mountain." Kabylia has no marked counterpart, unless one takes the lowlands of Algeria as its opposite. A region of southern Russia is called *Dagestan*, a Turkish name signifying "mountain land." An area of the Paropamisus Mountains in Afghanistan was, in the Middle Ages, called *Ghūr* or *Gharistan* "mountain land."[117] The Caucasus on Russia's southern rim is occupied by a variety of peoples whom the Russians collectively call *Gorcy* "mountaineers," while the northern slopes of the Carpathians are the domain of a Polish ethnic group called *Górale*. Both names mean "mountain folks."

Differentiation of regions into upper and lower is so common, natural, and logical that there is rarely any disagreement regarding the meaning of the attached qualifiers. For instance,

---

[114] Holder, *op. cit.*, I (1896), cols. 791–3, s.v. "Carni"; for the relevant Slavic words *see*, Vasmer, *REW*, I, p. 438, s.v. *gora* "mountain, forest"; and IV, pp. 274–5, s.v. *xrebet* "spine, ridge, mountain."

[115] *Cf.*, Vasmer, *REW*, IV, p. 262, s.v. "xorvat."

[116] Some recent scholars seek the original Croat homeland on the Iranian plateau, ignoring the evidence indicating that they had lived in North Central Eurasia *ab origine*.

[117] For location, *see*, *Hudūd al-ʾAlam*, p. XXIX, map, and *passim*.

when we examine such pairs as Obersachsen–Niedersachsen (Upper and Lower Saxony), Oberbayern–Niederbayern, Oberösterreich–Niederösterreich, Oberschlesien–Niederschlesien, etc., we understand that these regions were divided into upper and lower based on altitude, just as Roman Germania was divided into Superior and Inferior according to the lay of the land.[118]

However, there are instances where the logic of differentiation is not obvious. Unlike the Rhine which flowed in a more or less straight line from Upper Germany into Lower Germany, the Danube traversed the Roman province of Pannonia in a crooked fashion. Soon after it left Noricum and entered Pannonia the river made a sharp southward bend at Budapest, then again an equally sharp eastward turn at the Croatian city of Vukovar. So, when Roman administrators divided Pannonia into Superior and Inferior, they used the Danube's tributaries as a guide. Therefore, the province which they designated as Pannonia Inferior stretched along the Danube from Visegrad, near Budapest, to Belgrade. It included the lower valleys of the Danube's tributaries, the Sava and the Drava. Pannonia Superior extended westward along the Danube and the middle and upper valleys of its feeders into the Eastern Alps.[119]

In dividing Transdanubian Dacia into Dacia Superior and Inferior, the Romans followed the Danube as a guide. The river marked a more or less straight southern boundary of that province, just as today it separates Serbia and Bulgaria from the

---

[118]   The name Netherlands reflects the division once instituted by the Romans. The dialects of Germany also divide along the ancient border between Lower and Upper Germany into Low German and High German. Because High German became the literary language, today, many people believe it owes this designation to social rather than topographic altitude.

[119]   An example of confusion resulting from disregard of the function of the attributes denoting altitude may be seen in B. Grafenauer *et al.*, *Historija naroda Jugoslavije*, I (Zagreb, 1953), on the fold-out map facing page 144. Here, the terms "inferior" and "superior," which the authors encountered in the primary sources, where they were used to distinguish Pannonia according to altitude, were interpreted to mean "lower" and "upper" on a modern map with a northern orientation. Thus, they placed Upper Pannonia in the northern section of both the Upper and Lower Pannonia of the Romans, while indicating as Lower Pannonia the southern portions of Upper Pannonia and Lower Pannonia.

Banat of Timişoara (Vojvodina) and Rumania. The division of Dalmatia into Superior and Inferior appears logical only when we realize that the mountains in the superior portion are also higher.[120] The designation of northern Albania as Upper and southern as Lower follows the same logic. Upper Burgundy is truly situated on a higher ground than Lower Burgundy. Likewise, a region of Lithuania called *Aukštote* "highlands" lies higher than *Samogitia* "lowlands."

In the Slavic world there are many pairs of regions differentiated by attributes of altitude. For instance, Lusatia, the country of the Sorbs in Germany, is broken down into Upper and Lower Lusatia. In Slovenia, the pair *Gorensko–Dolensko* are colloquially used as equivalents of Upper and Lower Carniola. During the Middle Ages, the valley of the upper Bosna River, called *Vrhbosna* "high Bosna," became the seat of a Croatian banate of the same name. After the banate of Bosnia had expanded into the lowlands, the annexed region was called *Donji kraji* "lowlands." Today, the terms Upper and Lower Bosnia are commonly used. Upper Croatia comprises the Dinaric Mountain ranges, while Lower Croatia is demarcated by the Kupa, Sava, Danube, Drava, and Sutla rivers. *Felvidék* (Upper Hungary), comprising northern Hungary and Slovakia, was paired with the rest of the Kingdom of Saint Stephen, called *Delvidék* "the south." Finally, mention should be made of *Verxnjaja Rus'* "Upper Russia" and *Nizovaja Rus'* "Lower Russia." The term *Verxnjaja zemlja* "upper country" appears frequently in medieval Kievan sources as a designation for the region of Russia traversed by the upper Dnieper and the upper Volga.

The opposition up–down, so common in describing parts of towns and cities, is also used in distinguishing different and distant settlements with identical names. The logic behind the attributes of altitude is almost always clear. One example is the Russian city of Novgorod, established in Upper Russia. Centuries later, when Russian expansion had progressed down the Volga, another city by the name of Novgorod grew into

---

[120] C.B. Brandis, "Dacia," *PWRE*, IV.2 (1900), cols. 1948–76. On the divisions of Dalmatia, *see*, D. Mandić, *Crvena Hrvatska*, 2nd ed. (Chicago, 1972), ch. IV.

prominence. It was called *Nižnij* Novgorod ("lower") until it was renamed Gorky. Its original name has recently been restored.

We saw that some linguists derive the Germanic terms north and south from words for right and left. However, others trace their original meaning to down and up, respectively. This idea is attested in the celebrated name *Thule*, allegedly from the Celtic word *dhol* "below," which for centuries stood as a symbol of the ultimate north. Further, following this line of thought the ethnonym *Chauci*, from *hauhs* "high," arose because this Germanic people lived southward or "up" in relation to those who gave them this name.[121]

Modern maps are usually oriented to the north. Therefore, north is frequently used synonymously with "up." In fact, in Sanskrit, the primary meaning of the word *uttara-* "north" is "upper, higher." Therefore, the Indian state called Uttar Pradesh is both "upper" and "northern." In Sweden, the upper or northern province is called Uppland with its center at Uppsala (*upp* "up").[122] The ancient Romans frequently referred to the Adriatic as the Upper Sea, and to the Thyrrhenian as the Lower Sea,[123] following perhaps the same idea that the north was "up."

A section of a land may be perceived as hollow. The best known such regions are those to which the Greek adjective *koilē* "hollow" was attached. Thus, an area of Elis in Hellas was called *Coele Elis*. There was also *Coele Persis*, a hollow or lower area of that land. *Coele Syria* was the name given first to the valley between Mount Libanus and Mount Antilibanus, better known as the Bika Valley. Later, the whole of Phoenicia was called Coele Syria and distinguished from Syria proper.

Forest-Dwellers and Field-Dwellers

Differentiation of peoples into forest- and field-dwellers is also both ancient and universal. The Dorians of Hellas are perhaps

---

[121]   M. Ihm, "Chauci," *PWRE*, III.2 (1899), cols. 2201-2; G. Macdonald, "Thule," *PWRE*, VIA.1 (1936), cols. 627–30.

[122]   Uppsala is in the middle of modern Sweden, a few kilometers north of Stockholm. Earlier, when the center of the Swedish state was further south Uppsala was truly "up" and "north."

[123]   Burr, *op. cit.*, pp. 68–72.

the earliest attested "woodsmen" in Eurasia. In their wanderings through the South Balkans they came to a canton called Dōris or Dōreis. From there they expanded to other regions of Greece and were given the name *Dōrieis* after their temporary homeland.[124] Considered as rude barbarians by modern scholars, their name seems to signify "forest-dwellers."[125] The Thracians, who were also regarded as wild and warlike by their neighbors, and among whom the war-god Ares resided, lived in that part of the Balkan Peninsula which, in antiquity and the Middle Ages, was covered by dense forests. The Thracian ethnonym, *Thrax-Thrakes,* may be explained from the Greek adjective *trachos* "rugged." This adjective appears often in geographical names as an opposite of *pedinos* "level." For instance, Cilicia was divided into *Cilicia Tracheia* and *Cilicia Pedias*.[126] The eastern prong of the Crimean Peninsula, equivalent to the Kerch Peninsula, was known in antiquity as *Chersonēsos trachea* "rough peninsula."[127] The name of the largest Thracian people, *Odrysae* "forest-dwellers," had no marked counterpart.[128] We may accept the fact that the ethnonyms Dores and Odrysae truly signify "forest-dwellers," without identifying their counterparts. These names may have been coined by neighbors whose own domain was outside the forest and whose names functioned as the unmarked members of the respective pairs. Examples where only one member is marked are numerous.

The name of the Lugii people in Magna Germania derives from an Indo-European word for "forest," of which there are cognates in several languages. In Russian there is *lug* "grove," in Croatian *lugar* "forester," and in Latin *lucus* "grove."[129] We are encouraged to interpret the name Lugii as forest-dwellers because the same general area occupied by them in antiquity be-

---

[124] Herodotus, I.56.
[125] Fisk, *op. cit.,* s.v. "Doreis."
[126] Strabo, 14.5.1.
[127] Herodotus, IV.99.
[128] D. Detschew, *Die thrakischen Sprachreste* (Vienna, 1957), p. 338.
[129] *Cf.,* M. Schönfeld, "Lugii," *PWRE,* XIII (1926), cols. 1715–17; and T. Lehr-Spławiński, "Lugowie," *SSS,* III (1967), pp. 103–4.; *see* further, Vasmer, *REW,* II, p. 527, s.v. "lug."

came, in the Middle Ages, home to the Slavic Drevljane, whose name signifies forest-dwellers.[130]

Though the ethnicity of the Nemetes, who lived at the turn of the Christian era in the upper Rhine Valley, is hard to determine, their name appears to be of Celtic origin. Some scholars claim that it derives from the word *nemed* "noble," others have suggested *nemet* "forest," implying that the Nemetes were so called because they were seen as forest-dwellers by their neighbors. It has been argued that the Slavic name for Germans, *Němcy*, derives from the Nemetes rather than from *němoj* "dumb, mute," as is commonly believed. Even though linguistic laws permit the derivation of the Slavic name for Germans from the adjective mute, this etymology should be rejected in favor of the forest-dwelling Nemetes[131]

The name *Finn*, first recorded by Tacitus as Fenni, by Ptolemy as Phinnoi, is usually explained from the Gothic word *fani* "swamp." According to this view, the name was a collective designation for swamp-dwellers of northwestern Russia.[132]

The name *Pole* derives from *pole* "field."[133] The people called *Poljane* took leadership in establishing the state which became known as *Polska* in Polish, *Polonia* in Latin. But there is another name for Poland in Slavic and other languages. In Russian a

---

[130] *See* below, p. 101.

[131] There is no reason why the Slavs would regard their Germanic neighbors as a "mute people." People usually ridicule speakers of languages other than their own by pointing to some characteristic sound which they imitate in a distorted manner. For instance, to speakers of Greek all foreign languages sounded "barabara," which gave the term barbarian. Another example is the name *Digiči* used by Slovenes and Croats for the Italians. It is based on the Italian expression *dica* (pronounced diga) "say." Though the Nemetes were not a mighty people, it is quite possible that their name, originally meaning forest-dwellers in a language of their Celtic neighbors, became a general Celtic name for Germans. The Slavs then borrowed this ethnonym from the Celts, just as the East Romans borrowed it from the Slavs in the Middle Ages and the Ottoman Turks in modern times. *See*, A. Franke, "Nemetes," *PWRE*, XVI (1935), cols. 2382–5; *see* further, Vasmer, *REW*, III, p. 62, s.v. "nemec."

[132] M. Ihm, "Fenni," *PWRE*, VI (1909), col. 2186.

[133] S. Urbańczyk, "Polanie," *SSS*, IV (1970), p. 181, accepts the explanation proposed by the late medieval chronicler J. Długosz who wrote: "Polanie, id est campestres."

Pole was called *ljax*, his country *Ljad'skaja zemlja*; in Hungarian a Pole is called *Lengyel*, his country *Lengyelország*; in Turkish a Pole is called *Leh*, Poland *Lehistan*. Medieval Polish writers claimed Čech's brother Lech as the founder of Poland to explain the name *Lechy*. According to some scholars, the name *Lech* derives from the Slavic word *les"* "forest." If this were true, the Turkish name *Lehistan* "forest land" could be considered the opposite of the Latin name *Polonia* "field land," with which it would form a pair. However, according to another view, Lech's name is a diminutive form of **Lędĕnin"* (from **lędo* "land") "field-dweller."[134] If we accept this etymology, we could state that the Russian ethnonym *ljax* and the Polish name for themselves, *Polak*, both derive from words meaning a field-dweller.

There is no disagreement regarding the meaning of the name of the Slavic *Drevani* (Drevljane) who lived in the Laba/Elbe Valley and in the valleys of its tributaries, the Ilmenau and the Jetze; it means "forest-dwellers."[135] The Drevljane settled near that portion of Magna Germania which, in antiquity was inhabited by the Lugii. Perhaps the name Drevljane is a synonym of the ethnonym Lugii.

In the Pontic region settled the Gothic pair, the *Tervingi* and the *Greutungi*. Their names mean "forest-dwellers" and "sand (field)-dwellers, respectively."[136] The Russian Tivercy held in the Early Middle Ages approximately the same area where the Tervingi had halted for a while on their fateful migration from Scandinavia to Romania. The Slavic name also means forest-dwellers.[137]

In Gaul, the Oscidates were divided into the *Montani* and *Campestres*.[138]

---

[134] Vasmer, *REW*, II, pp. 549, 553, s.v. "ljada," "ljax"; *see* also, T. Lehr-Spławiński, "Lachowie," *SSS*, III (1967), p. 12; and K. Ślaski, "Lech-eponim, *SSS*, III (1967), pp. 31–2.

[135] T. Lehr-Spławiński and J. Nalepa, "Drzewianie," *SSS*, I (1961), p. 394. Their name lives as Drawehn, a hilly terrain between Uelzen and Lüchow.

[136] F. Altheim, "Greutungen," *BzN*, 7 (1956), pp. 81–93; *idem*, "Zum letzten Mal: Greutungen," *BzN*, 7 (1956), pp. 241–246; and Wolfram, *op. cit.*, pp. 24–6, notes 49,57,58.

[137] *See* below, p. 103.

[138] Pliny, *n.h.*, IV.108.

The Slavic domain abounds in forest-dweller–field-dweller pairs of ethnonyms, beginning with the earliest named of these, the Derriopes and the Agrianes in ancient Macedonia. The name *Derriopes* derives from a word recorded in Old Slavic as *drĕvo* "tree." We may take the neighboring *Agrianes*, from *ager* "field," as their counterparts.[139]

In the middle Dnieper Valley lived the people who founded Kiev and established the Russian state and church. Called *Poljane* "field-dwellers," their counterparts were the people whom they called *Drevljane* "forest-dwellers."[140]

To be noted is the fact that the Lithuanians call a Belorussian *Gudas* and his land *Gudija*. Some scholars derive the ethnonym from the name Goth, others from Getae, and still others from the Old Prussian **gudān* (*gudde* "Wald") "Waldbewohner."[141]

During Roman rule a division of Dacia was named Malvensis, an appellation deriving, we suggest, from the Albanian word *mal* "mountain." To corroborate this explanation, we point out that in the same general area a mountainous region of modern Rumania is appropriately called Muntenia.

Like peoples, rivers may also be distinguished into forest- and field-streams. For example, at Linz in Austria, the Danube meets the Aist River, formed from the Waldaist and Feldaist; the White Nile is formed from the *Baḥr al-ʿarab* "desert river" and the *Baḥr al-jabal* "mountain river."

The Mlava River (attested as Malava in the Middle Ages) flows from the mountains of eastern Serbia into the Danube. It has been suggested that the hydronym derives from the Albanian word *mal* "mountain."

The hydronym *Moldovă*, which gave its name to the Rumanian province of Moldavia and the sovereign Republic of Moldo-

---

[139] *See*, Hammond, *op. cit.*, maps 9 and 17 for location; for the explanation of the ethnonym Derriopes, *see*, Sakellariou, *op. cit.*, p. 44; on the Agrianes, *see*, V.I. Georgiev, *Trakite i tehnijat ezik* (Sofija, 1977), pp. 77–8.

[140] One of the major early sources on Russia, the *Russian Primary Chronicle (PVL)*, was written by field-dwellers who had nothing good to say about their forest-dwelling counterparts. Most modern scholars uncritically accept the bias of these Kievan field-dwellers.

[141] E. Fraenkel, *Litauisches etymologisches Wörterbuch* (Heidelberg, 1962), I, p. 174, s.v. "gudas."

va, derives from the Germanic words *wald* "forest" and *ahvo* "water." The name may have originated at a time when the valley of the Moldovă was inhabited by the Tervingi Goths, whose name means forest-dwellers.[142] In the Middle Ages, the same land was occupied by the Slavic Tivercy, whose name some scholars explain from an unattested hydronym *Tivr″, which they relate to the Tyras, the modern Dniester. According to this view, both the ethnonym and the hydronym may be explained from the Old Indian adjective *tīvrás* "quick, rapid." Because in some Old Russian sources the Tivercy are referred to as "interpreters," other linguists associate their name with a reconstructed Turkic noun *tiv-är* "interpreter."[143] It has been suggested that the Slavic ethnonym *Tivercy* derives from the self-designation *Tüürik* "Turk" by way of the Old Russian plural form *tyurcy*.[144] None of these explanations are fully satisfying, and the search continues. However, we propose that the resemblence between the ethnonyms Tivercy and Tervingi is too striking to be dismissed as accidental. Both names may be traced to a word for tree, just as the chief river which drained the land occupied by these people was named the "forest stream." In fact, to corroborate this suggestion we point out that in the same region Herodotus had mentioned a river named *Ordessus*.[145] This hydronym derives from the word *drus* "tree," attested also in the name *Odrysae*, the "forest-dwelling" Thracians.

In conclusion, we mention some ethnonyms and hydronyms which reflect the nature of the surrounding terrain but have no named opposites. Thus, Eurasian ethnonymy knows of Water Croats (Wasserkroaten) and Water Mongols. In Slavic areas, the adjectives *gnilyj* "putrid, stagnant," *suxoj* "dry," and *kamenyj* "stony" are commonly used attributes in hydronymy.

---

[142] *See* above, p. 101.
[143] Vasmer, *REW*, IV, p. 55, s.v. "tivercy."
[144] G.A. Xaburgaev, *Ètnonimija "povesti vremennyx let"* (Moscow, 1979), p. 155.
[145] IV.48.

MISCELLANEOUS MARKERS: Cold Scythia, Dromitae

Us Versus Them

From the most remote antiquity until our age, clans, tribes, nations, races, and religious and political sects have been comprehending and naming themselves and others in pairs of opposites: Us versus Them, Aryans–Dasyus, Jews–Goyim, Greeks–Barbarians, Romans–Barbarians, Christians–Outsiders (*hoi Exō*), Christians–Infidels, Muslims–Infidels (Giaours), Romanichal (Gypsies)–Gorgios (non-Gypsies), and so on. A similar idea is rendered by the ethnonyms Suiones, Semnones, and Suebi (Swabians) which signify "Wir selbst," implying separation from the rest of humanity.[146] The Russians once saw themselves as followers of the "true" religion, often besieged by the European "schismatics" whom they collectively called *latincy* and *nemcy*. This contributed to their self-perception as a besieged camp. They were also vulnerable to attacks by Muslims of Eurasia and the Balkans for whom they used the term *busurmane*. As we saw, the Russians, themselves, have, until recently, occupied the position of "them" in the imagination of their rivals and foes in the Western world.

Clothing and Food

Today, due to the rapidly advancing homogenization of the human race, we rarely draw boundaries according to people's dressing and eating customs. The past, of course, was quite different. Until recently, one could hear of a division of North Central Eurasia according to whether its peasants wore their shirts tucked into their breeches or let them hang loose and tie them with belts. France was divided along a wine-drinking versus beer-drinking line. In antiquity, with the Roman conquest of the Mediterranean basin came Roman dress and short hair for men. The wearing of a *toga* was a symbol of Romanitas, so the word *togatus* came to mean a Roman as opposed to a foreigner.

---

[146] M. Schönfeld, "Suebi," *PWRE*, XXVII.1 (1931, cols. 564–79, especially, p. 579.

Long hair was in fashion among Celts and other barbarians, short hair among Roman men. Consequently, the Celtic realm beyond the Alps, Gallia Transalpina, was first divided by the Roman conquerors and observers into *Gallia Comata* "Hairy Gaul" and *Gallia Togata* "Robed Gaul." Pliny uses the term *Capillati* "long-haired" for native peoples of the Alpes Maritimes around Nice.[147]

Unexplored or little known coasts were usually peopled in works of ancient geographers with imaginary tribes and nations of eaters of raw, and often human, flesh. A number of names are given according to the perception of a people's most common or unusual food. Thus there were the folks named *Ichthyophagi* "fish-eaters," living along the coasts of modern Iran and Pakistan. The ancients also spoke of the fish-eating Ethiopians. One branch of this imaginary race lived along the eastern approaches of the *Terra incognita* and fished in the Green Sea, *Prasodes thalassa*, the other was a coastal branch of the *Hesperii Aethiopes*.[148]

Some commentators place the *Lotophagi* "lotus-eaters" of Homer's *Odyssey* along the coast of Libya.[149] *Rhizophagi* "rice-eaters" was the name given to some tribes of Africa and Asia who were known or believed to be rice cultivators.[150] The whole coast of eastern Africa was peopled in geographical works of antiquity by "barbarians" and "cannibals."[151] Many authors who dealt with North Central Eurasia found in Scythia the *Hippemolgi* "mare-milk-drinkers," first mentioned in the *Iliad*,[152] the *Androphagi* "man-eaters," made popular by Herodotus,[153] as well as the *Phthirophagi* "bird-eaters" and the *Hippophagi* "horse-eaters."[154] In Ethiopia lived a people whom the Greeks called *Cynamolgi* "bitch-milkers."[155] In the ancient Persian province of Carmania lived the *Chelonophagi* "turtle-eaters," "who roof their

---

[147]   *n.h.*, III.47.
[148]   J. Tkač, "Ichthyophagi," *PWRE*, IX (1916), cols. 2524–31.
[149]   H. Lamer, "Lotophagen," *PWRE*, XIII (1926), cols. 1507–14.
[150]   E. Kiessling, "Rhizophagi," *PWRE*, 2nd series, I.1 (1920), col. 939.
[151]   Ptolemy, *Geography*, IV.ix; Tabula IV, Africae.
[152]   *Iliad*, XIII.1–6; Strabo, 7.3.2–3 and *passim*.
[153]   Herodotus, IV.18.100.102,106.119.125.
[154]   For "location," *see*, Ptolemy, *Geography*, Text and Tabulae.
[155]   Strabo, 16.4.10.

houses with the shells and live on the flesh of turtles."[156] In his description of that region of Russia which extended northward from the crest of the Caucasus, Strabo named some *Troglodytae* "cave-dwellers," and next to them the *Chamaecoetae* "people who sleep on the ground" and the *Polyphagi* "heavy-eaters."[157]

The custom of naming people after their characteristic, though incidental, food, continues to our day. For example, though the French do not subsist on a diet of snails and frogs' legs, but eat them only occasionally, some people use the derogatory term "frogs" for the French. The same may be said about the term "kraut" applied by those wishing to insult the Germans.

Such "ethnonyms" are, of course, marked members of pairs of opposites. The eating habits of the group that does the naming remain unspecified, which in itself is a statement of differentiation. Thus, the Cree people who coined the name *Eskimo* from *askimowew* "he eats it raw," implied that they ate it cooked. The Eskimos call themselves *Inuit*, and their land, recently declared as a Territory of Canada, is called *Nunavut* "our land."

Tame and Free (Savage)

People may designate themselves as free or may be so designated by others. It is frequently suggested that the ethnonym *Illyrii* signifies "free."[158] The ancient Romans presented themselves as liberators from Macedonian rule to some ethnic groups in Upper Macedonia, and, after they succeeded in detaching their cantons from the Macedonian Kingdom, called them "Free Macedonians."[159] After most of the Cilicians were conquered by the Roman general Pompey, the fortunate ones who had escaped slavery were called *Eleutherokilikes* "Free Cilicians."[160] While the Dacians in Roman Dacia were forced to endure Roman slavery, beyond the *limes* on the Someş River roamed their free

---

[156]   Pliny, *n.h.*, VI.109.
[157]   11.5.7.
[158]   A. Stipčević, *Iliri: Povijest, život, kultura*, 3rd ed. (Zagreb, 1991), p. 15.
[159]   Strabo, 7.7.8.
[160]   Cicero, *Ad Familiares*, XV.4

counterparts, the *Dacii Liberi*.[161] The ethnonym *Frank* appears to have been coined by the people themselves or by their neighbors and applied eventually to a number of Germanic peoples who were free of Roman bondage.[162]

The adjective "free" may have a bad connotation and be confused with "savage." This appears to have been the case with those Polovcians who were called *Dikie Polovcy* "savage Polovcians" by their Russian neighbors. These people seem to have been seen and named in contradistinction to the other Polovcians, the ones that were under a firm rule or were settled, for in Russian the steppe is called *dikoe pole* "wild field," so that its denizens may have been named "wild" as well.[163]

The "savages" may also be angry, and this fact may be reflected in their name by which they are known among their neighbors. This seems to be the origin of the name of the Germanic *Quadi*, from *quad* "anger,"[164] and the Slavic *Lutiči*, from *ljutij* "angry."[165]

Attributes of tameness versus madness or rage are also found in hydronymy. The river which the Germans call Moldau is known as the Vltava by Czech Slavs. The Slavic name derives from the Germanic words *wild* and *ahvo* "wild water."[166] In Silesia, several rivers are called Nysa/Neisse. The one that joins the Katzbach is called the *Wütende* Neisse. In Czechia, the Orlice River is formed from the *Divoká* "wild" and *Tichá* "silent" Orlice. In Russia flows the *Tixaja* "silent" Sosna, a tributary of the Sosna River. In Transylvania, a tributary of the Körös/Criş is called *Sebes* Körös/Crişul *Repede* "swift" Körös. In Bulgaria, two Kamčijas, one called *goljama* "big," the other *luda* "mad," come together to form the Kamčija.

---

[161] Bačić, *The Emergence of the Slavs*, p. 118.

[162] J.B. Bury, *The Invasion of Europe by the Barbarians* (London, 1927; Norton, New York, 1967), p. 10.

[163] P.B. Golden, "The Polovci Dikii," in *Eucharisterion* (O. Pritsak Festschrift) (Cambridge, Mass., 1979/80), pp. 296–309.

[164] P. Goessler, "Quadi," *PWRE*, XXIV.1 (1963), cols. 623–4.

[165] Herrmann, *op. cit.*, p. 11.

[166] Vasmer, *REW*, II, p. 642, s.v. "Moldavija."

Warm and Cold

Names of streams are often distinguished by the attributes cold
and warm. Thus, in Czechia the Vltava River is formed from the
Warm Vltava and Cold Vltava (*teplá* and *studená*), in Transylvania there is Someşul *cald* ("warm").

The opposition cold and warm is used by geographers who
think globally and divide the earth into zones according to the
temperature. Scythia, both Little and Great, along with other
regions of North Central Eurasia normally evoked cold weather
in the minds of people from the temperate zone. For this reason
the region often appeared with the modifier "cold." Some Nordic
writers, seeking "proof" of ancient glory for their homeland,
replaced the name *Scythia* with *Sweden*, ending up with Great
Sweden and Cold Sweden.[167]

Old and New

Among the most ancient and universal ways of distinguishing
paired geographical names is the opposition old versus new. The
ancient Greeks were unclear about their origins, but were sure
that their earliest homeland, called *Hē archaiotatē Hellas*, was
located in Epirus.[168] Herodotus called a region of Scythia "old,"
an indication that it was the "original" homeland of the Scythians.[169] The Saxons of Britain referred to their kinsmen on the
continent as Old Saxons.[170] In Rhomaean sources the "original"
homeland of the Bulgars was called black, great, and old
Bulgaria, while Balkan Bulgaria remained unmarked.[171] The
Spanish kingdom of Castille is made up of Castilla la Vieja and
Castilla la Nueva.

---

[167] A. Heusler, *Die gelehrte Urgeschichte im altisländischen Schrifttum*
(=*Abhandlungen d. Akad. d. Wiss. Hist.-phil. Kl.*) (Berlin, 1908). In his
Origin of Rus', pp. 27, 245–5, 267–8, and *passim*, O. Pritsak offers modern
substance to this medieval form.
[168] J. Miller, "Hellas," *PWRE*, VIII (1912), cols. 157–8.
[169] IV.99; *see* also, Dovatur *et al.*, *op. cit.*, pp. 336–7, n. 575, for
interpretations of the term.
[170] Bede, *Opera Historica*, V.ix, uses the expression *Antiqui Saxones*.
[171] Theophanes Confessor, *Chronographia*, p. 357.

Since the Age of the Great Discoveries, the *oikoumene* has been perceived bi-polarly as Old and New Worlds. As West Europeans colonized the New World they frequently named their colonies after their mother country, using the attribute "new" as a distinguisher. Thus came into being New Holland, New Spain, New England, New France, etc. In the course of the eighteenth century, after the Russians had captured from the Crimean Tatars and their Ottoman overlords the steppe land beyond the Dnieper cataracts and settled it with Slavs, an area of the newly acquired territory which was given to migrants from the Balkans was called New Serbia. The whole region, however, was named New Russia. New Russia covered approximately the same terrain as Inner Russia, the unmarked counterpart of Outer Russia in the tenth century.

Right and Left

One of the most ancient and universal ways of distinguishing the environment is to perceive objects as being on one's right or left. Depending on one's general orientation, the four quarters may be named front, back, right, or left, and geographical names and names of peoples may be coined in accordance with such an arrangement. We saw that the ancient Egyptians followed a southern orientation, so that within their scheme the Mediterranean Sea and its islands were "in the back," in the northern quarter which was synonymous with darkness. A peculiarity of the Egyptian custom was adoration of the west because it was to the right, and right was good, and denigration of the east because it was to the left, and left was bad. The ancient Semites, following an eastern orientation, ended up with the west in their back, the east in front of them, the south on their right, and the north on their left. As we saw, names of peoples and lands reflect this orientation, the most common ones being Benē Šim'āl and Benē Iamina and Yemen and Šim'āl (Syria).

Like the Semites, some Indo-European peoples identify the south with the right side, the north with the left. This notion is reflected in the name *Dekkan*, a plateau on the Indian Subcontinent situated between the Eastern Ghats and the Western

Ghats. The name was coined by speakers of an Indo-European language who followed an eastern orientation and for whom the south was to the right (the name derives from the Old Indian word *dakšina* "south, right side"). Modern Breton names *Ar mor dehou* "the sea on the right" and *Ar mor klei* "the sea on the left," signifying the South Sea and the North Sea, indicate that the Bretons follow an eastern orientation.

It is a universal custom to name a river's banks right and left by facing downstream. Several rivers in Slavia are named Desna (from Old Slavonic *desn"* "right"), including Dnieper's tributary the Desna. However, since the Desna joins the Dnieper on the left, some scholars claim the name is actually an antiphrasis for the hated left side. But, the left side could not be avoided, as shown by a number of streams named Šuja and Šujica (from Old Slavonic *šuj* "left").

Sacred Promontories

Ancient geographers often arbitrarily named coasts, promontories, and islands in regions which they knew only from hearsay or which they imagined. Thus, some works mention the Tamarus Promunturium along the coasts of the Yellow Sea. A gold island was placed in the same sea where Homer imagined Dawn's abode.[172] The coast of the Horn of Africa, known by some as Barbaria, was also distinguished as *Cinnamofera* "cinnamon-bearing region," while the Horn itself was called by the Egyptians "the horn of the world." The Greeks named it *Notou keras* "the horn of the god of the south wind," because they thought it was at the world's southern end. *Aromata promunturium* was the name given to this cape by later classical geographers, while modern explorers know it as Guardafui. The natives, themselves, call it Ras Asir.[173]

---

[172] The island was called Chryse (from *chrysos* "gold"); *see*, Bunbury, *op. cit.*, II, p. 364.

[173] *Ibid.*, II, pp. 320; *see* also, F. Windberg, "Notou keras," *PWRE*, XXXIII (1936), cols. 1120–3.

The Western Promontory, *Hesperium promunturium*, was the most westerly point in Africa.[174] Several sacred promontories may have been named by geographers to guide voyagers to the Western Sea and the Isles of the Blessed, and perhaps to set the stage for tales of mariners and explorers who had visited those distant regions. Thus, four sacred promontories were known in antiquity. The earliest appeared on Corsica at the time when voyagers from the east believed this island was at the end of the world. Modern Capo Corso is the site, Capo Sacro the name of the Greek *Hieron akron*. After Iberia's southwest tip had been discovered, it became the next sacred promontory, called today Cabo de Sâo Vicente. Ireland, which often was called the Sacred Island, also obtained a sacred promontory, placed at its southeast point.

The ancients believed that Achilles came to Phthia from Scythia and that his shade went to the White Island, off the coast of Scythia, to meet Helen's shade.[175] Since he was a horseman, they provided him with a racecourse. Called *Achilleōs dromos*, this place appears in most geographical works on Scythia. It has been identified with a spit called *Tenderovskaja kosa*, off *Beloberežje* "white coast." The west end of the racecourse was called *Hieron akron* "sacred promontory."[176] When the Rhomaeans became acquainted with Russian armies, among the several names they gave them was that of the *Dromitai*, or *Achilleiodromitai*, because they thought the Russians were Achilles' descendants since they lived near his racecourse and professed the same "Hellenic" religion as the Greek hero.[177]

---

[174] C.T. Fischer, "Hesperium promunturium," *PWRE*, VIII (1912), cols. 1248–9.
[175] This little island, called today *Zmejnij ostrov* "snake island," was known in antiquity as *Achilleōs nēsos* "Achilles' Island." *See*, W. Tomaschek, "Achilleos nesos," *PWRE*, I (1893), col. 221.
[176] W. Tomaschek, "Achilleos dromos," *PWRE*, I (1893), col. 221.
[177] *See,* Ch. VII, p. 334.

CHAPTER III

COLORS IN COSMOGRAPHY

Colors are an essential component of geographical and ethno-nymic nomenclatures of ancient and modern cultures and civilizations. Though numerous attempts have been made to explain their functions, there is no consensus on some of the basic questions regarding the origin of the custom of using colors to describe the *positio loci* of the named objects. Ernst Förstemann, perhaps the first European scholar who noticed attributes of color in geographical names, suggested that such use of colors was a Slavic custom. More than a hundred years ago he wrote:

> Rivers especially are often differentiated by the addition of words signifying colors. Thus we can find such old [river] names as Rotitruna and Wizzitruna, Witzmuone, Wizer regin; also the Elstra nigra, first mentioned by Thietmar. We commonly use such names as Black and White Elster, Red and White Main (Wismain, attested in 1541). In names other than those of rivers we seldom find color designations. ... *It seems that this method of naming was borrowed from the Slavic world where it flourishes.* (Italics added)[1]

Since Förstemann's time other scholars have tried to explain the function of colors in geographical names, and some have even offered arguments for the profusion of such names in Slavic language areas. While Förstemann thought the Germans had learned to use colors in this sense from the Slavs, some more recent scholars shift the origin of the custom of using colors in

---

[1] E. Förstemann, *Die deutschen Ortsnamen* (Nordhausen, 1863), pp. 216–17.

ethnonymy from the Slavs to their eastern neighbors. For instance, H. Ludat wrote:

> The application of attributes of color in names of peoples is, as mentioned earlier, limited to the eastern half of our continent [sc. Europe], where the steppe peoples are known to have played an important historical role. It is not found among other European families of peoples. ... Nevertheless, based on the preceding discussion, we are compelled to seek the source of the idea of applying colors in differentiating among names of peoples and lands in a non-European cultural milieu, that is, among the steppe peoples. One is encouraged to take this approach by recent linguistic and historical findings on the question of the [origin] of the Croats and Serbs.[2]

It has been opined that the Croats migrated to Europe from the Iranian plateau. One of the frequently used arguments to prove this hypothesis was their division into White and Red Croats, which today some scholars believe was originally an Iranian custom, not Slavic, contradicting Förstemann who thought it was Slavic. Further, it is widely held by modern authorities that all Slavic peoples were, at the beginning of the Middle Ages, ruled by the Huns and Avars. These Eurasian Turkic nomads used colors as symbols of the directions of the horizon and allegedly transmitted the idea to their Slavic "subjects."[3] The division of Russia into White, Red, and Black Russias is usually attributed to the nomads of Asia.

This chapter will show that colors are part of the cosmographic systems not only of the peoples of East and Central Asia but also of those of Southwest Asia, North Africa, and Europe. Even though there is no incontrovertible evidence that any ancient Western Eurasian people consciously and systematically

---

[2] H. Ludat, "Farbenbezeichnungen in Völkernamen: Ein Beitrag zu asiatisch-osteuropäischen Kulturbeziehungen," *Saeculum*, IV (1953), pp. 138–55; see further, G. Reichenkron, *Historische Latein-Altromanische Grammatik*, I (Wiesbaden, 1965), p. 345, where the "oriental connection" is overstated; F.Dvornik, *The Making of Central and Eastern Europe*, 2nd ed. (Gulf Breeze, Fla., 1974); and W. Mańczak, "Biała, Czarna i Czerwona Rus'," *International Journal of Slavic Linguistics and Poetics*, XIX/2 (1975), pp. 31–9.

[3] *Cf.*, Bačić, *The Emergence of the Slavs*, ch. 4, where the primary sources on Slav–nomad relations are examined.

used colors to indicate the directions of the horizon, the material discussed will suffice to conclude that they were not strangers to the idea. We shall survey some of these systems in order to understand the function of colors in such names as Red Sea and Black Russia, as well as in other names of places and peoples, beginning with the Sumerians whose name for themselves is a color word.

SUMER

In the Old World civilized life began in the alluvial plain of the lower Tigris and Euphrates rivers. The people who built there the cities of Eridu, Ur, Uruk, Lagash, Larsa, and many more, the same who either invented or perfected writing started by some mysterious autochthonous inhabitants of that land, and who first told myths of gods and men and wrote them down, are called the Sumerians. The name goes back through various filters to Shumer, a region in the lower basin of the Tigris and Euphrates. The name *Shumer* seems to be derived from the Akkadian word *shumu* "name, son," its Hebrew equivalent being *shem*, which is also the name of the eponym of the Semitic peoples, Shem, son of Noah.[4] Shinar, the place where the confusion of tongues took place, is also equated with the name Shumer.[5] Taking their "knowledge" from the Bible, medieval Europeans, including the Russians, traced their roots to the Plain of Shinar. Sumerian ideas of real and mythical geography antedate by millennia such thoughts as the Hebrews, Greeks, and other peoples expressed on the same subject, so that it is reasonable to point to Mesopotamia as their ultimate source.

It is generally accepted that the Sumerians immigrated to Lower Iraq in the second half of the fourth millennium BC. Because their language is of an agglutinative type, it has been suggested that their original homeland was somewhere in Upper Asia or Russia, in or close to the domain of the Uralic and Altaic peoples whose languages are also agglutinative. The country called Aratta, situated perhaps between Lake Urmia and

---

[4] *EJ*, XIV (1971), col. 1368.
[5] Kramer, *op. cit.*, pp. 297–8.

the Caspian Sea, has been proposed as the *Urheimat* of the Sumerians.[6]

Like other peoples who migrated from another place into their historical homeland, the Sumerians made no record of the event. Rather, they believed they were native to "the land" and that their political institutions were of local and divine origin. A Sumerian myth says that "sceptre, crown, tiara, and (shepherd's) crook lay before Anu in heaven." Symbolizing royal power, these objects were transferred from heaven to Eridu in Lower Iraq to sanctify the first antediluvian kingship established there. After the Great Flood the gods of the Sumerians restored royal authority on earth, appointing as their steward the king of the city of Kish, located upstream from Eridu and near future Babylon. Though many kings resided at cities other than Kish, those who aspired to be acknowledged as kings of the whole land of Sumer assumed the title "King of Kish."[7]

The land occupied by the Sumerians is known by Europeans as *Mesopotamia*, a Greek approximation of the native Semitic term *Naharain* "two rivers." Sumer and Akkad are also called Chaldaea and Babylonia. The region's Arab inhabitants see Mesopotamia as an island demarcated by the Tigris, the Sinjar Mountains, the Euphrates, and the Habur River, and call it *al-Jazira* "the island." This name is limited today to northern Iraq stretching upstream from Baghdad to the Turkish border. Al-Jazira is roughly coterminous with the ancient Roman and Persian province of Mesopotamia. The remainder of the Tigris–Euphrates basin goes by the names *Iraq* "lowland" and *Sawād* "black land."

The whole of the Tigris–Euphrates basin may be viewed as an island of cultivated land surrounded by the untillable desert and the mountains on the east, north, and west, and by the sea and the desert on the south. In fact, this image of a cultivated land in the midst of the desert has been popularized by the Hebrew story of the Garden of Eden, or paradise, watered by four rivers, two of which we readily recognize under the Hebrew names for

[6] Kramer, *op. cit.*, p. 42.
[7] Gadd, "The Cities of Babylonia," pp. 102, 109.

the Tigris and Euphrates. In fact, the name *Eden* comes from the Sumerian word *edin* "plain, steppe."[8]

According to Sumerologists,

> [T]he world known to the Sumerians extended no farther than India on the east; Anatolia, the Caucasus region, and the more westerly parts of central Asia on the north; the Mediterranean Sea on the west, although perhaps Cyprus and Crete might be included; and Egypt and Ethiopia on the south.[9]

Within this world the strictly Sumerian domain was bounded by the Persian Gulf (which their cultural heirs called the Lower Sea), the Red Desert, the Syrian Desert, the mountains of the north and the east. The Sumerians thought of their land as a unit even before it was politically unified. The common name for the assemblage of Sumerian city-kingdoms was *kalam* "the land," distinguished from *kur-kur* "foreign lands."[10] As we saw, the Land was divided into *Ki-Uri* and *Ki-en-gi*, or *Uri and Kengir*.[11] The Sumerians pictured the earth surrounded by the ocean, and appear to have always known of two seas. Their land verged on the southern sea, the Persian Gulf, and was relatively distant from other seas, so that often in Sumerian sources the term "sea" refers to the Persian Gulf.

Sumerian cosmography was based on two circles, outer and inner. In the outer circle were imaginary lands, which lay beyond the regions occupied by Sumer's neighbors. Thus, in the extreme east, the Sumerians imagined paradise which they named Dilmun. Originally, the Islands of Bahrain bore the name Dilmun, but, after the appellation acquired a fabulous meaning, it was transferred to a location beyond the Persian Gulf and perhaps beyond India. In the Epic of Gilgamesh Dilmun is located "at the mouth of the rivers," where the sun rose. No mortal man, other than the half-divine Gilgamesh, King of Uruk, ever visited Dilmun. To come to that distant place, the hero had to cross a wide desert, scale the Mountain of Sunrise guarded by

---

[8] *New Bible Dictionary*, 2nd ed. (Leicester, 1982), pp. 296–8.

[9] Kramer, *op. cit.*, p. 284.

[10]   Gadd, "The Cities of Babylonia," p. 106; and *idem*, "The Dynasty of Agade and the Gutian Invasion," p. 421.

[11]   *See* above, p. 92.

Man-Scorpion, walk through the Garden of the Gods, and cross the Ocean of Death. The only human beings he encountered on this journey, other than the monster Man-Scorpion, were Siduri, Urshanabi, and Utnapishtim and his wife. Siduri resided in the Garden of the Gods ruled by Utu/ Shamash, the sun-god. She may be compared to Circe of Greek mythology, just as Urshanabi, the ferryman who took Gilgamesh across the Ocean of Death to Dilmun, may be pointed out as the prototype for the Greek Charon. In that faraway place lived, in everlasting bliss, the survivor of the Great Flood. His Sumerian name was Ziusudra, signifying "faraway." In Babylonian he was called Utnapishtim.[12]

The Sumerians and Akkadians had relations with India, though it is difficult to gauge their nature and intensity. Records exist of ships sailing between Agade and Dilmun and of kings boasting of having campaigned in Dilmun. This Dilmun is usually identified with the Islands of Bahrain, rather than with Utnapishtim's dwelling place.

The Sumerians had contacts with Africa, to which they generally attached the names *Magan* and *Meluhha*. At first these names designated some areas of the Arabian Peninsula verging on the Persian Gulf, but were later shifted onto the continent of Africa. In the first millennium BC, the names Magan and Meluhha stood for the real land of Egypt and the semi-mythical "land of black people," identified with the Ethiopia of European sources.[13]

The Sumerians were separated from the Mediterranean Sea by a broad stretch of the Red Desert and the Syrian Desert, inhabited by the nomadic Amorites and other Semites. From these people they may have heard tales of a distant and terrifying western sea where the sun died in its daily journey from east to west. Beyond the sea or beyond the mountains was the Land of No Return, whereto the dead souls were transported by the Boat of the West, the Boat of Magilum. The Land of No Return was located in a vague and distant region, a realm of darkness, dust, and of somber colors, ruled by a somber god and his wife Queen

---

[12] For a discussion of the "location" of the Sumerian paradise, *see*, Kramer, *op. cit.*, pp. 281ff.

[13] Kramer, *op. cit.*, pp. 276–84.

Ereshkigal, formerly a sky-goddess and possibly a sister of Ishtar. Designated with logograms indicating "mountain" or "foreign land," the domain of the dead was the antithesis of "the land," the Sumerians' own country.[14]

Mountains surround Mesopotamia on the east and north, and this fact was reflected in the names of the land's two principal mountainous neighbors, Elam and Urartu.[15] However, the central place in the oronymy of the Sumerians and their Semitic successors was occupied by the mountains named *Mashu*, an Akkadian name meaning "twins," for the Mashu were the Mountain of Sunrise and the Mountain of Sunset.[16] They were guarded by Man-Scorpion. In the north of the real world was *Nisir* "mountain of salvation," where Utnapishtim had found refuge from the flood. It is identified either with the Pir Oman Gudrun Mountains in northern Iraq, or with Mount Ararat. The Cedar Forest and the Silver Mountain also appear frequently in Sumerian and Akkadian sources. The first name stands for the Amanus, the second for the Taurus ranges.[17] As their names indicate, the northern mountains were the source of many necessities needed by the lowlanders of the south, such as water, timber, ores, and human labor. For this reason the Mesopotamians called the northern quarter "the country of the living." Here lies the documented origin of the belief, evident from the extant literary monuments of other ancient and medieval Mediterranean cultures, that the peoples of the northern quarter were more fertile than those occupying the central belt of the earth.[18]

The Sumerians and their Semitic successors often arranged the world around them so that Sumer and Akkad occupied in reality and represented symbolically the south, Subartu the north, Elam the east, and Amurru the west.

---

[14]   Hooke, *op. cit.*, pp. 20–3.

[15]   *See* above, p. 93.

[16]   The idea and the name appeared in the Macedonian period as *Mazoi Borra* "Breasts of the North." See, Anderson, *op. cit.*, pp. 43–57.

[17]   Gadd, "The Dynasty of Agade and the Gutian Invasion," pp. 425–6.

[18]   Today, many from among the peoples living in the more developed North view with similar awe the fertility rates of the peoples living in the South.

On the west, the neighbors of the Sumerians were the Semitic nomads of the desert, whom they called *Martu*, a name identical with that of the god who presided over the western quarter. The Martu, or Amurru, the biblical Amorites, and their god did not live in houses, ate no grain, and consequently were considered inferior to the Sumerians. These "western barbarians" were hated by the Sumerians with the intensity with which the farmer has hated the shepherd ever since the farmer Enkimdu had once hated the shepherd Dumuzi.[19] Eventually, the name Amurru came to mean "nomads" generally.

On the east and the north, civilized Mesopotamia was flanked by semi-nomadic mountain pastoralists.

Relations between the advanced civilizations of Mesopotamia and the cultures of the more primitive peoples of Asia Minor, Upper Asia, the Iranian plateau, the Red Desert, and the Syrian Desert were tense and often hostile. We know from Sumerian sources that they despised their "barbaric" neighbors, not so much because they were ethnically different, but because, as lowland nomads and highland shepherds, their way of life was antithetical to that of the Sumerian tillers of the soil and city-dwellers.[20] The lowlanders feared their invasions and despised them for their lack of civilization, while envying their freedom and longing for their arrival as divine instruments of punishment of sinners.

The Sumerians saw themselves and their land as an island of civilization in a sea of barbarity. They occupied the southern quarter of a four-fold division of their world. The other three quarters belonged to peoples who were much less civilized and therefore hated or despised by the Sumerians. The peoples of the Indus and the Nile valleys were perhaps as advanced as the

---

[19]   Gadd, "The Cities of Babylonia," p. 100; Kramer, *The Sumerians*, p. 153.
[20]   Hostilities between the lowlanders of Mesopotamia and the peoples of Upper Asia and Iran have continued through the ages under various disguises. Today, the ancient battles are fought between lowland Turks, Syrians, Iraqis, and Iranians and the Kurdish mountaineers; between Sunni and Shiite Muslims. The mountaineers are despised by their lowland neighbors to the point where the latter refuse even to recognize their separate ethnicity. For example, until recently the very name "Kurd" was outlawed in Turkey and the Kurds were called "Mountain Turks."

Sumerians, but they were too distant and therefore could not disturb the bi-polar division of Southwest Asian humanity into those who had civilization and those who did not, those who ate grain and those who did not.

Placing themselves in its center, the Sumerians were perhaps the first people to divide the world according to the four cardinal points. The eastern quarter, where they imagined paradise, was ruled by the sun-god Utu, called Shamash in Akkadian, and by his bride Aya "dawn," the Greek Eos. The western quarter was the domain of the god Martu who was considered as uncivilized as the Amorites, the people named after him. No particular gods guarded the southern and northern quarters. However, the north appears to have been the domain of the divine monster Humbaba, ruler of the Country of the Living. By imagining their domain under the rule of Humbaba, the Sumerians were perhaps the earliest people settled in the central belt of the earth who saw the north as the cradle of awesome peoples. This view is expressed in their belles lettres, especially in the epic of Gilgamesh.[21]

Like other peoples, the Sumerians believed that the gods had created the human race, *nam-lulu* "humankind."[22] The Sumerian name for themselves was *Sag-ud-da*. Traditional scholars interpret this ethnonym as "black-heads" and hold that the color's function is descriptive. For instance, S. Kramer states that black served as contrast to the greenness of vegetation.[23] This explanation is problematic, for people normally do not contrast themselves with vegetation. Rather, they would wish to be distinguished from other people symbolized perhaps by other colors.

A scholar has proposed that the name Sag-ud-da should not be translated as "tête noire," but as "tête fière." Pursuing Hungarian connections with the Sumerians, he pointed out that the Sumerians' name for themselves also appeared as the name of a Scythian tribe. The latter, in turn, resembles the name of the Hungarian city of Szeged, reminding this scholar of the ancient

---

[21] Kramer, *op. cit.*, ch. 4; *idem, Sumerian Mythology* (New York, 1961); Gadd, "The Cities of Babylonia," pp. 100–05.

[22] Kramer, *Sumerian Mythology*, p. 61.

[23] Kramer, *The Sumerians*, pp. 285–6.

Sag-ud-da.[24] We add that, although, in the Middle Ages, some Balkan and Anatolian Slavs were called Sagudatae—an ethnonym almost identical with the Sumerians' name for themselves—we refrain from postulating ethnic identity between these Slavs and the builders of the oldest civilization in Lower Iraq.[25]

Pace Gastony, the traditional explanation of the name Sag-ud-da as Black Heads should not be outright rejected, because the human race has seen itself in terms of colors since the beginning of time. Citing a few examples, we point out that in a poem about rivalry between the state of Aratta and the Sumerian city-state of Uruk, a whole array of colors in reference to a man is mentioned. The ruler of Aratta asks his Sumerian counterpart to find a warrior who is "neither black nor white, neither brown, yellow, nor dappled."[26] It is possible that these colors were intended to symbolize the totality of the human race. We shall see that the Egyptians divided people according to four colors. Further, in Arabic the expression *sawād al-nās* "black people" and in Russian the noun *čern'* "the black" are used as synonyms for "the common people," while the Arabic phrase *al-hamr wa al-sūd* "the red and the black" means Arabs and Blacks, that is, all of humanity.[27] It is plausible that the Sumerians also used colors in representing the four quarters and their inhabitants, applying the color black for the center (just as the Chinese used the color yellow for the same purpose). Naturally, considering their own land to be in the center, they referred to themselves as Black Heads. Gastony may have grasped a secondary meaning of the name Sagudda, when he interpreted it as "proud-heads." The Sumerians may have preferred it in order to give their name a more lofty meaning than it originally had.

It is possible that the Sumerians introduced the black color attribute for the fertile land of Mesopotamia, and the color red as a symbol of the desert. Vestiges of such ancient nomenclature

---

[24]   C.G. Gostony, *Dictionnaire d'étymologie sumerienne et grammaire comparée* (Paris, 1975).

[25]   F. Sławski and W. Swoboda, "Sagudaci," *SSS*, V (1975), pp. 18–19. The authors do not mention the Sagudda of Iraq.

[26]   Kramer, *The Sumerians,* pp. 271–2.

[27]   For instance, to underscore the universal nature of Allah's message the Muslims teach that Muhammad was sent to the red and the black, *i.e.*, to all humankind.

may be seen in the contemporary designation *al-Suwād* "black land" for a portion of Iraq and in the appellation Red Desert, covering a large area of Iraq, Jordan, and Saudi Arabia. Further, the Red Desert may have been named in opposition to the Syrian Desert, to which the color black may have originally attached because of its northern location. Finally, it was either the Sumerians or their Semitic heirs who named Europe the "land of darkness" because it was located in the northern quarter.

Names of some of the more important earliest cities in Lower Mesopotamia have been explained within the languages spoken by their builders and first occupants. For example, the names Eridu, Ur, and Uruk derive from words meaning a "city." Though the cities were residences of kings and priests, and white is the universal symbol of priesthood (purity), we do not know whether this, or any color for that matter, played a role in Sumerian toponymy. One of the oldest temples in the region, the temple of Uruk, has been named White Temple by archaeologists, a modern designation due to its white-washed walls.[28]

EGYPT

Ancient Egypt's place in the affairs of the Old World and the New has been the subject of interminable scholarly debates and polemics ever since a priest of Ptah at White Wall (Memphis) told the Persian king Darius he could not set his statue next to that of the Egyptian pharaoh Sesostris. The priest insisted that Darius was not Sesostris' equal because the Egyptian pharaoh had conquered more of the world than had the Persian king. Also, the priest reminded Darius that he had retreated in shame from Scythia, whereas Sesostris had conquered that land. Herodotus believed the story, which other ancient writers approvingly copied out of his book. Until the nineteenth century it was generally thought that Sesostris, not Darius, had been the first foreign invader of Russia. Today, critical scholars treat the story

---

[28]   Mallowan, *op. cit.*, p. 360.

of Sesostris' conquest of Scythia as a product of native Egyptian pride, not a reflection of the historical reality.[29]

Egypt has also been brought into recent controversies regarding its geographical position and the role it played in the shaping of various civilizations. The expression *ex oriente lux* was understood to mean not only that the sun rose in the east but also that European civilization originated from Egypt and West Asia. Although the country belongs to the continent of Africa, as defined by modern geographers, this was not so in antiquity when a great and original civilization thrived in Egypt. Taking the Nile rather than the Arabian Gulf as a continental boundary, some ancient writers divided Egypt between Asia and Africa.[30] In the later Roman Empire Egypt was a diocese, composed of the provinces of Aegyptus, Thebais, Libya, and Cyrenaica. It was attached to the Prefecture of the East ruled from Constantinople. In fact, ancient Egypt was an integral part of the Mediterranean world where the people who occupied the Nile Delta had more in common with those who settled at the mouths of the Danube, Dnieper, or the Don than either had with the folks living at the sources of these rivers. Nevertheless, one is justified to treat Egypt both as an Asian and an African country, or rather Afroasian, just as Russia is counted both as a European and an Asian land, or Eurasian.

Ancient Egypt and its inhabitants were demarcated and governed by the Nile. The boundary between the land which can be tilled and the desert which cannot is sharp. The country we call Egypt consists primarily of the Delta and a strip of arable land on both banks of the Nile, which tapers off as one goes upstream. This river's broad delta and a narrow valley provided the necessities for a good life to a large number of people. On the east, the cultivated domain is flanked by the Eastern (or Arabian) Desert, on the west, by the Libyan. The Arabic name for Egypt, *Misrun*, means "cultivated land." It is in the dual form

---

[29]   M. Bernal in his *Black Athena*, accepts the priest's story as true (II, ch. V). Since Bernal's declared objective in writing this book is "to lessen European cultural arrogance," (I, p. 73), his colleagues have declared his arguments to be as fanciful as the story of Sesostris' conquests which the priest of Ptah had fabricated "to lessen Persian arrogance."

[30]   *Cf.*, Pliny, *n.h.*, V.47–8, and Ptolemy, *Geography*, II. Prologue.

because when Egypt was first politically organized it was divided into two parts, Upper and Lower Egypt.[31]

Like the Sumerians, the Egyptians saw their land as a cultivated island surrounded by desert occupied by nomads. Consequently, they called all their neighbors "nomads."[32] More specifically, the people who lived in the desert between the Nile Valley and the Red Sea and some tribes in the Levant were called "sand-dwellers."

The will to settle down and produce food by agriculture and animal husbandry, to change from savagery to barbarism, and to build civilization, came naturally and independently to people in different parts of the world. Though the ancient Egyptians believed they were autochthonous, their origins are sought beyond the confines of Egypt by scholars who hold that some essential elements of Egyptian civilization were brought from West Asia, more precisely from Anatolia and the Levant, by small groups of people. In predynastic Egypt oases of farmers existed in a sea of nomads and hunters-gatherers. Some farming communities may have arrived from the Levant, while others grew on altogether native foundations. Generally, settled communities were more common in the Delta than in Upper Egypt, indicating that the neolithic revolution had spread from north to south. Archaeologists have concluded that a single race lived in predynastic Egypt. Then the land was flooded by people with skulls measuring 139 mm., or 7 mm. broader than the skulls of the natives. Aegyptologists hold:

> The quantity and distribution of the skeletons hitherto found suggest that the 'Dynastic Race' entered Egypt in considerable numbers from the north, where the purest examples of their racial types have been discovered; this fact would suggest that the immigrants came from Asia, but it is doubtful whether the assertion sometimes made that they were Armenoids is anatomically justifiable. Before the end of the First Dynasty they had already penetrated southward as far as Abydos and were becoming merged into the general population—a process which appears to have been intensified with the passage of time. So long as the origin of this people remains unexplained, it is difficult to determine what fresh

[31]   *See* note 2 to the Loeb Classical Library edition of Manetho, p. 7.
[32]   I.E.S. Edwards, "The Early Dynastic Period in Egypt," *CAH*, I.2[3] (1971), p. 50.

knowledge they have brought with them to Egypt, but it is probable that a generous share of the credit for the acceleration in cultural progress observable at this time should be ascribed to their presence. Perhaps the Semitic elements in the structure and vocabulary of the Egyptian language were also introduced by them. Archaeological evidence suggests that they provided the ruling class and that they adapted their way of life to conform with the customs already prevailing in their new home; in this respect they set a precedent which was to be followed by successive invaders of the Nile Valley down to Roman times.[33]

The nature of contacts between Lower Mesopotamia and the Nile Valley indicates that Asia was the giver, Africa the receiver of cultural influences. This leads to the conclusion that groups of Sumerians and Akkadians had also migrated to Egypt. Entering the country by way of the Arabian Gulf and the Wadi Hammamat, they may have contributed to the unification of the Two Lands. Before the unification there were two kingdoms in Egypt, the northern and the southern, also called Lower and Upper Egypt. The two became one through conquest by the northern kingdom of the southern.

Unlike the Sumerian kings who were mere stewards of the deities of their imagination, the pharaohs of Egypt themselves were invested with divine attributes. The first kings bore the title of the god Horus, claiming thereby to be the deity's earthly manifestation. King Chephren of the Fourth Dynasty took the title "Son of Re," the sun-god, which became obligatory from the Fifth Dynasty on. The ascension of the new king was described by the annalists as "the rising of the King of Upper Egypt, rising of the King of Lower Egypt, union of the Two Lands and procession around the Wall," that is, White Wall, or Memphis. At death the pharaohs relinquished their divine title. The highest official after the king was the one in charge of the White House and the Red House, or respectively, the treasuries of Upper and Lower Egypt.

Like the Sumerians, the ancient Egyptians divided the world into four quarters. A god presided over each of the four cardinal points, though the deities changed places through history. The Egyptians appear not to have had a fixed system of colors as

---

[33] *Ibid.*, pp. 40–1.

symbols of the four quarters. As we saw, they oriented themselves to the south, so that for them east was left, west was
right.[34] Although in other cultures the east stands for everything
positive, in ancient Egypt, that quarter was considered bad because of its left direction, while the west, because it was to the
right was associated with life and beauty and called "the beautiful west," and "the country of the living." At the same time, the
extreme west, "the horn of the west," as the abode of sunset, was
enveloped in "thick darkness."[35] Osiris was the god-king of the
western quarter. The dominant imaginary natural feature in the
east was *B3h* "mountain of sunrise," in the west *M3nw*
"mountain of sunset." Like some other peoples, the ancient
Egyptians imagined the north, which in their world view
extended from the Delta toward Europe, as the abode of darkness. The extreme north or northeast known to the Egyptians
was in a vaguely defined region of Upper Asia called *Naharina*
and situated, as its name shows, between two rivers, the Tigris
and Euphrates. It was there that the Egyptians imagined the four
supports of heaven, while placing the Horn of the World in the
south, identified with the Ras Asir Cape in Somalia.[36]

The ancient Egyptians knew the names of five seas. We have
already discussed the sea they called the Great Circle, concluding that it was equivalent to the Circumambient Ocean of other
peoples. The sea named the "circle which runs around the
H3nb.w" is identified with the Mediterranean, while the identity
of the one named the "great circle Sk" remains elusive. The remaining two names are a color pair. The term *Km-wr* the "great
black" was applied to the Bitter Lakes. It is possible that the
color attribute reflects the northern location of these lakes rather
than the appearance of their waters. The appellation *W3d̲-wr* the
"great green" appears to have been applied more specifically to
the Mediterranean, and the choice of green may stem from the
belief that this sea was a part of the Circumambient Ocean, the

---

[34]   *See* above, p. 44.
[35]   E.A. Wallis Budge, *The Gods of the Egyptians*, in 2 vols. (London,
1904; Dover Publications, New York, 1969), I, p. 205.
[36]   H. Brugsch, *Die Geographie des alten Aegyptens nach den
altägytischen Denkmälern* (Leipzig, 1857–60; reprinted Amsterdam, 1970),
pp. 31–6.

symbolic color of which may have been green, as it is in Arabic.[37]

The Indian Ocean, on whose northwestern shore the ancient Egyptians placed the Horn of the World, was called the *Shar Sea*. It corresponds to the *Erythra thalassa* of Greek sources. Coptic translators of the Bible use the name Shar Sea for the sea which the Hebrews called *Yam suf* "sea of reeds," affirming their god had parted it to help them escape from the pursuing Egyptians. The ancient Egyptian name for the Sea of Reeds was the *Sea of Mertet*, named after Mert, the goddess of the VIII hour of the Night. The appellation seems to refer both to the Gulf of Suez and the Bitter Lakes.[38]

The division of the Nile Valley into Upper and Lower Egypt is very ancient, and both parts were attributed a color. For each the symbol of sovereignty was a crown: that of Lower Egypt a red wickerwork diadem and that of Upper Egypt a tall white helmet. Together the crowns stood for the unity of the kingdom, representing, respectively, the south and the north. Occasionally mentioned are green and blue crowns, but their function and symbolism are not clear.[39] Egypt, as a whole, was also represented by another set of colors, that of black and red. For instance, when sovereignty over the land would be transferred to a new pharaoh, the gods used the phrase: "We give you *Kemi* (the black land) and *Desher* (the red land)." In this case black stands for the cultivated domain, red for the desert.[40]

The ancient Greeks thought that the native name of Egypt, *Kemi* "black", reflected the country's soil. For example, Herodotus says:

> Egypt ... is a land of black and crumbling earth, as if it were alluvial deposit carried down the river from Aethiopia; but we know that the soil of Libya is redder and somewhat sandy, and Arabia and Syria are lands rather of clay and stones.[41]

[37] Burr, *op. cit.*, p. 82; Posener, *op. cit.*, p. 76.

[38] Wallis Budge, *op. cit.*, I, p. 480; II, p. 301; on the Sea of Reeds, *see*, *EJ*, XIV (1971), s.v. "Red Sea—Sea of Reeds," cols. 14–17.

[39] G. Steindorff, "Die blaue Königskrone," *Zeitschrift für ägyptische Sprache und Altertumskunde*, LIII (1917), pp. 59–74.

[40] Brugsch, *op. cit.*, p. 73.

[41] II.12.

Though modern scholars concur with the quoted passage, one wonders, if the ancient Egyptians had called their land by a color other than black, would not the Greeks have "seen" it as the land's dominant hue. But, once Herodotus had established Egypt as a "black" land in Greek literature, this color became its fixed epithet. Thus, Plutarch, states:

> and even Egypt itself, by reason of the extreme blackness of the soil, is called Chemia, the very name which is given to the black part or pupil of the eye.[42]

Stephen of Byzantium accompanies the name Aigyptos with the epithet *melambolos* "of black soil."[43] The ancient Hebrews accounted for the color black associated with the name Kemi by furnishing Ham (a name related to the Egyptian name for their own country), who was black and accursed because he had sodomized his father Noah in the ark. Ham's sons were Kush, Mizraim, Put, and Canaan.[44]

Diodorus Siculus reports a Theban version of Egypt's origins in which they claimed to be the oldest of humankind. Their king, whom Diodorus calls *Uchoreus* "he who endures" (a Greek translation of the native name Menes, Meni or Min, mentioned by Herodotus and Manetho), conquered Lower Egypt and founded a city there. Then he built a great temple to the god Ptah.[45] The oldest name for Uchoreus' city was *'Ineb-hedj* "white wall." The same city was better known by the name *Men-Nefer*, which the Akkadians rendered as Mempi, the Hebrews as Moph, and the Greeks as Memphis. The city's third name was derived from the shrine of its chief god Ptah, which the natives called *Hekuptah* and the Greeks Aegyptus.[46]

---

[42] *Isis and Osiris*, ch. 33.

[43] *Ethnica*, s.v. "Aigyptos."

[44] *EJ*, VII (1971), col. 1216. The Canaanites, though Semites and close relatives of the Hebrews, were affiliated to Ham and other Africans in the Hebrew scheme because they occupied the land the Hebrews claimed their own deity had promised to them.

[45] Diodorus Siculus, I.50—1; Herodotus, II.4,99; Manetho, *Aegyptiaca*, fr. 4,7.

[46] W.F. Albright and T.O. Lambdin, "The Evidence of Language," *CAH*, I.1³ (1970), pp. 149—50.

White Wall (Memphis) is perhaps the oldest recorded toponym distinguished by an attribute of color. The ancients, speculating about the reason for the color, concluded that the city was called white because its walls were built of white stone, while other cities were built of brick. Some modern authorities claim that Memphis was called white because it was built by a king of Upper Egypt symbolized by the white crown. However, these explanations are not satisfactory. Although Memphis was built by a king of a land symbolized by the color white, and though its walls looked white, the color attribute may stem from the city's function rather than its appearance. Memphis had a great temple dedicated to Ptah, and a college of priests who maintained the cult. It may have been the city's function as a religious center that earned it the epithet white, as this color is often associated with the priestly class. We shall see that numerous cities in Greece, Rome, Slavia, and Russia either derived from words for the color white or were associated with it, all perhaps in imitation of White Wall of Egypt.

The Egyptians saw their land as a domain of tillers of the soil surrounded mostly by uncultivated terrain, and for this reason they considered all other peoples as nomads. They also saw the human race, including themselves, in terms of colors. They believed that they were autochthonous inhabitants of the Nile Valley, a people sprung from the soil. They called themselves *Retu*, and used red as their symbolic color. The south was the domain of the black race, the *Neḥesu*. The east and the north belonged to the *'Aamu*, the yellow race (the biblical Amonites). Libya and other western regions were occupied by the *Temeḥu*, the white race.[47] To be noted is the fact that the ancestors of the Greeks and Arabs were designated as the yellow race by the Egyptians. Later, when the Slavs and Russians came into the field of vision of the descendants of these "yellow folks," the latter called them the "yellow people." Eventually this color was shifted eastward and attached to the people who built the Yellow Empire, situated in the valley of the Yellow River and on the shores of the Yellow Sea.

---

[47] *See*, Brugsch, *op. cit.*, section "Geographie der Nachbarländer Aegyptens," pp. 89–91, Table XV.

In the Mediterranean basin, the color purple has, over the millennia, been associated with royal dignity. The custom first appeared in thirteenth-century BC Egypt. From there it spread throughout the Mediterranean world and was ultimately adopted by Roman and Rhomaean ideology and iconography.[48]

INDIA

The Aryans came to the Indian Subcontinent in migratory waves from the north and west, settling first in the Indus Valley. Thence they expanded eastward and southward in a long struggle with the indigenous inhabitants. In their literature the natives are depicted as dark, snub-nosed people called *Dasyus* and *Dāsas* "demons, enemies," while in European sources dark-skinned Indians are called Aethiopes.[49]

Like other Indo-European groups that abandoned the "motherland" in search of new homes, the Aryans who established their supremacy and Hindu civilization in India have left no evidence that they knew about the location of their original homeland or that they wished to maintain contact with it. The migrations from the north, which the ancient Aryans did not care to record for posterity, are postulated by modern scholars. In the surviving literary monuments the Aryans' first homeland is a region of northern India drained by the Indus River and its tributaries and called *Sapta-sindhu* "land of seven rivers." The term refers to the same area as *Punjab* "land of five rivers" today. The fact that there is another "land of seven rivers," *Semirečje* in Kyrgyzstan and Kazakhstan verging on Lake Balkash, is not an argument that the Aryans of India came from there, only that people attach significance to the number seven.[50]

In the imagination of the Aryan peoples of India, the southern quarter was the gathering place of the dead, called the *pitarah*

---

[48]   H. Hunger, *Reich der neuen Mitte* (Graz–Vienna–Cologne, 1965), p. 84.

[49]   Herodotus, III.94. The name *Aithiopes* means "sun-burned" and it was applied by Europeans to dark-type people both of Africa and Asia.

[50]   The German name *Siebenbürgen*, designating Transylvania, echoes the seven Hungarian tribes who settled in Transylvania in the tenth century in or near the homeland of the native Slavic *Hepta genea* "seven tribes."

"(fore)fathers." In the north, beyond the Himalayas, in the land of the gods, lived the Uttara-Kuru, a happy race who resembled the Hyperboreans of the Greek imagination.[51]

Cosmological systems attested in India are complex but well-studied. The ancient Indians were exceedingly imaginative in describing the geography of the earth, heaven, hell, and much more. To simplify, one may say that at first they saw the dry land as a contiguous mass floating in a sea, comparable to the Circumambient Sea of the Sumerians, Greeks, and Arabs. Like the Sumerians, Indian cosmographers also imagined the dry land divided into four quarters. Their world had four continents situated at the cardinal points of the compass. These were: Purvavideha (E), Jambudvipa (S), Aparagodana (W) and Uttarakuru (N). Within this scheme, the ocean was also divided into four sections. Additional ways of picturing the cosmos attested in India were engendered by human imagination and pedantic accommodation to the magical numbers 3 and 7 and their combinations.

In Hinduism the central place in the cosmos is occupied by the mythical Mount Meru, whose eastern slopes are white, southern yellow, western black, and northern red.[52] This multicolored hill is evidence that the ancient Indians consciously and systematically used colors as symbols of the directions of the horizon.

The heavenly bodies are also associated with specific colors. Thus, the Sun, Moon, and Venus are white, Mars is red, Jupiter greenish-yellow, Mercury dark, and Saturn black.[53] Names of several Hindu gods are color appellations. Vishnu's name may derive from *vish* "to work," but the name of one of his incarnations, *Krishna*, means "black" in Sanskrit. *Shiva*'s name means "red" in a Dravidian language. (His other name, *Rudra*, signifies "roaring" in Sanskrit.) Included in the symbolism associated with the five-headed god Shiva-Rudra are the following phenomena:

---

[51] G.M. Bongard–Levin and F.A. Grantovskij, *Ot Skifii do Indii* (Moscow, 1983), pp. 45–7.
[52] W. Kirfel, *Die Kosmographie der Inder nach den Quellen dargestellt* (Bonn–Leipzig, 1920), pp. 18–19, 93.
[53] W. Kirfel, *Symbolik des Hinduismus und des Jainismus* (Stuttgart, 1959) (=*Symbolik der Religionen*, IV), p. 64.

Sadyojata (West, white), Vamadeva (North, red), Tatpurusha (East, yellow), Aghora (South, black), and Isana (Center, crystal-clear).[54] Similar symbolism appears in Mahayana Buddhism, and the five heavenly or meditating Buddhas are associated with the cardinal points, colors, seasons, and several metaphysical concepts. In this system the colors are white, blue, yellow, red, and green.[55]

Though it is hard to imagine today that the Indian castes have anything to do with skin color, the Hindu caste system is based on colors. In fact, the very word *varṇa* "caste" means "color." The early Hindus divided humanity into four divinely appointed castes: Brahmins, Kshatriyas (warriors), Vaishyas (merchants and craftsmen), and Shudras (non-Aryan servants and slaves). The color of the Brahmana is white, the Kshatriyas red, the Vaishyas yellow, and of the Shudras black.[56] Their descendants are divided into about a thousand subcastes and intercastes.

The four mythical ages are also represented by colors. The first age, *Krita Yuga*, corresponding to the Golden Age of other cultures, is symbolized by the color white. It is followed by *Treta Yuga* (Silver Age), symbolized by the color yellow, and *Dvapara Yuga* (Bronze Age) by the color red. The present (Iron Age), which in India began with the emergence of Buddhism, is called *Kali Yuga*, and its color is black.[57]

CHINA

The ancient Chinese ethnogonic myths make no mention of migrations from other lands. Their civilization, the Chinese believed, was created in the Yellow River Valley by a succession of wise rulers, the last of whom, Yu the Great, founded the Hsia

[54] *Ibid.*, 16–40.
[55] W. Kirfel, *Symbolik des Buddhismus* (Stuttgart, 1959) (=*Symbolik der Religionen*, V), pp. 42–44.
[56] Kirfel, *Symbolik des Hinduismus und des Jainismus*, p. 25.
[57] Kirfel, *Die Kosmographie der Inder*, pp. 91ff; *Symbolik des Hinduismus*, p. 37; for a comparison of color symbolism of mythical ages in other cultures, *see*, D.A. Mackenzie, "Color Symbolisms," *Folk-lore*, XXXIII (1922), June, No. II, pp. 136–69.

dynasty. Because its historicity has not been documented, the Hsia dynasty is regarded as mythical by specialists. Chinese history begins with the Shang dynasty, 1523–1027 BC, whose rule has been recorded in the so-called *Bamboo Annals*. This period corresponds to the Bronze Age in China. The Shang kings were sons of Heaven, their subjects were settled agriculturalists, who also raised sheep, goats, and cattle. They kept horses, but at first they used them to pull war chariots, not to ride upon. They had a writing system of 2000 characters. We do not know the extent of the Shang state, other than that it was located on the banks of the Yellow River. Its neighbors must have all been ethnically and linguistically related to the Shang subjects, but, since they did not recognize the Son of Heaven, they were called "barbarians."

One such "barbarian" state, having learned some rudiments of civilization from the Shang dynasty, conquered its cultural parent and took over the leadership. These were the Chou dynasty, 1122–256 BC. The Chou emerged in the valley of the Wei River as guardians of China's western border. The founder of the dynasty, Wen Wang, bore the title of "Chief of the West." His son, Wu Wang, set up his capital in the Wei Valley, near the later city of Ch'angan (modern Hsian).

The Chou were the first in a long series of western and northern neighbors of China who marshalled the raw human resources of their less developed, chiefly nomadic, lands to take over and rule the Chinese Empire of settled agriculturalists. In the High Middle Ages both China and Russia found themselves under the Mongols whose empire may be regarded as the culmination of the political development of the nomadic peoples of the Great Eurasian Steppe. We shall see that colors reflecting the quarters attached to four large ethno-political divisions of the Mongol sphere: black (N), the attribute of the Mongol Emperor; yellow (E or Center), symbolizing the Chinese Emperor, his land and people; red (S), designating the Persian Emperor; and white (W), attributed to the ruler of Russia.

Specialists in ancient cosmologies have learned primarily by studying Chinese sources that a cosmographic system of four cardinal points may be symbolized by colors. The Chinese system, though perhaps not the most ancient, is the most readily recognizable as a complete set of ideas among similar Eurasian and African cosmographic systems. In China, the colors are a part of the so-called bino-quinary series which supposedly embrace all phenomena in heaven and on earth. The binary principle is represented by *yin* and *yang*, the quinary set is shown in the following chart:

Cardinal Point	Planet	Hour	Season	Color
East	Jupiter	Morning	Spring	Blue-green
South	Mars	Noon	Summer	Red
West	Venus	Evening	Autumn	White
North	Mercury	Midnight	Winter	Black
Center	Saturn	—	—	Yellow[58]

The ancient Chinese divided both heaven and earth into five sections: a center, plus four peripheral segments. In the center of the world as they saw it, was their own domain, the Middle Kingdom. The color that has symbolized it for millennia is yellow.

It is generally assumed that the celebrated *Huang Ho* "yellow river," the chief river of the "yellow" empire established by the "yellow" race in a region of Asia which verges on the Yellow Sea, obtained its name from the color of its waters.[59] However, doubt is cast on the certainty that the river's name "describes its color" by the realization that the same river might have been called *Kara-moran* "black river" by China's Turkic neighbors.[60] Reconciling the contradiction, we propose that the Turks may have named the river black in accordance with their perception of it as a stream in the "black" direction of the horizon, the same

[58]   L. de Saussure, "Le Système cosmologique sino-iranien," *Journal Asiatique*, 202 (1923), pp. 335—97.

[59]   *See* for example, K.S. Latourette, *The Chinese: Their History and Culture*, (New York, 1962⁴), p. 4: "[T]he Yellow River, which, rising in the mountains and plateaus that fringe Tibet, by a devious route flows into the Yellow Sea. Its name describes its color, and this in turn is due to the vast amount of sediment which the river carries ..."

[60]   Marco Polo, *Travels* (Penguin's ed.), p. 167; *see* also, the H. Yule, H. Cordier edition of *The Travels*, 2 vols. (Dover ed., New York, 1993), I, map.

way the Chinese themselves had named it yellow because it was in the center whose symbol was that color.

Another great river of China is called *Yangtze* "blue river." Issuing from the mountains of the province of *Szechwan* "four rivers," it skirts the region called the Red Basin, while supposedly maintaining its blue appearance until it reaches the Yellow Sea. It is commonly believed that the Blue River is truly blue and that the Red Basin is red. Since we know that the Chinese saw the center as yellow, it is reasonable to postulate that they saw the Yellow River as the central member of a system of rivers, therefore yellow. Other rivers, including the Blue River, may have also been given the attributes of the respective colors on account of their relative position rather than the appearance of their waters.

Each of the four cardinal points of the compass had its own mountain, which made it necessary to have a high mountain in the middle as well, so that the emperor, as Son of Heaven, could communicate more readily with his superiors. Nature having failed to provide such a mountain in the center of ancient China, human imagination satisfied the symmetry by naming a hill "high mountain." However, the emperor traditionally offered his sacrifices on a higher mountain in the east, called the "blue mountain," because blue-green was the symbol of the east.[61]

It has been suggested that the Chinese bino-quinary system had developed in contact with the cosmological sciences of West Asia.

HELLAS

Like other peoples, the Greeks, too, were confused about their origins. Their eponym is Hellen, son of Deucalion and Pyrrha, the just couple who survived the Great Flood by taking refuge on Mount Parnassus. After the flood Hellen had three sons: Dorus, Xuthus (who begat Ion), and Aeolus. The boys grew up in Thessaly, between Mount Parnassus and Mount Ossa, in a

---

[61] de Saussure, *op. cit.*

region called Hellas after their father. They founded the Dorian,
Ionian, and Aeolian branches of Greeks. The story of the three
brothers born in Hellas is the autochthonous version of Greek
origins. Like the Chinese, Sumerians, Egyptians, Scythians, and
many other peoples, the Greeks thought they were native to their
country. At the same time, they sought the roots of their civilization beyond the confines of Hellas, in the more civilized east
and south, not in the less developed west and the barbaric north.

Greek stories of their origins have been subjected to close
scrutiny by varied exegesists and doubters from ancient Greek
writers to modern scholars applying scientific methodologies.
Contrary to the belief of the ancient Greeks, who thought themselves to be autochthonous there or descendants from semi-
divine immigrants from Egypt and Asia, modern scholars
maintain that they, originating in Russia, descended in several
migratory waves as goatherds and shepherds from the interior of
the Balkans into their historically known homeland in the
southern portion of that peninsula, forcing and pursuing the
autochthonous inhabitants into the mountains and across the sea
and the Aegean and Ionian islands to Asia Minor, Sicily, and
Italy.[62] A similar process was repeated when the Slavs conquered Greece from the Romans at the beginning of the Middle
Ages, causing masses of Rhomaeans to seek safety in these
same regions.

We saw that when people know or believe that they had come
into a new country from an original homeland they may distinguish the two lands by adding either the attribute "old" or
"great" to the country from which they had arrived, while leaving the new homeland unmarked. The case of the Greeks is
somewhat more complex, because throughout antiquity the land
which was known as *Megalē Hellas, Magna Graecia* was not
considered to be the pristine habitat of Balkan and Ionian
Greeks. Archaeology, history, and linguistics teach that the basic
population of Magna Graecia spoke Italic languages, not Greek.
Greeks came as colonists to Italy, as they did to other regions of
the Mediterranean basin, without ever Hellenizing the
countryside. In contradistinction to other pairs of countries
differentiated by the attribute of size, Magna Graecia appears to

---

[62]   R.J. Hopper, *The Early Greeks* (New York, 1976), pp. 16ff.

be so named for its numerous Greek cities founded there during the first half of the first millennium BC. Also, the designation "great" appears to signify "more distant."[63]

The name "Hellas" first appeared in the following verse of the *Iliad*:

> Now all those who dwelt about Pelasgian Argos,
> those who lived by Alos and Alope and at Trachis,
> those who held Phthia and Hellas the land of fair women,
> who were called Myrmidons and Hellenes and Achaians,
> of all these and their fifty ships the lord was Achilleus.[64]

Hellas *stricte* was inhabited by Hellenes, while the rest of the domain of Peleus and his son Achilles was settled by Myrmydons and Achaeans. Since the name Achaioi is used by Homer as one of the appellations of the Greeks, the Hellenes appear also to be called by that name, as when the poet says "There are many Achaian girls in the land of Hellas and Phthia."[65] Though it is not clear which ancient people the name Myrmidons designated, the Rhomaeans used it for the Russians of their day believing that Achilles had been their ancestor and had come to Hellas from Russia.[66]

Thessaly may have been the cradle of the first known Hellas and Hellenes, but it was in Epirus that some ancients placed Old Hellas, occupied by a people whom their Illyrian neighbors called Graeci. The meaning of the name Graeci has not been clarified, though this did not prevent the Greeks from fashioning Graecus to serve as their founder and to explain why among their western neighbors they were called Graeci, while they referred to themselves as Hellenes. It was in the land occupied by the people whom the Illyrians called Graeci that some ancient Hellenes discovered the original country by coalescing the ethnonyms Graeci and Hellenes. In a district of Epirus, called Ellopia, in the city of Dodona, near modern Ioanina, there was an ancient temple of Zeus, to whom Achilles prayed:

[63] *See* above, p. 84.
[64] *Iliad*, II.681–5.
[65] *Iliad*, IX.395.
[66] *See* below, Ch. VII.

'High Zeus, lord of Dodona, Pelasgian, living afar off,
brooding over wintry Dodona, your prophets about you
living, the Selloi who sleep on the ground with feet unwashed.
Hear me.'[67]

The scholiasts called this region *He archaiotate Hellas* "the oldest Hellas."[68] Aristotle, sure the Hellenes originated from there, says:

[T]he so-called flood of Deucalion took place largely in the Hellenic lands and particularly in old Hellas, that is, the country round Dodona and the Achelous, a river which has frequently changed its course. Here dwelt the Selloi and the people then called Greeks and now called Hellenes.[69]

Based on our earliest extant written sources, a sufficiently clear northern boundary of the Hellenic race in antiquity may be drawn. An almost straight line separating Greeks from barbarians ran from the Gulf of Ambracia to the Vale of Tempe and the estuary of the Peneus.[70]

The siege and destruction of Troy was the first and the only common enterprise of the ancient Hellenes. The men who sided with Helen's wronged husband came from lands inhabited by speakers of Greek. No barbarian warrior fought on the side of Menelaus in the Trojan War and no Greek, other than the abducted Helen could be found in the Trojan camp. In historical time, however, the Hellenes fought each other so fiercely that they were exhausted and unable to resist the Macedonians, who, having defeated them at the battle of Chaeronea in 338 BC, became masters of Greece and put an end to its history.

In antiquity, the name Hellas was used informally to designate an area of the southern Balkans where Greeks exerted political control, where Greek was spoken, and where the native people

---

[67]   *Iliad*, 16.233-35.
[68]   Miller, "Hellas."
[69]   *Meteoroligica*, I.xiv.352a. Some scholars derive the name "Hellas" from the district of Ellopia, while the majority rejects this interpretation and the location of Old Greece in Epirus as confused tradition, without however proposing a better answer why that region particularly was known as pristine Greece, Graecia prisca, by Greeks themselves.
[70]   *See,* map in *CAH*, II.2³, p. 682.

followed Greek customs, but no territory was ever known formally by the name Hellas, not even the city or district of Hellas in Thessaly. The name Thessaly prevailed there, as did other local and regional appellations throughout the domain of the original Hellenes. Old Hellas in Epirus did not exist under that name in the historical period, only in the imagination of those Greeks who considered it the cradle of the Hellenic race. Great Hellas in Italy and Sicily, never formed a political unit. Southern Italy and Sicily, peopled by Greeks and natives, was apportioned by the region's Roman conquerors among the provinces none of which bore the Hellenic name.

No ancient foreign conqueror ever used the name "Hellas" to designate a political entity. Greece's first "barbarian" conquerors, the Macedonians, led by the "thrice barbarous" Philip II, found the land fragmented into numerous city-states and leagues. The Macedonians maintained the *status quo*. The Romans conquered Hellas in 146 BC, but in the long centuries of their rule and administrative subdivisions of Greek lands they never used the name Hellas for any territorial entity they formed. In the organization of the empire carried out by Diocletian, the land we call Greece was divided between the Prefecture of Illyricum and the Prefecture of the East. The Greek portion of Illyricum was subjected to the Diocese of Macedonia, within which Achaea was the only province peopled perhaps by speakers of Greek. The other provinces of Macedonia—Epirus Vetus, Epirus Nova, and the two Macedonias—were inhabited by Illyrians and Macedonians, ancestors of today's Vlachs, Macedonians, and Albanians. It seems that the "barbarian" element predominated in all these with the exception perhaps of the southern portion of Epirus Vetus, which extended to the Gulf of Corinth. Most of the Aegean islands were organized into a province called Insulae and subjected to the Diocese of Asia which belonged to the Prefecture of the East.

The ancient Hellenes, who have been so romantically adored by Philhellenes of all ages, ceased being Hellenes once they entered the realm

> where there is neither Greek nor Jew, circumcision nor uncir-
> cumcision, Barbarian, Scythian, bond nor free: but Christ is all,
> and in all.[71]

Along with other gentiles, the Hellenes melted into a new people
who were by citizenship Romans, by religion Christians, and by
language and culture Rhomaeans. Membership in this group was
open to all who satisfied these three requirements. The center of
the new civilization built from these elements was
Constantinople. Ancient Byzantium was not a new Athens, for
it was officially designated as New Rome and poetically and
ideologically as New Jerusalem, while its people referred to
themselves as Rhomaioi. The name "Hellene" acquired a new
meaning in the Christian republic established by Constantine the
Great. Explaining this transformation, a leading authority on
Neo-Hellenism wrote:

> During the reign of Constantine the Great and his successor there
> was a spirit of toleration towards the diverse religions of the
> Empire. The new capital was in constant intellectual intercourse
> with Athens and probably with Corinth and Thebes. Yet the very
> name Hellene, because of its connotation with the ideas and
> religious beliefs of the ancient Greeks, was already becoming
> synonymous with pagan. As adherents of the Christian religion
> gradually multiplied in Greece they tended to eschew the
> appellation Hellene in favor of *Romaios*, Roman, the more so
> because of an overriding sense of imperial citizenship. The
> pejorative overtones of the word Hellene only inhibited its use,
> thus destroying its function as the primary symbol of national
> identity.[72]

The Slavic conquerors of Greece could not revive the Hellenic
name because they were Christians and in their languages the
name meant pagan. The Crusaders, the Catalans, and the Venetians, finding ancient Hellas inhabited by Slavs, Albanians,
Vlachs, and scattered speakers of Rhomaean (medieval Greek)
never used the ancient Hellenic name for any territorial entity
they controlled in the former Greek lands, but availed them-

---

[71] Col. 3:11.
[72] A.E. Vacalopoulos, *Origins of the Greek Nation: The Byzantine
Period, 1204—1461*, transl. by I. Moles (New Brunswick, N.J., 1970), p. 18.

selves of more recent Slavic and Vlach geographical nomenclature. Thus, the Peloponnese was called Morea, a Slavic name
meaning "sea land," Thessaly became Great Vallachia, Aetolia
Little Vallachia, while a good portion of the defunct East Roman
state was named Romania.

The name Rome, on the other hand, has had more appeal in
the Balkans. The Turks, who conquered New Rome in 1453,
preserved it by officially designating as Rum or Rumelia most
of the Balkan peninsula under their control and by lumping
together the native Christian peoples under the rubric of *Rum
millet* "Roman people." The Ottomans never called any of the
territorial political entities by the name Hellas.

The name Hellene today is used as a self-designation by citizens of the Republic of Greece, called Hellas, and by Christian
Orthodox people whose native language is Greek regardless of
where they reside. Hellas was established as the Kingdom of the
Hellenes in February 1832 by Russia, Britain, and France who
sent a Bavarian prince to rule the Morea, Attica, portion of the
mainland, and some islands wrested by native rebels and these
same powers from the Ottoman Turks. The "Hellene" subjects of
the German prince included not only Neo-Hellenic-speaking
Orthodox Christians, thus, Rhomaeans, but also masses of
Albanians, Vlachs, Slavs, Turks, and Romi (Gypsies).[73]

Though we have no evidence that the ancient Greeks used
colors as symbols of the directions of the horizon, it is clear that
words connoting color were a fundamental part of their
ethnonymic and geographical nomenclatures, some of which
have been the subject of lengthy debates.

The ancient Greeks called themselves *Hellenes*, while their
western neighbors knew them as *Graeci*. We do not know how
these names originated and we ignore their etymologies. We
assume that the first, as a self-designation, ought to be explained
from Greek, while the meaning of the second is sought in the

---

[73] Both the kingdom and the republic of the Hellenes have by
persuasion, propaganda, and frequently by brutal means been trying to
homogenize the population ruled from Athens. They have partly succeeded
with Christian Orthodox Vlachs, Slavs, and Albanians, but have utterly failed to Hellenize the Muslims. The Greek state does not tolerate nor acknowl-
edges the existence of Vlachs and Albanians on its territory, while the
Macedonians are euphemistically dismissed as "allophonous Greeks."

entirely unknown language of the Illyrians. The ancients satisfied themselves by supplying the eponyms Hellen and Graecus. They also explained in this manner the names of the major divisions of the Hellenic peoples, claiming that the Dorians, Ionians, and Aeolians were founded by Dorus, Ion, and Aeolus.

As seen above, the Dorian ethnonym signifies forest-dwellers.[74] The name Iones is a mystery. The domain of the Ionian Greeks extended from the eastern coast of Greece, across the islands, to the sea-board of Anatolia. There is no agreement about the etymology of Ion, the people's *hero eponymous*. Moreover, its Afroasian forms (*Ja-ma-na* in Assyrian, *Jaunā* in Old Persian, *Yavan* in Hebrew, *Yunanlı* in modern Turkish) suggest a source other than the attested Greek.[75] We would be at a dead-end etymologically with this name had the ancients not provided the name of Ion's father, *Xouthos*, an appellation denoting a color. The dictionary definition of *xouthos* is "of a color, between *xanthos*, 'yellow' and *pyrros*, 'red, yellowish, brown-yellowish'." It is possible that the Ionians were at first called the "yellow or the red ones" after Xouthos and that Ion was introduced later to explain the Afroasian variant of their name.

The name Aeoles opens up several etymological avenues. The adjective *aiolos* means "quick, swift," or "writhing" like a snake. Another meaning is "changeful of hue, gleamy, glowing." It is not, of course, possible to state with certainty which of these meanings was originally conveyed by the name Aeoles.

On modern maps that use the Latin script, the name Ionian is given to the sea between Epirus and Italy. The islands off the shores of western Greece are also called Ionian. The ancient Greeks extended the Ionian name through the whole length of the sea we call the Adriatic. This, western, Ionian name must not be confused with the Aegean and Anatolian Ionians, for, in Greek, the two names are distinguished from each other, just as the omega in *Iōn* is distinguished from the omicron in *ion*. The

---

[74] *See* above, p. 98.

[75] W. Röllig, "Ionier," *Reallexikon der Assyriologie*, V (Berlin–New York, 1976–80), p. 151. Ancient Afroasian peoples used their form of the name Iones not only for the Greeks in general but also for other Anatolian and Balkan peoples.

Ionian Sea is usually associated with Io who crossed it on her long and circuitous journey from Hellas to Egypt. However, it is possible that the Ionian Sea has nothing to do with Io, that the name derives from the noun *to ion* "the violet." The word is rare and it is not clear whether it meant the violet or another dark-blue flower. Nevertheless, the Adriatic has been called blue through the millennia. On early modern maps it was often identified as the Gulf of Venice. (The adjective *venetus* signifies "light blue."[76]) In Croatian, the Adriatic appears with the fixed epithet *plavi* "blue," as in *Plavi Jadran* the "blue Adria." The Croatian epithet, the sea's Greek name, and the derivation of the color (light) blue from the Venetian ethnonym may all reflect a color that was first attributed to the Adriatic by a people for whom that sea was located in the direction symbolized by that color.

A diligent searcher would find that quite a few names of settlements, peoples, and natural features which can be explained from Greek are words with color connotation and in some of them the color's function is positional. For example, in ancient Greece, several cities, as well as a district in the north-east Peloponnese, were called *Argos*. One of the common names for the Hellenes in Homer was the *Argives*, from Argos. Among the many etymologies offered to explain this toponym is a suggestion that it comes from the adjective *'argós* "white." Why white? Was the appellation Argos in referring to cities an independent Greek development, or was the idea borrowed from Egypt, from White Wall of Memphis? We note *en passant* that Nicosia, the name of today's capital of Cyprus, the island which has throughout its history been in close contact with the more civilized peoples of Africa and Asia, is a distortion of Leukosia (from *leukos* "white").

Though the Greek name for the Phoenicians, *Phoinikes* the "purple ones," may be a translation of some native name, it is also possible that it gained its color attribute through Phoenicia's easterly location in relation to Greece. Further, we suggest that the Greeks "adjusted" the name *Bryges* "hillsmen" to *Phryges* the "shiny ones," when the people who bore this name in the

---

[76] Today, a shade of blue is called Venetian. On the Veneti, *see* below, Ch. V.

western gloom of Macedonia migrated to the sunny hills and dales of Anatolia.[77]

In the Mediterranean world the winds are represented by colors. This idea goes back to remote antiquity when colors symbolized the directions from which the winds blew. The wind rose is a reminder that the winds and the directions of the horizon were once perceived with color attributes. Traces of this idea are found in the names of some winds in Greek and other languages. In Greek mythology, Aeolus, the god of the winds, dwelt in a cave on the Island of Lipari, off the coast of Sicily. His principal sons were the west, east, south, and north winds. The west wind is best known by its Greek name, *Zephyrus*. It is a gentle, sweet, soporific breeze, which may bring sweet death because zephyrus blows from *zophos* "the dark quarter, or the West."[78] The south wind is called *notios* in Greek, *africus* in Latin when it blows from Libya, *auster* when it comes from Egypt or the Levant. This wind is called *sirocco* (from Arabic *šrq* "east") in Italian, *jugo* in Croatian (from *jug* "south"). The Greeks used the name *Boreas* for the north wind. Among the Croats of the Adriatic coast the same wind is known as *bura*, a word related to Boreas, as is its Venetian equivalent, *bora*. In classical Latin the word for the north and the north wind, *aquilo*, derived either from *aquilus* "dark-colored, blackish," or from *aqua* "water."[79] Finally, in Turkish the strong northwest wind is called *kara yel* "black wind." Though in Turkish *kara* stands both for "black" and "strong," the *kara yel* should be compared to the Greek *zephyrus* and Latin *aquilus*.

Ancient Greek poets and philosophers likened the southern belt of the *oikoumene* to the sun, to the day in its middle (*mesēmbria* "middle of the day, south"), and to human life in its prime. The south was seen as an extension of the east, with which it was often merged in imagination. The colors sym-

---

[77] Herodotus, VII.73; *see* also, Bačić, "Of Bryges and Macedones."

[78] English balladeers once sang about the westerlies and Alfred Lord Tennyson wrote a song to it, which opens: "Sweet and low, sweet and low,/wind of the western sea."

[79] It seems that *aquila* "eagle" (feminine gender of the adjective *aquilus*) is called so because of that bird's black plumage. The city of Aquileia may owe this name to its location at the extreme north of Roman Italy, that is, in the direction of darkness, to paraphrase Homer.

bolizing the two quarters were purple and red. Students of Homer know also that the west and the north were often perceived as one by the Bard, who operated primarily with two directions of the horizon: sunrise and sunset.[80] More specifically, the west was symbolized by sunset, evening, and old age; the north by darkness, the night, and death. We saw that some of Homer's verses and Strabo's explanations are proof that the north and darkness were synonymous.[81]

In Mediterranean cultures the color black, the night, darkness, death, and hell are considered bad. People do not like to be associated with any of them, although they readily attribute these to their enemies. Synthesizing ancient Afroasian myths, the Greeks developed an elaborate geography of death, woe, lamentation, and the underworld. Like the Sumerians who imagined the abode of the dead located in a "foreign land" and under the jurisdiction of a god and his consort, Ereshkigal, the Greeks, too, appointed Hades, one of the twelve Olympians, also known as Pluto, to rule the underworld in company with his wife Persephone. Like the various abodes of the dead of their Afroasian teachers of this type of geography, the Greeks' own domain of death was imagined beyond the frontiers of Hellas. The divine couple's realm is called Hades after the husband, but the name Tartarus and Erebus are used either as synonyms of Hades as a whole, or as regions of it.

Whereas Hades was vaguely located "beneath sacred place of the earth," one reached it from Hellas by going toward darkness, or to the northern extremes of the Hellenic world. The last major river one crossed en route to the underworld was the Achelous whose god was overpowered by Heracles in Greek mythology, but which, in reality, drained Aetolia and Acarnania.[82] The streams directly connected with Hades and, naturally, situated beyond Hellas, were the *Acheron* "river of woe," *Cocytus* "river of lamentation," *Phlegeton* "river of fire," *Letho* "river of forgetfulness," and the *Styx* "by whose waters the gods swore

[80] Bunbury, *op. cit.*, Ch. III: "Homeric Geography," pp. 31–84.
[81] *See above*, Prologue and Strabo, 1.2.28.
[82] The ancient native name of this stream has not survived. Its medieval and modern name *Aspropotamo* "white river" is a Rhomaean translation of a Slavic hydronym.

their immutable oath." The Acheron was identified with a real Epirote river whose native name has not survived. The learned of Hellas, indifferent to the feelings of the native inhabitants of the Acheron's Valley, named one of the river's tributaries Phlegeton, another Cocytus, while those with a view to profit established and ran *Nekyomanteion* "oracle of the dead" close to Acheron's mouth. The ancient Greeks assigned Mount Olympus in Macedonia as permanent home for their gods, giving the name Styx to a stream which issued from the neighboring Mount Titarius also situated in "barbarian" territory.

We saw that, in the imagination of the Southwest Asian and North African peoples, Greece lay in the domain of darkness. The names *Peloponnesus* and the original name of the Island of Cephalenia may be regarded as remnants of this ancient Afroasian point of view. Pelops, the son of Tantalus, fled his native Asia and settled on a peninsula of Europe to which he gave his name. The name *Pelops* means "dark-faced," an appropriate color for a hero whose insular namesake was enveloped in the darkness of the north and west when viewed from Africa and Asia. West of the Peloponnese the island which the ancient Greeks called Cephalenia, the medieval Slavs Glavinica, was originally known as "black island."[83]

Naturally, the Greeks themselves displaced further north and west many natural features and peoples associated with the color black, just as they placed the abode of black death beyond their borders. Ancient Greek toponymy abounds in names of natural features derived from this color or differentiated by the attribute *melas* "black," some of which we survey here.

We have mentioned the Island of Korčula in Croatia, called Krkar by medieval Croats.[84] The Greeks knew two islands by the name of Corcyra, one being Corcyra, modern Corfu, which they had captured from the Liburnians, the other Corcyra was farther north and beyond their reach. The Greeks and Romans named the more distant island *Kerkyra melaina, Corcyra nigra*, some believing it owed the black attribute to its appearance. For example, Apollonius Rhodius says about this Corcyra: "sailors beholding it from the sea, all black with its sombre woods, call

[83]   Pliny, *n.h.*, IV.54.
[84]   *See* above, Prologue.

it Corcyra the Black."[85] Since the ancients thought that the function of color was always and only descriptive, never positional, the "sombre woods" suggested themselves as the reason for the otherwise inexplicable "blackness" of Croatian Corcyra. Modern commentators declare that Black Corcyra owed this name to the thick pine forests which allegedly once covered this island.[86] *Pace* Apollonius and his modern followers, we are not convinced that northern Corcyra was named black on account of its thick pine forests. Rather, we suggest, the island obtained its name because, viewed from the south, it was situated in the realm of darkness in relation to Corcyra, Corfu, just as Homer said that Ithaca lay toward darkness in relation to the neighboring islands. Had Homer known of two Ithacas he might have called the northern black.

Off the coast of Thrace, where the river Melas empties into the Aegean Sea, there is *Melas kolpos/Saros körfezi* "the black bay."[87] It is possible that this bay, crossed first by the Argonauts on their way from Thessaly to Colchis, acquired the color attribute because of its northern location.

Since the color black was considered a bad omen, we must not exclude the possibility that in ancient Greece it was attributed only to peoples and natural features sufficiently distant in geography or in emotions to avoid "contamination." We may corroborate this by pointing out how the Greek domain of death was transferred northward to the shores of ancient Russia. The same northern region which in Strabo's day was the domain of the Scythians had earlier been occupied by the Cimmerians. The river Styx and Hades were thought to be located in the land of these unfortunate people when they were visited by Odysseus and his companions.[88] Strabo states that Homer had placed the Cimmerians near Hades because the Ionians generally hated these northern barbarians.[89]

Greek tales about the voyage of the Argonauts abound in color symbolism which has given rise to a rich literature. The

---

[85]   *Argonautica*, IV.566–71.
[86]   *Enciklopedija Jugoslavije*, V (Zagreb, 1962), p. 311, s.v. "Korčula."
[87]   E. Oberhummer, "Melas kolpos," *PWRE*, XIX.1 (1931), cols. 439–40.
[88]   *Odyssey*, XI.14.
[89]   3.2.12.

story of the Argo, carrying men from the abode of sunset, sailing across the Black Bay, through the Blue Rocks, and along the coast of the Black Sea to the abode of Dawn in search of the Golden Fleece, may be interpreted as a poetical account of a conflict between the west, symbolized by the color white, and the shiny, red, or golden east. Even though there is no readily recognized logic in the distribution of the colors, we suggest the following scheme: West = white, North = black, East = red. The west, or Pelasgia, is represented symbolically by Pelasgian Argos, the "white city." The north, where the Black Bay, the Blue Rocks, the Black Sea, and Black Corcyra were situated, is appropriately all black. The objects and things associated with the east are depicted in bright colors. To name only a few, *Phrixus*, whose name means "shiny," was the *hero eponymous* of the Phrygians who are usually associated with the color red. Colchis, the destination of the Argonauts, was the abode of dawn and therefore all bright. The most shiny thing in the fabled east was *chrysomallos* the "golden fleece," the object of the quest.

Numerous explanations of the term Golden Fleece have been offered. Strabo, who defended the historicity of the voyage, argued that it was a poetical rendering of the fact that Colchis in his day, and even more so in former times, abounded in iron, silver, and gold, and that it was a rich country offering lucrative trade to long-distance merchants.[90] Appian stated that the natives washed gold in the streams that flowed from the Caucasus into the Black Sea by using sheepskins to scoop the sand and water. He concluded that this was the reason why Colchis became associated with the Golden Fleece.[91] Finally, a modern scholar has suggested that the ancients "imagined as a Golden Fleece that aureous hue which lies over all the country like, as it were, to an illumined dew upon the surface of the land."[92]

In Colchis, Phrixus' sons born to him by a native princess, were named *Phrontis* "thought," *Cytissorus*, of unclear etymology, *Melas* "black," and *Argus* "white." The names of the first

[90]   1.2.39.
[91]   *The Mithridatic Wars*, 103.
[92]   W.E.D. Allen, *A History of the Georgian People* (London, 1932; reprinted, New York, 1971), pp. 3–4.

two sons were not associated with any inhabited place or a natural feature. Argus of course is a frequently occurring name of cities in the southern Balkans, so that this son of Phrixus was readily accepted to be the founder of some of these. Melas' scope of course was more limited, for none among the Hellenes wished to associate themselves with the color black. So he settled in a region of Thrace drained by the Melas River which empties into the Melas Gulf, both called black perhaps because they were located in the direction of the north.

Placed within a broader geographical context, the Golden Fleece appears merely as one of the several "shiny" things and persons associated with Colchis. The main reason why the peoples of the southern Balkans connected Colchis with gold is that it was situated in the ultimate east known to them. In many cultures the east symbolizes good things, such as the abundance of fruit and vegetables, spices, metals of all kinds, but especially of gold. The earliest known people who believed in an eastern paradise were the Sumerians. In Hebrew cosmography the Garden of Eden was in the east and it was a place that abounded in everything delicious.

The Medes and Persians, who at one time were the most easterly people known to the Greeks, were also associated with gold. The Greeks claimed the Medes were founded by Medea, a native of Colchis, the land of the Golden Fleece, the Persians by Perseus, whom Zeus had begotten by means of a golden shower which he let rain on Danae. In Aeschylus, the epithet *chrysogonos* "begotten of gold" appears as a synonym for a Persian. The largest deposit of mythical gold in antiquity was "located" just to the north of Colchis, in the land of the one-eyed Arimaspians, one of the early "inhabitants" of Russia. Geographical and other works of antiquity and the Middle Ages always included a "golden island" in the Eastern Ocean.[93]

Returning to Colchis, we note that irrespective of the Golden Fleece the land must have appeared "shiny" to the Greeks. It was the "homeland" of dawn and the sun, and its ruler, King Aeetes, was the son of Helios. One of Aeetes' sons was called Apsyrtus,

---

[93] Based on the observed fact of nature that the sun, the source of life, rises in the east, Western Eurasians once thought that peoples of the east had a great appreciation for gold and other precious metals and stones.

but the Colchians called him Phaethon "because he outshone all
the youths." Dawn dwelt near Colchis, and Aeetes' Kingdom was
seen as the first land to be bathed in the rays of the sun every
day. It is certainly because of this connection with the sun, the
source of life, that Aeetes' daughter Medea was believed to
possess magical powers, including the secret of eternal youth.

In conclusion, in the tale of the voyage of the Argonauts,
Colchis, which later writers counted as part of Scythia, was
thought of as the domain of dawn, sun, and youth. Being located
in the east, it was also associated with gold. The golden attribute
impressed itself on voyagers arriving to Colchis from the west
because they fancied that Helios began his daily journey from
Colchis, and, while still young, bathed his beloved son Aeetes
and his kingdom with his divine, golden rays. But other
strangers coming to Colchis from Khorāsān, a province of
modern Iran whose name also means the "land of the sun," may
discover that Aeetes' Kingdom had altogether a different hue,
perhaps the one which they would associate with the west, north,
old age, and death. How relative all this may look to a native
Georgian standing at the watershed between the rivers that drain
Colchis and flow into the Black Sea and those that join the Kura
and empty into the Caspian! In his language, Colchis is called
Imier "that side," which his ancestors contrasted with *Amier*
"this side."[94]

ROME AND NEW ROME

The name "Rome" is frequently accompanied by such flattering
epithets as "eternal city," *Roma caput mundi* "capital of the
world," etc., and now and then by the malodorous attribute
Magna Cloaca "the great sewer," applied to the city by people
who thought it attracted the dregs of the world. Early Christian
propagandists hated Rome, calling it "Babylon the Great," and
depicted it as a whore decked in scarlet. Among Rome's more

[94]   Allen, *op. cit.*, p. 7.

neutral attributes is the word *urbs* "city," often used instead of the name Rome.[95]

The centrality of Rome in the imagination of Western humanity has, through the ages, attracted legions of scholars who have been devoting their lives to the search for its origins and early history. However, the beginning of Rome, as the beginning of Kiev, for example, and the meaning of the name are hidden beyond a thick veil spun from threads of ambiguities, myths, and legends.

White and Red Latins

At the time of the arrival of mythical Aeneas and his followers to Latium, where their descendants were to establish the Roman Empire, many cities were already in existence, but Alba Longa, the mother of Latin urbanity, and Rome, *caput mundi*, were yet to rise. Aeneas did not live to see this, but Rome's future was revealed to him in the underworld. The founding of Alba Longa was foretold by the river-god Tiber who said to the Trojan:

> "O seed of a race divine, thou who from foemen's hands bringest back to us our Trojan city, and preservest her towers for ever, thou long looked for on Laurentine ground and Latin fields, here thy home is sure—draw not back—and sure are thy gods! Nor be scared by threats of war; all the swelling wrath of Heaven has abated. Even now, lest thou deem these words the idle feigning of sleep, thou shalt find a huge sow lying under the oaks on the shore, just delivered of a litter of thirty young, the mother reclining on the ground white—white, too, the young about her teats. By this token in thirty revolving years shall Ascanius found a city, Alba of glorious name. Not doubtful is my prophecy.[96]

Varro says:

> The saying is that a sow should bear as many piglets as she has teats; if she bear less she will not pay for herself, and if she bear more it is a portent. It is recorded that the most ancient portent of

[95] The phrase *Urbi et orbi*, "to the city and the world," used by Roman Pontiffs, implies that there is one city in the world and its name is Rome.
[96] *Aeneid*, VIII.36–58.

this kind is the sow of Aeneas at Lavinium, which bore thirty white pigs; and the portent was fulfilled in that thirty years later the people of Lavinium founded the town of Alba. Traces of this sow and her pigs are to be seen even to this day; there are bronze images of them standing in public places even now, and the body of the sow is exhibited by the priests, having been kept in brine, according to their account.[97]

These stories about the founding of Alba are similar to the explanations offered by the common folks concerning the origin of the name Black Beaver in Croatia. Like the people of Lika who resorted to a black billy goat to explain the name Black Beaver, the ancient Romans involved the white sow and her white piglets into the founding of Alba Longa, the mother of Latin cities, explaining thus the attribute of color.

Some modern scholars claim that *Alba* is not a Latin but a Ligurian name meaning "mountain town" since it reminds them of the name Alps.[98] However, too little is known about the Ligurian language to verify this etymology. Nevertheless, the ancients *believed* that the name Alba meant white, and that is why both the common folks and the learned associated the city's founding and its name with the white sow and thirty white piglets. Regardless of the meaning of the name Alba, it is clear that the Romans understood it to mean white. Obviously, the same symbolism applies to the ethnonym Albani, which derives from Alba.

The etymology of the name *Roma* is unknown. The Romans derived it from Romulus, while some Greek writers claimed that the name meant "strong," because it resembled the Greek noun *rhōmē* "strength." Regardless of the name's origin, Rome, like Memphis, was also associated with the color white. Romulus' mother, Rhea, who came to Rome from Alba Longa, brought with her the symbolism of the white sow and the thirty white piglets. Furthermore, according to tradition, Romulus followed an Etruscan custom of marking the city's perimeter by plowing a furrow around it. The cow that pulled the plow was white. We should not dismiss the cow's color as an irrelevant detail. Perhaps the white sow and her white piglets and the white cow appeared in Latin myth out of the desire to attribute to the city,

---

[97]   *De re rustica*, II.iv.17–19.
[98]   C. Hülsen, "Alba Longa," *PWRE*, I.1 (1893), cols. 1301–2.

the seat of the religious authority, the flamen, the color white as the symbol of the priestly caste.

At the same time, we propose that the Albula, the original name of the Tiber, may have been attributed the color white as a symbol of the west.[99] In the early history of Latium, the Albula marked the western border of Ausonia, inhabited by Indo-Europeans. Beyond the Albula stretched Etruria. Furthermore, we may place the Albula River, the city of Alba Longa, the people Albani, the white sow with her young, and the white cow into a spatial relationship with the city of Ardea and its inhabitants, the Rutuli, located toward sunrise in relation to them. Indeed, Ardea has as much to do with the origins of Rome as does Alba, for some ancient Romans were "white," others were "red."

In mythical past, Ardea was ruled by King Turnus, the most ardent opponent and rival of Aeneas and his immigrants from the east. The two men fought both for the possession of Latium and for the hand of Lavinia, King Latinus's daughter. Turnus lost, and his city fell into the hands of the invaders in the manner described by Ovid:

> At length Venus saw her son's arms victorious and Turnus fell. Ardea fell, counted a powerful city in Turnus' lifetime. But after the outlander's sword destroyed it and warm ashes hid its ruins, from the confused mass a bird flew forth of a kind never seen before, and beat the ashes with its flapping wings. Its sound, its meagre look, its deathly paleness, all things which become a captured city, yes even the city's name remained in the bird; and Ardea's self is beaten in lamentation by its wings. (*ardea,* "a heron")[100]

Out of the ashes of Ardea emerged not only the fledgling wing-flapping heron, but also the color and the name of one of the four divisions of the Roman people. Ardea itself had been the capital city of the Rutuli whose ruler was Turnus. The etymology of the name *Rutuli* presents no difficulty since the ancients explained it from the adjective *rutilus* "red, golden, auburn." They knew, and most modern scholars agree, that the

---

[99]   H. Philipp, "Tiberis," *PWRE*, XXX.1 (1936), col. 793.
[100]   *Metamorphoses,* XIV.572–80.

ethnonym meant "reds."[101] This "redness" of the Rutuli may have originated in contradistinction to the "whiteness" of the Albani which stemmed from Alba Longa, the white sow and her young.

The Rutuli were one of three peoples who may owe their name to their southeasterly position, for they were situated south-east of a line running through Latium from Tusculum in the north to Lavinium and its port, the Temple of Venus, in the south. In our effort to understand the circumstances related to the name's origin, we may imagine some ancient observers, standing at Tusculum, facing east, and using a language belonging to the Indo-European family to name places and peoples within their field of vision. Behind them were the Albani, the Alban Hills, Lake Albano, Alba Longa, and the Albula-Tiber. The land, towns, and peoples in front of our ancient observers were, at daybreak, bathed in the rays of dawn. In the language of these Indo-Europeans, dawn may have been called *ausos (from *aues), the word which in the mouth of Cicero, their Latin descendant in Tusculum, became *aurora*. Looking still from Tusculum (and pronouncing *aurora* rather than *ausos), one's view could range on a clear day in the early morning as far as the eastern limits of Latium. The first easternmost Latini to be bathed in Aurora's rays were appropriately called the *Aurunci*, also known as the *Ausoni*. Both designations, signifying "dawn," are still used as the names of two mountains and two cities, Monti Ausoni and Monti Aurunci, situated east of Monti Albani, while the corresponding cities are called Aurunca and Ausonia.[102]

We suggest that the ethnonyms Arunci, Ausoni, and Rutuli are semantically related since all three are associated with dawn as standing for the east. The names Aurunci and Ausoni incorporate the original concept of dawn, which is light, while the name Rutuli derives from the idea of redness associated with dawn, with the sun's rise, and with the east. It is perhaps at the early stage of naming that the most easterly city of the Latins, the city of Antium, modern Anzio, was established and appropriately named the "front" or "anti" city.

[101] H. Philipp, "Rutuli," *PWRE*, XXV.1 (1914), cols. 1282–3.
[102] C. Hülsen, "Aurunca, Aurunci, Ausones, Ausonia, Ausonium mare," *PWRE*, II.2 (1896), cols. 2554, 2561–2.

The ethnonym Ausoni is reflected in the name of the sea between the Balkan and Apennine peninsulas which at first was called the Ausonian, then the Sicilian, and finally the Ionian Sea. The whole of Italy was often called *Ausonia*. The name was adopted by the Rhomaeans who fancied themselves as heirs of the Roman Empire. But Italy had two additional names, Saturnia and Hesperia, which mean the opposite of Ausonia. The name *Saturnia* comes from that of Saturn or Cronus who was symbolized by the color black, death, and the north. *Hesperia* was the land of the evening star, Hesper. Clearly, the pair Albani—Rutuli was coined by people with microregional view, while the pair Hesperia—Ausonia reflects a macroregional orientation.

Red, White, Blue, and Green Romans

The ancient inhabitants of Lower Mesopotamia named themselves after the color black. Though their city-states warred with each other, to outsiders they must have presented a united front as Black Heads. The Egyptians, who depicted themselves as a people with a single color, red, attributed the color white to Upper Egypt, red to Lower Egypt. In Rome the situation was more complex, for in a much smaller area more colors were used to separate the people.

The ancient Romans were themselves not clear about the origin, significance, and number of colors they used in four-horse chariot races. In historical times, the primary and perhaps the only function of the colors was to differentiate among the competing charioteers in the circus. Some writers of late antiquity believed that the colors had been introduced by Romulus who built a circus. In order to divide the people who sought to murder him because he had killed his brother Remus, he instituted races of quadrigas in honor of the sun and the four elements. Each element was symbolized by a color. The population of Rome became divided, with every man and woman displaying their preferred colors. Differentiation led to hostility toward others and their colors, which made them unable to combine against Romulus and difficult to live in peace with each other. The original and traditional red and white, symbolizing perhaps the eastern and the western Latini, called the Rutuli and the Albani, were eclipsed under the empire by the new cosmopolitan divisions into Veneti and Prasini, blues and greens.

The traditional two colors had been sufficient for the Romans to hate each other because people could be divided bi-polarly into Us versus Them. When there are more colors hatred is less concentrated. The addition of new colors was experienced by the Roman people as confusing and unnecessary innovations. The emperors who loved "new colors" were depicted as monsters by contemporary writers. Caligula and Nero loved the new color green. They were bad. Domitian introduced two additional colors, gold and purple, and he also was remembered as a tyrant. On the other hand, a good emperor, such as Marcus Aurelius, stated that he was above the colors, that he supported neither greens nor blues.[103] The fact that he used only two colors is evidence of the tendency of people toward color polarization.

The importance of the colors used in chariot races in republican and imperial Rome transcends entertainment and sportsmanship. People may hate each other for real or imaginary reasons without acting out their feelings. But, when they openly adopt colors that are different from the ones their enemies prefer, the hatred flares up. Whatever their original function may have been, under the empire the colors served as visible rallying bases for the organization of factions whose activities were not limited to the circus, but rather permeated the private and public life of Roman citizens. They may be termed the political parties of the time.

[103] I.5.

Colors were also associated with the planets, the elements, the seasons, and the gods, as shown in the following table:[104]

	Color				
English	**Latin**	**Greek**	**god**	**element**	**season**
white	albati	leukoi	Jupiter	air	winter
red	russati	erythroi	Mars	fire	summer
green	virides	antheroi/ prasinoi	Venus	earth	spring
blue	veneti	kallainoi/ venetoi	Saturn or Neptune	water	autumn

The question of the origin and function of these four colors in the history of Rome and New Rome is one of the more studied themes in European history. The subject is attractive and popular, the sources are rather plentiful, so that a diligent inquirer can hope to arrive at meaningful and interesting conclusions. These fall neatly into two main groups based on how an author interprets the function of the colors. One group claims the colors perform a single function, the other argues they serve several functions. The writers who belong to the first group see the colors exclusively as a way of identifying teams of four-horse chariots in Roman circus races. In modern scholarship this view was established by Edward Gibbon. Most scholars still accept Gibbon's eloquent paraphrase of Procopius' description of clashes between Blues and Greens in the East Roman Empire under Justinian, and rarely venture to look at the colors beyond the circus.[105] Only a few belong to the second group. In late antiquity, Johannes Lydus saw more in the colors than simply the banners displayed at horse-races.[106] In modern times, Gavro

---

[104]   A. Cameron, *Circus Factions* (Oxford, 1978), p. 64, where the ancient and modern authorities are discussed.
[105]   *The Decline and Fall of the Roman Empire*, XL.ii.
[106]   *De mensibus*, IV.25; Cameron, *op. cit.*, pp. 60–1.

Manojlović, George Dumézil, and A. Levčenko have argued for a broader interpretation of the colors than the Roman circus.

George Dumézil interpreted the information provided by Johannes Lydus to propose that the colors represented at first a tripartite division of Roman society. The ancient Egyptian caste system was allegedly copied by the Athenians and passed on to the Romans. Johannes Lydus states that there were originally three colors in Rome: white, red, and green. The color blue was added later. According to Dumézil, in Rome the three colors stood for a tripartite division of an Indo-European people into priests (represented by the color white), warriors (whose color was red), and producers (symbolized by the color green).[107] But, the sources quoted by Dumézil indicate that there were flags of three colors in ancient Rome: white, red, and blue. There was no green flag. These flags, which were hoisted on the Capitol to summon the people to a gathering, were called *album, roseum,* and *caeruleum.*[108]

Tertullian states that at first only two colors, *albus* and *russeus,* white and red, were displayed in the four-horse chariot races initiated by Romulus. Also, he adds that white stood for winter, red for summer.[109] The two colors in chariot races may reflect the two-fold division of the people of Latium into Albani and Rutuli. The three-colored flags may symbolize not only these two peoples, but also the division of the Romans into main socio-economic classes.

Though there are oblique references to more than two colors in connection with chariot races, it cannot be demonstrated exactly when the color green was added. It seems that from the beginning this color had three names: *chrysocolla,* a word of Greek origin meaning "gold-soldered," *prasinus,* another Greek word signifying "green, or leek-green," and the Latin word *viridis* "green." In Greek the name remained *prasinos.* We do not know when the fourth color appeared in the races and under what name. If it was blue, was the classical Latin word *caeruleus* used or the later *venetus*? The Latin adjective *venetus*

---

[107] G. Dumézil, *Rituel indo-européen à Rome* (Paris, 1954), pp. 53–7.
[108] White, red, and blue in numerous permutations are now the colors of the many tricolor flags of European nations.
[109] *De Spectaculis,* IX.5.

derives from the ethnonym *Veneti*. Though we shall argue that the name Veneti may be traced back to an adjective signifying "white" in a Celtic language, in Latin *venetus* came to mean "blue" and it was used synonymously with *caeruleus*. In Greek *venetos* appeared as a synonym for *kallainos* "like the kalais," a precious stone of greenish blue. Six colors were in use under the Emperor Domitian, for Suetonius says that he introduced two additional colors to the existing four. The new colors were *aureus* "gold" and *purpureus* "purple." They were dropped from the horse races after Domitian's death.[110]

Veneti and Prasini in East Rome

The circus colors acquired an expanded meaning in New Rome. Edward Gibbon used the quarrels between the factions, which often led to bloody riots, as evidence that New Rome was more capable of aping the vices of her older sister than of imitating her virtues.[111] Since then scholars who have dealt with the topic, have treated the clashes between Blues and Greens (as the factions are called in English) as irrational outbursts of passionate spectators at horse races. Levčenko, wishing to give political meaning to these clashes, interpreted the factional strife as a form of class struggle. We reject this view because the sources contradict it, since it is clear that both major factions numbered among their supporters individuals from the lowest to the highest ranks.[112] Manojlović argued that the factions represented deep divisions among the people of Constantinople. Although he may have erred on a few points, he should be praised for expanding the meaning of the color factions beyond the circus.[113]

---

[110]   Suetonius, *Domitian*, VII.1.

[111]   *Op. cit., loc. cit.*

[112]   M.V. Levčenko, "Venety i prasiny v Vizantii v v–vii vv.," *Vizantijskij vremennik*, I (1947), pp. 164–83.

[113]   G. Manojlović, "Le peuple de Constantinople de 400 à 800 après J.C.," *Byzantion*, XI (1936), pp. 617–716.

Although four colors continued to be displayed in the hippodrome of Constantinople and other cities of the East Roman Empire, the people were divided after the two principal factions into Veneti and Prasini (Blues and Greens). In Constantinople, the *rhousioi* "reds" merged with prasini, the *leukoi* "whites" with veneti.[114] A bi-polar division of the population was most visible at the horse races, where the colors were displayed and where cheering and jeering were loud and frequently hostile. However, in our opinion, this polarization affected entire society and served as a clear geographical, cultural, religious, linguistic, and political divide. On the whole, Veneti stood for Europe, Prasini for Asia. Of course, occasionally a Syriac-speaking monophysite citizen of East Rome might have been a Venetus and a Greek- or Latin-speaking Orthodox person from the Balkans a Prasinus. Nevertheless, the majority of the East Roman population was separated into easterners or Prasini and westerners or Veneti by the Bosporus and the Dardanelles. The same line separating Veneti from Prasini also separated Europe from Asia, West from East.

The peoples of the East Roman Empire never reached a decent level of tolerance of each other, continually quarrelling over various points of political, economic, or religious nature. Only a few emperors were able to imitate Marcus Aurelius and rise above the factions, but most were as ardent in their support of their preferred colors as were the common people. New Rome was constantly racked by veritable civil wars between Veneti and Prasini, westerners and easterners. These took on many aspects, most of them religious in nature, until the whole state and the capital were conquered by Muslim Turks marching under the green flag of Islam.

SLAVIA

The Slavs began to record their thoughts and actions in their own language, a Macedonian idiom spoken in Salonica and its environs in the ninth century AD. Therefore, having no written

---

[114] Cameron, *op. cit.*, p. 65.

record upon which to base meaningful statements concerning ancient Slavic cosmography, we depend on writings in languages of their neighbors to elucidate Slavic origins. However, the timelessness of folklore permits us to project into the past some folk beliefs recorded in modern times. For example, the peasants who live in the mountains and valleys of the Black Timok and White Timok in eastern Serbia believe that the world is held up by four bulls. The colors of these bulls are distributed to the four cardinal points so that: Red bull = S, black bull = N, white bull = W, and blue bull = E.[115]

Though the name *Slav* first appeared in the middle of the first Christian millennium in the Danube Basin at the frontier of Romania and Barbaricum, the ethnonym *Venedae* and its cognates, by which the various Slavic peoples were and still are known, has been traced to the dawn of history in several regions of western Eurasia. It is related to the name *Eneti*, which made its first appearance in a written source when Homer's *Iliad* was committed to writing. The late classical form *Venedae* gave *Wenden* and served as the collective Germanic name for Slavs, and in the form of *Venäläinen* it still serves as the Finnish designation for a Russian. We shall show that the ethnonym Venedae, a color word, signifying "whites," had a directional counterpart in the ethnonym *Antae* "front people." These names might have originated in a Slavic milieu, but in historical times they appear to have been more popular among the Slavs' neighbors, when the Slavs themselves seem to have preferred their own peculiar method of dividing peoples into Whites and Reds. We shall suggest that the Slavic equivalent of the form Venedae was the name *Belcae* (possibly "whites"), first recorded in the third century BC. The native Slavic equivalent of the name Antae is an ethnonym that derives from a word for the color red, variously recorded as *Rosomoni* (Jordanes, sixth century), *Harūs* (Zachariah Rhetor, sixth century), *al-Rūs* (Muslim writers, seventh century), Rhos and Ruzzi (western Christian writers, ninth century), hoi Rhōs (East Roman writers, ninth century), and *Rusii* (Liudprand of Cremona, tenth century). The name *Russi* is not the only color ethnonym from medieval Slavia. In

---

[115] M. Filipović, "Nazivanje strana sveta i naroda po bojama," *Zbornik za društvene nauke Matice Srpske*, XXIX (1961), pp. 69–77.

the mid-tenth century, the peoples who lived in the eastern Balkans knew the western Croats and Serbs as White Croats and White Serbs. In Kiev, the western Croats were called *Beloxorvate* "White Croats." As we shall see, in the Middle Ages, Croatia was divided into Red Croatia and White Croatia. Finally, in modern times Russia was divided into Red, White, and Black Russias.

We have seen that there is a tendency to declare all names of Slavic peoples and cities which are words denoting colors as part of a Turco-Tartar cultural heritage. While this may be true of certain names, there is no evidence that the cities to be discussed presently owe their color attributes to speakers of Altaic languages. The custom of naming state centers after the color white was very popular among the ancient Slavs, as several royal or ducal residences and coronation centers in medieval Slavia testify. Of these the following are worthy of mention:

Belgrade, the seat of a medieval Hungarian banate and today the capital of Serbia, is perhaps the best known "white city." It was first recorded under this name in 878 AD as a medieval Slavic appellation for the ancient Singidunum, last mentioned in the sixth century.[116]

Medieval Hungarian kings were crowned in *Székesfehérvár* (from the Hungarian *székes* "seat," *fehér* "white," and *vár* "city"), known in German as *Stuhlweissenburg*. Both names appear to be translations of the Croatian name for the same city: *Stolni Biograd*. The Magyars arrived into their new homeland at the beginning of the tenth century. By then several Croatian rulers had resided at Stolni Biograd.[117] The shamanist Magyars forced Christian Croats to retreat to the Dinaric Alps and to transfer the seat of their kingdom to the Dalmatian coast. There, another Biograd soon emerged in the vicinity of Zadar in White Croatia. Kings of Dalmatian Croatia were crowned there, including King Colomanus of Hungary, who, in 1102, ascended the throne of Dalmatian Croatia. For this reason the city was officially called

---

[116]　F. Dvornik, *Les Slaves, Byzance et Rome au ixe siècle* (Paris, 1926), p. 277 and note 1.

[117]　On Slavs in the Danube Basin in the Early Middle Ages, *see*, Bačić, *The Emergence of the Slavs*; and *idem*, "Some Notes on the Early History of the Serbs."

Urbs regia or *Belgradum supra mare* and colloquially *Biograd na moru* "white city on the sea."

In medieval Transylvania a Belgrad was the seat of princely power. In Rumanian, the city is called *Alba Iulia*, in Hungarian *Gyula-Fehérvár* and in German *Weissenburg*. In all these languages the Slavic name *Belgrad* is translated accurately as "white city."

In medieval Carinthia, Beljak emerged as an important center out of the ruins of Roman Bilachium. The city's German name, *Villach*, is an adaptation of the Slavic one, which means "white water," and is attested in inscriptions and narrative texts dating from Roman rule, thus before the arrival into the area of the first speakers of a Turkic language.[118]

In ancient Illyria there was a city whose name was recorded as *Byllis* by Julius Caesar and other writers. When Illyria became Slavia, the name changed to *Belgrad*. Interpreting the Slavic attribute as "beautiful," the local Vlachs and the Rhomaeans named this center of medieval Slavia *Poulcheriopolis*, its Albanian inhabitants call it Berat.[119]

Medieval Slavia extended westward through the modern Croatian–Slovenian region of Istra as far as the Tilment/Tagliamento River in the province of Friuli–Venezia Giulia. A city named *Belgrad* stood on the banks of the Tilment and appears to have served as a seat of the regional princes ruling this region of medieval Slavia, known today as Beneška Slovenija. In central Istra a similar function appears to have been performed by a city once called *Bellegradus* and known today as the village of *Belaj*, located in the vicinity of the city of Pazin, Istra's traditional center.[120]

Also, in the Middle Ages, in the land of the Russian Tivercy and Ugliči flourished a city by the name of *Belgrad*, called by today's Ukrainians *Bilhorod Dnistrovkyi*. The Rhomaeans, Turks, and Rumanians translate accurately the city's Slavic name and call the place *Asprokastron/Leukopolichnē*, *Akkerman*, *Cetatea*

---

[118]   J. Bačić, "On the Etymology of Beljak," *Slovene Studies*, III/1 (1981), pp. 23–9.

[119]   Caesar, *De bello civile*, III.40; *Tabula Imperii Romani K34*, s.v. "Byllis"; and J. Nalepa, "Belgrad w Albanii," *SSS*, I (1961), p. 102.

[120]   Editorial board, "Běl″gord″," *SSS*, I (1961), pp. 101–2.

Albă, respectively. The people who looked at this region of medieval Slavia from the south appear to have been more familiar with Belgrad's counterpart on the left bank of the Dniester called *Čern'* by native Slavs, *Maurokastron, Mavro-castro*, and *Castel Nero* by the Rhomaeans, Venetians, and Genoese.[121]

In the Middle Ages the Pomeranian princes resided at the city of *Białogard*.[122]

Finally, after the Slavs, having failed to capture Constantinople in the seventh century, settled in the city's vicinity, they established a town on the Black Sea coast, a short distance from the coveted seat of the Rhomaean tsar, which they called Tsarigrad, and named it *Belgrad* as an ersatz for the real thing. The Rhomaeans renamed it *Velogradion*.[123]

It has been argued that the names of these Belgrads originated within a Turkic cosmographic system, that behind every Belgrad is an equivalent name in a Turkic language.[124] However, there is no evidence in the sources that this was the case. Rather, many of these "white cities" flourished long before the arrival of the Huns, the earliest migrants from Asia who supposedly spoke a Turkic language. Among these are Aegae in Macedonia and Vienna in medieval Slavia, modern Austria.

According to legend reported by Herodotus, Perdiccas, the founder of the Argead dynasty, came from Illyria to Lebaea, the seat of the Macedonian king, who unwittingly, though, transferred royal power to the migrant.[125] Then, Perdiccas,

> wishing to increase the strength of his kingdom, sent to Delphi to consult the oracle. And the Pythian priestess replied to him:
>
> Stands o'er a wealthy land a might of kings
> Of Temenus' right noble line,
> Of Aegis-bearing Zeus. But swiftly go
> To Bottiaïs, rich in flocks; and then

---

[121] W. Swoboda, "Biełgorod Dniestrowski," *SSS*, VII.2 Suppl. (A–C) (1984), pp. 451–2; Vasmer, *REW*, I, pp. 65–6, s.v. "Akkerman."

[122] A. Wędzki, "Białogard," *SSS*, I (1961), p. 111.

[123] *See*, note 120 above.

[124] Reichenkron, *op. cit. loc. cit.*

[125] Herodotus, VIII.137; *see* also, J. Bačić, "The Sixteen-Pointed Star," *Macedonia, Curiosum Mundi*, I.2 (1993), p. 3.

Where thou shalt see white-horned goats, with fleece
Like snow, resting at dawn, make sacrifice
Unto the blessed gods upon that spot
And raise the chief city of a state.[126]

The city Perdiccas was commanded to found is *Aegae* "goat's town." The city's "whiteness," though not reflected in its name, is confirmed by the color of the goats, after which it was named. In Macedonia the white goat, like the white sow in Latium, transferred its attribute of color to the region's political center.

The name of the city of Vienna goes back to the Roman and perhaps Celtic *Vindobona*. Linguists have analyzed the toponym as **uind-* "white" in Celtic, *ob* from *ab* "water," and the formative suffix *-ona*, attested in the names of the cities Arab*ona*, Sal*ona*, Nar*ona*, etc.[127] Thus, if the name Vindobona truly means "white-water-city," it could have derived from the hydronym **Vindab*, the ancient name of the little stream that meets the Danube at Vienna and is known today as the Wienfluss. Again, the naming of the river and the city must have been the work of speakers of Indo-European languages, rather than Turkic.

It is clear that the ancient Slavs had a predilection for "white cities." The fact that so many of these were centers of Slavic principalities and kingdoms should not be dismissed as accidental. Although they may have truly looked white-stoned, or whitewashed settlements surrounded by hamlets, villages, and towns built of mud, brick, and wood, these "white cities" in Slavia appear to have obtained their names not only by reason of their white appearance, but also from their intended function as centers of political and religious power, rather than from their relative geographic positions in relation to some presumed color counterparts.

But, if we must look for a cultural milieu which inspired the builders and namers of the various Belgrads in Slavia, why not look south, where urban life first flourished? Perhaps the namers of these Slavic cities were inspired by Rome, demarcated by a furrow plowed by a white cow, or by Alba Longa whose founding was presaged by a white sow and thirty white piglets,

---

[126] Diodorus Siculus, 7.16.
[127] Bačić, "On the Etymology of Beljak."

or by the white goats of Aegae in Macedonia. Also the Slavs may have called their capital cities white, in imitation of the numerous Argoses or "white cities" in Hellas or in honor of Argos Oresticum of Macedonia. Finally, if we must have a prototype for the Slavic "white cities," why not look for it in Egypt, at White Wall (Memphis), which had been built and named long before these "white cities," or any cities for that matter, were founded in Hellas, Macedonia, Rome, and Slavia? Certainly, some of the mentioned "white cities" of Slavia were built and named independently of Turks and Mongols, especially those which lay in ruins for centuries before descendants of Genghis Khan took up residence at Karakorum, the city which, some scholars have suggested was the color counterpart of all Belgrads. Furthermore, some of these cities, such as the Belgrads on the Tilment, in Istra, in Pomerania, Albania, and on the Adriatic coast, were too distant from the Turkic peoples for the latter to have any significant influence in their rise and in the coining of their names.

While the discussed cities named Belgrad appear not to have color counterparts, we have shown that the Slavic Croats of Lika used colors to indicate relative geographic positions of settlements. As further evidence that the Croats who lived in the heart of medieval Slavia used the colors white and black to differentiate between two homonymous settlements, we adduce the names *Bakonybél* and *Bakonycsernye* (Bakony is the name of a neighboring mountain, *bél* derives from the Slavic adjective *běl'* "white," *csernye* from the Slavic *č'rna* "black"), two villages in today's Hungary, in the vicinity of Székesfehérvár/Stolni Biograd.[128]

The Colors of Russia

The name *Russi*, at the root of which we propose is a word for the color red, became, in the course of history, a self-designation for a variety of peoples inhabiting an enormous land. It replaced numerous ethnonyms which either disappeared or acquired new meanings. Some of these were also color words, for the Russian

[128] L. Kiss, *Földrajzi nevek etimológiai szótára* (Budapest, 1980), pp. 76–7.

land has also been associated with colors other than red. We shall show that the Red Sea was called "red" only by people who looked at it from the north, "green" by those who approached it from the west. Likewise, we shall suggest here that the red color attribute in Russia was given by observers standing at a particular angle to it, possibly west or north. We should treat the red angle as merely one out of four color angles of looking at Russia and allow for the possibility that namers viewing that land from the other three angles attributed different colors to the land and its people. In fact they did, as will be shown below.

While Russia was known as Great Scythia and Sarmatia Europaea, the color attributed to it by those who looked at it from the south was black because it was in the direction of darkness (north) from them. Black was the sea that washed Russia's shores, black were the first named people from that land, the Cimmerians, black were the cloaks worn by that land's northern inhabitants, the Melanchlaeni, and possibly by the Sauromatae or Sarmatians, the black dog Cerberus, and black Hades were transferred to the shores of Russia after they could no longer be tolerated at the frontiers of Hellas. In the Middle Ages, black was the color which West Europeans attributed to the *Tatars* of Russia, changing it to *Tartars* to approximate more closely black *Tartarus*. As Marco Polo journeyed to Karakorum he designated as the "Land of Darkness" a good portion of North Eurasia next to Great Russia.[129]

Though seen from the south, Russia was dark or black, when observed from the east it was white because it was located in the quarter which its eastern neighbors associated with that color. Thus, in the High Middle Ages, the ruler of the Russian portion of North Eurasia was known as *Belyj tsar'* "white emperor." It has been suggested that the Muscovite monarch was given this epithet because he was "free" or because he wore a white mitre on ceremonial occasions.[130] However, these explanations overlook the fact that the Tsar of all Russia remained for a long

---

[129] *The Travels* (Penguin edition), pp. 10–11 on the name Tartars and p. 331 on the Land of Darkness.

[130] F.A. Brokgaus and I.A. Efron, *Enciklopedičeskij slovar'* (St.Petersburg, 1891), V, p. 249, s.v. "Belyj tsar'."

time the most westerly (therefore "white") ruler with whom the Central and East Asian peoples had contact, and that the name appears to have been coined by Russia's eastern neighbors to whom the tsar's presumed freedom and his white mitre would not be as significant factors in calling him "white" as would the fact that he governed the "white" or the western quarter of the world known to them. He was not so designated because he was a "white" man, a Caucasian or a European, but because he was the western counterpart of the Yellow or Central Emperor, who ruled the Middle Kingdom, symbolized by the color yellow. Within the same color scheme the Mongol monarch who ruled the northern (seen from China) quarter was called the Black Emperor, while the Persian ruler was appropriately designated the Red Emperor, for his domain was situated in the southern quarter, which was represented by the color red.[131]

As far as is known, Russian political life did not begin with a Belgrad as the land's political center, but one appeared in the Middle Ages. The chronicler says that St. Vladimir had 800 concubines. He kept 300 in Vyšgorod,[132] 200 at Berestovo and 300 at Belgorod.[133] Then under the year 991 the chronicler made this entry:

> Vladimir founded the city of Belgorod, and peopled it from other towns, bringing to it many settlers. For he was extremely fond of this city.[134]

This passage shows that this medieval Russian prince shared with other Slavs the desire to reside at a "white city."

---

[131] Other explanations for these color attributes are also possible and have been entertained by scholars. For example, the Black Emperor, who resided at Karakorum, may have obtained this epithet because of his power, for in Turkic languages black signifies "strong" as well as the direction of the horizon. *See*, I. Laude-Cirtautas, *Der Gebrauch der Farbbezeichnung in den Türkdialekten* (Wiesbaden, 1961).

[132] The name means "upper city, or city on a hill," and it occurs in many Slavic lands; for instance, in Hungary upstream from Budapest is the city of Visegrad; there is a Višegrad on the Drina in Bosnia, etc.

[133] He had these women, supposedly, before he accepted baptism and a Byzantine princess for wife, that is, before 988.

[134] *PVL*, p. 119.

When Moscow first appeared in a written source, in 1147, it was a minor town belonging to a principality which, in turn, was part of an assemblage of principalities presided over by the grand duke of Kiev. Moscow became the center of Russian economic, religious, and political life after the Mongols, having destroyed Kiev, had made most of Russia virtually or nominally subject to their emperor who resided at Karakorum. Moscow is poetically known as *Belokamennaja* "white-stoned," and one of the sections of the old town is called *Belyj gorod* "white city." While it is tempting to see the names Karakorum and Belyj gorod as a color pair where the colors symbolize the directions of the horizon, this should be rejected for the following reason: In Turkic languages the adjective *kara* has a variety of meanings, among them "strong, big," and it is perhaps this connotation that we should seek in the name Karakorum. The attribute white given to Moscow is perhaps descriptive. With its white stone buildings Moscow stood out among settlements with wooden structures, which normally are of a somber hue. It is a coincidence that the White Tsar ruled from Moskva Belokamennaja.

From 1917 until recently, the color associated with Russia had been red. Adopted by the victorious Bolshevik party during the Civil War that followed the fall of the monarchy in February 1917, this red stood for the red flag and red star as symbols of international communism. The chief opponents of Reds were monarchists who became known as Whites. Some peasant groups, known as Greens, tried to make their voice heard above the anarchy. Anarchy, itself, was promoted as a political alternative by associations of anarchists whose color of choice was black.

During the Soviet era of Russian history, it was occasionally suggested, though not always facetiously, that fate had willed that the seat of the eastern or "red" empire be at Red Square, while its western counterpart resides at the White House. Rejecting such interpretations, we wish to point out that the buildings which stand in the heart of Moscow around and near Red Square are painted with a variety of colors, not only red. Dominant among these are the golden-yellow color of the cupolas of the churches and roofs of some buildings, followed by various shades of red, orange, and white with which the façades of towers and other buildings are covered. From among this spectrum of colors we are at a loss to choose one to symbolize the architectural ensemble and may simply call the square "beautiful." Indeed, in Old Russian, Red Square had originally been called the "beautiful" square. Later, it became known as "red" square, owing to the similarity between the adjectives *krasivyj* "beautiful" and *krasnyj* "red." Thus, the colors attributed to Moscow, that is, red in the name Red Square, white-stoned as an epithet of the city, and golden-domed as a symbol of its numerous churches, are descriptive, not positional. As to the White House in Washington, its color symbolizes purity and honesty, not the west. Like the ancient Egyptian priests who officiated within White Wall (Memphis), the successive occupants of the White House had it painted white to make sure that the dwelling live up to the people's image of it.[135]

The erstwhile color contrast between two superpowers of the past has recently been blurred by the rise of a "white house" in Moscow, as the building that houses the Russian Parliament is called.[136]

MISCELLANEA

A bino-quinary system of colors attested in Iran has been called Sino-Iranian by L. de Saussure who also suggested that its ultimate origins may be found neither in China nor in Iran but in Mesopotamia. Regardless of whether East Asia or West Asia be considered as the cradle of the idea of attributing colors to the cardinal points of the compass, it is evident that the Iranians

[135] Purple, red, yellow, or orange have also served as preferred official colors of several Eurasian empires as shown by the color of façades of government buildings there. For instance, due to the profuse application of the color yellow in this manner, the Austro-Hungarian state was nicknamed the Yellow Monarchy.

[136] In the fall of 1993 the façade of the Russian Parliament building was blackened by fires set by the building's defenders and artillery shells launched by the forces loyal to Russia's president.

and the peoples of the Altaic language family were facilitated by their location to share if not in the creation then in the diffusion of the notions.

Our knowledge of the use of colors as symbols of the directions of the horizon in pre-Islamic Iran is imperfect. Although de Saussure stresses the system's Chinese connections, he also points out several basic modifications in Iran of the "pristine" system due to native developments and foreign influences. In regards to the planets, the color symbolism, similar to that attested in China, was also known to the ancient Iranians. Unfortunately, we lack positive evidence that colors were used as symbols of the directions of the horizon by the ancient peoples of Iran in their naming of peoples, settlements, and natural features. A frequently adduced indication that the regions of the world were symbolized by colors is Herodotus' description of Ecbatana. The historian says:

> But having obtained the power, he [sc. King Deioces] constrained the Medes to make him one stronghold and to fortify this more strongly than all the rest. This too the Medes did for him: so he built the great and mighty circles of walls within walls which are now called Agbatana. This fortress is so planned that each circle of walls is higher than the next outer circle by no more than the height of its battlements; to which end the site itself being on a hill in the plain, somewhat helps, but chiefly it was accomplished by art. There are seven circles in all; within the innermost circle are the king's dwellings and the treasuries; and the longest wall is about the length of the wall that surrounds the city of Athens. The battlements of the first circle are white, of the second black, of the third circle purple, of the fourth blue, and of the fifth orange: thus the battlements of five circles are painted with colors; and the battlements of the last two circles are coated, these with silver and those with gold.[137]

Like their Indo-Aryan cousins, the Aryan peoples of Iran appear to have used colors to divide humanity into castes, for their word for caste was *pishtra* "color."

The ancient Hebrews were surrounded by many nations whom they collectively called *Goyim*. The land in which they wanted to settle down was *Canaan* "red land." South of Canaan extend-

---

[137] I.98.

ed *Edom* another "red land."[138] Though there is no incontrovertible evidence that the Hebrews used colors to indicate the
directions of the horizon, a passage in the book of the Prophet
Zechariah suggests that they might have not been strangers to
the idea. Zechariah says:

> And I turned, and lifted up mine eyes, and looked, and behold,
> there came four chariots, out from between two mountains; and
> the mountains were mountains of brass. In the first chariot were
> red horses; and in the second chariot black horses; and in the third
> chariot white horses; and in the fourth chariot grizzled and bay
> horses. Then I answered and said unto the angel that talked with
> me, What are these, my lord? And the angel answered and said
> unto me, These are the four spirits of the heavens, which go forth
> from standing before the Lord of all the earth. The black horses
> which are therein go forth into the north country; and the white go
> forth after them; and the grizzled go forth toward the south
> country. And the bay went forth, and sought to go that they might
> walk to and from through the earth: and he said, Get you hence,
> walk to and fro through the earth. So they walked to and fro
> through the earth. Then cried he upon me, and spake unto me,
> saying, Behold, these that go toward the north country have
> quieted my spirit in the north country.[139]

The prophet and his angel did not tell us where the red horses
went. Some biblical exegesists see in the colors of the horses a
fixed system, whether it be the directions of the horizon or the
Hindu ages of human history that are also represented by colors.
Colored horses were made famous by St. John the Divine in his
Apocalypse, where they represent the historical epochs
symbolized by colors.

Even though it appears that the Germanic peoples had, from
antiquity, relied primarily on a system derived from their words
for the evening star and the morning star, and from the words
"right" and "left" to achieve the same purpose for which other
peoples used colors, this does not exclude the possibility that the
fashion of naming after colors had once blossomed among them
as well before it was replaced by the system of four words

---

[138]   Later, the Hebrews used the ethnonym Canaanite as a word for slave,
while the Diaspora Jews use the name Edom for all lands except the
Promised Land.
[139]   Zech. 6:1–8.

which ultimately gave our modern English terms: east, west, north, and south.

The Turkic and Mongol peoples, whose ancestral homeland is situated in the heart of Asia, have throughout their history made a number of uses of colors, including their application as symbols of the cardinal points.[140] Of interest for this topic are the facts that some of these divide both heaven and earth into segments to which they assign different colors. For example, the Soyat people in Siberia imagine the sky being held by a pillar resembling a tent pole.

> The pole's end rises above the top of the yurt and its end is decorated with blue, white, and yellow cloths, representing the colors of the celestial regions. This pole is sacred; it is regarded almost as a god. At its foot stands a small stone altar, on which offerings are placed.[141]

Among the Mayas of Mesoamerica the four cardinal points each have assigned a color: S = yellow, E = red, N = white, W = black. The Zunis of New Mexico

> had seven village-wards of phratries based on the four cardinal points, the zenith, nadir, and center. The North was associated with wind, water, war, and yellow; the South with fire, summer, tillage, and red; the East with frost, autumn, magic, and white; the West with water, spring, peace, and blue. Each section, made up of three clans was linked with three birds or beasts, except the Centre, which had a single clan and one creature (the macaw).[142]

One could adduce additional examples from all over the world to show that colors are systematically and consciously used as symbols of the directions of the horizon. In fact, as we were collecting information for this study, two colleagues, both of the University of Oregon, wrote about their encounter with colors

---

[140]   Laude-Cirtautas, *op. cit.*
[141]   M. Eliade, *Shamanism*, transl. by W.R. Trask (Princeton, N.J., 1964), p. 261.
[142]   J. Lindsey, *Origins of Astrology* (London, 1971), p. 21.

and the directions of the horizon. Ronald Wixman sent the following message from South East Asia:

> I spoke to a specialist on Chinese culture and he explained the Chinese color scheme in place names. It is also used in jade objects to denote directions. Here is the scheme:

N
Black Jade
Black Turtle

W	Center	E
White Jade	Yellow Jade	Green Jade
White Tiger	Earth, Dirt	Green Dragon

S
Red or Brown Jade
Red Bird

At about the same time William Loy wrote:

> Last week in Phoenix I thought of you when an Apache Indian said that directions were linked to colors as follows:
>
> black = East; blue = South; yellow = West; white = North.
>
> He is Edgar Perry, the author of the Apache dictionary. He is director of the Apache Cultural Center, White Mountain Indian Reservation in Arizona.

CONCLUSION

We believe it has been established here that colors have been used since remote antiquity to represent the directions of the horizon in both Old and New Worlds. The cardinal points of the compass are represented by specific colors not only in folklore but also in high cultures and civilizations and also both by people whose views are limited to their native valleys and mountains as well as by others who think globally. One may justifiably claim that differentiation by color is perhaps the oldest and the most widespread amongst the various methods of distinguishing natural features, settlements, and peoples. However, as we have seen, no universally accepted laws apply; that is, there is no fixed order, and different cultures assign different colors to different cardinal points. This makes our task of explicating the meaning of attributes of color in geographical names and in ethnonyms very difficult. Also, not knowing for certain whether the original namegiver had intended a given object's name to reflect its relative position, we are inclined to detect the "color" in every object with a color attribute.

But, if a plea to common sense be in order, in dealing with such names, it should not be directed against, but rather in favor of accepting the possibility that colors may reflect geographical position as well as appearance of the named objects. One may even wax melancholy by reading works of writers who have, since antiquity, been trying to unravel the significance of colors in geographical names and in names of peoples, because they failed to realize that colors may symbolize both the geographical location of the objects named, as well as to reflect their physical appearance. The few scholars who recognize colors as standing for the directions of the horizon usually weaken their arguments by involving some vague and distant "Asian" namegiver.[143] Perhaps most scholars seek the origin of color attributes in geographical names and in names of peoples in Asia because many reputable Orientalists and Turcologists have argued convincingly that the Chinese, Iranians, and Turks have, since ancient times, used colors as symbols of the directions of the horizon. Some go as far as to state categorically that the Slavs and other North Central Eurasian peoples were ignorant of this idea.[144]

A skeptic might still insist that, even in names coined by Asians, the colors do not necessarily reflect the *positio loci* of the named objects by pointing out that no one has produced evidence of a people's conscious and systematic application of

---

[143] For example, A. Room in *Place-Names of the World* (Newton Abbot, Devon, 1974), s.v. "Black Sea, Red Sea, and White Sea" proposes cautiously that color adjectives may symbolize the cardinal points adding: "as many Asian languages have colour names for different parts of the world."

[144] Ludat, *op. cit., loc. cit.*

colors as symbols of the directions of the horizon in an actual process of naming. This is not surprising, for we are rarely permitted to witness, even through written records of some past observers, the coining of a geographical name or an ethnonym. Almost all material of that nature in Eurasia and in the Mediterranean basin has been recorded by nametakers who lived generations after some unknown namegivers had done their work.

Faute de mieux, we wish to draw attention to a document which might serve as such evidence. It comes from the *Regnum Slavorum*, written by an anonymous Catholic priest or monk at the end of the twelfth century in Bar/Antibari in Red Croatia, known today as Montenegro (*Crna Gora* "Black Mountain"):

> And thus came the cardinals and the bishops to the field of Duvno [sc. a town in Bosnia], where they found the king who received them with great honor and reverence. Then the king ordered the people of his realm to convene in the same field. While the people were assembling, there arrived Leo and John, the noble and wise envoys of the Emperor Michael [sc. Michael III of East Rome], and other wise men, whom the king and the cardinals received with proper dignity. Having all convened, they began to deliberate both in Latin and in Slavic, as ordered by Honorius, the Pope's envoy, and the most Christian King Budimir. The congress lasted twelve days. ... At this same congress were read ancient diplomas, in both Greek and Latin, which had been sent by the Pope and the Emperor, for the people to hear how the emperors of old had divided provinces, regions, and lands. And the king and the people were pleased. After the congress had come to a close on the twelfth day, the king was crowned in the manner of Roman kings (*more Romanorum regum*) by Honorius, the papal envoy, and by the cardinals and bishops, and there was a great joy amongst his people in his whole kingdom. ... Thereupon he issued diplomas and privileges and divided his kingdom into regions and provinces and drew their borders in accordance with the ancient diplomas which had been read before the people, and in this manner: the region which is traversed by the rivers that flow from the mountains toward the south (*meridianam plagam*) he called the Maritime province; the region which slopes toward the north and through which the rivers from the mountains flow to join the mighty Danube River he called Surbia. Then he divided the Maritime province twofold. The land which extends from Duvno, where the king resided and where the congress was held, as far as Vinodol [near modern Rijeka] he called White Croatia (*vocavit Croatiam Albam*), which is also called Lower Dalmatia (*Dalmatia*

Inferior). ... Likewise, from Duvno as far as Bambalona, which is now called Durazzo, the land was named Red Croatia (*Croatiam Rubeam vocavit*), which is also known as Upper Dalmatia (*Dalmatia Superior*).[145]

We have adduced this passage as proof that at least two colors, red and white, were consciously used by medieval Croats for the purpose of identifying the eastern, or southeastern, and the western, or northwestern, sections of their kingdom, their *positio loci,* not their *qualitas corporis.* We ought to interpret the adjective red accompanying the Croatian name to mean Eastern (or Southeastern) Croatia, the adjective white added to the same country as Western (or Northwestern) Croatia, just as we readily interpret their Latin equivalents *superior* and *inferior* that modify the name Dalmatia to mean upper and lower in altitude, and just as, without hesitation, we interpret the words east and west attached to the Saxon ethnonym to mean Eastern and Western Saxons.

Though we only have direct evidence from medieval Croatia, the use of colors as symbols of the directions of the horizon was indirectly attested, in antiquity, in the Italic, Hellenic, and Celtic language areas. It is possible that the custom had once held sway from one end of Eurasia to the other, from the Ocean out of which the sun rises to the one which contains his bed, to paraphrase Homer. By insisting that the use of colors as symbols of the directions of the horizon be considered both an ancient and a universal custom, it is hoped that it will be taken into account as an autochthonously European, as well as Asian, African, and Native American tradition.

Based on this evidence, we should be permitted to include ancient Croatia and all Slavia in the area of Eurasia where colors were consciously used to designate the directions of the horizon. Furthermore, since in this enormous territory the Chinese are the most easterly, the Croats the most westerly peoples among the multitude of peoples and cultures of Eurasia who made use of colors as symbols of the cardinal points, we propose that the scheme not be designated as the intellectual

---

[145] Diocleas Presbyter, *Regnum Slavorum,* ed. by F. Šišić (Belgrade—Zagreb, 1928), pp. 304–6.

property of any particular people or civilization, but rather as a universal idea shared by many. For this reason, we are taking the liberty to suggest that de Saussure's term "sino-iranien" be geographically amplified into "Sino-Croatian."

CHAPTER IV

COLORS IN GEOGRAPHICAL NAMES

This chapter discusses some geographical names which derive from words denoting color as well as others that are modified by color adjectives. Because most of these names are found in works of ancient writers who lived several centuries *before* the arrival to Europe of the first speakers of an Altaic language, such as the Huns who appeared at the beginning of the Christian era, they may serve here as evidence that the manner of naming after colors is an undatable autochthonous North African and West Eurasian tradition rather than a dated borrowing from peoples of Central and East Asia. It is hoped that this effort will be regarded as a contribution to our understanding of some "inexplicable" toponyms and ethnonyms such as Red Sea, Black Sea, Red Russia, White Russia, Black Russia, and the Russi. The pertinent material is grouped into four sections: thalassonymy, hydronymy, oronymy, and toponymy. Colors in ethnonymy are discussed in Chapter V.

THALASSONYMY: Names of seas, shores, capes, islands

The Red Sea

The gulf which stretches from the Suez Canal to the Bab el-Mandeb is labeled "Red Sea" on modern maps. But throughout antiquity and the Middle Ages this name was actually used to cover a much larger body of water which encompassed the whole of the Indian Ocean, including its parts that are called today the Arabian Sea, the Gulf of Oman, and the Persian Gulf.

The gulf which today is called the Red Sea was, prior to the modern age, known primarily as the Arabian Gulf. Therefore, in searching for the meaning of the color attribute in the name Red Sea one must proceed from the ancient content of the designation rather than focus on its modern restriction, from the Indian Ocean, not from the Arabian Gulf.

In classical sources the Indian or Southern Ocean was occasionally called after the south wind; its more common, perhaps more poetic, and even more ancient name was *Erythra thalassa, Mare rubrum* "red sea." Herodotus is the earliest authority on the Greek name for this body of water. In the opening passage of his book he introduces a pair of designations consisting of Our Sea (the Mediterranean) and the Red Sea (the Indian Ocean). The passage reads:

> The Persian learned men say that the Phoenicians were the cause of the feud [sc. the war between Asians and Europeans]. These (they say) came to our sea from the sea which is called Red (*apo tēs Erythrēs kaleomenēs thalassēs apikomenous epi tēnde tēn thalassan*), and having settled in the country which they still occupy, at once began to make long voyages.[1]

According to Herodotus, the Phoenicians, themselves, affirmed they had migrated from the shores of the Red Sea to those of the Mediterranean:

> These Phoenicians dwelt in old time, as they themselves say, by the Red Sea (*epi tē Erythrē thalassē*); passing over from thence, they now inhabit the seacoast of Syria; that part of Syria and as much of it as reaches to Egypt, is all called Palestine.[2]

The presumably original homeland of the Phoenicians was not washed by the Arabian but by the Persian Gulf, as will become apparent presently. The Persian Gulf, *Persikos kolpos, Sinus Persicus*, was in fact the Red Sea. This can be seen from Herodotus' description of the Euphrates as: "a wide, deep, and swift river, flowing from Armenia and issuing into the Red Sea"; and again from his remark on the Gyndes River, modern Dyala,

---

[1] I.1.
[2] VII.89.

which rises in the mountains of the Matieni and flows through the Dardanean country into another river, the Tigris, which again passes the city of Opis and issues into the Red Sea.[3]

In reporting on the fate of captive Milesians, Herodotus clearly states what he meant by the name Red Sea:

> After that [sc. the taking of Miletus by the Persians], the captive Milesians were brought to Susa. King Darius did them no further hurt, but settled them by the sea called Red (*epi tē Erythrē kaleomenē thalassē*), in the city called Ampe, whereby flows the river Tigris as it issues into the sea.[4]

The island of Qeshm (ancient Oaracta) and other neighboring islands, located in what we call the Persian Gulf and the Gulf of Oman, belonged to the fourteenth province of Persia, and were, according to Herodotus, in the Red Sea (*en tē Erythrē thalassē*).[5] These islands and their inhabitants are mentioned in Herodotus' catalog of the Persian armies:

> The island tribes that came from the Red Sea (*ek tēs Erythrēs thalassēs epomena*), and from the islands where the king plants those who are called Exiles, wore dress and armour likest to the Median.[6]

This passage proves that in Herodotus' day the sea called red washed the shores of Persia. At the same time, Herodotus uses the term Red Sea for the southern portion of the Circumambient Ocean all the way to the Yellow Sea. He states:

> So much for the parts of Asia west of the Persians (*apo Perseōn ta pros hesperēn*). But what is beyond the Persians, and Medes, and Saspires, and Colchians, eastward and toward the rising sun (*ta pros ēō te kai hēlion anatellonta*), this is bounded on the one hand by the Red Sea, and to the north by the Caspian Sea, and the river Araxes, that flows towards the sun's rising.[7]

---

[3] I.180, 189.
[4] VI.20.
[5] III.93.
[6] VII.80.
[7] IV.40.

Herodotus did not limit the designation "Red Sea" to the
Persian Gulf, but rather extended it over a large section of the
Circumambient Ocean, consisting of three parts: 1) "the sea
whereon the Greeks sail" (sc. the Mediterranean); 2) "the sea
beyond the Pillars of Heracles, which they call Atlantic"; and 3)
the Red Sea. These, he says "are all one: but the Caspian is
separate and by itself."[8]

Further, Herodotus applies the name "Red Sea" synonymously
with the term *Notia thalassa* "southern sea," just as he uses the
expression *Boreia thalassa* "northern sea" as a synonym for the
Mediterranean Sea, which includes the Greek Sea, Our Sea, and
occasionally the Black Sea. The following passage shows that he
saw the Red Sea as a directional counterpart of the Mediterranean:

> The land where the Persians dwell reaches to the southern sea,
> that sea which is called Red; beyond these to the north are the
> Medes, and beyond the Medes the Saspires, and beyond the
> Saspires the Colchians, whose country reaches to the northern sea
> (*epi tēn boreiēn thalassan*) into which issues the river Phasis; so
> these four nations dwell between the one sea and the other.[9]

The historian also gives the location of the Red Sea in relation
to Arabia and Egypt:

> Beyond and above Heliopolis Egypt is a narrow land. For it is
> bounded on the one side by the mountains of Arabia, which bear
> from the north to the south, ever stretching southward towards the
> sea called the Red Sea (*ap' arktou pros mesambriēn te kai noton,
> aiei anō teinon es tēn Erythrēn kaleomenēn thalassan*).[10]

The fact that in this passage Herodotus refers to the Arabian
Gulf as the Red Sea does not contradict his statements that the
Persian Gulf, too, was known as the Red Sea. The following

---

[8] I.203.
[9] IV.37.
[10] II.8.

passage shows that he considered the Arabian Gulf as an arm of one continuous body of water called the Red Sea:

> Now in Arabia, not far from Egypt, there is a gulf of the sea entering in from the sea called Red (*kolpos thalassēs esechōn ek tēs Erythrēs kaleomenēs thalassēs*), of which the length and narrowness is such as I shall show: for length, it is a forty days' voyage for a ship rowed by oars from its inner end out to the wide sea; and for breadth, it is half a day's voyage at the widest.[11]

Like the Persian Gulf, the Arabian Gulf, too, was regarded as a bay of the Red Sea. In fact, in a passage on the building of a canal between the Nile and the Arabian Gulf, Herodotus uses the term Red Sea to cover both the Arabian Gulf and the Indian Ocean. He says:

> Psammetichus had a son Necos, who became king of Egypt. It was he who began the making of the canal into the Red Sea, which was finished by Darius the Persian. This is four days' voyage in length, and it was dug wide enough for two triremes to move in it rowed abreast. It is fed by the Nile, and is carried from a little above Bubastis by the Arabian town of Patumus; it issues into the Red Sea. The beginning of the digging was in the part of the Egyptian plain which is nearest to Arabia; the mountains that extend to Memphis (in which mountains are the stone quarries) come close to this plain; the canal is led along the lower slope of these mountains in a long reach from west to east; passing then into a ravine it bears southward out of the hill country towards the Arabian Gulf. Now the shortest and most direct passage from the northern to the southern or Red Sea is from the Casian promontory, which is the boundary between Egypt and Syria, to the Arabian Gulf, and this is a distance of one thousand furlongs, neither more nor less; this is the most direct way, but the canal is by much longer, inasmuch as it is more crooked.[12]

Clearly, Herodotus viewed the Red Sea as the southern section of the Circumambient Ocean and as a directional counterpart of the *Boreia thalassa* "northern sea."

Just as he uses the name Red Sea for the Persian Gulf, so in the following passage Herodotus applies it to the Arabian Gulf,

[11]   II.11.
[12]   II.158.

while the rest of the southern section of the Circumambient Ocean he calls the Southern Sea:

> For Libya [sc. Africa] shows clearly that it is encompassed by the sea, save only where it borders on Asia; and this was proved first (as far as we know) by Necos king of Egypt. He, when he had made an end of digging the canal which leads from the Nile to the Arabian Gulf, sent Phoenicians in ships, charging them to sail on their return voyage past the Pillars of Heracles till they should come into the northern sea and so to Egypt. So the Phoenicians set out from the Red Sea and sailed the southern sea; whenever autumn came they would put in and sow the land, to whatever part of Libya they might come, and there await the harvest; then, having gathered in the crop, they sailed on, so that after two years had passed, it was in the third that they rounded the Pillars of Heracles and came to Egypt.[13]

Those modern commentators who believe that the Arabian Gulf was the original Red Sea could not have reached this conclusion from Herodotus. Their belief rests on the authority of Aegyptologists quoted by H. Berger who declared:

> Concerning the appellation Red Sea which was much investigated already in antiquity, I accept the enlightened explanation of Aegyptologists. They recognize in the Red Sea the Sea of the Red Land, a name appearing so frequently in Egyptian inscriptions as a designation for Arabia, a land neighboring on the Black Land of Egypt.[14]

Berger also quotes Pindar and Aeschylus, writers who flourished during the century which claims Herodotus, to amplify his theory.[15] Here is Pindar:

> And they [sc. the Argonauts] reached the streams of Ocean, and the Red Sea, and the race of the Lemnian wives who slew their lords (*en t'Okeanou pelagessi migen pontō t' Erythrō/ Lamnian t' ethnei gynaikōn androphonōn*).[16]

---

[13]   IV.42.
[14]   *Geschichte der wissenschaftlichen Erdkunde der Griechen*, 2nd ed. (Leipzig, 1903), p. 59.
[15]   *Ibid.*, pp. 58–9.
[16]   *Pythian Odes*, IV.251–4.

Pace Berger, the quoted passage proves merely that the Greeks thought that between the Circumambient Ocean and the Mediterranean Sea, where the island of Lemnos was located, was a body of water called the Red Sea. Pindar should not be used as the authority that the Arabian Gulf was the Red Sea, that it was the only sea that bore this name, nor that the name originated on the shores of this bay. Aeschylus mentions the Red Sea in his *Prometheus Unbound*, a work which has come down to us in fragments. Here is the fragment in question quoted by Strabo:

> *phoinikopedon t' erythras hieron*
> *cheuma thalassēs,*
> *chalkomaraugon te par' Okeanō*
> *limnan pantotrophon Aithiopōn,*
> *hin' ho pantoptas Hēlios aiei*
> *chrōt' athanaton kamaton th' hippōn*
> *thermais hydatos*
> *malakou prochoais anapauei.*

> ("The sacred flood of the Red Sea with its bed of scarlet sands, and the mere on the shore of Oceanus that dazzles with its gleam of brass and furnishes all nourishment to Ethiopians, where the Sun, who sees all things, gives rest to his tired steeds and refreshes his immortal body in warm outpourings of soft water.")[17]

Again, nothing indicates that Aeschylus applied the name Red Sea only to the Arabian Gulf, nor that the name originated there.

To conclude, there should be no disagreement about the term *Erythra thalassa* because Herodotus uses it clearly to designate the Persian Gulf, Gulf of Oman, Arabian Sea, Arabian Gulf, Indian Ocean, and occasionally the Southern Sea in general. He often comprehended these seas as one, as the southern section of the Circumambient Ocean, and as a directional counterpart of the "northern sea." No classical writer contradicts Herodotus. The geographical knowledge of the time was summed up in the following statement:

> Arabia Felix is terminated on the north by the designated border of Arabia Petraea and Arabia Deserta; on the northeast by a part

[17] 1.2.27.

of the Persian gulf; on the west by the Arabian gulf; on the south by the Red sea.[18]

The name *Erythra thalassa* appeared in the Greek language at the time when the primary, or perhaps the only, function of the attribute of color in geographical names was thought to be descriptive. The object which the name designated was accepted as red by poets, while philosophers initiated a search for the source of its color. In the passage quoted above, Aeschylus uses the adjective *erythra* for the sea and *phoinikopedon* "scarlet" for its bed, expecting his readers to agree that the Southern Sea truly looked red, or scarlet.

Since the Greeks believed that the Persian Gulf was the original Red Sea, their etymological efforts went in that direction. Ctesias of Cnidus was one of the first investigators to account for the sea's color attribute. His and other writers' views on the matter of the Red Sea are discussed by Strabo who says:

> For example, he [sc. Artemidorus] says that some writers call the sea "Erythra" from the colour it presents as the result of reflection, whether from the rays of the sun when it is in the zenith, or from the mountains, which have been reddened by the scorching heat; for, he continues, conjecture runs both ways about the cause; but Ctesias the Cnidian reports a spring, consisting of red and ochre-coloured water (*ereuthes kai miltōdes hydōr*), as emptying into the sea; and Agatharcides, a fellow-citizen of Ctesias, reports from a certain Boxus, of Persian descent, that when a herd of horses had been driven out of the country by a passion-frenzied lioness as far as the sea and from there the herd had crossed over to a certain island, a certain Persian, Erythras by name, built a raft and was the first man to cross to the island; and that when he saw that it was beautifully adapted to habitation, he drove the herd back to Persis, sent forth colonists to that island and to the others and to the coast, and caused the sea to be named after himself; but other writers, he says, declare that Erythras was the son of Perseus, and that he ruled over this region.[19]

The sea in question is a section of the *Erythra thalassa* of the ancients which modern cartographers divide between the Persian Gulf and the Gulf of Oman. Ctesias must have heard of the red-

---

[18] Ptolemy, *Geography*, VI.vii, p. 137 of Stevenson's translation.
[19] 16.4.20.

colored spring during his sojourn in Persia. Artemidorus' explanation should be understood as applying to the same sea, while the explanations furnished by Agatharcides and other writers clearly point to Persia and its shores as the origin and the cause of the sea's name.

The name *Phoinikē* "Phoenicia" appears to derive from a Semitic source, and the color scarlet-red in Greek reflects some native Asian hue. It is possible that this gave rise to the belief that the Phoenicians had originated from the shores of the Persian Gulf or the Red Sea, which Strabo, though skeptical of such beliefs, identifies with the Persian Gulf, saying:

> For some of them [sc. the writers criticized] say that even the Sidonians who are our neighbours are colonists from the Sidonians on Oceanus, and they actually add the reason why our Sidonians are called Phoenicians, namely, because the colour of the Persian Gulf is "red" (*thalatta erythra*).[20]

Let us conclude this brief survey of ancient authorities on the name of the Red Sea with Arrian:

> They said that in this island [sc. Oaracta, modern Qeshm] the tomb of the first chief of this territory was shown; his name was Erythres, and hence came the name of the sea (*ounoma de autō Erythrēn einai, ap' hotou kai tēn epōnymiēn tē thalassē tautē einai, Erythrēn kaleesthai*).[21]

The island of Qeshm, is situated in the Strait of Hormuz, at the point where the waters of the Persian Gulf mix with those of the Gulf of Oman and the open sea, the true *Erythra thalassa* of antiquity.

We saw that Herodotus occasionally applies to the Arabian Gulf the same name *Erythra thalassa,* which he generally uses for the Indian Ocean as a whole and for the Persian Gulf in particular. The Arabian Gulf, which regularly obtains its waters, marine life, storms, and the like from the open sea (the Red Sea of the ancients) ultimately came to be known as the only Red Sea, like a son appropriating the father's name and qualities. The

[20]   1.2.35.
[21]   Arrian, *Indica*, 37.3.

attribute of the color red, which has, in the course of time become limited to the Arabian Gulf, has not ceased to stir the imagination of poets and scientists, as is evidenced by a rich literature of explanations of that gulf's relatively recent but "unusual" name. However, it must be stressed that the Arabian Gulf was elevated into the Red Sea by translators.

Since the Arabian Gulf demarcates Africa from Asia and Egypt from Palestine and Sinai, it has seen much traffic throughout history. In mythical time, the Hebrew patriarchs migrated to the land of Goshem by way of the isthmus separating the Mediterranean Sea from the Arabian Gulf. Centuries later some of their descendants fled Egypt by a more southerly route that required crossing the sea which the Egyptians knew as the Great Black or as the Sea of Mertet. In ancient Hebrew sagas the flight was facilitated by Yahweh who caused the waters of the sea to recede to let his people pass over dry land. Once they were all safe on the Asian side, the deity brought the waters back in order to block the pursuing Egyptians from capturing the escapees. The Alexandrian Jews, once believed to have been commissioned by the Macedonian king of Egypt, Ptolemy II Philadelphus (285–247 BC), to translate their lore into Koine, the *lingua franca* of the Macedonian Empire, rendered the Hebrew term *Yam suf* "sea of reeds," the sea which Yahweh had parted and which must be identical with the Great Black of the Egyptians, as *Erythra thalassa.*[22]

Forgetting that the Persian Gulf as well as the Indian Ocean had also been called Red Sea by the ancients, the Graeco-Roman Christians gradually limited the designation to the Arabian Gulf alone.[23] The name Arabian Gulf, commonly used in antiquity,

---

[22]   *EJ*, XIV (1971), s.v. "Red Sea—Sea of Reeds," cols. 14–17; on ancient Hebrew thalassonymy, *see*, Burr, *op. cit.*, pp. 80–95; and Stadelmann, *op. cit.*, pp. 154–60; P. Green, in his *Alexander to Actium* (Berkeley, Calif., 1990), p. 317, states that the motive for translation "was the increasing inability of the Greek-speaking Alexandrian Jews to understand either Hebrew or Aramaic."

[23]   The Egyptian Christians translate the name *Erythra thalassa* as the "Sea of Shar," which is equivalent to the Indian Ocean.

has disappeared from modern cartography, having been replaced by the name Red Sea.[24]

Trying to explain the red attribute applied exclusively by imprecise translators to this sea, some claim that it came from the blood of the smitten Egyptians, while others seek natural explanations.

It is widely believed today that the ancient Greeks learned the name Red Sea from the Egyptians who had allegedly transferred the attribute to the adjacent sea from Red Land, the name used by them to designate the Desert of the South, as opposed to Egypt proper, called the Black Land.[25] If we accept this explanation, we still have to account for the attribute red in the *true* Red Sea of our classical sources, that is, the Persian Gulf and the whole Indian Ocean. It is clear that the native peoples of Southwest Asia called these bodies of water Red Sea, but there is no indication that they borrowed from the Egyptians either the name or the idea of using colors as symbols of the directions of the horizon in coining geographical names.

For this reason explanations of the name Red Sea provided by modern commentators are largely irrelevant because they usually shift and restrict the designations *Erythra thalassa* and *Mare rubrum* to the Arabian Gulf and seek there the source of the presumed color of its waters.

Finally, scientists declare that the Red Sea, that is, the Arabian Gulf, is not red but blue-green in appearance:

> Die Farbe des Roten Meeres ist blaugrün, in der Nähe der Untiefen grün; seinen Namen trägt es wegen des zeitweisen Auftretens einer rot erscheinenden Alge (Trichodesmium erythraeum), deren Chlorophyll durch rote Pigmente überdeckt wird.[26]

[24] Certain Arab nationalists dislike the name Persian Gulf and would like to rename it the Arabian Gulf. If they want to "improve" upon the geographical nomenclature of Southwest Asia, they should replace the appellation Red Sea with the ancient name *Sinus Arabicus.*

[25] Berger, *op. cit.*, p. 59; *see* also, Stewart, *op. cit.*, pp. 172ff for an interesting solution of the problem of the sea's name.

[26] *Westermann Lexikon der Geographie*, ed. by W. Tietze and E. Weigt (Braunschweig, 1970), III, p. 1073.

Although aimed at the wrong sea, the above explanation of the name Red Sea is generally plausible. A sea could be named red either because it is red permanently or only occasionally. However, we reject it because the designation Red Sea was, as we saw, throughout antiquity, used for the Persian Gulf, Gulf of Oman, Arabian Sea, Indian Ocean, and only occasionally for the Arabian Gulf (our Red Sea). Therefore, the derivative "redness" of the Arabian Gulf must be referred to the original "redness" of these other seas, the true *Erythra thalassa*.

The English term *Erythraean Sea* and its Italian version *Mare Eritreo*, used in popular literature, derive from the affected Latin term *Erythraeum mare*, used synonymously, in antiquity, with *Mare rubrum* and *Erythra thalassa*. Unfortunately, the name Erythraean Sea now frequently appears parallel with the name Red Sea, as if denoting a separate sea. The confusion increased after the creation of Eritrea, which, in the opinion of some, gave its name to the sea. Rather the opposite is true, since Eritrea was established as Colonia Eritrea by Italian imperialists on January 1, 1890, as an administrative unit comprising territory conquered from the peoples of Ethiopia. Italian administrators imposed the name Eritrea on a coastal region of Ethiopia believing the sea that washed its shores was the "Erythraean" Sea.

The Green Sea

In Arabic geographical works the name *al-Baḥr al-akhḍar* "green sea" was used generally for the Circumambient Ocean (*al-Baḥr al-muḥīt*) and more restrictively to distinguish the Atlantic Ocean, Southern Sea, Indian Ocean, and the Yellow Sea from other seas.[27] In other words, the Arabs once called "green" also that portion of the Great Ocean, which bathed their lands from the east and the south, while the peoples living in the north called the same sea "red." The Arabic name, recorded during the Middle Ages, may go back into antiquity when the southern

---

[27]   *See,* al-Mas'ūdī's view described in G.H.T. Kimble, *Geography in the Middle Ages* (London, 1938), p. 53. The Arabs may have taken the Egyptian designation the Great Green and applied it to the encompassing body of water, which included the Yellow Sea.

section of the Indian Ocean was called *Prasōdēs thalassa* "green sea."

Scholars argue that the name originated among the Greeks, who, supposedly struck by the sea's green color, applied to it one of their words for "green," *prasaios, prasinos* (from *prason* "a leek," Latin *porrum*).[28] The Green Sea can not be precisely identified because pertinent extant classical sources are both sparse and vague. All that we know about its location is that it stretched from the coast of East Africa to the Subcontinent of India.[29] The adjective *prason,* occurs also in the name of the most southeasterly promontory of Africa known to the Mediterranean peoples, *Prason akrōtērion* "green promontory,[30] and in the name of a bay around Ceylon (Sri Lanka), *Prasōdēs kolpos.*[31]

Because the Green Sea was far from the Graeco-Roman world, it was scarcely known and only occasionally mentioned by writers who used Greek and Latin. But, once the sea had come to be known as "leek-green," some people "saw" its green color. Thus, both Marcus of Heraclea and the Anonymous Geographus state that the color attribute reflects the sea's leek-green surface.[32] But, Pliny calls this same sea the Red Sea and the Azanian Sea.[33] He says that the sea around the *Coliacum promunturium*, Cape Comorin, is of a deep green color, *colore perviridi*, and that thickets of trees grow there, the tops of which are brushed by rudders of passing vessels.[34] In general, ex-

---

[28]   H. Treidler, "Prasōdēs thalassa," *PWRE*, XXII (1954), cols. 1705–19).

[29]   For location, *see, ibid.* and Ptolemy, *Geography*, VII. iii–iv.

[30]   *Ibid.; see* also, H. Treidler, "Prason," *PWRE*, XXII (1954), cols. 1705–19.

[31]   Ptolemy, *Geography*, VII.iv; *see* also, H. Treidler, "Prasōdēs kolpos," *PWRE*, XXII (1954), cols. 1703–05.

[32]   Quoted in Treidler, "Prasōdēs thalassa." Modern scholars agree with their opinion.

[33]   *n.h.*, VI.108; the name Azanian Sea means "the parched sea," deriving either from the Greek verb *azanō* "to dry, parch up," or from the Arabic *Zanj* "black." Today, black nationalists use the name Azania for the country others call the Republic of South Africa.

[34]   *Ibid.*, VI.87. Pliny's informants may have had in mind some mangrove swamps off the tip of India. This local greenness does not explain the green color of the Indian Ocean off the coast of East Africa.

planations of this nature, stemming from a received name rather than from observation, ought to be treated with reservation.

We do not know the origin of the name *Prasōdēs thalassa*, but the possibility exists that the color is a Greek rendering of the Arabic word *akhḍar* "green" or *azraq* "blue." We suggest that ancient Greek mariners learned the name for the whole of the Indian Ocean from Arabs or other native peoples to whom it was the Green Sea, not because it looked green but because it stretched to the east, the direction which they symbolically represented by that color.

The naming of these natural features may have originated among the Arabs, or another people in whose language green symbolized a direction of the horizon, most likely the east. The names Green Sea, Green Promontory, and Green Bay may have sprung from the mind of some namegiver with a broad view, say, an unknown African Ptolemy, who needed an eastern counterpart for the *Occidentalis Oceanus*, which extended toward sunset from the shores inhabited by the *Hesperii Aethiopes*, and an eastern counterpart for the *Hesperium Promunturium*, situated somewhere along the coast of the imaginary "western" Ethiopians.[35]

The ancient appellation Green Sea was known to the medieval Arabs. For example, Ibn Khaldun calls the Mediterranean the Roman Sea or the Syrian Sea. For our Red Sea (the ancient Arabian Gulf) he uses the name the Sea of al-Qulzum, after the city of al-Qulzum, and to the Persian Gulf he applies the name Green Sea.[36]

The Red and Green Seas Are One

Expressing no wonderment at the name Red Sea, Herodotus took it as something quite common, well-known, almost ordinary. The red color attribute of that sea in his *Histories* describes not the physical appearance of the sea, not its *qualitas corporis*, but its geographical location, its *positio loci*. The fact that the

---

[35]   Ptolemy, *Geography*, IV.vi, vii.
[36]   Ibn Khaldun, *Muqaddimah*, transl. by F. Rosenthal (Princeton, N.J., 1967), pp. 49–52.

Persian Gulf, which was called the Red Sea by Herodotus and other writers, has been known as the Green Gulf by the Arabs, forces us to affirm that neither of the attributes of color reflects the appearance of its waters. Rather, the Persian Gulf and the Indian Ocean were "seen" as the "red" sea by the namegiver who lived along the sea's northern shores and for whom their geographical location, the south, was symbolized by the color red, while this same sea was "seen" as "green" by the people who viewed it from the west and for whom the east was equivalent to the green color.

In other words, the true function of the color in the name Red Sea becomes evident when we realize that the same body of water was known in antiquity as the Green Sea, and that a bay of the ancient Red Sea, or a section of the ancient Green Sea is still called Green Sea by the Arabs. The descriptive explanation of "green" in the designation Green Sea is counterindicated by the fact that this same sea was known as the Red Sea by others.

The logical solution that offers itself is to ascribe to both these color adjectives a positional rather than a descriptive function. The original purpose of each color was to define the sea's *positio loci*, not its *qualitas corporis*. The Indian Ocean was called Red Sea by the people for whom it was the southern sea, Green Sea by those for whom it was the eastern sea.[37]

In conclusion, the explanations attributing to the colors in the names Red Sea and Green Sea a purely descriptive function offered by classical and modern writers cannot be accepted. Without taking into account that such modifiers frequently carry other than descriptive meaning we cannot fully understand these names. If we had no other ground on which to reject the descriptive functions of these colors, the fact that the sea which was called Red Sea by the people for whom it was the southern sea has also, since ancient times, been known as the Green Sea by those living along its western shores would suffice.

---

[37]   It cannot be shown to the satisfaction of all that the leek-green color adjectives attached to names of natural features from East Africa to India always symbolize the east, because directional counterparts of the objects so designated cannot immediately be identified.

The Black Sea

We saw that Herodotus and other ancient writers considered the Red Sea as the southern segment of the Circumambient Ocean. Its limits remained unknown to Mediterranean peoples until the Great Discoveries at the dawn of the modern age. It is quite different with the Red Sea's northern counterparts, the Mediterranean and the Black seas. Although sections of their shores, especially those distant from the Aegean basin, remained long hidden from view and associated with mythical personages and events, these seas had by the middle of the first millennium BC become well-known and well-charted by seafaring peoples, especially Phoenicians and Greeks.

Many diverse nations have occupied the shores of the Black Sea. Some of them, like the Tauri in antiquity and the Russians in the Middle Ages, ruled its waves, traded with foreign lands, and occasionally raided the vessels of merchants and adventurers who came from distant shores. Others, especially those who lived by pastoral nomadism, avoided the sea altogether.

It is plausible that the earliest native peoples of the Black Sea basin knew only that sea, and, like the Sumerians who at first knew only the Red Sea (the Persian Gulf) and named it the Great Water, they may have referred to it merely as "the sea." Consequently, they would have had no need to attach a modifier to their word for the sea. This seems to be the way how the Greeks came to refer to the Black Sea as *pontos* "the sea."

We depend exclusively on Greek and Roman writers for the names of and information about the Black Sea in antiquity, since records made by other ancient literate peoples have not come down to us. Though Homer does not mention the Black Sea by name, he makes references to some of the inhabitants living on its shores and to Jason the Argonaut, the mythical voyager from Thessaly, who had brought to Hellas not only the Golden Fleece but also a more clear knowledge of the Black Sea and the peoples occupying its southern coasts. Later, when the Greeks began to sail and settle along the sea's northern shore, they came into contact with other peoples. Among these were the Tauri whose piratical activities, hatred of foreigners and their customs were believed to have prompted the early Greeks to name the Black Sea *Axenos* or *Axeinos Pontos* "the inhospitable sea."[38]

The earliest known Greek colonies along the shores of the Black Sea date from the seventh century BC. The first extant Greek writers who mention the Black Sea, namely, Pindar and Euripides, use the adjective *axeinos* "inhospitable" and its antonym *euxeinos* "hospitable," whereas Herodotus employs the latter exclusively.[39] Centuries later, Ovid, while languishing in Tomi, exiled from his warm and beloved Italy, found the term "hospitable" inappropriate. In a poem composed on the occasion of his birthday, he implores his *genius natalis* to rescue him from his exile or let him end his life, "so long as all but the remotest part of the world, the Pontus, falsely called Euxine, possesses me."[40] In a poem addressed to a friend, Ovid clarifies his whereabouts and the sea's place in Graeco-Roman mythology:

> The cold shores of the Pontus Euxinus keep me; by men of old it was called Axenus. For its waters are tossed by no moderate winds and there are no quiet harbours visited by foreign ships. Round about are tribes eager for plunder and bloodshed, and the land is not less to be feared than the treacherous sea. They whom you hear as rejoicing in men's gore dwell almost beneath the axis of the same constellation as myself, and not far away from me is the place where the Tauric altar of the quivered goddess is sprinkled with the blood of murder.[41]

Strabo agrees with Ovid concerning the earlier name and reputation of the Black Sea and explains how both had changed, saying:

> ... at that time [sc. Homer's] this sea was not navigable, and was called Axine (Axenon) because of its wintry storms and the ferocity of the tribes that lived around it, and particularly the Scythians, in that they sacrificed strangers, ate their flesh, and

---

[38] C.M. Danoff, "Pontos Euxeinos," *PWRE*, Suppl. IX (1962), cols. 866ff, especially Sections 11, 13, 14, 19.

[39] Pindar, *Pythian Odes*, IV.362; *Nemian Odes*, IV.79; Euripides, *Iphigenia in Taurica*, 125; Herodotus, *passim*; *see* further, Danoff, "Pontos Euxeinos," cols. 950–5.

[40] *Tristia*, III.xiii.25–8.

[41] *Ibid.*, IV.iv.55–64.

used their skulls as drinking-cups; but later it was called "Euxine," when the Ionians founded cities on the seaboard.[42]

Modern scholars, on the whole, accepted Strabo's explanation for the reason of the change from "inhospitable" to "hospitable" until an investigator resumed the search for the original name and its meaning by proposing that the Greeks had learned the name of the Black Sea from the Thracians. Further, he argued that the Inhospitable Sea was perceived and named as a counterpart of a "hospitable" sea, which he claims had been the epithet of the Hellespont.[43] This opinion has not gained acceptance.[44] It is generally agreed today that the Greek word *axenos* "inhospitable" derives, by way of folk-etymology, from the Old Iranian word *axšaena* "black or dark-blue."[45] This theory is reinforced by the fact that in the Pontic languages, including the Slavic ones, Turkish, and modern Greek, the Pontus Euxinus of antiquity is known as the *Black* Sea.[46]

Since the ancients thought that the Black Sea had originally been known as the Inhospitable Sea, being ignorant of the name's Old Iranian origin, their explanations were focused on discovering the reason for that epithet. The moderns, on the other hand, having established the Iranian connection, seek the reason why the same sea had been named "dark." As with the Red Sea, the consequence has brought forth the cause, and scholars declare (some use Baedeker's as authority) that the Black Sea does in fact look *schwarz-blau*, and seem to be contented with the following solution: the sea looks dark-blue, therefore it was named the Black Sea. Scientists concur: "Die

[42]   7.3.6.

[43]   A.C. Moorhouse, "The Name of the Euxine Pontus," *Classical Quarterly*, XXXIV (1940), pp. 123–8.

[44]   W.S. Allen, "The Name of the Black Sea in Greek," *Classical Quarterly*, XLI (1947), pp. 86–8.

[45]   E. Boisacq, "Le nom de la mer Noire en grec ancien," *Revue belge de philologie et d'histoire*, III (1924), pp. 317–19; see also, Danoff, *op. cit.*

[46]   The Pontus Euxinus was first specifically called black, or, rather, dark by Constantine Porphyrogenitus in his description of White Croatia. He says that White Croatian merchants come down to the sea "which is called 'dark' (*skoteinē*)." *See*, his *DAI*, ch. 32; for first appearances of the name in other languages, *see*, *EI*, IV, s.v. "Kara Deniz."

Sauerstoffarmut und Anreicherung an H_2S gab zum Namen Schwarzes Meer Anlass."[47]

Following this explanation we should imagine an ancient person, who, upon seeing the Black Sea for the first time and being struck by its dark appearance, called the sea black and made the color adjective a part of the sea's name either to stress its blackness *an und für sich* or to distinguish its blackness from the color of another sea. Yet, we should not be contented and must search for an explanation which would not only satisfy ancient inhabitants of the Pontic region, but would also be acceptable to modern Turks, Bulgarians, Macedonians, Greeks, and Arabs in whose languages the Black Sea is not perceived simply as black *an und für sich* but in contradistinction to the White Sea, their name for the Mediterranean.[48] In other words, we ought not to accept an explanation for the presumed "blackness" in the Black Sea while ignoring the "whiteness" in its western counterpart, for these two colors cannot be isolated from each other, just as the two seas are not independent of each other. While many believe that the Black Sea owes its name to the color of its waters, no one has seriously argued the "whiteness" of the Mediterranean although some of the peoples who today live on its shores call it the "white sea." Are we reluctant to call the Mediterranean white because Homer had called it "wine-dark"?

We suggest that the Black Sea owes its black color attribute to its northern location. The people who named it were not necessarily Iranians, nor is the Greek adjective *euxenos* a folk-etymology of the Old Iranian *axšaena*.

In our search for the origin of the name Black Sea we must not overlook the *Symplēgades petrai, Kyaneai nēsoi,* or *Planctae* "clashing rocks, blue isles." This natural or imaginary feature first appeared in tales of the voyage of the Argonauts. On their way from Pelasgia in Thessaly to Colchis, the voyagers sailed across *Melas kolpos* "black gulf" to Lemnos. From there they proceeded through the Hellespont and the Bosporus into the Black Sea. The sea's entrance was guarded by the Blue Isles

---

[47] *Westermann Lexikon der Geographie,* IV (1970), p. 150.
[48] It seems that the names *al-Baḥr al-abyaḍ, Asprē thalassa* and *Bjalo more* are translations of the Turkish *Akdeniz* "white sea."

ready to crush their ship. At the time the *Odyssey* was written
down they were an obligatory obstacle in tales of dangerous
voyages. Circe warned Odysseus about them but the hero did not
relate to the Phaeacians how he passed between the Clashing
Rocks.[49]

Although by the time Euripides was writing *Iphigenia in
Tauris* the whole coast of the Black Sea had been settled by
Greek colonists, the region was still a place where unusual
events could be imagined in works of fiction. The Clashing
Rocks are mentioned several times in this play. Their location
at the Thracian Bosporus, where Io had made her traditional
crossing, is described by a temple maiden as follows:

> O Clashing Rocks, under whose shadow the dark
> Threat waits, though through this cleft
> Io fled safe, in her disguise as heifer
> Pursued by the sharp stinging of the gadfly
> Fled beyond Europe's land
> And Europe's sea, fled safe but sick at heart,
> Away from home and kin,
> Into the alien wilderness of Asia,
> What sort of men would leave the holy streams
>   of Dirce or the reeds
> Green-growing in Eurotas, to explore
> A bitter beach, to dare these ominous rocks
> Where the seas meet in fog,
> Where Artemis, among Her colonnades
> Demanding sacrifice,
> Receives upon her altar human blood?[50]

On his way to Scythia at the head of a mighty multinational
army, the Persian king Darius the Great made a side trip to the
shore of the Black Sea to view the Rocks, "which the Greeks
say did formerly move upon the waters." The Ionian fleet in Persian service passed between them on its way to the mouth of the
Danube.[51] In Herodotus' story of Darius's expedition the Blue

---

[49]   *Odyssey*, XII.59–72.
[50]   Euripides, *Iphigenia in Tauris*, 392–406; the English is from W.
Bynner's translation, published in *The Complete Greek Tragedies: Euripides*,
II, ed. by D. Greene and O. Lattimore (Chicago, 1956).
[51]   Herodotus, IV.85, 89.

Rocks are one of the several bad omens which accompany its progress and presage its ignominious end.

The Blue Isles may have been some offshore rocks at the entrance to the Black Sea. Since no islands are visible there now, some scholars propose that they have been submerged, while others maintain that they stood, in antiquity, for icebergs. Whether real or imaginary, after they were established in Greek myth, the Blue Isles lived in people's imagination as fearsome guardians at the entrance to the Black Sea. Voyagers who followed the Argonauts into that sea's waters were obligated to pass between the Clashing Rocks or else be crushed by them. It is logical to suppose that the same people who first sighted or imagined these islands and saw them as blue saw the sea they guarded in the same color. In fact, Sophocles calls the sea around the Blue Isles *Kyanea pelagē* "blue sea."[52] Also, at the opposite end of the Pontus Euxinus the dark color was associated with the Sea of Azov, the ancient Maeotis, which native Scythians called *Temarunda*. Pliny translated this name as "the mother of the sea," but modern linguists read it as *temarun* "dark sea" (from Old Indian *támas,* Russian *temnyj* "dark," and *árṇa* "sea").[53] It is very likely that the Black Sea, including the Sea of Azov which may be considered its bay, was called blue, dark-blue, or black because of its northern location. That is, the color in this case stands for the *positio loci* of the sea rather than the appearance of its waters.

One is tempted to pair the Black Sea with the Red Sea and consider the first the northern, the second the southern sea. However, the two seas were probably not originally comprehended and named as a pair. The peoples of the Aegean basin may have, at first, attributed the color black to the northern portion of the Aegean Sea, such as the Melas kolpos, and only later transferred this hue to the Pontus Euxinus and still later to the Sea of Azov. On the other hand, the peoples of the Fertile Crescent and Upper Asia may have named another body of water black or blue merely to indicate its northern location. This could have been one of the several lakes of Upper Asia and eastern Anatolia, most likely Lake Urmia, whose ancient name

---

[52] *Antigone*, 968.
[53] Pliny, *n.h.*, VI.20.

in Old Armenian was *Kapoit-azow (Capauta)*, which Strabo, translating the adjective as *kyanē* "blue," interpreted as "blue lake."[54] Another possibility is *Gökçegöl*, a lake in Armenia whose Turkish name signifies "blue lake."

When we compare the dark color attributes in the names of these bays, seas, and lakes with the equally dark connotations associated with the Violet Sea (the Blue Adriatic) we are prompted to refer them all to their common and obvious northern locations in relation to the people who coined the names rather than to the appearance of the designated objects.

The name Black Sea may have originated among the Babylonians, Assyrians, Egyptians, Phoenicians, Medes, Persians, or among any people who dwelt south of the sea, including the Greeks. The sea was called black, not because it looked black, but because it was located in "the direction of darkness." If we were to insist on a color prototype, the Great Black of the Egyptians would serve the purpose. Once the Greeks came to know the sea well, and after they had settled along its shores, they avoided the attribute of the color black, replacing it with the epithet "inhospitable" as a milder substitute for the awesome color. With time, even that epithet became inappropriate, so its antonym, "hospitable," came into vogue and remained in use until the color black reasserted itself in its name in the Dark Ages, when those East Roman Christians who spoke Greek adopted the name *Maurē thalassa* for the Pontus Euxinus. Since we have argued that the Greeks and other Aegean basin peoples had named the sea black or dark blue, we cannot accept the popular explanation of the Greek adjective *axenos* as a folk etymology of the unattested Persian *axšaena*.

The White Sea

Our Mediterranean observers remained poorly informed about the regions of Europe which lay beyond the Rhine and the Danube. Also, with the exception of the coasts of the Black Sea, their knowledge of modern Ukraine and Russia was, throughout antiquity, insignificant and vague. Eastern Europe

---

[54]   11.14.8; *see* note 4 of the Loeb Library edition.

continued, well into the Middle Ages, to be peopled, in the imagination of southerners, with one-eyed Arimaspians, Griffins, Man-Eaters, Black-Cloaks, and other more or less fictitious peoples. For the sake of simplicity they regularly applied to the whole landmass, as far as the Arctic Ocean, the name of the most powerful steppe nomads described by Herodotus, the Scythians, whose place was later taken by Sarmatians, and still later by Russians.

The northern section of the Circumambient Ocean had no particular name in works of early writers. Later, however, the names of the peoples who were believed to have occupied its coasts were extended onto the sea as well. Thus, Pomponius Mela divides the entire northern segment of the Ocean into two parts: the *Britannicus oceanus* and *Scythicus oceanus*;[55] Ptolemy uses the names: *Germanicus, Hyperboreus, Duecaledonius*, and *Sarmaticus oceanus*.[56] Both writers describe Thule and Scandia as islands in the northern sea. Still other authors attach to this sea the epithets "frozen, Cronian" (from Cronus/Saturn), and "dead."[57] In modern times portions of the same ocean have been known as the Arctic Ocean, Ice Sea, *Ledovityj okean* in Russian, and *Mare glacialis* in Latin. A gulf of the Arctic Ocean is known today as *Beloe more* "white sea."[58]

The Baltic Sea

The sea known to us as the Baltic appeared at first in Graeco-Roman sources as the Suevian Sea, named so after the Suevi, Suabians, a Germanic people.[59] When Ptolemy was collecting his data the southern shores of the Baltic Sea were occupied by Slavs called Venedae, so he called it *Ouenedikos kolpos*

---

[55]   *See*, a map according to the views of Pomponius Mela in Bunbury, *op. cit.*, facing p. 360.

[56]   Ptolemy, *Geography*, Tabulae Europae, I, VIII.

[57]   *See*, for example, Pliny, *n.h.*, IV.94–5.

[58]   Room, *op. cit.*, s.v. "White Sea," explains the term "white" as "north."

[59]   Tacitus, *Germania*, 45, and the fold-out map attached to the Loeb Classical Library edition; *see* further, Bunbury, *op. cit.*, map facing p. 440; and H. Ludat, "Ostsee und Mare Balticum," *Zeitschrift des Vereins für Schleswig Holsteinsche Geschichte*, 76 (1952), pp. 1–23.

"Venedicus gulf," stating that it was a bay of the Sarmatian Ocean.[60] The sea's modern name is best understood in the languages of the nations who inhabit its southeastern shores, the Lithuanians and Latvians, known also as Balts. Although several explanations have been suggested for the name *Balt*, there is no reason why we ought not to accept the obvious fact that it means "white." In Latvian the sea's name is *Balta jūra* "white sea," from *balts* "white" and *jūra* "sea." The Latvians and other Baltic peoples viewed this sea from the east or south and named it the White Sea, because it was located in the direction of "whiteness," which in their ancient cultures symbolized the west or the north.

The same Baltic Sea, which is the "white" sea to the people who occupy its southeastern shores, has been known as "the eastern sea" by the Germanic peoples who control the sea's western approaches. Thus, in Old Norse the Baltic was called *Austrmar*, in Old Icelandic and Danish *Eystrasalt*, in Anglo-Saxon *Eastsae*, etc. In Latin documents which follow the Germanic point of view the term is *Mare orientale*. Under the influence of the Germanic languages even some peoples for whom the Baltic is the western sea use the term "eastern sea." For instance, in Finnish the Baltic is called *Itameri* "east sea." In tsarist Russia it was common to call the Baltic the *Ostzejskoe more* and the people who lived along its shore the *Ostzejcy*. The Estonians, however, have not accepted these designations and use the name *Laanemeri* "west sea," for the sea which from their point of view stretches toward sundown.[61]

******

Based on information gleaned from poets and philosophers from antiquity till modern times, we may state with a comfortable degree of certainty that North African and West Eurasian peoples applied the ancient and universal system of colors in naming the seas within their field of vision. The oldest pair of

---

[60] *Geography*, III.v.
[61] K. Inno, "Mare Balticum and Balticum," *Journal of Baltic Studies*, X.2 (1979), pp. 135–47.

thalassonyms distinguished by attributes of color are the Great Green and the Great Black of the ancient Egyptians, followed by the *Erythra thalassa*, the Southwest Asian and Balkan name for the Indian Ocean, the same which some ancient Arabian or African people knew as the Green Sea (*Prasōdēs thalassa*). The designation *Erythra thalassa*, referring to the southern segment of the Circumambient Ocean, was intelligible to speakers of Greek and Latin who called it red, although they did not know why it was red. Likewise, the designation Green Sea, referring to the eastern segment of the same Circumambient Ocean, was intelligible to the peoples of East Africa.

The use of colors in thalassonymy continued in the Middle Ages when the name *al-Bahr al-akhdar* appeared as presumably an Arab equivalent of the Great Green and *Prasōdēs thalassa*. While several bodies of water had the black attribute in antiquity, toady's Black Sea, however, was known among the learned of Hellas and Romania by the Greek name *Pontos Euxinos*, an antiphrasis of *Axenos Pontos*, itself a substitute for a word denoting the color black. The elegant, literate, Greek neologism, *Pontos Euxinos*, ultimately failed to replace the old, common name, and in all modern languages, including Greek, that sea is called "black," having regained its original attribute of color. The attribute white is attested in the names of the White Sea and the Baltic Sea, as well as in Turkish, Bulgarian, Macedonian, Arabic, and modern Greek names for the Mediterranean Sea.

Though we cannot claim that the attributes of color in the discussed thalassonyms are part of a deliberate effort, nevertheless their distribution is such that the following scheme suggests itself: Green=East (attested first as *W3d-wr* in ancient Egyptian sources as an appellation for the Circumambient Ocean and later in Greek and medieval Arabic sources as the *Prasōdēs thalassa* and *al-Bahr al-akhdar* and designating its eastern segment); Red=South (attested in the name *Erythra thalassa*); Black=North (attested in the ancient names *Km-wr, Melas kolpos, Plavi Jadran, Kyanea pelage, Temarunda*, and *Kapoit-azow*, in the tenth century as *Skoteinē thalassa*, and today in the universal name Black Sea); White=West (attested since antiquity in the Slavic, Baltic, and other languages as the names of the Baltic

Sea and the White Sea and in modern times in the Turkish and other people's names for the Mediterranean Sea).

Shores, Capes, Islands

Names of some coasts can be traced to words designating colors. It is believed that the *Côte d'Azur* (from the Arabic *azraq* "blue, azure") obtained this name from its appearance. However, in this instance, the attributed color could also stand for the east, which is the function it plays in the name *al-Bahr al-azraq* "Blue Nile." The Costa Azul in Portugal was also named by Arabs who do not seem to have designated its color counterpart. We would be more certain about this question if we could indicate a "white" or western counterpart for these coasts, as we do in the Blue Nile's western opposite, the White Nile. Nevertheless, the Costa Blanca on the Iberian Peninsula might be offered as a color counterpart for the Côte d'Azur.

The eastern regions of the Mediterranean Basin are known among West Europeans and North Americans by a number of names, such as the Middle East, Near East, Anatolia, and Levant, whose classical equivalents are *Anatolē* and *Oriens.* These terms were introduced by those ancients who believed they occupied the center of the earth, concluding they were equally distant from sunrise and sunset, Eos and Hesper. Other names for the same regions show traces of red and purple color attributes as symbols of the east as well as the south. For example, the Greek name *Phoinikē* "Phoenicia, purple land" is such a name.[62] Another example is the Greek form and explanation of the most powerful Anatolian people, the *Phryges*, from the verb *phrygō* "to shine."

The bright color attribute associated with Anatolia should perhaps be contrasted with the color black associated with the names of natural features in the northern direction, such as the Black Bay and the Black River (the *Melas*). It is possible that these colors symbolize the direction of the horizon, rather than the physical appearance of the designated objects.

---

[62]   O. Eissfeldt, "Phoiniker und Phoinikia," *PWRE*, XX.1 (1941), cols. 350–80.

Many stretches of seacoasts are known by their Greek names which mean "white strand or coast." Thus, a coastal area of Thrace was known as *Leukē Aktē* "white strand."[63] There was also a *Leukē Aktē*, in Egypt west of Alexandria, which owed its name to the white appearance of the soil. The name survives today in the Arabic designation *Ras al-abyaḍ* "white cape," a part of *Ras al-Kanais*.[64] Another *Ras al-abyaḍ*, in Tunisia, is so called because of its white rocks. The coast of Acarnania was called *Leucas* before the Trojan War. In historical time the name designated a peninsula of Acarnania, which became the Island of Leucas after the Corinthians had dug a canal through its isthmus. There is a cape on Leucas, called *Leucatos*, from which Sapho is believed to have leapt into the sea.

Many other white capes may have obtained their names from their appearance, but surely in some the attributed color reflects their location in relation to the people who had named them. Such an example may be *Capo di Leuca* on the heel of Italy whose name derives from the Greek adjective *leukos*. It may owe its white color to its western location in relation to the homeland of the Greeks who named it.

Before the Croatian Island of Korčula was named black by Croats' Greek neighbors,[65] Europe and the central ancient Greek domain, the Peloponnese, had been attributed the same color by the peoples of North Africa and Southwest Asia. Since their field of vision appears not to have ranged beyond the islands of Cyprus and Crete, they were not familiar with the contours of Europe. In the darkness extending from their shores to the North Pole they pictured the region we call Europe as a series of islands, occupied by awesome savages mixed in with the souls of the Southwest Asian dead ferried thither by the Boat of Magilum. The Semites appear to have applied to this dark quarter the name *Ereb* "darkness, the west," which the Greeks turned into Europa. Surely, the "island" of Europe was named black because it was in the direction of darkness in relation to those who named it.[66]

Herodotus, VII.25; and Strabo, Book VII, Fragment 55.
[64] Strabo, 17.1.14.
[65] *See* above, p. 146.
[66] *See* below, p. 216.

The Peloponnesus, "island of Pelops," was named after a refugee from Phrygia, whose name derives from a word for the color black (*pelops* "dark-colored"). We suggest that, like Europe, the Peloponnesus obtained its name at the time when the namegiving people believed it was the most northerly or the most westerly island they knew. The pertinent namers may have well been the Hypachaei of Cilicia[67] or those who held the Island of Rhodes, which, situated in the southeastern extremity of the Hellenic world, might have been perceived as a counterpart of the Peloponnese. It certainly was its color counterpart, for its name comes from a word for the rose. It is perhaps the island's geographical location in the direction of "redness" that engendered the belief that it was the home of the rose and rose cultivation, as well as the Isle of the Sun.[68]

The Peloponnesians, believing their island was in the center of the world, shifted the color black onto an island extending from their western shores in the direction of darkness. The island so distinguished must have been Cephalenia, because Pliny states that it had once been called Black Island.[69]

In the eastern corner of the Pontic coast, in Colchis, names of several peoples and places were accompanied by symbols of dawn and sunrise. It is there that Greek mythographers placed the Golden Fleece, Medea, King Aetes, and the Island of Aeaea, the dwelling place of Dawn. In keeping with the geography of Greek mythology dawn and youth—Medea had the secret of eternal youth—were relegated to Colchis where the ancients placed the extreme east. We may take the Crimean or Tauric Peninsula as a geographical counterpart of Dawn within the Black Sea region. There, gloom, cold, darkness, and death hovered over the shore, held by the hated Cimmerians, the dreaded Tauri, the feared Scythians, and ultimately by the supposedly inscrutable Russians. North of the coastal areas lived the *Melanchlaeni* "black-cloaks," who may have obtained this name on account of their geographical location, rather than from

---

[67] Herodotus, VII.92.

[68] H.v. Gaertingen, "Rhodos," *PWRE*, Suppl. V (1931), col. 740.

[69] Pliny, *n.h.*, IV.54; medieval Slavic inhabitants of ancient Hellas changed the name to Glavinica; *see*, Vasmer, *Die Slaven in Griechenland*, pp. 78–9.

the color of their mantles.[70] But, in the western corner of the Black Sea was *Leukē* "white island," where the shades of Achilles and Helen were united.[71] The Slavic name for the northwestern coast of the Black Sea, *Belobrežje* "white coast," may harken back to this ancient nomenclature.[72]

The Isle of *Albion*, in the ultimate "extreme" northwest, is widely believed to have been named white after the White Cliffs of Dover by voyagers coming to its shores from the continent. But, since the earliest contacts between the primitive peoples occupying Great Britain in antiquity and the advanced Mediterranean civilizations took place in Cornwall and other southwestern areas where tin was mined, some dissenters, seeking other source of the color attribute, point out that the celebrated white cliffs would not have been observed by sailors coming from the south and landing in Cornwall. The name *Cassiterides* "tin islands" is evidence not only of the purpose of their voyages, but also an indication that, like the ancient Afroasians, they, too, may have imagined the northwestern regions of the world as a series of islands.[73]

The name Albion did not necessarily apply to the whole of Great Britain, but only to the southern regions, coextensive with modern England and Wales. The northern portion of Albion, which may have been imagined as a separate island, emerged out of antiquity and the Middle Ages as Scotland, named, presumably after an Irish people called Scotti. Though the etymology of the ethnonym has not been decided upon, it is very tempting to compare the name Scotti to the Greek word *skotos* "darkness."[74] Accepting this explanation we may argue that the Isle of Albion obtained its white color attribute from the people looking at it from the continent of Europe. Like the ancient

[70] Herodotus, IV.107, says: "The Black-cloaks all wear black raiment, whence they take their name."

[71] E. Bonnell, *Beiträge zur Altertumskunde Russlands*, 2 vols. (St. Petersburg, 1882), I, p. 11; II, pp. 512–13.

[72] For location, *see*, PVL, pp. 76, 90 and note 73.

[73] On the earliest contacts between the Mediterranean Basin cultures and Britain, *see*, Pytheas of Marseilles, *Fragmente*, transl. as *Ueber das Weltmeer*, ed. by D. Stichtenoth (Cologne-Graz, 1959), *passim* and especially the fold-out map; and Bunbury, *op. cit.*, II, pp. 196ff.

[74] *Cf.*, Holder, *op. cit.*, II, col. 1406.

Afroasians and the Greeks, the ancient inhabitants of Albion attributed the color black to that peninsula of their island which extended in the direction of darkness, that is, Scotland.

When Mediterranean explorers discovered the Scandinavian Peninsula, they believed it was an island called Scandia. Among the several etymologies proposed for this name, the one which explains it from the Gothic word *skadus*, Greek *skotos* "darkness" is of course quite appealing and useful.[75] Situated next to Thule, in the extreme north, Scandia was attributed the color black because of its location in the darkest recesses of the northern quarter.

If we be allowed to suggest that ancient Eurasians with a global view had named some significant islands within their field of vision, we would propose the following color arrangement: E/S = red or rose, represented by Rhodes; W = white, occupied by Albion; N = black, the color attribute of Europe, the Peloponnesus, Cephalenia, Black Corcyra, Scotland, and Scandia.

Somewhere in that huge and uncharted void off the coasts of Europe and Africa the ancient Egyptians imagined the Isles of the Blessed, where the dead gathered. Elaborating on this African myth, Greek mythographers added a garden of golden apples guarded by the Daughters of Night.

HYDRONYMY: Names of Rivers and Lakes

We saw that among the ways of differentiating between homonymous rivers, especially between streams which come together to form a larger river, is the opposition little versus great. Among the examples adduced is the pair Timachus Maior and Timachus Minor so differentiated in late antiquity.[76] Today, these streams are called *Crni* "black" Timok and *Beli* "white" Timok. They come together at Zaječar to form the Timok River. It is clear that in Serbian the attributes of color can serve to

---

[75]   J. Svennung, *Scandinavia und Scandia: Lateinisch-Nordische Namenstudien* (Uppsala—Wiesbaden, 1963), p. 20.

[76]   *See* above, p. 79.

differentiate between homonymous streams, the function performed by their Latin equivalents *minor* and *maior.*[77]

There is no doubt that the colors attributed to the two rivers which come together at Khartoum to form the Nile, namely, the White Nile, which flows from the west, and the Blue Nile (formerly known as the Green Nile), which flows from the east, from the direction of the Green Sea, describe the rivers' geographical locations rather than the colors of their waters.[78]

In addition to the Timok and the Nile, numerous other homonymous hydronyms are differentiated by attributes of color whose function appears to designate the streams' relative geographical positions rather than the appearance of their waters. To continue with Balkan rivers, such pairs are, for example, the Drin, which is formed at Kukës in Albania from the waters of the *Crni Drin/Drini i Zi* "black Drin" and the *Beli Drin/Drini i Bardhë* "white Drin." In Serbia there are the *Bela Reka* "white river" and the *Crnojka* "blackish river." The *Bijeli* "white" Rzav and *Crveni* "red" Rzav meet at Dobrun in Bosnia and flow as the Rzav into the Drina near Višegrad. In Croatia, the Korana is formed from the *Crna Rijeka* "black river" and *Bijela Rijeka* "white river." As it descends toward the Pannonian Plain, the Korana breaks into several lakes and waterfalls called Plitvice. In eastern Bulgaria, the *Beli* Lom and the *Černi* Lom join to form the Ruski Lom, which flows by the city of Ruse into the Danube. This Lom is called "Ruski" to be distinguished from the other Lom that meets the Danube at the city of Lom. In western Bulgaria, the Iskâr River is formed from the waters of the *Černi* "black" Iskâr the *Beli* Iskâr. In Macedonia, the Mesta is formed from the *Černa* Mesta and the *Bela* Mesta. Originating in the Bihar Mountains, the *Fekete/Negru* "black" Körös/Criş and the *Fehér/Alb* "white" Körös/Criş come together at the city of Gyula in today's Hungary to form the Körös. (The Körös receives another stream which is called Körös/Criş *Sebes/Repede* "swift" for distinction.) In Ukraine the *Belyi*

---

[77]   The hydronym Timok, itself, means "black water." *See,* V. Georgiev, *Trakite i tehnijat ezik* (Sofia, 1977), p. 161. The people who live in the region of Serbia drained by the Timok River believe that four colored bulls hold the world; *see,* above, p. 161.

[78]   *EI,* III (1936), s.v. "al-Nil."

Čeremoš and the *Čornyi* Čeremoš form the Čeremoš River. The Tisa River is formed in Subcarpathian Ukraine from the *Čorna* Tysa and the *Bila* Tysa. In Slovakia the *Biely* Váh and *Cierny* Váh join and form the Váh River. From Poland to Slovakia flows the *Czarna* Orawa, where it meets the *Biela* Orava to form the Orava River, a tributary of the Váh. In Poland the *Biały* Dunajec and the *Czarny* Dunajec meet at Nowy Targ to form the Dunajec. In Germany the Schoeps, Elster, Traun, Main, Regen, and the Saar rivers are formed from color branches as follows: *Weisse* and *Schwarze* Schoeps, *Weisse* and *Schwarze* Elster, *Rote* and *Weisse* Traun, *Roter* and *Weisser* Main, *Weisser* and *Schwarzer* Regen, and the *Rote* and *Weisse* Saar.

The Danube receives the *Cerna* "black" River at Orşova in Rumania. A tributary of the Cerna's is called the *Bela* "white," which joins it at Băile Herculane.

Moving beyond Europe, we note the better known color hydronyms: the Black and White Irtyš which form the Irtyš in Siberia; near Jelalabad in Afghanistan the *Surukh-rud* "red river" receives the *Karasu* "black water"; in Africa, the state of Upper Volta, Burkina Faso, is drained by the Black Volta and the White Volta which join in Ghana to form the Volta River; in the neighboring country of the Ivory Coast, one of the tributaries of the Bandama River is called the White Bandama; the chief stream of North Vietnam is called the Red River, while the region is drained by two other major rivers with color attributes, the Black River and the White River; the Amazon receives the *Rio Negro* which in turn receives the *Rio Branco*.

On the basis of the examples cited, it is not possible to state categorically that the colors always indicate a direction of the horizon, because it is difficult to establish definite correlations between the colors and the cardinal points of the compass. Of the mentioned color pairs only the two branches of the Nile and the two which form the Elster stand in a clear east-west relation to each other. In both cases the white branches flow from the west, the blue or black from the east. In other cases the general alignment varies and also most rivers meander, so that they stand in different spatial relationship in different sections of their course. Nevertheless, it seems plausible that in some hydronyms the colors designate the directions of the horizon rather than the color of their waters.

Some color hydronyms may have been perceived and named as directional pairs, even though the rivers themselves are not connected to each other. Numerous names of rivers all over the world are obvious color words or are revealed to be such upon etymological investigation. It is natural that some of the colors are descriptive, but others must be positional. We have already mentioned the Yellow River of China, called Black River by the Mongols. This should encourage us to speculate whether there are other such names where the function of the colors is relative or positional, not fixed or descriptive.

The Volga has been known by different names among the many races that have lived on its banks. The Greeks, approximating perhaps some Iranian appellation, called it Rha. The etymology of the Russian name Volga is doubtful. Some derive it from the Proto-Slavic word *v'lga "humidity," others, tracing the name to a Finno-Ugric language, argue it comes from the Finnish adjective *valkea* "white." One of the tributaries of the Volga is the Kama and one of Kama's tributaries is called the *Belaja* "white" Kama. The Kama is known by the local Tatars as the *Ak* "white" Idyl, so that the Volga itself may be considered its color counterpart, since its Tatar name is *Kara* "black" Idyl.[79] We know that the Volga has been called the Black River by the Turkic peoples since the sixth century AD because a contemporary, Theophylact Simocatta, records its name as Til, from Itil, and explained it as *Melana* "black."[80] Later in the Middle Ages, Itil was the name of the Khazar capital, derived certainly from the river on whose banks it was built. The same city was called *al-Baydā* "white city" by the Arabs, *Belaveža* "white gate" by the Russians.[81]

The *Melas* River which flows into the Black Gulf may have obtained its name, which means "black," because, looking from the Thracian coast, it was the river that came from the north, that is, from the direction of darkness.

Ancient writers mention a river named *Axiopa* between the Danube and the Dniester. The Axiopa has not been identified

---

[79] Vasmer, *REW*, I, pp. 336–7, s.v. "Volga"; and II, p. 172, s.v. "Kama."

[80] *Historiae*, VII.7, pp. 283–4.

[81] J. Marquart, *Osteuropäische und ostasiatische Streifzüge* (Leipzig, 1903), pp. 1–5.

with any modern hydronym, but it has been suggested that the name means "black water." However, centuries later Constantine Porphyrogenitus noted in the same region of Russia an *Aspros potamos* "white river."[82] These may be two different rivers, a color pair, or one stream observed from different angles.

Macedonia's two chief rivers are the Vardar/Axius and the Bistrica/Haliacmon. Homer introduces the Axius as a river "whose stream on all earth is the loveliest water."[83] The name may have reminded the poet of the Greek word *axios* "worthy, valuable." However, it has been suggested that the hydronym Axius derives from the Old Iranian word *axšaena*, which the Greeks approximated to their own *axenos* "inhospitable" when referring to the sea, and as *axios* when relating to the river. A tributary of the Axius was called Erigon in antiquity. Like Axius, *Erigon*, called by native Macedonians *Crna Reka* "black river," also appears to derive from a word designating the color black, for instance, the Thracian *eregno* "dark."[84]

The classical name of the other major Macedonian river, the Haliacmon, is of obscure etymology, while its Slavic name Bistrica means "clear, or swift river."

The peasants and shepherds of Macedonia who lived in the valleys of the Axius and the Haliacmon seemingly saw these rivers as a black–white color pair. We surmise this from the following remark by Theophrastus:

> [T]hose who wish white young to be born lead their beasts to the Haliacmon, but to the Axius if they wish the young to be black or dark.[85]

Failing to consult the ancient writers, the Turks use the name Vardar for the Axius, while referring to the Haliacmon either as Bistrica or as *Karasu* "black water."

Many lake names have attributes of color reflecting the surrounding natural features, vegetation, animals, etc. However, there are instances where the function of the color cannot readily

---

[82] *DAI*, ch. 9; and *Commentary*, p. 57.
[83] *Iliad*, II.848–50.
[84] Georgiev, *op. cit.*, pp. 77–8.
[85] Quoted by Pliny, *n.h.*, XXXI.10.

be accounted for. For example, in northern Minnesota there is Red Lake, divided into Upper Red Lake and Lower Red Lake. The lake is drained by the Red Lake River, a tributary of the Red River. In northern Russia there is *Beloozero* "white lake." We can assume that the Minnesotan hydronym has its roots in an Indian language, while the Russian name coexists with the Finnish term *Valkea Järvi* "white lake." It is impossible to establish the function of the color attribute in these names, that is, whether it is simply descriptive or relates to a direction of the horizon.

The many blue, white, and black lakes all over the world may have been named on account of the appearance of their waters. However, we have argued that Lake Urmia's Armenian name may reflect its northern geographical position since it was the northernmost body of water known to the peoples of Mesopotamia, and the Armenian name may be a translation of some more ancient appellation. The same may be stated concerning Gökçegöl.

Curious is the case of the lake known as Lychnitis in antiquity and as Ohrid or *Belo Ezero* "white lake" by today's Macedonians. Though it is the source of the Black Drin, being situated west of Lake Prespa, the color attribute in its name may follow from Belo Ezero's western location in relation to Lake Prespa.

The Bodensee, was known in antiquity as *Lacus Venetus*. The name Veneti, as will be shown, derives from a word meaning "whites." The lake obtained its name when the Veneti occupied its shores, and the people's name was transferred to their lake.

ORONYMY: Names of Mountains

The world's oronymy includes a very high number of color attributes in all languages, from the Blue Mountains of Oregon, Black Hills of South Dakota, Green Mountains and White Mountains of Vermont, Montenegro (Crna Gora in Red Croatia and another Crna Gora in northern Macedonia) to numerous black, *kara*, and white, *ak*, mountains, *dağlar*, in the Turkic regions of Eurasia. Many ancient writers speak of mountains and mountain ranges which had entered the science of geography from myth. Some were imagined at the center, others at the edges of the known world, still others were believed to be the abode of gods or were made of gold. Many of them carry color attributes in their names or the names themselves designate colors.[86]

Without a clear knowledge of a given mountain's physical appearance and the approximate dates and locations of name-giving it is difficult to arrive at meaningful conclusions concerning the function of colors in oronymy. Nevertheless, we wish to consider here two cases where the color may indicate a mountain's location rather than its physical appearance. The first one is the westernmost mountain on Crete, which from antiquity has been called White Mountain, the birthplace of Zeus.[87] The fact that there is no readily recognizable color counterpart for this mountain ought not to be used as evidence that the white mountain of Crete obtained its name because it really appeared white. To the contrary, it is possible that in this and similar other cases the color attribute refers to geographical position rather than to appearance.

The second oronym is found in the Carpathians, a branch of which is known as the Little Carpathians, another as the White Carpathians. It is tempting to pair the White Carpathians, called *Bílé Karpaty* by the Slovaks, *Fehér Kárpátok* by the Hungarians, on the western border of Slovakia, identical with the western border of pre-1918 Hungary, with the Tatra Mountains in central and eastern Slovakia and northern Hungary. Further, the oronym *Tatra* may be likened to the name of Mount Titarium situated between Greece and Macedonia. As the source of the black river Styx, this mountain surely was also seen as black.[88]

Al-Jabal al-akhḍar "green mountains" in eastern Libya and in Oman have no color counterparts. The color appears to symbolize the east, because it is very unlikely that these particular mountains were greener than other mountains lacking the "green" distinction. The Green Mountains of Oman may owe their appellation to the neighboring Green Gulf, the name given by Arabs to the Persian Gulf and the Sea of Oman.

---

[86]   The importance of mountains in cosmography is discussed by Kirfel, *Die Kosmographie der Inder*, pp. 14ff.

[87]   Strabo, 10.4.4.

[88]   *Iliad*, 2.750–54.

The name *Lebanon* (from **laban+ ān-*) means "white mountain." It is believed that the color attribute reflects the snows that cover these mountains.[89] The same is true of the Caucasus which the Scythians called *Croucasis* "white with snow."[90]

TOPONYMY: *Names of Cities and Lands*

In our discussion of colors in Slavic cosmography we have rejected the temptation, to which some scholars have succumbed, to place all the numerous Belgrads in Slavia in spatial relations to Karakorum, suggesting rather that the color white attributed to them reflects their function as centers of religious and political power. However, we have offered the pairs Black Beaver–White Stones in Croatia and Bakonybél–Bakonycsernye in Hungary as examples of the use of color attributes for the directions of the horizon in toponymy. Here we adduce some additional examples where the colors might be positional rather than descriptive. In the valley of the Northern Bug River the towns of Czerwień (red) and Bełz (white) played significant roles in medieval history. There is no agreement regarding the function of the colors associated with the names of these towns.[91] In medieval Russia the city of Černigov (modern Ukrainian Černihiv), situated northeast of Kiev, may have been given its black color on account of its location.[92] The Hungarian city of Csongrád was given this name (originally, **Č'rn"grad"* "black city") by Danubian Slavs perhaps because it was in the direction of darkness or north of Belgrad on the Danube.[93] Csongrád may have been seen and named as the eastern color counterpart of Stolni Biograd or as the northern opposite of Belgrade.

---

[89]   M. Weippert, "Libanon," *Reallexikon der Assyriologie und vorderasiatischen Archäologie*, VI (1980–83), pp. 641–42.

[90]   Pliny, *n.h.*, VI.50.

[91]   M. Rudnicki and A. Poppe, "Bełz," *SSS*, I (1961), pp. 102–3; W. Kuraszkiewicz and T. Wąsowicz, "Czerwień," *ibidem*, p. 301.

[92]   M. Rudnicki and W. Kowalenko, "Czernihów," *SSS*, I (1961), pp. 298–9.

[93]   Kiss, *op. cit.*, pp. 166–7.

We saw that names of lands are derived from words for the cardinal points of the compass, from names of natural features, from ethnonyms, etc. Here are mentioned briefly some such names that derive from words for colors and those that are differentiated by color attributes, beginning with Europe, the land of darkness.

The ancient Greeks saw the *oikoumene* as a continuous land-mass divided into three parts: Asia, Libya, and Europe. The name *Asia* first appeared in Hittite documents as *Asuwa*, desig-nating a state in western Anatolia. In Homer's day Asia was confined to a portion of the Cayster River Valley.[94] The name *Libya* was originally a Greek name for an area of North Africa occupied by the people called Tjemehu by the Egyptians, Libyes by the Greeks. Ultimately the name Libya extended over the whole continent which we know as Africa.[95] The Latin name *Africa* derives either from the name of the town of Afer near Carthage or from the name of a Berber people.[96] Thus, the names of these two Old World continents are local native names which had become generalized in the languages of their European neighbors. Just as the peoples of Asia and Africa had no common name for their continents, so the Europeans lacked a common designation for theirs until they borrowed it from their more advanced Asian neighbors for whom Europe was the land of darkness because of its location.[97]

Though numerous explanations of the name Europa have been offered over the centuries, we choose to follow the ancient Greeks who derived it from *Europē*, Phoenix' daughter born in the Phoenician city of Tyre. The lady was abducted by Zeus, disguised as a bull, and taken to Crete whose queen she later became.[98] Among the etymologies proposed, the one which traces the name *Europa* to the Akkadian expression *erēb šamši* "darkness," and "the sun," that is, "the west," seems quite plausi-ble, and almost certain when we consider that Europa's father was Phoenix, her brother was prince Cadmus, whose name is

---

[94]   *Iliad*, 2.461; Georgacas, *op. cit.*
[95]   Stewart, *op. cit.*, p. 211; Edwards, *op. cit.*, p. 7.
[96]   Stewart, *op. cit.*, pp. 211ff.
[97]   *Ibid.*, p. 208ff.
[98]   Moschus, *Europa*.

reflected in the ethnonym Kadmonites, who lived *v'kedmah* "in front" or "to the east" of those who named them.[99] Seen from Tyre, Europe was the black, or the western, land, the front land was occupied by the Bene Qedem, Kadmonites, or Easterners, known also as the Saracens.

We have discussed the colors attributed to Egypt as a whole (black), to the two main divisions of the land (red to Lower Egypt, white to Upper Egypt), and red to the neighboring desert.[100]

The ancient Hebrews moved in and around lands named after the color red. To their south was *Edom/Idumaea*, truly a red land, for the Hebrews furnished a *hero eponymous* by the name of Esau, known also as Edom, to be the land's founder. He had a red complexion, red hair, and liked red lentils, because the people he founded settled in that quarter which their namegivers represented by the color red.[101] Their northern neighbor was Phoenicia, a land associated with the color purple. The land which their deity promised to give to them was part of the land of *Canaan* "red land."[102] Medieval Jews referred to the Slavs, Russians, and other northern peoples as Canaanites and their language as *lešn Kena'an* "Canaanitish."[103] Continuing this ancient Southwest Asian nomenclature, some observant Jews of the Diaspora refer to any land but *Eretz Israel* as Edom.

In late antiquity, a region of the Iranian plateau known also as Arachosia appeared under the Greek name *Indikē Leukē* "White India." We reject the explanation that the color reflects the white complexion of the region's inhabitants and suggest that it stands for the west or northwest in relation to the rest of India which remained unmarked.[104]

[99]   Stewart, *op. cit.*, pp. 209–210.

[100]   *See* above, p. 127.

[101]   Gen. 25:19–33; G. Beer, "Idumaea," *PWRE*, IX (1916), cols. 913–18; and Stewart, *op. cit.*, pp. 173–4.

[102]   Stadelmann, *op. cit.*, p. 10ff.

[103]   T. Kowalski, *Relacja Ibrāhīma ibn Ja'kūba z podróży do krajów słowiańskich w przekazie Al-Bekrīego* (Cracow, 1946) (=*Monumenta Poloniae historica*, n.s. t. 1), pp. 28-30.

[104]   A. Forbiger, *Handbuch der alten Geographie aus den Quellen bearbeitet*, 3 vols. (Leipzig, 1842–77), II (1843), pp. 536, 539, n. 80.

Toward the end of the seventh century the Bulgars, who had
settled in the Kuban steppe-land north of the Caucasus, were
attacked by the Khazars. A branch of the Bulgars escaped westward to the Danube area, another moved northward to the
middle Volga Valley. In Rhomaean sources the Kuban Bulgaria
appears with the modifiers: great, old, and black. It has already
been suggested that the original Bulgaria was called great
because to Balkan Bulgars it was the old country which also was
more distant, unmeasured by them, and located in the great
unknown.[105] Here, we add that the same land was called black
because it was located in the direction of darkness or to the
north in relation to the Balkan Bulgars and their neighbors.

The domain of the Vlachs in the Balkans broke down into
White and Black Valachias. This originally Slavic nomenclature
was recorded by the Rhomaeans and the Ottomans who used the
expressions *Maurovlachia* and *Kara Eflak* and *Kara Bogdan*, respectively, as well as by Venice where the term *Morlacchia*, designating the domain of transhumance pastoralists in Dalmatia,
was used.[106]

It may be appropriate to mention here briefly that Russia,
which will be treated later in more detail, was divided twofold
in the work of Constantine Porphyrogenitus. He speaks of Outer,
$Ex\bar{o}$, Russia in opposition to a presumed Inner Russia.[107] Later,
the attributes great and little were used. Both these divisions
originated among Russia's southern neighbors. In the late Middle
Ages and well into the modern age there existed a tricolor
division of Russia: red, white, and black. Today, only the name
Belarus "White Russia," as the westernmost area of Russia,
survives, while its color counterparts, Black Russia and Red
Russia are known simply as Russia and Ukraine.[108] The colors

---

[105] *See* above, pp. 81, 83.

[106] D. Mandić, "Postanak Vlaha," in *Rasprave i prilozi iz stare hrvatske
povijesti* (Rome, 1963), pp. 515–67.

[107] The name Outer Russia has caused some confusion, because it lacks
a counterpart in an Inner Russia; see, Constantine Porphyrogenitus, *DAI*, ch.
9; *Commentary*, pp. 25–6.

[108] Borščak, *op. cit.*; Mańczak, *op. cit.*; Ju.K. Begunov, "Weisse Rus' und
Weissrussen in einer Deutschen Chronik des 15. Jahrhunderts," *Forschungen
zur Osteuropäischen Geschichte*, XXVII (1980), pp. 299–305; and this
author's "Phantastische russische Familienwappen in der Deutschen 'Chronik

attributed to these divisions of Russia symbolize the cardinal points, just as the white and red color attributes in the divisions of medieval Croatia stand for the west and east, respectively.

des Constanzer Concils' aus den ersten Viertel des 15. Jahrhunderts," in the same periodical, XXX (1982), pp. 51–60.

CHAPTER V

COLORS IN ETHNONYMY

Names with attributes of color discussed so far designate natural features and human settlements, mute objects which have no perception of and no names for themselves. Generally, such objects obtain their appellations suddenly when they are first seen, imagined, or, in case of settlements, as they are being built. Individuals receive their names at birth from their earthly creators, their parents. This is not the case with clans, tribes, peoples, and nations, whose ethnogonies, ethnogeneses, and christenings are usually slow and complex processes, so that they are normally named long after their "birth." Also, the coming onto the world's stage of a new people, like the birth of a child, is often noted by others well before the people born become aware of their own separate existence signified by a common name.

Some peoples are known by the same name at home and beyond their borders, while others use one name at home (*Selbstbennenung*) and are known by one or more different names among their neighbors (*Andersbennenung*). A typical example of the first case are the Macedonians, who have been known both at home and abroad by the same name since the Argeadae dynasty established a state under the name of Macedon in the eighth century BC. The second case may be illustrated by their neighbors, those who call themselves Hellenes, but whom the Europeans know as Greeks, the Anatolians as Yunanlı.

Names of peoples may be fashioned from things heavenly or sublunary, from gods or demons, from odors which they supposedly exude, from the size or shape of their noses, or from the length of their hair. Regardless of the origin of a people's name, when a self-designation, they often give it a lofty meaning which is not normally shared by their neighbors, who tend to believe that the name must mean at best something ordinary, or even something bad.[1]

In addition to the mostly binary methods of distinguishing the homonymous ethnonyms discussed in Chapter II, colors, too, have been used from antiquity till today to differentiate ethnic groups with identical names. Using a combination of criteria, such as physical appearance and geographical origin (as in white or Caucasian), scientists classify the human race into main categories and sub-categories, reduced in common parlance according to people's colors to yellow, white, red, and black. The ancient Mediterranean basin folks had only vague notions about the peoples who, today, rightly or wrongly, are referred to as the yellow race. Within their own sphere they recognized only the black and white branches of humanity, ascribing their different complexions to the effects of climate. Thus, blacks were believed to be black because of excessive heat in their belt of the *oikoumene*. All Old World peoples were ignorant of Native Americans, who were misnamed Red Indians when they were "discovered" by modern Europeans.

From time immemorial, human beings have been perceiving and classifying each other in terms of the color of their hair, eyes, or skin. Among European whites, individuals often have nicknames which reflect their complexion, the most common being those derived from words for black, dark, yellow, blue, blond, white, and red.[2] The function of color in such personal names is either neutrally descriptive or emotive. Persons are given color attributes because of their *qualitas corporis*, but red, black, and white may also be used in reference to character. For instance, in the German-speaking realms a red-haired individual is deemed dangerous, as seen from the popular saying: *Rote Haare, Gott bewahre!*

In Homer, some color attributes accompany personal names, often as fixed epithets, as for example "the golden-haired

---

[1] *See,* the Sciri–Soulones names, above, p. 88.
[2] In ancient Rome some men were called *Niger* "black," and the Latin name *Rufus* "red" is still universally popular.

Achaeans." In Croatian epic songs the head that is cut off is normally accompanied by the fixed epithet *rusa* "russet." The line *I rusu mu odrubiše glavu* "And they cut off his russet head" appears frequently in such poetry. We saw that the ancient Indians and Iranians used colors not only as symbols of the cardinal points, but also as a basis for social organization, the caste system.[3]

The ethnonym *Aithiopes* "sunburnt" was a collective Greek appellation for the dark-skinned peoples. In Africa the term encompassed a much broader range of humanity than does its modern equivalent, Ethiopians. The Aethiopes were further subdivided into eastern and western Aethiopes. The name was used for non-African dark people as well, as for instance by Herodotus when he refers to the Aethiopes of Asia, meaning the dark-skinned Dravidian peoples of India.[4]

When contrasting the peoples of the south with those of the north, Mediterranean writers used the name Aethiopes to represent the south and to serve as a directional and color counterpart to the most populous nation of North Central Eurasia which, at a given time, stood for the north. Thus, Xenophanes of Colophon (ca. 565–470 BC), observing that people made gods in their own image, wrote: "The Aethiop saith that his Gods are snub-nosed and black, the Thracian that his have blue eyes and red hair."[5] Later, writers regarded the Scythians as the true counterparts of the Aethiopes.[6] Medieval Muslims made similar observations by contrasting African blacks with Slavs because they saw the latter as the principal European people in their day.[7]

[3] *See* above, Ch. III.

[4] Herodotus, III.94.

[5] Fragment 16; *see* further, F.M. Snowden, Jr., *Blacks in Antiquity* (Cambridge, Mass., 1970), p. 25.

[6] Strabo, 1.2.28.

[7] *See* below, Ch. VIII.

In this chapter we examine some ethnonyms which derive from words denoting color and some of those that are accompanied by color designators, in order to reach a better understanding of the significance of colors in the names of certain peoples of North Central Eurasia and of Russia in particular.

BLACK-HEADS—WHITE SYRIANS

We saw that the Sumerians called themselves *Sag-ud-da* "black-heads." Today, the Australian aborigines refer to themselves as *Kori* "black fellows." The name of the African *Gaetuli* often appears with the attribute *melas* "black," *i.e.*, *Melanogaetuli*. It is plausible that they were called "black" because they appeared so to European whites.[8] The same Saharan region, once occupied by the Melanogaetuli, is today the domain of the *Tuaregs*, called "blue men" by their neighbors. The common explanation for this appellation is that the indigo of their blue caftans, rubbing on their skin, makes them look blue. The function of the color attribute in the name of these modern Africans seems to be purely descriptive.

There are many peoples who lived in the direction opposite to Africa, *i.e.*, in the north, or toward darkness, in a region which has always been the domain of whites, yet carry the attribute black in their names. Thus, for example, ancient writers speak profusely of the *Melanchlaeni* "black cloaks" who were supposedly given this name due to their black overcoats. They also knew well the *Sauromatae* or *Sarmatae*, whose name, too, may mean "black-overcoats." We, however, suggest that, rather than being descriptive, the black attribute attached to these names is positional. These people were called black because they lived in the north in relation to the folks who named them, those living *wo die Zitronen blühn*. In fact, we saw that the latter eventually transferred to the same northern quarter the

---

[8] Strabo, 7.3.2; Ptolemy, *Geography*, IV.vi, Tabula IV, Africae; H. Dessau, "Gaetuli," *PWRE*, VII (1912), cols. 464–5.

black river Styx, black Hades, the black dog Cerberus, black night, black cold, black death, and the black Cimmerians.[9]

We saw that the ancients associated the Phoenicians with the color purple inherent in the Greek form of their name, and believed that they originated from the shores of the Red Sea. We have argued that the color connotation in the name of the sea symbolized the south. Indeed, the Phoenician ethnonym reflects the same direction of the horizon as does the Red Sea.

The *Edomites* "reds" dwelt in the direction of the sun, the desert, and "redness" in relation to the Hebrews, prompting the latter to create *Esau*, a man with reddish hair who liked red lentils, to be their founder. Also, the name *Canaanites* "reds" reflected that people's geographical location in relation to those who had named them.

Perhaps the oldest known people who were distinguished from their namesakes by an attribute of color were the White Syrians. Those Syrians (and/or Assyrians) who settled in Cappadocia Pontica, became eventually known as *Leukosyroi* "White Syrians." Apollonius Rhodius, writing in the third— second century BC about the mythical voyage of the Argonauts, calls the land around Sinope the "Assyrian land." He applies the same name to an area stretching between the estuaries of the Halys, and the Iris rivers. The scholiasts added the designation *Leukosyria* to the name of this Assyrian land to indicate that it was more common than the one used by Apollonius.[10] Strabo quotes Pindar as evidence that a region of Cappadocia known as Themyscira had belonged to the Syrians in antiquity. By Strabo's time the Pontic Syrians had become known as White Syrians. The geographer explains:

> As for the Paphlagonians, they are bounded on the east by the Halys River, "which," according to Herodotus, "flows from the south between the Syrians and the Paphlagonians and empties into the Euxine Sea, as it is called"; by "Syrians," however, he means the "Cappadocians," and in fact they are still to-day called "White

[9] We hope to treat this and other ethnonyms of ancient Russia in a separate study.

[10] Apollonius Rhodius, *Argonautica*, II.946–8; 963–4; W. Ruge, "Leukosyroi," *PWRE*, XII.2 (1925), cols. 2291–3.

Syrians" (*Leukosyroi*), while those outside the Taurus are called
"Syrians." As compared with those this side of the Taurus, those
outside have a tanned complexion, while those this side do not,
and for this reason received the appellation "white."[11]

Two explanations of the "whiteness" of the Pontic Syrians have
been offered by modern commentators. One, following Strabo,
refers the color attribute to the supposedly light complexion of
the Pontic Syrians. The other involves the root *Lukki-*, *Lyko-*, the
presumed bases of the names of the river Lycus, of the countries
of Lycia and Lycaonia, etc., which the Greeks allegedly
rendered through the process of folk-etymology as *leukon*,
"white."[12] In other words, those who defend the second version
of the color's origin imagine that some ancient namegiver attributed the color white to the Pontic Syrians because they lived
in a region abounding in names which, through folk-etymology,
became associated with the Greek adjective "white," not because
the Assyrians of Anatolia were truly a whiter branch of the
Syrian nation. We find both explanations unconvincing.

If the Pontic Syrians were the only people differentiated from
their relatives and namesakes by the attribute "white," we would
have no ground upon which to reject these explanations.
However, in light of the conclusions we reached in Chapters III
and IV, it is more plausible that the "*leuko-*" part of the name
Leukosyroi became attached to the name Assyroi or Syroi to indicate that these people lived west of other Syrians. Indeed, one
can not seriously entertain the postulation that, having mixed
with the people in Anatolia, the complexion of the immigrants
from the Fertile Crescent had truly taken on a paler shade. In
other words, the white attribute in the designation *Leukosyroi*
has to refer to their westerly location.

This appellation may have been coined by the Medes after
they had conquered Assyria and established their control as far
west as the Halys River. From the Median point of view, beyond
that river extended the domain of their rivals, the Lydians.
Under Lydian rule lived a branch of the Syrian nation whom the

[11]   Strabo, 12.3.9.
[12]   Ruge, *op. cit.*

Medes named White Syrians for distinction. In Herodotus' day the new appellation had not yet become common, so he called these people "the Syrians of the valleys of the Thermodon and the Parthenius," designating the main branch of the Syrian people as the "Syrians of Palestine."[13] But in Strabo's, Appian's,[14] and Ptolemy's[15] time the name White Syrians was current at least among the people's neighbors. The original positional meaning of the color attribute had given way to a descriptive interpretation, and the people's complexion was indicated as the reason for the color attribute.[16]

Centuries after the White Syrians had lost their ethnicity and name by assimilating with their Anatolian neighbors, the white color attribute acquired a fresh meaning when Constantine Porphyrogenitus declared that the ancient inhabitants of the Rhomaean province of Armeniacon (Roman Cappadocia Pontica) had been called *Leukosyroi* "White Syrians" in contrast to the *Melanosyroi* "Black Syrians," a term coined by Porphyrogenitus for color symmetry.[17]

A few years after Porphyrogenitus wrote the above, Liudprand of Cremona discovered the color connotation in the Russian ethnonym and attributed it to the people's appearance. To clarify the origin and meaning of the name Russi we begin our search in ancient Paphlagonia, situated slightly west of the homeland of the White Syrians, and occupied in Homer's days by a people called Eneti. Since this ethnonym is regarded by most authorities as the *Urform* of the name Venedae (and, of course of Austr-Winðar), it is necessary to discuss its various metamorphoses while weighing the possibility that it was carried by Anatolian migrants to Slavia, Italy, Gaul, Venedia, and Antia.

---

[13]   Herodotus, II.104.
[14]   Appian, *Mithridatic Wars*, 69.
[15]   Ptolemy, *Geography*, V.vi.
[16]   *Cf.*, A.H. Krappe, "The Leucosyrians," *Armenian Quarterly*, I/1 (1946), pp. 101–7.
[17]   *De thematibus*, II. 35–6.

THE VENEDAE–THE ANTAE, WHITES–REDS

Ever since they began to record their thoughts and actions in their own language, the Russians have known that they were both Russians and Slavs, with the two names used synonymously. The name Slav has, since the beginning of the Middle Ages, been both a general foreign name for and a self-designation by peoples of Europe east of the rivers Tilment/ Tagliamento, Aniža/Enns, Salava/Saale, and Laba/Elbe, called also the Trieste–Hamburg line. The Slavs, a conglomerate of closely related peoples regarded as an ethno-linguistic monolith by outsiders, have throughout their history been aware of their common origin. Other general designations for the Slavic peoples current among their neighbors, but apparently not used as *Selbstbennenung* in historical times, included the names Venedae and Antae. The name Venedae survives into our days in colloquial German as *Wenden/Winden* "Slavs" and in Estonian as *Venelane* "Russian" and *Venemaa* "Russia" (the Finnish equivalents are *Venäläinen* and *Venäjä*). The name Antae designated peoples who lived *anti* "in the front, at the end" of the Venedae and other Slavic peoples. It has not survived. Since the name Venedae is the earliest attested of many names applied to the Russians by their neighbors, we begin by tracing its origin.

The name *Venedae*, which yielded *Wenden* in German, *Venäläinen* in Finnish, resembles numerous geographical names and ethnonyms attested through the whole Indo-European language area, from India to Great Britain, from Paphlagonia to the Baltic, and from Homer to this day. The current scholarly consensus is that they are related to the names Veneti and Eneti, and that they all derive either from the Italo-Celtic *ven-e-to-* (from the root **ven-* "desire, love"[18]), or from the Celtic *uindo-s* "white, beautiful" (Breton *gwen* "white").[19] In the Roman and East Roman empires the adjective *venetus/ouenetos,* deriving from the ethnonym Veneti, took on the meaning of "(light) blue" and was attributed to a faction at the hippodromes.[20]

---

[18]   F. Sławski and G. Labuda, "Wenedowie," *SSS*, VI (1977), pp. 373–8.
[19]   P. Merlat, "Veneti," *PWRE*, XXXII.1 (1955), cols. 707–8.
[20]   *See*, above, pp. 155–60.

The Finnic name for Russia is related to the names of the modern Italian provinces of Veneto and Friuli-Venezia Giulia, to the name Wendland in Lower Saxony, and to the name of the province of Vendée in France. Closer scrutiny reveals a number of names of peoples, settlements, and natural features which derive from *ven-e-to* or *uindo-s*. With the exception of the Adriatic Veneti,[21] no other people whose name derives from *ven-* or *uindo-s* have left sufficient evidence about their language to determine their family affiliation. However, we are justified in claiming some of the peoples so designated for the Slavic family because today two languages, both belonging to the Slavic branch of the Indo-European family, may be called "Venetic." One is *Venäjän kieli*, the Finnish name for the language of the Russians, the other is *Wendisch*, a colloquial German name for the language of the Slavs of the former German Democratic Republic.[22]

The ubiquitousness of the names Eneti (Heneti), Veneti, Venedae is, perhaps, the reason why so many writers, from the ancient Greeks to modern scholars, have been offering explanations based on the assumption that the identity or similarity of names presupposes the identity of peoples, and that the appearance of same or similar names in from each other distant regions is the result of migrations. This path is not followed here, for we are not insisting that all ethnonyms that may be analyzed as "white" or "beautiful" designate the same ethnic group, or that the people so designated migrated from some common original homeland. Rather, we submit that ancient namegivers used these appellations for certain peoples because of their relative geographical position, irrespective of their affiliation.

---

[21]   Traces of their language are found in votive inscriptions written in a script borrowed from the Etruscans. Venetic was presumably spoken in the Po Valley from an unknown date until that region of Italy was conquered by the Romans, and the natives switched to Latin.

[22]   In the past, other languages of the Polabian Slavs as well as that spoken by the Sorbs of East Germany and the language of the Slovenes used to be designated as *Wendisch* and *Windisch* by the Germans. Although today Sorbian is officially called *Sorbisch* and Slovene *Slovenisch* by Germans, colloquially the Wendisch name survives as a reminder that in the past the Slavs were called *Wenden* by their Germanic neighbors.

We suggest that the Slavic ethnonyms Venedae and Antae be examined against the background of similar names of natural features, settlements, and peoples. Joining those scholars who explain the name Venedae from the Celtic word *uindo-s* "white," we invite them to consider our suggestion that the name Antae derives from the preposition *anti*, attested in this and similar forms in a variety of languages throughout the Indo-European area. The name does not have to be "Slavic" to designate Slavs, for there is no evidence that the people called Antae ever used the name themselves. This is only natural, for it would be strange for a people to call themselves "the anti" people. The ethnonym Antae, like such "ethnonyms" as "fish-eaters, man-eaters, cave-dwellers," etc., is the product of the imagination of others, not of the people named.

The Eneti–Antenor

The earliest attested namesakes of the Venedae, Venelased, Wenden, and Austr-Winðar are the Eneti of Paphlagonia. They are mentioned in the following verse of the *Iliad*:

> Pylaimones the wild heart was leader of the
> Paphlagones,
> from the land of the Enetoi where the wild
> mules are engendered,
> those who held Kytoros and those who dwelt
> about Sesamos,
> those whose renowned homes were about
> Parthenios river,
> and Kromna and Aigialos and high Erythinoi.[23]

The name *Enetoi* was another designation for the Paphlagones, whose domain extended from the Black Sea southward, slightly past the city of Gangra. On the west, Paphlagonia was

---

[23]   *Iliad*, II.851–5; *see* also, Strabo, 12.3.10.

demarcated by the Parthenius River, on the east by the Halys.[24]
The towns mentioned in the quoted verses were and remained
minor settlements on the coast of Paphlagonia. Only Sesamus,
eventually renamed Amastris, grew into an important city and
played a role in the history of Russia.[25] Although, according to
the indications given by Homer, the Eneti lived in Paphlagonia,
near the mythical Amazons and the historical White Syrians,
later writers found no Eneti in that area.

The fact that no Eneti were found in historical times in
Paphlagonia gave rise to speculations. Did Herodotus ignore the
Paphlagonian Eneti because he felt no need to include all the
peoples found in Homer? Yet, he mentions the Eneti of Illyria
and those of northern Italy. According to Strabo, Zenodatus had
amended Homer's phrase "from the Enetoi" to "from Enete"
claiming that the poet had in mind not a people but a place.
Others, refusing to amend Homer but wanting to account for the
people's disappearance, argued that the Eneti had joined the
raiding Cimmerians and, "driven to the Adriatic Sea," reappeared
there as the Veneti. Strabo states his own opinion as follows:

> But the thing upon which there is general agreement is, that the
> Eneti, to whom Pylaemones belonged, were the most notable tribe
> of the Paphlagonians, and that, furthermore, these made the
> expedition with him in very great numbers, but, losing their
> leader, crossed over to Thrace after the capture of Troy, and on
> their wanderings went to the Enetian country, as it is now called.
> According to some writers, Antenor and his children took part in
> the expedition and settled at the recess of the Adriatic, as
> mentioned by me in my account of Italy. It is therefore reasonable
> to suppose that it was on this account that the Eneti disappeared
> and are not to be seen in Paphlagonia.[26]

---

[24]   In antiquity, the Halys River was frequently recognized as a political
or cultural boundary.

[25]   Dvornik, *Les Slaves,* p. 58, n. 1.

[26]   12.3.9.

The Eneti—the Antani

Expanding upon Strabo's abbreviated description of the migration of the Eneti, we intend to show that the Eneti and their positional counterparts, the Antae, who symbolically appeared in Asia Minor under the anthroponym Antenor, were ensconced in Macedonia as neighbors of the Dardani, a people with a name almost identical with those of Troy whom the Eneti had come to help against the Greek assailants.

The Balkan route of the migration of the Eneti from Paphlagonia and Troy to the Adriatic appears to be confirmed by Herodotus who mentions the Eneti twice in his book. First, he refers to them as "the Eneti in Illyria."[27] Then, he names the Eneti in connection with the Danubian Syginnae whose borders "reach as far as the Eneti on the Adriatic Sea."[28] The latter Eneti were those of northern Italy whose easternmost domain stretched as far as the Tilment/Tagliamento River, the medieval boundary between Slavs and speakers of Romance dialects. It is not clear whether in Herodotus' day the Balkan and Apennine Eneti had more in common than the name.

Another mention of the Balkan Eneti occurs in Appian. After his victory over Mithridates' armies in Greece, the Roman general Sulla, deciding to secure the borders of Roman Macedonia,

> marched against the Eneti, the Dardani, and the Sinti, tribes on the border of Macedonia, who were continually invading the country, and devastated their territory. In this way he exercised his soldiers and enriched them at the same time.[29]

These Eneti, identical with those mentioned by Herodotus, were a Balkan people and neighbors of the Dardani, who lived in the present-day Republics of Macedonia and Kosova. The available data indicate that, from the time of Herodotus to that of Sulla, the Eneti were a Balkan people whose ancestors might have

---

[27] I.196.
[28] I.196.
[29] *Mithridatic War*, 55.

migrated from Paphlagonia, perhaps in company of their erstwhile allies, the Dardanians of Troy.

We suggest that the true meaning of the name Eneti in Macedonia is confirmed by their positional opposites, the Antani, a subdivision of an Illyrian people called Atintani. Whereas for the Eneti of Asia Minor we assume a positional opposite symbolically represented by Antenor, in the Balkans the real Antani served that purpose. The name Antani reemerged in the sixth century simultaneously in the Balkans and in Russia in the form of Antae. A Macedonian city called Antania by Constantine Porphyrogenitus is evidence of a continuous presence of this people in the Balkans.[30] The Macedonian Eneti and Antani, along with numerous other peoples mentioned by Greek and Roman writers, were submerged by Slavs in the Early Middle Ages, and their particular names vanished. However, the name Eneti reappeared in the Balkans when a twelfth-century Rhomaean writer, Anna Komnena, reintroduced on the pages of history a people whose name resembles that of the ancient Eneti. In a marginal note she added to her description of the Battle of Dyrrachium (1107), Anna defines the Adriatic Sea as:

> A vast body of almost land-locked water, of great length, dividing our land from Italy and extending as far as the barbarian Vetones with a bend to the northeast. Opposite them is the land of the Apulians.[31]

By their location indicated here, the Vetones were coastal inhabitants of Illyria who, at that time, were called Croats. Recently, a scholar argued that the Vetones were in fact the Venedae, and that this was the name for the Balkan Serbs who had allegedly originated from Baltic Venedia.[32] We reject this opinion because we have shown that evidence for a migration of Balkan Slavs from beyond the Carpathians is lacking.[33] Further, since neither

---

[30]   *See* above, Ch. II, p. 64, note 22.
[31]   *Alexiad*, XII.9.
[32]   R. Novaković, *Odakle su Srbi došli na Balkan* (Belgrade, 1977), pp. 107–12.
[33]   Bačić, *The Emergence of the Slavs*, p. 302.

the Serbs nor any other South Slavic people used the name Venedae as self-designation in the High Middle Ages, Anna Komnena could not have heard it from them. It is likely that Anna found the name Eneti in Herodotus, Appian, or some other ancient writer and applied it to the people who called themselves Croats. She did this frequently, as may be seen from a number of archaic names she uses for the various peoples who in her day were known by their "new barbaric" names. Probably, she reasoned that, since she could not find it in Herodotus, the Croatian ethnonym, as a "barbaric" innovation, had to be avoided. Instead, she may have found the names Eneti, Heneti, Veneti, which, due perhaps to scribal error eventually turned into Vetones.[34]

The Veneti—Antenor, Andiantes, the Vindelici

In Strabo's day, the Po Valley was divided into Gallia Cispadana and Gallia Transpadana. Since the Celts were the dominant people on both sides of the Alps, northern Italy was also called Cisalpine Gaul in order to be distinguished from Transalpine Gaul, an area covering modern France, Belgium, Luxembourg, and parts of Germany. Besides the various Celtic peoples, other ethnic groups lived in Cisalpine Gaul including the "autochthonous" Ligurians, as well as the Heneti or Veneti. Concerning their origins Strabo says:

> Now these Celti are indeed of the same race as the Transalpine Celti, but concerning the Heneti there are two different accounts: Some say that the Heneti too are colonists of those Celti of like name who live on the ocean-coast; while others say that certain of the Heneti of Paphlagonia escaped hither with Antenor from the Trojan war, and, as testimony to this, adduce their devotion to the breeding o horses—a devotion which now, indeed, has wholly disappeared, although formerly it was prized among them, from the fact of their ancient rivalry in the matter of producing mares for mule-breeding. Homer, too, recalls this fact: "From the land of

---

[34] It is unlikely that Anna had in mind the Vettones who lived in ancient Portugal (*see*, Lucan, *Pharsalia*, IV.9).

the Heneti, whence the breed of the wild mules." Again, Dionysius, the tyrant of Sicily, collected his stud of prize-horses from here, and consequently not only did the fame of the Henetian foal-breeding reach the Greeks but the breed itself was held in high esteem by them for a long time.[35]

And in a section on Gaul, where he speaks of the Veneti (Ounetoi) who were a coastal branch of the Belgae, the geographer writes:

> It is these Veneti, I think, who settled the colony that is on the Adriatic (for about all the Celti that are in Italy migrated from the transalpine land, just as did the Boii and Senones), although, on account of the likeness of name, people call them Paphlagonians. I do not speak positively, however, for with reference to such matters probability suffices.[36]

It is clear that Strabo was puzzled about the origin of the Adriatic Veneti. As a native Anatolian, he was emotionally neutral and not too eager to defend the Asian, that is, the more illustrious descent of these western barbarians. Therefore, he was willing to accept the opinion that they had migrated from the barbarous Atlantic. On the other hand, the Roman historian Livy, desiring illustrious ancestors for his own people, accepted the belief that the Veneti, led by Antenor, had immigrated to Italy from Troy. He says:

> First of all, then, it is generally agreed that when Troy was taken vengeance was wreaked upon the other Trojans, but that two, Aeneas and Antenor, were spared all the penalties of war by the Achivi, owing to long-standing claims of hospitality, and because they had always advocated peace and the giving back of Helen. They then experienced various vicissitudes. Antenor, with a company of Eneti who had been expelled from Paphlagonia in a revolution and were looking for a home and a leader—for they had lost their king, Pylaemenes, at Troy—came to the inmost bay of

[35]   5.1.4. *See* further, J. Untermann, "Veneti," *PWRE*, Suppl. XV (1978), cols. 855—98.
[36]   4.4.2.

the Adriatic. There, driving out the Euganei, who dwelt between the sea and the Alps, the Eneti and Trojans took possession of those lands. And in fact the place where they first landed is called Troy, and the district is therefore known as Trojan, while the people as a whole are called the Veneti.[37]

Modern scholars reject Livy's Paphlagonian origin of the Veneti, as they reject the Trojan origin of the Romans. A frequently adduced argument against placing the original Venetic homeland in Anatolia is the fact that their language and culture supposedly do not show Anatolian elements. True, but we must allow for the possibility that they lost such elements en route through the Balkans where they picked up new ones. Though the ancient belief in the Anatolian origin of the Veneti rested on the similarity of their name with that of the Eneti, nevertheless, a migration of the Veneti from east to west has perhaps a historical basis, since in western Eurasia civilization expanded from east to west and from south to north carried by people moving in these directions.

According to classical tradition, the Eneti were led west by Antenor, who was a Trojan, not an Enetian, and a counsellor of King Priam. We mention this because the other names which closely resemble the original Eneti/Veneti appear paired together with names that approximate that of Antenor. We saw that the Eneti of Macedonia were paired with the Antani. We shall also see that the presumably Celtic Veneti in Gaul had the Andes for neighbors, while those who clearly belonged to the Slavic family may be paired with the Antae. The anthroponym *Antenor* ("opposite or front man") perhaps stands for an ethnonym, which, like the names Antani, Andes, and Antae, also derives from the preposition *anti*. It is noteworthy that near Mantua, in Gallia Transpadana, stood the town of Andes, Virgil's birthplace, called Pietola today. However, we suggest that the Adriatic Veneti be paired with the Andiantes of the Croatian province of Slavonia.[38]

[37] I.1.1–3.
[38] *See* below, pp. 252–3.

From their Adriatic homeland the Veneti appear to have
expanded northward. We saw that Livy said that the people
whom Antenor had led to the Adriatic pushed the native
Euganeans into the Alps, where they were known to have lived
in historical times.[39] The Alps, as mountains generally, served
as refuge for people who could not stand the pressure in the
lowlands. Today, as a result of this process, the Alps offer an
ethnic mosaic made of speakers of Romance, Germanic, and
Slavic languages. In antiquity, the ethnic picture was also
complex, when the Alpine country of modern Italy, Switzerland,
Germany, Austria, and Slovenia was inhabited by a variety of
peoples. The Rhaeti, Carni, Norici, and Tauri, who were considered autochthonous, received and gradually absorbed Celtic
immigrants from the west and Italic, Celtic, and Venetic
refugees fleeing Roman conquerors of Cisalpine Gaul and
Venetia.

In historical times a people called Vindelici also settled in the
Alps, and they appear to be related to the Veneti.[40] We have
already suggested that this ethnonym is a diminutive form of the
name Veneti. The Alpine Vindelici or Vindolici obtained their
name because they were perceived as a branch of the Veneti.
We propose that the Vindelici descended from those Veneti
whom the Romans, pushing from the south, and the Celts,
penetrating their country from the west and north, had expelled
from their native Venetia. Since other peoples moved from south
to north before the advancing Romans, we may assume that
some Veneti were among them, and that their name changed to
Vindelici in their new country. To corroborate this statement, we
point to the fate of the Boii, a people expelled from the Po
Valley and pushed across the Alps into Pannonia by the
victorious Romans. They eventually found rest in the upper
Laba/Elbe Valley where the name Bohemia, signifying "home of
the Boii," testifies to their sojourn. Further, a branch of the Boii
were called Boisci, a diminutive form of the ethnonym Boii. It
is natural to suppose that some Veneti also migrated northward,
although this migration is not recorded in the extant sources.
The name of the emigrants was consistently rendered as

---

39   I.1.
40   R. Heuberger, "Vindelici," *PWRE*, IXA.1 (1961), cols. 1–17.

Vindelici or *Vindolici* in Latin, *Uindolikioi* in Greek, and, from them, the eastern portion of Rhaetia was informally known as Vindelicia. The pair Venetia–Vindelicia should be compared to the neighboring pair Carniola–Carantania, where the diminutive and augmentative suffixes differentiate homonymous lands occupied by the Carni, ancestors of the Croats and Slovenes.

The Vindelici have left behind a number of place names that bear witness to their presence. Chief among these is Augusta Vindelicum, modern Augsburg. Other less known toponyms in Bavaria, Austria, Italy, and Switzerland derive from the ethnonym Wind or Wend. Since this was the German name for Slavs, it is not always possible to make precise conclusions concerning the origin of such names, that is, whether they go back to the Italic Veneti or to the Slavic Venedae. For instance, the ancient name of the Bodensee, Lacus Venetus, testifies only to the fact that there was a time when the people who lived along its shores were called Veneti by their neighbors. These may have been the same people who were otherwise known as the Vindelici. In Austria, the mountain peak Gross Wenediger was named either after the Adriatic Veneti, the Alpine Vindelici, or after the Slavic Venedae. On the other hand, the German name of the town of Windischgrätz, known also as Slovenj Gradec, in Styria (today, Slovenia), clearly derives from the German name for Slavs and the Slavic word *gradec* (diminutive) "town."

The ancients have transmitted down to us very little inform-ation about the origin of the Vindelici. The Romans discovered, defeated, and subjected the Vindelici to their rule. Polybius, Pliny, Tacitus, and Dio speak of them in connection with Roman warlike activities in the Alps. Horace mentions the Vindelici in the following verses:

> even such was Drusus as the Vindelici beheld him waging war beneath the Rhaetian Alps. Whence was derived the custom that through all recorded time arms their right hands with the Amazonian battle-axe, I have forborne to seek, nor is it vouchsafed to know all things; but the hordes long victorious on many a field were vanquished by the young hero's wisdom, and

were made to feel the potency of head and heart fitly nurtured beneath an auspicious roof, and of Augustus' fatherly devotion to the youthful Neros.[41]

The Amazonian battle-axe points in the direction of Anatolia, where, in Homer's day, the Eneti, the namesakes of the Veneti, lived as neighbors of the women warriors. We may interpret this poetic evidence as a vague hint that Horace thought the Vindelici and the Veneti had originated from Asia Minor.

Summing up our conclusions, we may say: Having encountered identical or similar names of peoples in distant from each other regions of the world, the ancients reasoned that the peoples themselves must have migrated from one common homeland. Since their name appears to be identical with that of the Paphlagonian Eneti and the Atlantic Veneti, some ancients "knew" the Adriatic Veneti were immigrants either from Asia Minor or from the shores of the Atlantic Ocean. Livy, and perhaps Horace, sought the original homeland of the Veneti in Asia. They are justified because the Asian Eneti were known long before their namesakes of northern Italy. Judging by their language, the Adriatic Veneti belonged to the Italic branch of the Indo-European family, though some dissenters suggest they were Illyrians. It is commonly believed that the Italic peoples, including the Veneti, came to the Apennine Peninsula from the Middle Danube Basin or from the Balkan Peninsula. Some contemporary scholars have been directing our attention to the Transcarpathian homeland of the Venedae, in modern Poland, as the country of origin of both the Eneti and all the Veneti.[42]

As to the Vindelici, though clearly a branch of the Veneti, it is difficult to separate them from the Rhaeti, for both peoples seem to have settled in a mosaic-like fashion, mingling among each other and other peoples. After conquering the country, the Romans simplified the ethnic picture, and, by ignoring the Vindelici and other peoples, named the province Rhaetia. Later, they divided the land into Rhaetia I and II. The Romans are justly reproached for practicing the policy of *divide et impera*.

---

[41]   *Odes*, IV.iv.18.
[42]   *See* below, p. 263.

However, in the Alps and the Balkans they also practiced the policy of *e pluribus unum*. Not only did they unite the lands of the Rhaeti, Vindelici, and other peoples into one Rhaetia, but they also made this province, for the purpose of taxation and customs, a part of the already enlarged province of Illyria. For this reason the Vindelici have been treated as "Illyrians" by some modern scholars. It has also been suggested that they were Celts. Although the name Vindelici may be Celtic, this fact alone is not sufficiently indicative of their nationality, especially since the Celtic form may be an adaptation of some vanished native ethnonym. Nevertheless, by attaching Vindelicia to Illyria, the Romans may have recognized and acknowledged some ethno-linguistic kinship between the inhabitants of the two lands. Expanding upon this theme, we suggest that the Adriatic Veneti and the Vindelici were related to the Andiantes and the Antani, their positional counterparts in Slavonia and Macedonia, and to the Eneti, their namesakes in Macedonia, while the ultimate roots of all these groups go back to the Eneti of Paphlagonia and to their leader Antenor.

The Veneti—the Andes, and the Venelli

It is generally agreed that the Celts arrived in Gaul, Iberia, to the Isle of Albion, and Ireland from their homeland in the upper Rhine and upper Danube valleys, to which, in turn, they came from the steppes of Russia. Gaul was established on the pages of history through Caesar's celebrated treaties *De Bello Gallico*, written in the winter of 52–51 BC. In the opening lines, memorized by generations of school children, the conqueror of Gaul says:

> Gaul is a whole divided into three parts, one of which is inhabited by the Belgae, another by the Aquitani, and a third by a people called in their own tongue Celtae, in the Latin Galli. All these are different one from another in language, institutions, and laws. The Galli (Gauls) are separated from the Aquitani by the river Garonne, from the Belgae by the Marne and the Seine. Of all these peoples the Belgae are the most courageous, because they are farthest removed from the culture and the civilization of the Province, and least often visited by merchants introducing the

commodities that make for effeminacy; and also because they are nearest to the Germans dwelling beyond the Rhine, with whom they are continually at war.[43]

Gallia was a name used by foreigners for modern France, Belgium, and Luxembourg which in antiquity were occupied by Gauls and other peoples. We do not know whether the Gauls or their neighbors had a common name for the same land or whether they even saw it as a whole. Starting from the south, the direction of the Roman conquest, the first part of Gaul that was annexed to the Roman state was the region around the city of Narbonne. It was made into a Roman province in 121 BC and named *Provincia Narbonensis*. In common parlance it was known as *Provincia*, from which the name *Provence* derives. Also, that section of Gaul was known as *Gallia togata* "robed Gaul" in opposition to *Gallia comata* "hairy Gaul." The name *Aquitania* appears to be a Latin translation of some native term signifying "waterland or coastland."[44] Belgica was named after the Belgae, a people whose name some scholars liken to the Belcae, introduced by Pytheas of Marseille.[45] The ethnonym Belgae is commonly explained from the Celtic word *belgae* "strong."[46] In characterizing the Belgae as the most courageous among the Celts and contrasting them with the effeminate inhabitants of Provincia, Caesar shared the prevailing belief

---

[43] I.1.

[44] The name Aquitania may be compared to numerous similar names, such as Slavic regions named after the sea, *more*, and, of course, to the coastal region of Belgica known as *Armorica* "sealand."

[45] *See* below, p. 246.

[46] M. Ihm, "Belgae," *PWRE*, III.1 (1897), col. 207. The ethnonym has also reminded some scholars of the Old Irish *bolgaim* "I swell," others of the Old High German *belgan*, Middle High German *belgen* "to swell, be angry," in the sense of puffy, angry or strong ones. The commonly accepted explanation of the name Belgae as the "strong ones" may be a folk etymology, a self-flattering interpretation of an ethnonym which may also derive from a word for the color white. At the time of Caesar's campaigns the Belgae were the most northerly and most westerly Celts who may have obtained their name on account of their geographical location in relation to other Celts and to other Indo-Europeans.

among the civilized peoples of Southwest Asia, the Balkans, and Rome of his time that savagery and warlike traits increased with distance from centers of civilization. As a man of action and a warrior, he admired the warlike character of the Belgae, but as a civilized southerner, he considered their way of life primitive and inferior to his own.

The names Veneti and Andes appear for the first time in the following passage:

> At the same season Publius Crassus, whom he [sc. Caesar] had despatched with one legion against the Veneti, Venelli, Osismi, Curiosilitae, Esubii, Aulerici, and Redones, the maritime states which border upon the Ocean, reported that all those states had been brought into subjection to the power of Rome. ... As soon as the legions had been withdrawn to winter quarters among the Carnutes, the Andes, the Turones, and such states as were near the scenes of the recent campaign, he himself [sc. Caesar] set out for Italy.[47]

The two peoples are mentioned again in connection with a rebellion of the defeated Gauls. The war broke out as Publius Crassus, commander of the Seventh Legion, was

> wintering by the Ocean in the country of the Andes. As there was a lack of corn in those parts, he despatched several commandants and tribunes into the neighbouring states to seek it. Of these officers Titus Terrasidius was sent among the Esubii, Marcus Trebius Gallus among the Curiosolites, Quintus Velanius with Titus Silius among the Veneti.[48]

The Andes were also called Andecavi, while their chief city was known as Andes, the modern Angers.[49] We take the Veneti and the Andes of Gaul as a pair because of the similarity of these

---

[47] Caesar, *De Bello Gallico*, II.34–5; P. Merlat, "Veneti," PWRE, VIIIA.1 (1955), cols. 705–83.
[48] Caesar, *De Bello Gallico*, III.7.
[49] M. Ihm, "Andecavi," *PWRE*, I.2 (1894). col. 2121.

ethnonyms with the Paphlagonian Eneti– *Antae (symbolically represented by Antenor), the Macedonian Eneti–Antani, the Adriatic Veneti–the Italic *Antes (attested as the anthroponym Antenor and the toponym Andes) and the Slavonian Andiantes, and, as will be shown, with the Venedae–Antae pair of Germany, Poland, Belarus, Ukraine, and Russia. This similarity should not be dismissed as a coincidence, even though there is no positive proof that these sets of the paired names, in fact, designated peoples who were related to each other. However, regardless of their ethnolinguistic affiliation, these people might have been perceived and named by observers who belonged to the linguistic group which used the color white as a symbol of a direction of the horizon, possibly the west or the north, while designating as "anti" objects located to the east or simply opposite. If this explanation is correct, the names of the Paphlagonian, Macedonian, Adriatic, Atlantic, and Baltic Eneti, Veneti (Heneti), and Venedae may signify "whites," that is, "western folks," whereas that of the *Antai, Antani, Andiantes, Andes, and Antae would mean "frontal folks," that is, "easterners."

The Atlantic Veneti may also be viewed in relation to the Venelli who dwelt north of them. The element *-elli*, being a diminutive suffix, it served as a differentiator between the two ethnonyms, the function assigned to the element *-elici* in the pair Veneti-Vindelici just discussed.[50] We have included both pairs in our discussion of ethnonyms differentiated by size.

Appreciating the role played by the Veneti in the affairs of Gaul and in the rebellion against the Roman invaders, Caesar wrote:

> These Veneti exercise by far the most extensive authority over all the sea-coast in those districts, for they have numerous ships, in which it is their custom to sail to Britain, and they excel the rest in the theory and practice of navigation. As the sea is very boisterous, and open, with but a few harbours here and there which they hold themselves, they have as tributaries almost all those whose custom is to sail that sea. It was the Veneti who took the first step, by detaining Silius and Velanius, supposing that

[50]   H. Bannert, "Venelli," *PWRE*, Suppl. XV (1978), col. 851.

through them they should recover their own hostages whom they had given to Crassus. ... Moreover, they urged the remaining states to choose rather to abide in the liberty received from their ancestors than to endure Roman slavery. The whole sea-coast was rapidly won to their opinion, and they despatched a deputation in common to Publius Crassus, bidding him restore their hostages if he would receive back his own officers.[51]

With the resources of Gallia Togata and of the whole Roman Empire at his disposal, Caesar took personal command of the war against the Veneti and their coalition, which included: the Osismi, Lexovii, Namnetes, Ambiliati, Morini, Diablintes, and Menapii.[52] The Veneti also obtained auxiliaries from Britain. Caesar built battleships on the Liger River, the modern Loire, and assembled there a powerful force to crush the Veneti. The latter were not only expert seafarers, but also had numerous fortified towns.

While Caesar was waging war on the Veneti, Sabinus,

with the force received from Caesar, reached the borders of the Venelli. Their chief, Viridovix, held the supreme command of all the revolted states, from which he had raised an army, and large levies besides. Further, in the last few days the Aulerci, Eburovices, and the Lexovii, after putting their senate to death because they refused to approve the war, closed their gates and joined Viridovix. Moreover, from every corner of Gaul a great host of desperadoes and brigands had gathered, whom the hope of plunder and the passion for war seduced from the daily toil of agriculture.[53]

Sabinus triumphed over the Venelli, Caesar over the Veneti. Caesar describes his total victory over the Veneti:

This engagement finished the campaign against the Veneti and the whole sea-coast. For, on the one hand, all the fighting men,

[51]   *De Bello Gallico*, III.8.
[52]   The Menapii lived in what is today coastal Belgium. Their name contains the Indo-European root word *ap* "water."
[53]   *De Bello Gallico*, III.17; *see* also, Bannert, *op. cit.*, cols. 850–5.

nay, all the older men who had any sagacity or distinction, had there assembled; on the other, they had collected in one place every single ship they had anywhere; and after such losses the rest of their men had no point to retire to, no means of defending the towns. Accordingly they surrendered themselves and all they had to Caesar. He decided that their punishment must be the more severe in order that the privilege of deputies might be more carefully preserved by the natives for the future. He therefore put the whole of their senate to the sword, and sold the rest of the men as slaves.[54]

The defeat at the hands of the Romans and their allies meant the end of the Veneti as an independent force in this portion of Europe.

It would be wrong to suppose that all of the people of Armorica submitted to the Roman yoke without first trying to escape to freedom. Countless Celts crossed the Channel to the Isle of Albion from the pursuing Romans. In fact, the ethnonymy of that island points strongly in the direction of Gaul. There were the Pictones in Aquitania, and the Picti in Scotland, the Parisii in Belgica and their namesakes in Yorkshire, and the mighty Belgae on the continent and their offshoots across the Channel, to name the most remarkable pairs of names. The pair Veneti and Andes also appeared, obliquely though, in Roman Britain, as proven by the name *Castrum Ventorum* "fort of the Veneti," called Winchester today, and by the ethnonyms Brigantes, Decantae, Novantae, and Trinovantes in which we may recognize the element *antes/antae*.

As Roman Britain succumbed under the pressure of Angles, Saxons, and Jutes at the beginning of the Middle Ages, masses of people fled to the continent. In the same corner of Armorica, which centuries earlier some Veneti had to abandon for safety in Britain, the refugees from Britannia established a Celtic enclave which became known as Bretagne in honor of the fatherland they had lost to the Germanic invaders. However, the old name Armorica survives as the name for all of Bretagne, western Normandy, and Vendée.

---

[54]   *De Bello Gallico*, III.16.

Whether groups of Veneti and other Armorican peoples, fleeing from the Romans, settled along the Baltic coast or in any other region of Slavia cannot be said with certainty. The possibility should not be excluded in view of the fact that Celts generally were found in antiquity not only in their presumed homeland, but also in Anatolia, on the Crimea, in the Balkans, in Italy, and in the west from the Pillars of Heracles to Ireland and Scotland. It is a reasonable assumption that some Veneti, Venelli, and Andes also took refuge in Slavia fleeing the horrors and blessings of the *Pax Romana*.

As a practical man, Caesar was interested in how to bring the Veneti under Roman control, not in their past. Strabo, who wrote after Gaul had been conquered by the Romans and annexed to their empire, had more information on its peoples, and tried to understand their origins. As we saw earlier, puzzled by the identity of the names of the Adriatic and the Atlantic Veneti, he suggested that the Adriatic ones had migrated from Paphlagonia. Then, in the section of his work dealing with Italy, he sided with those who claimed the same people had come to Italy along with other Celts from Transalpine Gaul.

The defeated and enslaved peoples of Gaul, including the Veneti, Venelli, Andes, and others, became, with time, Romanized. In the course of the Middle Ages some accepted the name of the Germanic invaders and conquerors of Gaul, the Franks. However, the name Veneti lives on in a portion of that people's ancient land called Vendée. The Vendéens made an impression on eighteenth century France as fierce opponents of the Revolution. They defended the *ancien régime* of France, not the liberties of ancient Venetia. Today, the descendants of the Veneti and other conquered peoples of ancient Gaul, while referring to themselves as *Français*, after their medieval conquerors, the Franks, chant praises to their more distant ancestors, *les Gaulois*, in the language which derives from the one imposed upon these same ancestors by their Roman conquerors.

The Venedae–the Antae

We now turn to the ethnonym Venedae, the basis for the general Germanic designation for the Slavs and the Finnic name for the Russians, and their positional opposites, the Antae.[55] The regions where the namesakes of the Venedae and the Antae had settled were relatively well known to the Mediterranean peoples by the beginning of the first Christian century. The Venedae and the northern, or Russian, branch of the Antae, on the other hand, lived in that region of North Central Eurasia which remained *terra incognita* into the Middle Ages. Migrations of the Goths, Gepids, Heruli, Burgundians, Vandals, and other Germanic peoples via Scythia and Sarmatia, Venedia and Antia to Romania are relatively well known because these peoples wreaked havoc in the Roman Empire at the time when literacy was still sufficiently common for some writers to record their origins and *res gestae*. At the same time, masses of people, escaping from Roman pressure, crossed the Danube and settled in today's Slovakia, Czechia, East Germany, Poland, Ukraine, Belarus, Russia, and in the Baltic lands. But neither the Romans, nor the refugees, nor the people among whom they settled recorded the events.

The earliest information on the homeland of the Venedae was provided by Pytheas of Massilia (Marseille) who journeyed to northern Europe in the fourth century BC. Fragments of his work survive in brief citations by other writers. In imitation of Herodotus, Pytheas called all northern peoples Scythians and extended their domain to the Atlantic Ocean and the North German Sea. Further, he said that the Scythians were almost all called Belcae.[56] If we identify the Belcae with the Belgae of later sources, we must assume that Pytheas extended the latter's domain and name eastward into Scythia. However, Pytheas' Belcae may have been a distinct "Scythian" people, their name

[55]   N. Polaschek, "Venedae," *PWRE*, XXXII.1 (1955), cols. 698–9; Sławski and Labuda, "Wenedowie," *loc. cit.*; T. Lehr-Spławiński, S. Jasnosz, W. Kowalenko, and S. Roman, "Antowie," *SSS*, I (1975), pp. 35-8.
[56]   Quoted in Pomponius Mela, *Cosmographia; see* also, C.F.C. Hawkes, *Pytheas: Europe and the Greek Explorers* (Oxford, 1977); and Phytheas of Marseilles, *Fragmente*, transl. as *Ueber das Weltmeer*, ed. D. Stichenoth.

deriving from some "Scythian" word for the color white. We saw that in their own languages the Baltic Lithuanians and Latvians attributed the color white to the sea which washes their shores. It should be regarded as natural that some peoples who lived in the lands verging on this "white" sea were also called "white." A number of hydronyms and ethnonyms in the region inhabited by the Belcae and the Venedae derive from Baltic, Germanic, and Slavic words for the color white. Therefore, we ought to feel comfortable with the suggestion that the name *Belcae* is also of the same origin, that it derives from a word for the color white—perhaps from the Slavic *bĕlyj* "white"—and that the ethnonyms Balti and Venedae, both meaning "whites," are its late classical, medieval, and modern equivalents or synonyms.

At the beginning of the Christian era, the Roman Empire controlled the shores of the Mediterranean Sea and much of the hinterland. On the west, having annexed the Pillars of Heracles, conquered Iberia and Gaul, the Roman state reached what could be counted as natural frontiers. But beyond the coasts of the lands washed by the Western Ocean, lay the unapproachable Isles of the Blessed. Across the narrow channel beckoned the island called Albion and Britain. Its immense wealth motivated the Romans to invade and plunder it in the reign of Claudius. On the north, the Roman state never reached a natural and stable border. Caesar's conquest extended as far as the Rhine. Augustus and his generals brought the Roman eagles to the banks of the Danube, but their efforts to extend the Roman domain to the Laba (Elbe) River were unsuccessful.

Europe extending between the Laba (Elbe), the Roman *limes*, the Baltic Sea (which the ancients thought was the Northern Ocean, with Scandia and Ultima Thule as islands in it), the upper Volga and Don and down the Don to the Sea of Azov, remained as if hidden from the view of classical writers. To fill the unknown with familiar names some ethnonyms were extended far beyond the ethnic boundaries of the peoples they designated. Often names of known peoples were interspersed with names of wholly invented or fabulous ones. Space was found for ethnonyms that had appeared in Homer and Herodotus in that area, regardless of whether the people themselves existed at the time of writing or had since disappeared.

Centuries passed before another Mediterranean writer offered a survey of northern ethnography, namely, Pliny in his *Historia naturalis*. In describing roughly modern Poland, Pliny says:

> Some authorities report that these regions as far as the river Vistula are inhabited by the Sarmati, Venedi, Sciri and Hirri, and that there is a gulf named Cylipenus, with the island of Latris at its mouth, and then another gulf, that of Lagnus, at which is the frontier of the Cimbri.[57]

The name Sarmati is a general appellation for the nomadic peoples of North Central Eurasia, the Sciri and Hirri are regarded as Germanic tribes, while the Venedi are declared to be Slavs. We suggest that they be equated with Pytheas' Belcae for the following reason. Pliny's information about Germany, including, according to some authorities, the name Germani, itself, was obtained through the Celts. It is quite possible that some Slavic ethnonyms are intelligible only when we take into account the Celtic filter through which they reached the Romans. The name Venedae may be a Celtic version of Belcae.[58]

The next time the Venedae appeared is in Tacitus' work *Germania*. Though the Roman historian never visited Germania, he was able to gain knowledge from written sources and first-hand reports brought by Roman soldiers, merchants, and other travellers, as well as from numerous Celts and Germans living in and journeying through the Roman Empire. Following Tacitus, modern scholars assume a three-fold ethno-linguistic division of the Germanic race. Their common ancestor Mannus had three sons, the *heroes eponymoi* of the Ingaevones, who inhabited Jutland and Scandinavia, the Istaevones, who took the region along the Lower Rhine, and the Herminones, who occupied the central areas of Germany. Among the Hermiones

---

[57]   IV.97.
[58]   When interpreting Slavic ethnonyms, the majority of scholars assume these must be intelligible in Slavic. When they are not, like the name Antae, this is used as argument that the people named were not Slavs. Yet, the Venedae, whose name is also believed to be non-Slavic, are considered to have been Slavs.

the principal group were the Suebians. The basic population in the middle Elbe basin were the Lugii (Lusatians) whose ethnolinguistic affiliation cannot be established for lack of evidence, their name signifying "forest-dwellers."[59]

However, that the southerners generally were in the dark regarding the ethnography of the area is well illustrated by Tacitus' uncertainty whether the Venedae (Venethi) were Germans or Sarmatians. He says:

> As for the tribes of the Peucini, Venethi, and Fenni, I am in doubt whether to count them as Germans or Sarmatians, though the Peucini, whom some men call Bastarnae, in language, manner of life, fixity of habitation, and house-building, conduct themselves as Germans. All are dirty and their chiefs are lethargic: the faces of the chiefs, too, owing to intermarriage, wear to some extent the degraded aspect of Sarmatians: while the Venethi have contracted many Sarmatian habits; they are brigands, infesting all the hills and forests which rise between the Peucini and the Fenni.
>
> And yet these peoples are preferably entered as Germans, since they have fixed abodes, and carry shields, and delight to use their feet and to run fast: all of which traits are opposite to those of the Sarmatians, who live in wagons and on horseback.[60]

The quoted passage shows that Tacitus considered the Venethi (Venedae) as a people who were neither completely German nor Sarmatian. But because he operated with a bi-polar division of northern Barbaricum into Germania and Sarmatia, he had to decide into which of the two to place them, as if *tertium non datur*. So he used their way of life to classify them as Germans. He tells us nothing about the language of the Venedae.

The historian's statement that the Venedae were brigands ranging through "the hills and forests which rise between the Peucini and the Fenni, that is, through the northward and eastward sloping Carpathians, Volhynia, and the Valdai Hills, may be taken as an indication that they were newcomers into that area. We make this supposition because it is more likely that newcomers would engage in brigandage than an old ·

---

[59] *See* above, pp. 99–100.
[60] *Germania*, 46.1–2.

autochthonous people. Though the area occupied or merely crisscrossed in plundering raids by the Venethi was extensive, they had not yet reached the coast of the Baltic Sea, which was held by Suebi, Rugii, and Gutones.

The Fenni are identified with the hunters-gatherers who dwelt in the forest zone of Russia, and the Peucini, in Tacitus' day, dwelt at the mouths of the Danube. The Suebi, after whom the Baltic was called the Suebian Sea, are well-known from other sources. The original Suebian homeland was situated before Julius Caesar's time, ca. 101 BC, in the middle Laba/Elbe Valley. To the Suebian grouping belonged also the Semnones, Hermunduri, Marcomani, and Quadi, as well as the Trebochi, Vangiones, and Nemetes. The Suebi migrated into today's Poland from their original homeland in Germany, carrying along their name, a self-designation which some scholar interpret as "Wir selbst."[61] The Gutones, in whose name we see the augmentative suffix were the continental cousins of the Gauti of Sweden.[62] The ethnicity of the Rugii and of their counterparts, the Ulmerugi "insular Rugii," has been the subject of an ongoing debate. We note here the fact that in the Middle Ages some western Christian writers applied the name Rugii for the Russians of their day.[63]

By the time Ptolemy collected his information on Sarmatia Europaea the Venedae were so well established in the region that the Baltic Sea was called the Venedicus Bay and a section of the Carpathian ranges was called the Venedici Mountains in their honor. We saw that Ptolemy uses the differentiator *megista ethnē* to distinguish these distant Venedae from others of the same name who lived closer to Romania or within its borders. As the counterpart of these Greater Venedae we have suggested the Venadi Sarmatae who, in the first century AD, occupied an area extending from the Eastern Carpathians to the Dniester River.[64]

---

[61]   *See* above, p. 104.

[62]   *See* above, p. 87.

[63]   Jordanes, *Getica*, 24, 26 and *passim*, notes 59, 64 of the Skržinskaja edition.

[64]   Ptolemy, *Geography*, III.v; *Tabula Peutingeriana*, segments VIII.1,4; *see* also, Labuda, "Wenedowie," p. 374.

The Venedae mentioned by Pliny, Tacitus, and Ptolemy lived in that portion of North Central Eurasia which the ancients called Sarmatia Europaea. These northern Sarmatian Venedae occupied modern Poland east of the Vistula, and were classified by Tacitus as Germans because they were not nomads. Ptolemy refers to them as the Greatest Venedae because he wished to distinguish them from their namesakes in Bessarabia or from the Roman Venedae.

Our first medieval source on the Venedae is Jordanes, who uses the form Venethi. In the mid-sixth century, when Jordanes wrote his *Getica*, the Venethi held a "great expanse of land," extending from the source of the Vistula and the northern foothills of the Carpathians toward the Baltic Sea. Assigning a quantitative function to the modifier used by Ptolemy, Jordanes calls the Venedae *"natio populosa."*[65] The Gothic historian claims that the Venethi were among the numerous peoples defeated by the Gothic king Hermanaricus.[66] He may have been inspired by Ammianus Marcellinus' brief statement that Hermanaricus had been bellicose and feared by his neighbors[67] to compose a list of peoples he had supposedly brought under his rule. Since the list includes numerous and distant Scythian peoples some of whom may have never seen a Goth, it is doubtful whether Hermanaricus was able to overwhelm the mighty and populous nation of the Venedae.

Suebian presence in Magna Germania between the Elbe and the Vistula must have been quite remarkable, for Tacitus says that the Odra was a river of the Suebians, and the Baltic the Suebian Sea. However, already Ptolemy refers to the Baltic as the Venetic Bay. Half a millennium later Germans vanished from Magna Germania east of the Elbe, and the region became a part of Slavia. This momentous change occurred without literate observers recording it. Nevertheless, based on our knowledge of events along the line that separated Romans from their northern neighbors, the Celts, Illyrians, Dalmatians, Pannonians, and others, there should be no objection to postulating a mass migration of Macedonian Eneti, Adriatic

---

[65]   *Getica*, 34.
[66]   *Ibid.*, 116–20.
[67]   Ammianus Marcellinus, XXXI.3.1.

Veneti, Alpine Vindelici, and Atlantic Veneti and Venelli to Magna Germania and Sarmatia Europaea. Masses of people fled northward from the Roman wave that was encroaching upon their land and persons. Perhaps the Venedae mentioned by Pliny, Tacitus, and Ptolemy were also refugees from the south, which fact might well be reflected in their name, so similar to the names of some of their cousins conquered by the Romans.

It seems that from the first century of the Christian era it was customary among Mediterranean writers to designate as either Germania Magna or Sarmatia Europaea that portion of North Central Eurasia which from the sixth century onwards would be a part of Slavia. Germania Magna was a term popularized by Strabo, Ptolemy, and other Roman writers wishing to distinguish the area of Europe peopled by Germans who remained outside Roman rule from those who lived in Roman Germania. But the German element controlled firmly only that portion of Germania Magna which ended at the Laba/Elbe. The name Venedae became the general name for Slavs in the Germanic languages. As the Slavs conquered Magna Germania as far west as the Laba/Elbe and the Salava/Saale rivers, this name spread westward, so that from ca. 500 AD the ethnonyms Venedae and Slavs began to be applied to that portion of former Germania Magna which extended from these rivers on the west to the Vistula River on the east. Generally, the Slavs of ancient Magna Germania were called Wenden by their Germanic neighbors in the Middle Ages, while those of Sarmatia became differentiated as Austr-Winðar. In the Middle Ages, an area of Slavia west of the Laba/Elbe was called *Alba Patria, Belsem, or Belxa terra* "white land."[68] Another, or the same, area was called *Wenedonia.*[69] These names, perhaps, reflect the ancient Slavic attribute *bělyj*, attested in the name *Belcae* brought to the pages of history by Pytheas of Marseilles. The name Venedae still survives in the name *Wendland*, a region near Hannover, and in colloquial German as *Winden/Wenden*.

The name *Antae*, clearly designating a Slavic people, first appeared in the sixth-century AD Rhomaean and Latin sources.

---

[68] T. Lehr-Spławiński and J. Nalepa, "Biała ziemia," *SSS*, I (1961), p. 111.

[69] G. Labuda, "Wenedonia," *SSS*, VI (1977), pp. 372–3.

It was one of the several names used by foreigners to indicate groups of North Central Eurasian people, some settled in the Balkans, others holding an area which has, since the ninth century, been known as Russia. The Antae are regarded as the eastern branch of the Slavs and ancestors of the Ukrainians and Russians. Since we believe that the name derives from the word *anti*, it is not profitable to seek its explanation in the language of the people themselves as many scholars have done, but rather in the languages of their neighbors.

The Antae were so closely related to the Slavs that the two peoples were often considered as one by contemporary observers, just as later the Russians and Slavs were believed to be one people. Nevertheless, the "un-Slavic"-sounding name Antae has given rise to a number of theories about the origin of the people.[70] Here an attempt is made to locate the Antae as precisely as possible, while trying to clarify their name.

We have already discussed the Antani of Macedonia (Slavia Nova) and their namesakes in Italy and Gaul. Pursuing this ethnonym in Slavia Antiqua and Antia, we note that Strabo and other classical writers mention the Andizitii/ Andizetes/Andiantes, a people living in the lower Drava Valley where the ethnonym Slav appeared in the sixth Christian century. A city in the same region was called Antianis/ Antiana/Antina, located near modern Vukovar in Croatia, and a settlement at Zagreb bore the name Andautonia.[71] Both the people and the city owed their name to their eastern or frontal position in relation to their namers. The name Antae, in the form Andes, a man's name, is found on several inscriptions from other regions of Croatia, more specifically from Lika, Turkish Croatia, and Dalmatia. The name Vend has also been found on many inscriptions in this region. The forms are Venamois, Vendemius, Vendes, Vendo, Venndo (a woman's name) and Venetus. One inscription from

---

[70] For the various explanations of the name Antae, *see*: G. Vernadsky and M. Karpovich, *A History of Russia*, Vol. I by G. Vernadsky, *Ancient Russia*, pp. 104–7; B. Struminskyj, "Were the Antes Eastern Slavs?", in *Eucharisterion to O. Pritsak* (Cambridge, Mass., 1979/80) pp. 786–96; Lehr-Spławiński *et al.*, "Antowie," *loc. cit.*; and Xaburgaev, *op. cit.*, pp. 99–101.

[71] Strabo, 7.5.3. On Pannonia generally, *see*, A. Mócsy, "Pannonia," *PWRE*, Suppl. IX (1962), cols. 516–776; and his *Pannonia and Upper Moesia*, transl. by S. Frere (London–Boston, 1974).

Bihać in Bosnia (Turkish Croatia) has: *Vendes Dennata Andentis* "Vende, daughter of Andes." These names are seen as Celtic by some scholars, Ilyrian by others.

The earliest record of a "Scythian" ethnonym which resembles that of the Antae is found in Pliny. In his description of the lands north of the Black Sea, Pliny takes us across the fabled Rhipaean Mountains to the Scythian Ocean whose shores were occupied by the Hyperboreans. South of that happy people dwelt the sacred race of the Arimphaei. Beyond them

> we come directly to the Scythians, Cimmerians, Cissi, Anthi, Georgi, and a race of Amazons, the last reaching to the Caspian and Hyrcanian Sea.[72]

The name *Anthi* resembles closely the name *Antae* or *Antes*, but we are not able to place these people on the map of Eurasia. At the same time, we cannot exclude the possibility that the name designates the same Slavic people who were later known as the Antae and still later as the Russians. Noting in passing the apparent proximity of the Anthi and the Amazons, we add that the women warriors seem to have remained close to the ancestors of the Russians through the Middle Ages.[73]

The next writer to mention the Antae is Jordanes who uses the form *Antes*. They appear in a passage about the Ostrogoths, whose king, Hermanaric, committed suicide after his people had been defeated by the Huns. Jordanes states that his successor, King Vinitharius, liberated groups of the Ostrogoths from the Huns and led them into the land of the Antae. Though the Goths were defeated by the Antae, they allegedly crucified their king Boz together with his sons and seventy princes. At the basis of this tale are facts known from other sources: that the Ostrogoths were routed and enslaved by the Huns; that some of the defeated people escaped in many directions, including the Roman Empire. It is possible that certain Gothic escapees made it to the land of the Antae, and, not being allowed to settle down, committed

[72] *n.h.*, VI.35.
[73] *See* below, p. 291.

violent acts. Since King Boz, his sons, and seventy (a symbolic number!) princes appear only in Jordanes, whose *Getica* glorifies the Goths, we have reason to doubt the historicity of their crucifixion by Vinitharius.[74]

In a passage describing the mid-sixth century ethnic situation in Scythia, Jordanes says that the Antae lived in the curve of the Black Sea, in the Dniester—Dnieper mesopotamia.[75] The East Roman historian Procopius speaks several times about the homeland of the Antae. First, in connection with the Slavs and Huns. The Antae lived, along with these two peoples, north of the Danube not far from its banks.[76] Second, when he says that the Antae and the Slavs occupy most of the other bank of the Danube.[77] Third, when he describes the peoples of Scythia:

> And above the Saginae are settled numerous Hunnic tribes. And from there onward the country has received the name of Eulysia, and barbarian peoples hold both the coast and the interior of this land, as far as the so-called Maeotic Lake and the Tanais River which empties into the lake. And this lake has its outlet at the coast of the Euxine Sea. Now the people who are settled there were named in ancient times Cimmerians, but now they are called Utigurs. And above them to the north the countless tribes of the Antae are settled.[78]

These Antae appear to be identical with those mentioned by Jordanes and perhaps with the Anthi of Pliny. We may state with a degree of certainty that the forest—steppe ecological belt which runs between the Dniester and the Dnieper and perhaps eastward as far as the Don was occupied, in the middle of the sixth century AD, by a people who were known to their southern neighbors as the Antes or Antae. The homeland of these Antae was rather distant from the frontiers of the Roman Empire. Pliny, Jordanes, and Procopius, the only writers who mention

[74] *Getica*, 246–7.
[75] *Getica*, 35–36.
[76] *Libri de bellis*, VII.xiv.29–30.
[77] *Ibid.*, V.xxvii.
[78] *Ibid.*, VIII.iv.6–9.

them, appear to have known little more about them than their name.

However, in sixth-century Rhomaean sources, the name Antae occurs quite frequently. Antae cavalry units fought for Justinian and Rome against the Goths in Italy, in Upper Asia against Persia, and in the Balkans as Rhomaean allies against Rome's foes. We have shown elsewhere that these Antae lived between the Danube and the Dniester, in Black Wallachia and Black Bogdania, and were distinct from the Antae who occupied the forest–steppe zone of Ukraine and Russia.[79] The Great Scythian Antae must be distinguished from their namesakes on the Danube, as East Slavs are usually distinguished from their southern and western cousins. As a land of settled communities, separated from the Black Sea coast by a broad belt of steppe country inhabited by a variety of nomadic, mostly Turkic, peoples, Great Scythian Antia was of marginal importance and interest for the Rhomaeans. The Antae could, when necessary, be bribed to attack the nomads in the rear. However, the Rhomaeans could neither raid nor attack this Antia without the cooperation of the nomads. On the other hand, Danubian Antia was a neighbor of the Rhomaean Empire and it played an important role in the affairs of the Danube Basin, the Balkans, and the Pontic area. The Balkan and Danubian Antae were defeated by the Rhomaean General Germanus, and from around the year 545 they were settled in and around the city of Turris, somewhere in the lower Dniester Valley. Although these Antae do not seem to have been *foederati*, they entered into a *quid pro quo* agreement with the Emperor Justinian, who styled himself *Anticus*.

The name Antae has impressed some scholars as so "alien" to Slavic ethnonymy that they have used this fact as evidence that the people it designated were also not Slavs. Various etymologies have been proposed, but none has been able to stand the test of criticism. Among the better known solutions is the widespread belief that the names Venedae and Antae are merely variants of the Slavic ethnonym *Vjatiči*.[80] If we accept this

---

[79]   Bačić, *The Emergence of the Slavs*, ch. 3. The southern and northern Antias may be compared to two Scythias, Little–Great, and to two sets of Russias, Inner–Outer and Little–Great.

solution for the Venedae and Antae, we still would have to explain the other similar pairs of ethnonyms. Also, even if it can be shown that the Vjatiči came to be known as the Venedae and as the Venelased in Estonian, while the same people were known as the Antae in the sources of the southerners, we still have to explain the name of the Antae of Black Wallachia, Black Bogdania, and other Balkan and Danubian areas who were rather distant from the Vjatiči, not to speak of the other similar pairs elsewhere. Therefore, this solution, though economical and appealing, cannot be accepted.

There is a trend in recent Antae studies to root these people in the Great Eurasian Steppe, either as alleged masters of the neighboring and presumably nameless and ahistorical masses of settled agriculturalists known as Slavs, or themselves as slaves of still other nomadic warriors. George Vernadsky saw the name Antae as an oblique case of the ethnonym As-Antas, declined on the pattern of the Greek word *gigas-gigantes* "giant."[81] His solution has not found acceptance in the scholarly community. Yet, though Vernadsky's etymology has been rejected, his belief that the Antae were a branch of the As people has been widely accepted. The anthroponym Antas found on a third century AD inscription at Kerch, and the presence of the As (according to Vernadsky As=Antas) people in the same general area have strengthened the beliefs of the learned that the "original" homeland of the Antae is to be sought in the Sarmatian steppe, occupied at the beginning of the Christian era by the As (Alan) peoples. Supposedly, these Antae did not speak a dialect of Proto-Slavic, but rather became Slavicized after they had allegedly established their rule over some Slavic tribes, who then came to be known by the "Sarmatian" names of Croats and Serbs. Further, the As are frequently projected into the past under the name Sarmatae and Sauromatae and are declared to be Iranians.[82] We reject these equations as unsupported in the sources.

Though nothing is known about the language spoken by the Avars there is an "Avar" etymology explaining the ethnonym

[80] *See* references in Vasmer, *REW*, I, p. 376, s.v. "vjatiči."
[81] *Ancient Russia*, pp. 104–7.
[82] Dvornik, *The Making of Central and Eastern Europe*, pp. 277–97.

Antae from the Turkic word *ant* "oath" (in Mongol *anda/and* means "blood brother," *pobratim* in Russian). According to this view, the Avars, arriving from Asia, subdued some Slavs and turned them into "*anty*," that is, forced them to be their blood-brothers. The name then was borrowed by the Rhomaeans from the Avars. The Antae "disappeared" after the conquered Slavs, who had been forced by the Avars to be their slaves, rebelled against their masters or older brothers and ceased to be their bloodbrothers, thus ceasing to be "anty."[83] Our analysis of Avar–Slav and Avar–Antae relations contradicts this and other modern writers' theories regarding the early history of the Antae. It must be remembered that the name Antae designating a people related to the Slavs appeared in Rhomaean writings *before* the arrival of the Avars to Europe. At the time when the Avar nomads still roamed the steppes of Central Asia under the rule of the Kök Turks, the Antae were known to the Rhomaeans as an old and independent Danubian people. Their cavalry and infantry units fought in Italy against the Goths and for the greater glory of Rome; one of their conationals, General Chilbudius, was an accomplished strategist in the service of East Rome against his own people as well as against the Slavs; and, finally, the Emperor Justinian styled himself *Anticus* and made an alliance with the Antae while still a young man. He first saw an Avar when he was to depart from the affairs of this world, being advanced in years.[84]

Recently, a scholar proposed that these Antae were not Slavs but Goths. He based his evidence on what he believed is a Germanic origin of the name of one Ant, Chilbudius.[85] The

---

[83]   F.P. Filin, *Obrazovanie jazyka vostočnyx slavjan* (Moscow–Leningrad, 1962), p. 61.

[84]   Bačić, *The Emergence*, pp. 201–301.

[85]   Strumins'kij, *op. cit.*, pp. 786–796.

fatuousness of this kind of reasoning had already been pointed out by Jordanes:

> Let no one who is ignorant cavil at the fact that the tribes of men use many names, the Romans from the Macedonians, Greeks from the Romans, the Sarmatians from the Germans and the Goths frequently from the Huns.[86]

If we could derive the name Antae from that of As, a very doubtful procedure, then we need not involve the As from the shores of the Black Sea, for we find in the Middle Danube Basin several names which can be associated with both the As and the Antae. In addition to the As–Alans who gave their name to one of the principal passes in the Caucasus, Dār-i Alān or Daryal Pass, the Ir people of Georgia and Russia whom the Russians call Osseti (Ossetians), the city of Iași in Moldavia, which derives from the ethnonym As, there were the nomadic Iazyge in Hungary (a region of Hungary is today called Jaszság), while farther west, in the Drava Valley around Aquae Balisae, modern Daruvar, and Aquae Iasae, Varaždinske Toplice (all in Croatia), lived their agricultural relatives, the Iasii. However, the ethnonym Antae appears to have nothing to do with the ethnonym Iasii. Both are attested independently of each other, not only in the Danube Basin but in many other parts of Eurasia.

Some scholars are puzzled by the brevity of Antae's existence on the pages of history, their name vanishing at the end of the sixth century, never to appear again. They seemed to have been obliterated more thoroughly than the Avars themselves, their alleged overlords. This fact strengthens our hypothesis that this name was used more by their neighbors than by the Antae themselves.

****

Summing up we may say that, in antiquity, in areas distant from each other, many identical or similar ethnonyms have been recorded. The ancients usually took this as evidence of migrations of peoples. The names Eneti, Veneti (Heneti), and

---

[86] *Getica*, 58–59.

Venedae, on the one hand, and Antenor, Antani, Andiantes, Andes, and Antae, on the other, sound very close, but the peoples to whom they were applied may have been unrelated. Although most scholars agree that the name Veneti is of Celtic origin, ultimately signifying "whites," a consensus on the color's function is lacking. We suggest it was not descriptive but positional, just as the white color attributed to the Syrians of Anatolia referred to their geographical location, not to the color of their skin. We wish the following to serve as corroboration of our thesis.

The Eneti in Paphlagonia were one of several Anatolian peoples whose names may be derived from color words. We have already discussed the Phrygians whose name was changed from Bryges to Phryges to reflect their easterly location in relation to the people who named them. The Eneti lived northeast of the Phrygians on the shores of the sea that was black. Their land could be reached from the Aegean basin by passing between the Blue Rocks. The Eneti, according to some authorities, joined the Cimmerians, who came from the black quarter of the world and who were associated with the color black. Finally, the Eneti lived west of the White Syrians. All this makes it highly probable that their name is also a color word, and that the function of the color is positional.

We saw that, while ignoring the Eneti of Asia Minor, Herodotus used this name for two distinct peoples, one of whom lived on the Balkan Peninsula, the other on the Apennine.

The Balkan Eneti had their positional counterparts in the Antani. The Adriatic Veneti may have been paired with the mythical *Antae whose eponym Antenor led the Eneti on their westward migration, as well as in relation to the Andiantes of Slavonia whose directional counterparts they were. Also, the Veneti may have been termed whites or western folks independently of any counterparts. It should be emphasized that before the establishment of Phoenician and Greek colonies in western Mediterranean, the Bay of Adria was considered the most westerly part of the world known to the Aegean peoples. Therefore, the Veneti lived in what to the Greeks and other peoples of the eastern Mediterranean was the true west, Hesperia, the land of the evening star. The Veneti may have obtained their name because they were the most westerly people known to those who gave them this name. Their land was perceived by observers who lived close to dawn as the abode of sunset, the planet Venus. Venetia was washed by the Cronian Sea, symbolized by the color black. The term Violet Sea, used by ancient Greeks for the Adriatic, belongs to this color symbolism. We saw also that in Old and New Rome the adjective *venetus*, which comes from the ethnonym *Veneti*, acquired the meaning of "light blue."

As to the form, it is possible that the Adriatic Eneti may have been called Veneti from the start. Their name may have originated independently of the Eneti and it may have reached Herodotus via some Celtic informer. Since Celts were then dwelling in the upper Danube Valley, it is possible that they had named both the Balkan and Adriatic Eneti, or had translated into their language some native ethnonyms. The Celts may have used the form Veneti for the names, but Herodotus "adjusted" it to the Greek ear, either to correspond more closely to the Homeric Eneti, or because the Greeks of his day distorted barbaric words in the manner which turned the Veneti into Eneti.

We do not know what name the Veneti used to refer to themselves. It is possible that this name was originally given to them by others and that, with time, it became their self-designation, because the Veneti appear to have been known throughout the Mediterranean world by this name, as it may be deduced from numerous tombstone inscriptions, votive inscriptions and other textual evidence left by men and women who called themselves Veneti.

The Atlantic Veneti appear to have derived their name from a word for the color white because of their geographical location as the most westerly people in Gaul. The Andes who lived east or in front of them may owe their name to their frontal or "anti" location in relation to the Veneti.

The name Venedae/Venethi appears to have been borrowed by Germans from Celts and applied to a third group, the Slavs.[87] At

---

[87] Similarly, the Slavs borrowed the name Vlach from the Germans, who used it originally to designate a Celtic people, the Volcae. Then in all Slavic languages the name became the common and general appellation for the Italians and Romance-speaking or Romanized peoples of the Balkan Peninsula and the Danube Basin.

the same time, we must allow for the possibility that the Celtic name, as applied to the Slavs, was a translation from some Slavic name that stood for the color white. There is no better candidate than the name Belcae, the name which may derive from the Slavic adjective *bělyj* "white." The Belcae, when they were observed by Pytheas, were surely the most westerly or northwesterly of the Scythians. The Venedi who appeared in Tacitus' *Germania* were the northwestern branch of the Slavic race. The color in the Slavic or Celtic form of their name appears to symbolize the people's geographical location in the north, the west, or in the northwest.

Our witnesses that the Venedae, and perhaps other peoples similarly named, were Slavs are the Finnic and Germanic peoples, because they have continually used their forms of this name exclusively for them. Thanks to Jordanes we know that as early as the sixth century AD the Venedae of the North European Plain were Slavs by language and customs. Therefore, our starting point is that century. But the Venedae appeared north of the Carpathians as early as the first century AD. Are we to consider them also as Slavs? Most scholars do. Some, as we saw, go as far as to project the name Venedae and the people it designated either as Slavs or as Indo-Europeans to the second millennium BC. However, there is reason to believe only that from the first Christian millennium the Venedae north of the Carpathians spoke a dialect of Slavic. They were migrants from a common Slavic homeland in the Balkans and the Danube Basin, which they had been forced to abandon under the pressure of the retreating Celts and the advancing Romans.

Interesting parallels between the destinies of the Atlantic Veneti and the Baltic Venedae may be offered as suggestive of something more than a mere similarity of names and circumstances. First, the land inhabited by the Atlantic Veneti has been known as *Armorica* since the days of Caesar. The name, deriving from a word for the sea, signifies "coastal region." The Venedae, before they were incorporated into the Polish and German states, consisted of many tribes, chief of whom were the Pomeranians. Their name signifies "sea-coast people" in Slavic. The Baltic coast of Poland and Germany is still known as Pomerania after them. Second, in the Middle Ages, in the land of the Atlantic Veneti, inhabited then by Bretons, flourished a city called Veneda. It was mentioned by the monk Ermold the Black, who, in 818, accompanied the King Louis the Pious in his campaign against the Bretons. Although Ermold said that the city was at the estuary of the Loire, its location has not been established.[88] At the same time, in the land of the Baltic Vene-dae there was the celebrated city of Vineta. Destroyed by Danes, Vineta's site has not been located, though recent research points to the mouth of the Odra River.[89]

The Adriatic, Atlantic, and the Baltic Veneti and Venedae have exhibited exceptional talent for seafaring. The first to do this were the Atlantic Veneti, who, according to Caesar, were a seafaring people *par excellence*. The Baltic Venedae were a re-nowned maritime power until they were overwhelmed by Danes and later subdued by Germans. As to the Adriatic Veneti, while still linguistically a separate group, they appear not to have engaged in maritime activities. Their talent surfaced in the Middle Ages when Venice, the city which continues the ancient name of the Veneti, became the mistress of the Adriatic and the leading naval power in the Mediterranean.

The ethnicity of the Paphlagonian, Macedonian, Adriatic, and Atlantic Eneti and Veneti has not been settled and the search for their believed common origin continues in our time. We saw that Strabo looked to Asia Minor as well as to Gaul for the original homeland of the Adriatic Veneti. More than a hundred years ago, J. Šafařík correctly concluded that the Slavs had first appeared in history under the name Venedae and included not only the latter by also the Veneti in his monumental and unsurpassed work on Slavic antiquities.[90] Today, scholars use evidence other than mere similarity or even identity of names in their search for a people's origins. However, the results are usually controversial. Here are briefly mentioned some attempts at solving the mystery of the Eneti, Veneti, and Venedae.

Ignoring their namesakes of Paphlagonia and Macedonia, H. Fleischer believed the Adriatic, Baltic, and Atlantic Veneti were one people, who, though not Germanic, descended from a

---

[88] P. Merlat, "Veneda," *PWRE*, XXXII.1 (1955), cols. 697–8.
[89] L. Leciejewicz, "Wineta," *SSS*, VI (1977), p. 472.
[90] J. Šafařík, *Slawische Alterthümer*, 2 vols. (Leipzig, 1843–4), I, especially, pp. 65–92, 223–65.

common Veneto-Germanic ancestor.[91] Focusing on the element
-*eti*, while also ignoring the Macedonian Eneti, a scholar
proposed that the Veneti originated in Transcaucasia, where
several ethnonyms also have this element, for instance, the
Svaneti, Osseti, Meskheti and others. According to his view, the
Eneti migrated from their original Caucasian homeland to
Paphlagonia, the Adriatic, and ultimately to the Atlantic.[92] While
overlooking all the Antae and the Eneti of Macedonia, Polish
scholars reverse the migratory directions and regard the Atlantic
Veneti, the Adriatic Veneti, and the Paphlagonian Eneti as
migrants from their common original homeland in Poland and
Thuringia.[93]

Other scholars are more reserved, so there is no general
agreement concerning the ethnicity of these peoples with the
same or similar names. Though most have always regarded the
Atlantic Veneti as Celts, we saw that they have also been
considered as Slavic, Caucasian, and "Germano-Venetic." The
question of the origin of the Atlantic Veneti cannot be answered.
Although they lived in Gaul surrounded by Celts, we cannot be
sure they, themselves, were Celts. On the other hand, the only
reason why so many scholars have tried to unveil the mystery of
their origins is their ubiquitousness. Had the name Veneti or
Eneti not appeared in different parts of the world we would have
no reason to speculate about the ethnicity of these peoples and
would not try to find their common original homeland.

On the basis of the information gathered from ancient writers,
we are unable to state whether the Eneti in Paphlagonia, the
Eneti (and the Vetones) in the Balkans, the Veneti in Italy and
Gaul, and the Venedae in the Vistula Valley belonged to one
and the same ethno-linguistic group. We may surmise that they
all spoke languages which are descended from a common Indo-
European idiom. But beyond that we are in the dark. Though we
lack positive evidence that the various groups of peoples who
bore these names had migrated from a common Enetic/Venetic
homeland, nevertheless, since it is suggested here that while in
antiquity some people migrated from Europe to Asia, others

---

[91]   H. Fleischer, *Mannus*, XIV (1922), pp. 58ff.
[92]   *See,* reference in Merlat, "Veneti," cols. 707–8.
[93]   Labuda, "Wenedowie," p. 375 (map).

moved from Asia to Europe, the hypothesis that the Venedae arrived to their ultimate homeland in the Vistula Valley, in the land of darkness, from the sunny dales of Paphlagonia, by way of Macedonia, the Po Valley, Lacus Venetus (Bodensee), and the Atlantic coast of Gaul, ought to be considered. Future archaeological and linguistic studies may confirm this hypothesis. In the meantime, the identity and similarity of names remains the only ground upon which rests the claim that the Eneti, Veneti (Heneti), and Venedae belonged to the same ethnolinguistic group. It seems that two millennia after these names were first recorded we cannot do better than to settle for probabilities in matters of their bearers' ethnic origins, to paraphrase Strabo.[94] Nevertheless, it seems that any meaningful search for the origin of these names must embrace the names derived from *anti*.

Numerous spatially perceived pairs of names of natural features and settlements were differentiated by marking one of the members with *anti*. We have added the pairs Eneti– Antenor in Anatolia, Eneti–Antani in Macedonia, Veneti– Antenor (*Andes) and Andiantes on the Adriatic and in Slavonia, Veneti–Andes in Gaul, and we now add the Venedae–Antae pair of Sarmatia Europaea. There may be more such pairs where only one member is marked. In this category we have discussed one of the oldest known peoples in the Mediterranean world, the Cadmonites, who obtained their name on account of their "frontal" position, while the people who named them remained unmarked. Rather than searching through the chronologically and spatially distant languages of East and Central Asia for the origin of the name Antae, we suggest that the ethnonym Cadmonites be taken into account as a possible prototype, especially since their eponym Cadmus, having wandered through ancient Macedonia found rest in Red Croatia. The name of the Macedonian Antani might be a Balkan adaptation of the Semitic Kadmoni, both meaning "those in front," that is, in front of an observer following an eastern orientation.

To conclude, we have seen that several ethnonyms derive from words signifying white. Likewise, there is a profusion of names of natural features, cities, and peoples in which we are

---

[94]   4.4.1.

permitted to recognize the preposition *anti*. We have argued that east of the Veneti in Gaul were the Andes, just as east of the Venedae in Sarmatia lived the Antae. The name *Venedae* derives from a Celtic word for "white," and it stands for the west, symbolized by the color white. The name *Antae* signifies "the people who live in front," or "at the end," or "easterners," all in relation to those who, as westerners, are designated with the color white. This manner of naming goes back to the remote past, and we should not be surprised at finding it applied in ethnonymy.

Concerning the Russians, we may state that, in the middle of the first century AD, some of their ancestors appeared in written sources under the names Venedi, Venethi, Venedae. They occupied a portion of the North European Plain north and east of the Carpathians. These names are variants of the names Eneti and Veneti (Heneti) attested in Anatolia, Macedonia, Italy, and Gaul. Pliny may be regarded as the first writer who recorded the Russians under the name from which the Finnish name for Russia, Venäjä, derives. Pliny also speaks of the Anthi, whom we may also consider as ancestors and namesakes of the sixth century Antae (Antes). Since the seventh century the Antae were known by several names which can be explained from the Slavic languages. Those who lived in the forest—steppe zone of Sarmatia Europaea were called *Severjane* "northern folks." Their Danubian relatives were known to the Rhomaeans first as *Severoi* and *Hepta genea* "seven tribes," then as Great Moravians, Serbs, and Bulgarians. In the Late Middle Ages, the Antae who occupied the lower Dniester Valley were called Ugliči and Tivercy. The Antae and other Slavs who lived east or southeast in relation to their namers were also collectively called Russi or Reds.

RED CROATS—WHITE CROATS

Returning to the south and back in time to antiquity, we note that, if we draw a line from the Upper Nile through the Aegean and on to the Dnieper and look for ethnonyms with color attributes, we find a large number of them both east and west of this divide. To start with Africa, we recall that the Egyptians attributed the color red to themselves, other colors to their neighbors. While the Sumerians used the color black as their particular attribute, northwest of their land extended the huge Red Desert of Iraq, Saudi Arabia, and Jordan. Its fringes were occupied by the Edomites and the Canaanites, whose names derive from words for the color red. Then there were the Phoenicians, whose name is associated with Phoenix and the purple dye. When the Bryges, whose name means "highlanders," moved to Anatolia, the Greeks renamed them *Phryges* "shiny ones" and furnished Phrixus to serve as their eponym.[95]

In Great Scythia there was an abundance of color names. Viewed from the south, the majority of such names were associated with the color black. Looking from the east a few names were distinguished by the color white, among which were the *Roxolani* "light Alans," named so because they were the western or northern Alans, the light hue standing for the north or the west, just as the names of the northwesterly seas derive from the color white. We saw that the westernmost Scythian peoples were at first called *Belcae*, then one of the western peoples of Sarmatia came to be known as the *Venedae*, which, we argued is a translation into Celtic of the name Belcae.

Among the Turkic peoples color differentiation in ethnonymy is very common, and it is generally believed that the function of the colors is positional, not descriptive. The Huns were the first Turkic-speaking people to come into the field of vision of literate Mediterranean observers. Several writers of late antiquity mention a branch of the Hunnic nation whom they call *Leukohunnoi* "white Huns" and whom they and some modern scholars identify with the Hephthalites.[96] Although the ethnic content behind the latter name, as well as the meaning of the attribute white in the Hunnic name, are still the subject of lively discussions among specialists, we should agree with those who interpret the appellation White Huns as Western Huns.[97] This

---

[95]   Some of their descendants today are called *Kizilbash* "red heads" by their neighbors because they wear red hats.

[96]   A. Lippold, "Hephthalitai," *PWRE*, Suppl. XIV (1974), cols. 127–37.

[97]   The literature is given in Lippold's article; *see* especially, F. Altheim and R. Stiehl, *Geschichte Mittelasiens im Altertum*, with contributions by various authors (Berlin, 1970), pp. 690ff.

explanation may be accepted without a search for the White Huns' color counterparts. The other Huns may have been known simply as the Huns.

There is no need to discuss at length here the names of all Turkic peoples that followed the Huns in their migration from sunrise toward sunset, from the depths of Asia to the Carpathians, the Eastern Alps, the Dinaric Alps, and the Balkan Mountains. It suffices to touch briefly upon those whose names frequently appeared in the sources with color attributes.

We have already mentioned the Bulgars and their homeland in the Kuban steppe, called Black, Old, or Great Bulgaria. These appellations originated among the emigrants who had established a Bulgar state between the lower Danube and the foothills of the Balkan Mountain ranges. Danubian or Balkan Bulgaria was known simply as Bulgaria, the color black being attributed to that country's northern namesake. By the time the Russians had acquired an alphabet for their own language and had begun recording their observations Kuban Bulgaria had become absorbed by Khazaria and Balkan Bulgaria had become a province of the East Roman Empire. But, north of the Sea of Azov lived the *Černye Bolgary* "black Bulgars."[98] Their namesakes on the Volga whom the Arabs called Outer Bulgars were known in Kiev as *Serebryannye Bolgary* "silver Bulgars."[99] Although scholars have proposed a number of explanations for the meaning of the color attribute in the Bulgar ethnonym, it is suggested here that they be rejected as insufficient. Rather the color black should be interpreted as a symbol of the directions of the horizon, so that we may translate the ethnonyms Black Bulgars as Northern Bulgars. We ought to do this with the same readiness with which we interpret the names Essex as East Saxons, Wessex as West Saxons, and Norfolk as the Northern Folks.

The Khazars, another Turkic people, who succeeded the Bulgars as the dominant nomadic power in the Kuban steppe and

---

[98] *PVL, passim.*; T. Lewicki, "Bułgarzy Czarni," *SSS*, I (1961), p. 202.
[99] Beševliev, *op. cit.*, p. 155.

along the lower valleys of the Don and the Volga, were differentiated into White Khazars and Black Khazars. Al-Istakhrī says:

> The Khazars do not resemble the Turks. They are black-haired, and are of two kinds, one called the Kara Khazars, who are swarthy verging on deep black as if they were a kind of Indian, and a white kind, who are strikingly handsome.[100]

This explanation is difficult to accept, for it is unlikely that the Khazar nation had split into two groups based on complexion or good looks. It is more plausible that, following the ancient Turkic custom of using colors as symbols of the directions of the horizon, one group of Khazars became known as Black Khazars, the other as White Khazars, with the attributes of color reflecting their relative geographical locations. We may render these names as Eastern or Northern Khazars and Western or Southern Khazars. When Istakhrī heard the names, not understanding the function of the attributes of color, he concluded that the Black Khazars must be swarthy, while the White Khazars must be handsome, because they were white. Like Othelo, this Moor, too, thought "White is beautiful," implying that black was not.

While they lived in the steppes of southern Russia, the Magyars were called *Sabartoi asphaloi*. The Sabartoi who migrated to Azerbaijan and kept their name are perhaps identical with the people called Sevordi who in the eighth century lived in the Kura Valley. Porphyrogenitus calls them *Serbotians*, saying they were also known as *Maura paidia* "black children."[101] Their kinsmen who moved to the Danube Valley were named *Belye Ugry* "white Hungarians" by the Kievan chronicler. *Pace* Ludat, there is no evidence that Danubian Hungarians were also divided into White Hungarians and Black Hungarians by the Danube or the Tisza.[102]

---

[100] Quoted in D.M. Dunlop, *The History of the Jewish Khazars* (Princeton, N.J., 1954), p. 96.
[101] *DAI*, ch. 38; *De Ceremoniis*, 687, 13–14.
[102] Ludat, "Farbenbezeichnung in Völkernamen," p. 143, note 18, and p. 153, note 84. *Cf.*, Macartney, *op. cit.*, pp. 86–92. Excursus III, pp. 174–6.

The Magyars were forced to abandon their country in the Pontic steppe by the westward-pushing Pečenegs, the Patsinaks of Rhomaean sources.[103] When these and other steppe peoples were, in turn, conquered by the next wave, the Polovtsians or the Cumans, masses of refugees who escaped northward and settled among the Russian Slavs along the middle Dnieper became known in Russian sources as *Čërnye klobuki* "black-hats."[104] Did they really wear black hats, or did they put them on upon embarking on their melancholy journey toward darkness remains an unanswered question. It is certain that the conquerors of their homeland, the Cumans, whose name in Turkic means yellow, were known in medieval western sources as "pale faces." Their country continued to be called Cumania long after they had been overpowered by the next nomadic wave, the Tatars.[105] Though the name Tatar is of Mongol origin,[106] West European Christians adjusted it to resemble more closely black Tartarus (a division of Hades), for the Tatars were seen as the sowers of death, just as earlier the Cimmerians, their predecessors in the regions of "darkness," had been surrounded by things black in the imagination of their enemies because of their northern homeland and presumed savagery.[107] The Tatars themselves were split into the White and the Black Tatars.[108]

Great Tartary abounded in ethnonyms which appeared in the sources with attributes of color. Among these are the Black Kirghiz, Blue Turks, Yellow Uigurs, etc.

Before the Ottoman Turks had conquered the Balkan Peninsula, some Vlachs were called *Maurovlachoi, Nigri Latini* "black Vlachs."[109] During the Ottoman ascendancy two northern

---

[103]   *DAI, passim.*

[104]   *PVL, passim; see* also, *EI,* II (1927), pp. 736–7, s.v. "Karakalpak."

[105]   On the destruction of Comania by the Tatars, *see, The Journey of Friar John of Pian de Carpini,* in *Contemporaries of Marco Polo,* ed. by M. Komroff (New York, 1928), pp. 36–37.

[106]   E.H. Parker, *A Thousand Years of the Tartars* (London, 1895).

[107]   *See,* the Introduction to the Penguin edition of *The Travels of Marco Polo,* by R. Latham, pp. 7–29.

[108]   Parker, *op. cit.,* p. 97, on the White Tartars; Ludat, "Farbenbe-zeichnungen in Völkernamen," on both.

[109]   *Enciklopedija Jugoslavije,* VI (Zagreb, 1963), s.v. "Morlaci," pp. 162–3.

Vlach (Rumanian) principalities and their inhabitants were attributed the color black, *kara*: Kara Eflak and Kara Bogdan. In Venetian documents the region of Lika, where Black Beaver is situated, and the neighboring districts of Croatia were known as *Morlachia* and the people as *Morlachi* "black Vlachs" (from Maurovlachoi). There is no doubt that the Vlachs of Rumania and Lika were called black because they were the most northerly groups of that people.

The custom of differentiating peoples by colors was so common in ancient North Central Eurasia that even the Goths, on their way from Scandinavia to Romania via Scythia, seem to have been subjected to it. We saw that the once united Gothic nation, after it settled in Great Scythia was divided into *Greutungi* and *Tervingi* "field- or sand-dwellers" and "forest-dwellers," respectively. The division of the same people into *Ostrogotha* and *Visigotha* began in Scythia and was apparently finalized in Romania.[110] In the literary monuments of the Germanic peoples the names *Hreidgotha* and *Balagotha/Walagothi* appeared, reflecting the native custom of naming after colors. The Hreidgotha was the "Scythian" name of the Ostrogoths, the Balagotha were the Visigoths. The name Hreidgotha was shortened to *Hreida*, meaning "reds" or "glorious."[111] We suggest that the first meaning is the equivalent to the name Russi. The Balagotha came also to be known as the *Balingi*. This name appeared in a variety of distorted forms: *Balingi, Valingi, Gualingi,* all reflecting the uncertainty of Latin writers in how to treat the Greek, Slavic, and Germanic *b*.[112] Furthermore, in Slavia the name was subjected to additional change in that *l* was replaced with *r*, a common phenomenon found in many names and words that were borrowed from one language to another over the centuries in Slavia, Great Scythia, and in the interface of Romania and Barbaricum. The original form *Balingi* became *Varangi* in Slavic languages, *Varangoi* in Rhomaean. In East Slavic the name further changed to *Varjagi*.

---

[110]   Wolfram, *op. cit.*, pp. 25–6.
[111]   Pritsak, *op. cit.*, p. 214–20 and *passim*.
[112]   W. Goffart, "The Supposedly 'Frankish' Table of Nations: An Edition and Study," *Frühmittelalterliche Studien*, XVII (1983), pp. 98–130, especially, pp. 120–2, 126.

In medieval Russia, the whole northwestern quarter of the world was designated with the name Varjag. Thus, the Baltic Sea became the Varjag Sea. The name passed into Arabic where it gave *al-Baḥr al-Barank*. The Black Sea came thus to be called the Russian Sea. Here we have a matched color pair of names. The northern or western sea was white, the southern or eastern sea was red, for the ethnonyms Varjagi and Russi appear to be a color pair, where the first means "whites," the second "reds." Further, in medieval Russia, numerous peoples of western Europe who were not Slavs were called Varjagi. Of course the people so designated never used the name themselves. It is futile to look for a specific European nation whose name resembles the name Varjagi, for the latter derives from the form Balagotha, which, in turn, was an alternate name for the Goths who called themselves Visigotha in their language.

After the fall of the West Roman Empire, the Slavs, who call themselves *Hrvati* (Croats) assembled at Duvno, the ancient capital of Dalmatia, to define the political and ecclesiastical subdivisions of their country. The Croat king declared that Croatia which stretched toward sunrise be called Red Croatia, the other stretching toward sunset be called White Croatia. The Croat nation accepted these appellations, for they took them as natural, their own traditional way of indicating the directions of the horizon, just as they knew that other peoples used other ways for the same purpose. Had the Croat king been of Germanic stock, he would have split Croatia into eastern and western sections, after Eos and Hesper; had he been a Roman he would have divided his realm according to altitude and called it Croatia Superior and Croatia Inferior. The fact that Red Croatia was also called Dalmatia Superior, White Croatia Dalmatia Inferior proves that the function of the color attributed to each group of the Croats is relative. It is not likely that the Croats were divided into Red and White Croats because of their looks, rather the colors stand for each group's geographical position, east and west.

Even a cursory survey of the literature dealing with ethnonys shows that there is no consensus regarding the origin and function of color attributes in ethnic names, just as there is no generally acceptable explanation of the same phenomenon in geographical names. It would serve no purpose to discuss here all the varied and contradictory explanations and theories concerning the true meaning of colors in ethnonymy, especially since most of them are based on insufficient evidence. Although we have no way of showing to the satisfaction of all that, for example, the White Khazars were not more handsome than their Black Khazar cousins, we suggest that colors in ethnonymy may serve other than the descriptive functions. The scholars who insist the custom of naming after colors was not primordially Slavic but a rather dated borrowing from the Iranian and Turkic peoples should explain when and how the exchange was made. In the meantime, we suggest that colors in ethnonymy be examined with the possibility that we are dealing with the universal Sino–Croatian system discussed in Chapter III.

Resting on reasonable certainty concerning the positional function of the attributes of color in the Croatian ethnonym, we suggest that Liudprand of Cremona's remark on the name Rusii be modified to read: They are called Rusii because of their geographical location.

CHAPTER VI

RUSSI

RHOS, GOG AND MAGOG

Ezekiel and other ancient Hebrew prophets, who so vividly described events of the latter days as they "saw" them, have exerted a tremendous influence on a sizeable portion of literary, artistic, and other achievements of western peoples. In their visionary scenarios, some of them assigned a prominent role to the peoples of the north. It all began under King Ahab when Yahweh ordered the prophet Elijah to anoint a Hebrew king and one to their northern neighbors, the Aramaeans, who will wreak frightful havoc among the children of Israel as punishment for their sins. Isaiah makes Yahweh use the warlike Assyrians for a similar purpose. Although the prophet does not specifically name the executors of divine punishment, it is clear from the context that he had the Assyrians in mind. Jeremiah is also vague, for he, too, fails to name the awesome northern nation which he makes Yahweh dangle like a sword of Damocles over the heads of the Israelites, giving license to exegesists to speculate. Ezekiel's eschatological visions are our sole source on Rhōs and his involvement with Gog and Magog in the affairs of Southwest Asia. The koine version of the Book of Ezekiel is the cornerstone on which rests the connection between the Russians and the "end of days," as well as the source of the learned form of the name Russi, that is, Harūs, hoi Rhōs, and al-Rūs. Russia came to play a role in the imagined Armageddon through the believed connection of Rhōs both with Gog and Magog and with the Russians.

Of interest for our topic is Ezekiel's elaboration upon the ancient theme of universal destruction and a fuller involvement of the northern quarter in the imagined events. The prophet "saw" the day when Yahweh will have had annihilated all the sinners of Israel. Then, as the righteous Remnant is living peacefully in the center of the earth at and near Mount Zion, Yahweh orders Ezekiel to prophesy against Gog, King of Magog, saying:

> And the word of the Lord came unto me, saying, Son of man, set thy face against Gog, the land of Magog, the chief prince of Meshech and Tubal, and prophesy against him, and say, Thus saith the Lord God; Behold, I am against thee, O Gog, the chief prince of Meshech and Tubal: and I will turn thee back, and put hooks into thy jaws, and I will bring thee forth, and all thine army, horses and horsemen, all of them clothed with all sorts of armor, even a great company with bucklers and shields, all of them handling swords: Persia, Ethiopia, and Libya with them; all of them with shield and helmet: Gomer, and all his bands; the house of Togar'mah of the north quarters, and all his bands and many people with thee.[1]

The armies of the whole known world led by Gog march against the Remnant of Israel, "people got out of peoples," who at that time, after they had been thoroughly purified, engage in animal husbandry and agriculture and lead peaceful lives. The drama heightens as Ezekiel repeatedly contrasts the peaceful, unwarlike and purified Israelites with the fierce warlike character of Gog and his armies, and their desire to plunder Yahweh's people. Yahweh orders Ezekiel to speak thus to Gog:

> In that day when my people of Israel dwelleth safely, shalt thou not know it? And thou shalt come from thy place out of the north parts, thou, and many people with thee, all of them riding upon horses, a great company, and a mighty army: and thou shalt come up against my people of Israel, as a cloud to cover the land; it shall be in the latter days, and I will bring thee against my land, that the heathen may know me, when I shall be sanctified in thee, O Gog, before their eyes.[2]

---

[1] Ezekiel 38:1-6.
[2] Ezekiel 38:14-16.

Yahweh will annihilate Gog and his armies. In Ezekiel 39 the horrible massacre of the warriors of the whole world led by Gog is repeated and expounded. The chapter opens with Yahweh urging Ezekiel to prophesy against Gog saying:

> Behold, I am against thee, O Gog, the chief prince of Meshech and Tubal: and I will turn thee back, and leave but the sixth part of thee, and will cause thee to come up from the north parts, and will bring thee upon the mountains of Israel.[3]

There the invaders will perish. Gog, his armies, and the people that will be with him will be massacred and offered by Yahweh as carrion to birds of prey and wild beasts. Yahweh will rain fire on the land of Magog and those who "dwell carelessly in the isles," so that they may know that he is the Lord.

Following these events the inhabitants of the cities of Israel will come out and for seven years they will be busy disposing of the corpses of the international armies that their god will have destroyed. In "the valley of the passengers [sc. the valley of the Abarim], east of the sea," will be the burial place of Gog and his multitudes. The valley will be renamed *Haman-Gog* "the multitude of Gog"; there is already the city of Haman in that valley.

Gog and Magog are probably some of the most debated biblical names, while their supposed leader, Rhōs, is even more controversial. To the enormous exegetical literature we wish to add our interpretation of how these names originated, aimed at clarifying some unsettled questions from Russia's past. The King James' version of the Bible knows one name only which looks like Rhōs. It is Rosh (Ros in Greek, Ros in Latin, Rš in Hebrew) who, along with his brothers Muppim, Huppim, and others, is named as a son of Benjamin.[4] The name Rhōs does not appear in the King James' version because the seventeenth-century English translators of the Bible depended principally on the authority of St. Jerome, a native of White Croatia and the author of the Vulgate. In western Europe his Latin version of the Bible remained until modern times the principal, if not the only,

---

[3] Ezekiel 39:1-3.
[4] Gen.46:21.

authoritative translation from Hebrew and Greek of both the Old and New Testaments. The English Bible has no name Rhōs because it is absent from the Vulgate. The first English-language version of the Bible which mentions Rhōs is a translation of the Septuagint by Charles Lee Benton, published in London in 1851. Benton's Ezekiel 38:2:

> And the word of the Lord came to me, saying, Son of man, lift thy face against Gog, and the land of Magog, Rhos, prince of Mesoch and Thobel, and prophesy against him, and say to him, Thus saith the Lord.

Ezekiel 39:1 of the same translation:

> Therefore, thou son of man, prophesy against Gog, and say Thus saith the Lord God; Behold I am against thee, O Gog, Rhos, prince of Meshech and Tubal.

The difference between the two passages quoted from this translation of the Septuagint and the King James' version and the Vulgate is that St. Jerome understood the Hebrew word *rš* as "head," rather than as a proper name. His version of the same passage reads:

> fili hominis pone faciam tuam contra Gog terram Magog
> principem capitis Mosoch et Thubal
> et vaticinare de eo et dices ad eum
> haec dicit Dominus Deus
> ecce ego ad te Gog principem capitis Mosoch et
> Thubal(Ezechiel 38:2)

> tu autem fili hominis vaticinare adversum Gog et dices
> haec dicit Dominus Deus
> ecce ego super te Gog principem capitis
> Mosoch et Thubal (Ezechiel 39:1)

In English the term *princeps capitis* appears as "chief prince." In Croatian and in other Slavic languages which follow St. Jerome the phrase is *veliki knez, velikij knjaz* "grand duke."

Until recently it was believed that St. Jerome was correct in translating the Hebrew words *rš malik Mesech wa Thubal* as *princeps capitis Mosoch et Thubal*. Scholars were fortified in this belief because, with the exception of Benjamin's son Rosh, no proper name that resembles Rhos appears elsewhere in the Bible. However, more recent translations of Isaiah include the name Roš. Thus, a new version of Isaiah 66:19 reads:

> And I will set a sign among them, and I will send those that escape of them into the nations, to Tarshish, Pul (rather than Pud), and Lud, Mošek, Roš (the names Mošek and Roš replace the phrase "that draw the bow" of earlier translations), Tubal and Javan, to the isles afar off, that have not heard my name, neither have seen my glory; and they shall declare my glory among the Gentiles.

In the Septuagint the peoples and places listed are:

> kai kataleipso ep' auton semeina kai exapostelo eks auton sesosmenous eis ta ethne, eis Tharsis kai Phud kai Lud kai Mosoch kai Thobel kai eis ten Hellada kai eis tas nesous tas porro. ...

The Vulgate:

> et ponam in eis signum et mittam ex eis qui solvati fuerint ad gentes in mari, in Africa in Lydia tenentes sagittam in Italiam et Graeciam ad insulas longe. ...

It is clear that liberties were taken by various translators with the names of peoples and places to be visited by Yahweh's emissaries. St. Jerome understood Tarshish to mean "the sea," Phut (rather than Pud) as Africa (Libya in Greek) and Lud as Lydia. He followed the Septuagint in ignoring Roš, while the Mosoch and Thobel he translated as *tenentes sagittam* "that draw the bow." Javan and the islands he rendered as "Greece, Italy, and the far away islands," although the Hebrew prophet may have had no knowledge of Italy at all. For the sake of comparison and as evidence that the translators of the King James' version followed St. Jerome here is the passage as they understood it:

> And I will set a sign among them, and I will send those that escape of them unto the nations, to Tarshish, Pul, and Lud, that draw the bow, to Tubal, and Javan, to the isles afar off...

St. Jerome's translation is both literal and accurate. The names Mosoch, Thobel and perhaps Roš were difficult to render into

Latin. They would have been meaningless to his readers if they were left as proper names. Somehow he must have obtained additional information about them either from his Palestinian informants, other texts, or from a marginal gloss. He had reason to believe that the named peoples were horsemen and accomplished archers. In Ezekiel 38 and 39 he translated *rš malik* as "chief prince." In Isaiah 66:19 he replaced the word or name *rš* along with the incomprehensible names Mosoch and Thobel with a phrase *"tenentes sagittam"* that describes the warlike character of these people as perceived by their neighbors, the Hebrews, Assyrians, and other Afroasians.

The fact that Roš appears in the company of Meshech and Thubal, the Muški and Tabal of Assyrian documents, may be an indication of his identity. It is quite plausible that *rš* stands neither for the word "head," nor for a people, but that it is rather the name of one of the four kings of Urartu, named Rusas.[5] In any case, it is admissible to search for Roš, whether the name designates an individual or a people, in the same general area where the other warlike tribes and nations known to the ancient Hebrews lived. That is, north of Palestine, in Anatolia, Upper Asia, or Transcaucasia. That is, at the southern fringes of Russia.

It remains to clarify the names of Gog and Magog. The question of Gog and Magog is complicated for a number of reasons. Magog is mentioned in Genesis 10:2 as a son of Japheth, one of his five sons without indicated descendants. Josephus Flavius made him into the founder of the otherwise unknown Magogians, whom, he states, the Greeks called Scythians.[6] The similarity between the pair Gog and Magog and the pair Getae and Massagetae must have impressed itself upon those scholars who place an equation sign between the two sets.

The pair Gog and Magog belong to the category of names differentiated by specifically marking one member of the pair with the syllable *ma-*. The best solution of the question of the meaning and purpose of this procedure is to be found in the

---

[5] R.D. Barnett, "Phrygia and the Peoples of Anatolia in the Iron Age," *CAH*, II.2³ (1975), pp.425–6; Vernadsky, *The Origin of Russia*, p. 189, n. 2.

[6] *Jewish Antiquities*, I. 123; *see also* Anderson, *op. cit.*, pp. 4-8.

ancient and still applied Levantine method of referring to a set of objects for which one wishes to show disrespect or with which one is impatient, or about which one wishes to appear vague. For example, the modern Turks and Jews practice this method quite a lot in everyday speech. In Turkish, if one wishes to name, say, two cities but does not care to specify the name of the second, one says "Istanbul, Mistanbul," "Bursa, Mursa." Depending on the context this could mean either "Istanbul or some other city," or "I do not care whether it be Istanbul or another city." We propose that the pair Gog and Magog as they appear in the Book of Ezekiel be also interpreted in this manner. The biblical Gog and Magog appear to have settled in or near a northeastern region which the Assyrians designated as Zamua and Mazamua.[7]

Regardless of the origin and early meaning of the pair Gog and Magog, it appears that, as used by Ezekiel, they did not designate any specific persons or people, but were rather intended as a brief and contemptuous label for the warlike multitudes of the north.

From Ezekiel onward Gog and Magog had a rich life in the imagination of the Hebrews and their ideological heirs, the early Christians and Muslims. The names were applied freely and loosely, for they were not restricted to any specific geographical or ethnic meaning. The flexibility with which the ancient Hebrews could apply the phrase "Gog and Magog" is evident from the fact that in the Hebrew Sibylline Oracles they are used to designate a country between the rivers of Ethiopia, a country full of blood and scheduled to be devastated. In the Haggadah Gog and Magog appear as the enemies of the Lord at the end of time. Here they are two names for one single nation. Gog and Magog were often moved not only across the geographical expanse of the known world but also through time. Introduced at first as future enemies of Israel, the names could easily be

---

[7] There are many names of this nature. For instance, in the Persian Empire a satrapy called Saka, rhyming with another one called Maka: Saka-Maka. The name Saka derives from the Persian name for the nomads of the Eurasian steppe, known as Sacae or Scythians in Europe. The Muslims imagined near the land of the Gog and Magog the peoples called Čin and Mačin. *See,* Anderson, *op. cit.,* p. 6, note 6.

attached to any present or future people or city which the fancy of the eschatologist envisaged, as well as to be taken into the past as far as the days of Moses and applied to a people who then were hostile to the Hebrews. In fact, Moses is supposed to have seen Gog and his multitudinous host advancing against Israel in the valley of Jericho.[8]

As St. Jerome struggled to render the Book of Ezekiel into Latin and get meaning out of the confused ethnic geography, he realized that Gog and Magog were not used by the prophet to designate any specific people but rather forces of evil, or "pseudo-knowledge that sets itself up against the truth."

In the national consciousness of the peoples of Egypt and Southwest Asia the extreme north, comprising Upper Asia, Anatolia, and Transcaucasia, was engraved as the quarter from which armies of men in chariots or on horseback regularly came south with hostile intentions. The "men of the north," were collectively and continuously called the *Umman Manda* "the great horde" in Baylonia.[9] The earliest recorded invaders from the north were the unnamed horde which swept through Sumer in the third millennium BC. They were followed by peoples known individually as the Gutians, who invaded and conquered Sumer and Akkad, the Hyksos, who invaded Egypt and ruled it for two centuries, the Hittites, who sacked Babylon in 1559 BC, the Kassites, who conquered and ruled Babylon for 450 years, the Cimmerians and Scythians, who crisscrossed the civilized world with hostile intentions, and finally the Medes and Persians, who conquered the Fertile Crescent and Egypt and held them under their rule when Ezekiel prophesied. These invasions from the north must have left a powerful impression on the common peoples in North Africa and Southwest Asia and, of course, on those who intellectualized the broad issues of life and death. This millennial process continued after Ezekiel into the Middle Ages when the Goths, Huns, Avars, Khazars, and Russians forced their way through the Derbent Gate. It ended with the invasions of Mongols in the High Middle Ages. This imprecisely recorded and vaguely remembered history of

---

[8] *EJ*, VII, cols. 691–3.
[9] Lehhmann-Haupt, "Kimmerier," col. 417; this scholar suggests that the term *manda* may be a folk-etymology of the Iranian tribe Mandai(a).

invasions from the north was the reason why St. Jerome interpreted the names Roš, Moshoch, and Thobal of Isaiah 66:19 as *tenentes sagittam* "that draw the bow." Regardless of the ultimate place of origin of these peoples, it is a fact of geography that they had to pass by the land of the Muški and Tubal peoples of Upper Asia and through the land ruled by several kings named Rusas on their way to Lower Asia, Palestine, and Egypt.

Hostilities and antagonism between North and South in Southwest Asia and Egypt were a result of an uneven level of cultural development of the two quarters. In Mesopotamia, the south, comprising the lower basins of the Tigris and Euphrates rivers, was the center of the earliest known cities, of civilization, while the north remained relatively underdeveloped. The transhumance-type of mountain pastoralism is still an important aspect of the economy and culture in the upper valleys of these and other rivers, where once the kingdom of Urartu thrived. In the imagination of the literate peoples of Southwest Asia and Egypt, Russia and all of Europe were the abode of extreme and unknown barbarity, for they lay beyond Anatolia and Upper Asia whose inhabitants were known, hated, feared, and at times admired by their more civilized southern neighbors. As its very name in the Semitic languages shows, Europe was truly a "land of darkness."

The southerners fought numerous battles against the northern invaders whose military characteristics were arrows, cavalry, and great numbers of soldiers. Some among the blase, sophisticated, or disgruntled among the southerners yearned poetically for the coming of the northerners to purge the sinners in the supposedly corrupt and sinful southern lands. Expanding upon the belles-lettres and folklore of their Mesopotamian antecedents, the Hebrew eschatologists saw the peoples of the northern quarter as instruments of Yahweh in his periodic purges of sinners in the whole civilized world.

To the Egyptians the extreme north was in Greece, Anatolia, and Upper Asia. To the Sumerians and their successor states and civilizations it was in Upper Asia drained by the Upper Euphrates and Tigris and called appropriately Urartu "uplands." The Hebrews imagined the north in the land of Gog and Magog, also somewhere in Upper Asia. Though these civilized ancient peoples provide valuable information on the peoples of ancient Russia, they observed them only as they prepared for military campaigns against the south. The southerners believed that Upper Asia was their gathering place. Their disinterest in them as people is shown by the generic names they used, such as *Umman Manda* "great horde," Gog and Magog, "those that draw the bow," etc. Nevertheless, in the midst of this ancient mosaic of awesome peoples, many medieval and modern observers readily identify the Russians.

THE RUSSIANS AND ARMAGEDDON

Revelation of John the Divine is our only source on Armageddon. In order to see whether the author intended that Russia play a role at the battle of Armageddon, it is necessary to picture him within his own political, ideological, and cultural milieu and to cast the geography of Revelation against the contemporary geographical knowledge.

Our author flourished at the end of the first century AD. His book appears to have been written during the reign of the Roman Emperor Domitian (81–96). He calls himself John and says he was an exile on the island of Patmos. Nothing else is known about the man. It was once believed that he was John, the son of Zabedee and brother of James, one of the twelve apostles of Jesus. This view is not widely held nowadays. Whereas the Apostle had been an Aramaic-speaking Jew who may have not known Greek, the author of Revelation, on the other hand, appears to have known both Greek and Hebrew. In his day Christianity was still predominately a Jewish sect, so there is no ground upon which to claim him for another nationality.

John ran afoul of Roman law, not as a Jew but as a Christian. The Jews had traditionally been exempt from the emperor worship. The Christians, being mostly Jews, at the beginning were also exempt. As non-Jews became the majority of Christians they could no longer claim exemption on the ground of Jewish ethnicity. Yet, they refused to take part in the cult of the state and the emperor. Nero (54–58) had tried to destroy them but had failed. After his death there emerged the belief in *Nero redivivus*, that is, that Nero would come back to continue the slaughter of Christians. This task was carried out by some of his successors until Constantine the Great became a Christian himself. Domitian, John's earthly lord, is counted among the more ardent enemies of Christians.

At the beginning of the first Christian millennium the geographical field of vision of knowledgeable Romans ranged beyond the frontiers of Romania, but it did not completely include the whole Old World. Most of Europe was still *terra incognita* to such giants as Strabo. Central, East, and South Asia were still unexplored, as was Sub-Saharan Africa. A politically aware Roman subject, as our author may have been, most likely knew that the center of the world was occupied by the Roman Empire. The state was surrounded by unorganized masses of barbarian clans, tribes, and federations. However, within the domain of the barbarians, called Barbaricum, a few nations lived under strong monarchies. In Asia, the empire of the Parthians was both a powerful state and a permanent rival of Rome. In Africa, after the conquest of Egypt, Lybia and Mauretania, no major power challenged Roman domination, though the mysterious and unknown Ethiopia loomed much larger in the imagination of the Mediterranean peoples than its ability to challenge Rome warranted. After they had pushed their frontiers to the Humber, Rhine, and the Danube and established the *limes* there, the Romans believed they ruled Europe. But beyond the border lived many peoples, most of whom had strong reasons to hate Rome. The Romans knew them collectively as Celts, Germans, Dacians, and Sarmatians. In the ocean they saw, or so they believed, numerous islands, some real like Ireland, others fabulous, like the Isle of the Blessed. But no organized power could challenge Roman authority from these islands. Dacia under King Burebista resisted and challenged Roman domination in the middle and lower Danube valley. It was destroyed by Trajan, after Revelation had been composed. Great Scythia, known also as Sarmatia, was peopled by a multitude of nomadic host. At the time of the writing of Revelation the name given to these peoples in the popular literature of the Levant and Egypt was Gog and Magog. It must be stressed that St. John the Divine and his contemporaries had only vague ideas about Russia and were unaware of the existence of the continent of America in the western hemisphere and of Australia and Antarctica in the southern.

The Book of Revelation consists of three sections. First, the general cover letter describes the content of the enclosure. It is the revelation of "things which must surely come to pass," conveyed by the deity via angels to John who states that he saw all that which is written in the book. He is merely passing it along to the seven churches, saying that those who will hear and keep the prophecy are blessed, "for the time is at hand."

The second section consists of letters to the seven prominent bishoprics of Asia Minor dictated by the corresponding angel.

The third section is the main body of the text of the Apocalypse.[10] The message is confused and confusing to say the least. The book opens with our author still in the place of confinement at Patmos. John looked up and saw a door opened in heaven. A trumpet-like voice asked him to come up to be shown "things which must be hereafter." He obeyed, came to the throne in heaven. He describes it borrowing passages, words, phrases, and images from Exodus and Ezekiel.

The clash that would lead to Armageddon, like the one that led to the Trojan War, began in heaven. Of interest for our topic is the episode instigated by the so-called sixth angel, who

> poured out his vial upon the great river Euphrates; and the water thereof was dried up, that the way of the kings of the east might be prepared. And I saw three unclean spirits like frogs come out of the mouth of the dragon, and out of the mouth of the beast, and out of the mouth of the false prophet. For they are the spirits of devils, working miracles, which go forth unto the kings of the earth and of the whole world, to gather them to the battle of that great day of God Almighty. ... And he gathered them together into a place called in the Hebrew tongue Armageddon.[11]

It would be methodologically incorrect to interpret the above passage out of its temporal, ideological, political, geographic,

---

[10] Logically, a copy was to be attached to each of the seven letters sent to each of the seven churches. Nothing is known of this. A few centuries after, however, in the Christian world there was a profusion of copies of Revelation. It became one of the most controversial tracts of Christian literature. Its status as part of the Biblical canon is still questioned by some.

[11] Rev. 16:12–16.

and cultural context. At the time of the writing of Revelation the Roman Empire was at the height of its power. No human being could know when it would fall, though many, including John, wished this to happen soon. The angel who preceded the Armageddon angel, the fifth, had only succeeded in causing some damage to Rome but no total destruction. Therefore when the sixth angel did his work of making the Euphrates dry up in order for "the kings of the east" to march into the Roman Empire, our author could have had only Parthia in mind. John may have believed that there were many more kings in the east, but there is no evidence that he was aware of any peoples or kings beyond Parthia. In other words, Russia, Central Asia, China, Japan, India, and Southeast Asia lay beyond his ken.

The unholy trinity of the Dragon, the Beast, and the False Prophet emitted the unclean spirits who, in turn caused "the kings of the whole world" to march to Armageddon. Naturally, the kings that gathered at Armageddon were those whose lands lay at the borders of the Roman Empire. Nothing is said here about Russia or the northern quarter. The day of Armageddon is "that great day of God," known also by Old Testament prophets as "the latter day" or "that day."

The name "Armageddon," which appears only once in the whole literary corpus of the peoples of West Asia, has been a puzzlement to scholars. It seems logical that John had in mind either the city or the plain of Megiddo or Magedo in Canaan, which appeared several times in the Old Testament. It was at Megiddo that the Canaanite kings were defeated by the Hebrews.[12] It was there that king Josia perished.[13] The immediate model for John was "the mourning for Hadadrimon in the valley of Megiddon."[14] Megiddo was in the plain of Jezreel near Mount Carmel. It is widely believed that the name Armageddon derives from the Hebrew word *har* "mountain" and Megiddo, thus, "the Mountain of Megiddo." The mountain is Carmel, called by the Hebrews *Har Karmel* "mountain orchard," or "pleasant woodland." It is not very likely that the author had changed the hallowed name of Mount Carmel to that of the

12 Jdgs. 5:19.
13 4 Kings 23:29; 2 Chr. 35:22-25.
14 Zech. 12:11.

Mount of Megiddo. Nor is it likely that he meant the town itself, though it does stand on a hill. It is more logical to presume that he conflated two different literary references. One was the great mourning at Megiddon mentioned by Zechariah, the other is the convention established by Old Testament eschatologists, especially by Ezekiel, that the decisive battle between Yahweh and his chosen people and the nations of the earth take place in and around a mountain. Old Testament eschatologists imagined Mount Zion as the locale, while John moved the imaginary battlefield to Armageddon.

While the armies of good and evil (white and red) waited at Armageddon ready for battle, the supreme deity in John's mind intervened by sending out the seventh angel who poured out his vial into the air. Then the voice came out of the temple saying: "It is done." This was accompanied by the customary voices, thundering, lightnings, and an earthquake greater than men had ever experienced. Uppermost in our author's mind was Rome which he hated. Therefore he begins his description of the final destruction of the world by the breakup of the great city into three parts. The cities of gentiles fell.[15] The islands and the mountains disappeared, and a great hail fell upon mankind. All this had already happened in the imagination of Old Testament eschatologists.

The victory of the white horsemen and his white army over the red army is not the final victory. There is still the Red Dragon, alias Satan. An angel came down with the key to the bottomless pit and a chain. He captured Satan and chained him in the pit for a thousand years. This signals the beginning of the millennium. During this period Jesus of Nazareth, the King of Kings, shall reign unopposed. The souls of the martyred Christians and of those who did not worship the Beast, nor his image, nor had received his mark on their foreheads or arms, shall live and reign with him for the duration of the millennium. The rest of mankind shall be dead and damned. Their death shall

---

[15] This should mean all the cities in the world. There were no other than gentile cities at that time, for the earthly Jerusalem and other cities and villages in Palestine were ruled by the Romans and were counted as gentile cities.

be spiritual, since there must be people on earth physically alive
for Satan to do his last trick with them.

At the expiration of the millennium

> Satan shall be loosed out of his prison, and shall go out to deceive
> the nations which are in the four quarters of the earth, Gog and
> Magog, to gather them together for battle: the number of whom is
> as the sand of the sea. And they went up on the breadth of the
> earth, and compassed the camp of the saints about, and the
> beloved city: and fire came down from God out of heaven, and
> devoured them. And the devil that deceived them was cast into the
> lake of fire and brimstone, where the beast and the false prophet
> are, and shall be tormented day and night for ever and ever.

There is no explanation why Satan was released, unless it is to
bring perdition to the rest of mankind, to those who lived
beyond the frontiers of Rome. Much has been made in the
literature about the Gog and Magog of this passage. Some
interpreters of Revelation imagine them as Russians and the
place of their destruction they call Armageddon. Although some
Hebrew eschatologists, who preceded John, and the Koran,
which followed it, place Gog and Magog in the northern quarter,
John says clearly that they were the nations who inhabited *all
four quarters*, not just one. The expression "Gog and Magog"
may be a label he used for the "them" portion of humanity,
similar to the words *goyim* of the ancient Hebrews and modern
Jews and *barbaroi* of the Greeks. The Gog and Magog in the
above passage came out to lay siege to the camp of the saints
and the beloved city. This is kingdom of Jesus and his saints
with Jerusalem as its capital. The opposites here are the saints
versus Gog and Magog, the beloved city versus the four
quarters. To limit Gog and Magog of this passage first to the
northern quarter then to the Russians would be to violate both
the letter and the spirit of Revelation.

To conclude, when John had his visions at the end of the first
Christian century the names Gog and Magog were well known
in Southwest Asia and Egypt. They were a part of the vocabulary of the common man, not merely technical terms used by
writers of eschatological literature. We must assume that John
was a Jewish follower of Jesus and that he was steeped in the
eschatological lore of his and other peoples. The names Gog and
Magog of Revelation are identical with the names that appear in

Ezekiel. The identity between the two sets of names goes only as far as the form, that is, the labels, whereas the ethnic content is as imprecise in Revelation as it is in the book of Ezekiel.

We saw that a connection between Russia and Muscovy with Gog and Magog by way of Rhōs and Meshech has no basis in the Scriptures as they are understood by serious scholars. The most that we could concede on this point to those who insist that the prophets, although they used names of vaguely known peoples of Upper Asia, had intended to convey "symbolically" the meaning of the totality of what today stands for Russia. Once we do this, however, we leave free scholarly inquiry and enter the realm of the occult. As far as Russia and Armageddon go a connection is even weaker.

The battle at Armageddon was imagined by the eschatologist as a clash between the red armies of Rome and Parthia and the white army of Jesus. In the red armies gathered for the "semifinal" battle at Armageddon there was no mention of either Rhōs, Gog and Magog and not even of the northern quarter. The northern quarter, and therefore the region where Russia later emerged, sent no warriors to Armageddon. People who consider the Book of Revelation as divine truth ought not to fear, but love, Armageddon, for it leads to the Millennium. They should not fear Russia and its possible unilateral intervention, for it will enter the final fray only as a member of the world-wide confederation of Gog and Magog who inhabit all four quarters. This event shall take place at the expiration of the Millennium as an inexplicable preparation for Doomsday, which those whose names are in the book of life should greet with joy.

ROSOMONI, HARŪS, RUZZI

In the mid-sixth century of the Christian era, while Justinian, a native of Slavia nova, ruled the Roman Empire from the city of his fellow countryman, Constantine, the Gothic historian Jordanes recorded the Russian name in the form of *Rosomoni* "red men," calling the people it designated "gens infida."[16]

---

[16]   *Getica*, 129; note 389, pp. 279–80 of E.Č. Skržinskaja's edition.

At approximately the same time, the Russian name appears in another source, which we quote *in extenso*:

Now Ptolemy Philadelphus, king of Egypt, as the Chronicle of Eusebius of Caesarea declares, two hundred and eighty years and more before the birth of our Lord, at the beginning of his reign, set the Jewish captives in Egypt free and sent offerings to Jerusalem to Isra`el (El'azar is meant), who was priest at that time; and he assembled seventy men learned in the law and had the Holy Scriptures translated from the Hebrew tongue into Greek; and he stored them up and kept them with him; for in this matter he was indeed moved by God, in order to prepare for the calling of the nations who should attain to knowledge, that they might be true worshippers of the glorious Trinity through the ministration of the Spirit.

Yet again about the space of one hundred and thirty years after him Ptolemy Philometor also was honourably moved and exerted himself, and by means of ambassadors and letters and presents, which he sent and dispatched to the rulers of the countries of the nations, he urged them to write down and send to him the limits of the lands under their sway and of the neighbouring peoples, and also a description of their habitations and their customs. And they wrote and sent them to him except the northern region extending to the East and to the West. And we have thought it necessary to write it out here at the end for the understanding of the discerning. And the account is as follows: .....

This description of the peoples of the world was made, as recorded above, by the exertions of Ptolemy Philometor and in the thirtieth year of his reign, one hundred and fifty years before the birth of our Saviour, so that the space of time from that day to the present, which is the twenty-eighth year of the reign of Justinian, the serene king of our days, the eight hundred and sixty-sixth year of Alexander, and the three hundred and thirty-third Olympiad, will be found (sc. 555 A.D.) to be a space of seven hundred and eleven years. In such a space of time, therefore, how many cities have been built and added among all peoples in the world from the time of Ptolemy down to the present day, and especially since the birth of our Saviour! And peace has reigned among nations and kindreds and tongues, and they have not observed their former custom, nor has nation stood up to make war or to use their swords against nation, nor have they contended in battle, in that the prophecy has been fulfilled in them which says, "They shall beat their swords into plowshares and their spears into pruning-hooks."

And besides these there are also in this northern region five believing peoples, and their bishops are twenty-four, and their Catholic lives at D'win, the chief city of Persian Armenia. The name of their Catholic was Gregory, a righteous and a distinguished man.

Further Gurzan (Georgia), a country in Armenia, and its language is like Greek; and they have a Christian prince, who is subject to the king of Persia.

Further the country of Arran in the country of Armenia, with a language of its own, a believing people, and there are also heathens living in it.

Further the country of Sisagan, with a language of its own, a believing people, and there are also heathens living in it.

The country of Bazgun (Abasgia), with a language of its own, which adjoins and extends to the Caspian Gates and sea, the Gates in the land of the Huns. And beyond the Gates are the Bulgarians with their own language, a heathen and barbarous people, and they have cities; and the men of the race of Dadu (?), and they live on the mountains and have strongholds; the Unnogur, a people living in tents, the Ogor, the Sabir, the Bulgarian, the Khorthrigor, the Avar, the Khasar, the Dirmar, the Sarurgur (?), the Bagarsik (?) the Khulas (?), the Abdel, the Ephthalite, these thirteen people dwelling in tents; and they live on the flesh of cattle and fish and wild beasts and by arms; and beyond them the tribe of the pigmies and of the dog-men, and north-west of them the Amazons, women with one breast each, who live entirely by themselves and fight in arms and on horseback; and there is no male among them, but when they wish to pair, they go in peaceful fashion to a tribe near their country and hold intercourse with them for a month of days and return to their country; and when they bear a child, if it is a male, they kill it, and if it is a female, they preserve it alive; and in this way they keep up their ranks. And the tribe which lives near them is the Harus (?), tall, big-limbed men, who have no weapons of war, and horses cannot carry them because of the bigness of their limbs. And to the east again verging on the north are three other black tribes.[17]

The Syriac form *Harūs* is derived from the *Rhōs* of the Septuagint. Since the Harūs were considered as neighbors of the Amazons and other mythical and real peoples who were imagined or in fact lived north of the Caucasus and beyond the

[17] Zachariah Rhetor, *Ecclesiastical History*, XII, vii; the English is from *The Syriac Chronicle known as that of Zachariah of Mitylene*, transl. F.J. Hamilton and E.W. Brooks (London, 1899), pp. 325–328, Harūs, p. 328; the Syriac text in *Historia Ecclesiastica*, ed. E.W. Brooks (Paris, 1919) (=*Corpus Scriptorum Christianorum Orientalium; Scriptores Syri, Series Tertia*, Vol. VI).

Derbent Gate, in Russia, we suggest that they be equated to the Rosomoni of Jordanes, as well as to the Anthi of Pliny. At the basis of both these names is the native form *rusyj. The latter converged with the form Rhōs from the Septuagint, itself a transcription of the Hebrew rš "head." The unreal Rhōs of Ezekiel were readily located in southern Russia because there lived a real people whose name resembles them closely, namely the Russi.

The Slavic form of the name Russi was more faithfully recorded in a work ascribed to an unknown ninth-century Bavarian geographer. Writing in Latin, this author mentions a people by the name of *Ruzzi* who must be identical with the Russi.[18]

RUSINI—RUTHENI

In the Middle Ages, the Slavs added the suffix -in to the name Rus' to render it *Rusin-Rusii*.[19] The name Rusini became Rutheni in Latin.

The medieval and modern names Rusini-Rutheni in Slavia are obviously similar to at least two ancient ethnonyms: Rutuli in Italy[20] and Ruteni in Gaul. The name Rutuli did not survive the Roman Empire as a self-designation of any people. Like so many names of tribes and nations it also vanished. The Ruteni of Gaul, however, have had a very interesting literary afterlife. Like the names of their namesakes in Latium and in Slavia, their ethnonym also appears to derive from the same root word for the color red.

At the time of the Roman conquest of their land, the Ruteni lived along the western foothills of the Cemmenus Mountains and between the rivers Tarn and Lot. Among the neighbors of

---

[18] Anonymous Bavarus Geographus, *Descriptio civitatum ad septentrionalem plagam Danubii* , ed. B. Horák and D. Trávníček (Prague, 1956) (=*Rozpravy Českoslov. Akad. Věd.* 66/2), p. 3.

[19] The formation of Rusin from Rus is regular and common in the Slavic languages. Rus-Rusin may be compared to Srb-Srbin, Hrvat-Hrvatin, Cigan-Ciganin, Arap-Arapin, etc.

[20] *See* above, p. 153-4.

the Ruteni were the people called Antobroges whose political center was at the city named Antobrix. West of the Ruteni were the Volcae who occupied the country between the lower valley of the Tarn and the northern foot of the Pyrenees. Their, chief city was Tolosa, modern Toulouse. The Ruteni and the Volcae were conquered by the Romans, and their lands made part of the Roman Empire.[21]

We have already stated that the so-called Celtic version of the origin of Rus' is based on the similarity between the name Ruteni in southern Gaul and Rutheni in Slavia. Those scholars who defend it ought to be consistent and add the Rutuli in Latium as ethnonymic ancestors of the Russians.

Later, in the Middle Ages, both the Ruteni and the Volcae, who by then were a Romance-speaking people, became quite notorious. The Ruteni expanded, "Rutenizing" the eastern branch of the Volcae and establishing the province or state of Roussillon. Roussillon changed hands between France and Spain until it was definitively annexed by the French king in 1659. Under the Republic, Roussillon was divided into *départements* and the name disappeared. It has recently been revived as the name of the Région Languedoc-Roussillon. The ethnonym Ruteni survives also as the name of the city of Rodez and the name of the region of Rouergue of which this city is the center. The descendants of the Volcae, whose medieval capital was known as Albi, were called the Albigensians.

In the High Middle Ages, the Rutenian name reappeared in Great Britain. In his *History of the Kings of Britain*, Geoffrey of Monmouth has much to say about the Ruteni. They were first mentioned in connection with Geoffrey's interpretation of Caesar's description of his conquest of Gaul and his invasion of Britain. In this description, the Roman conqueror launched his invasion of that island from "the seacoast of the Ruteni." This of course is an anachronism, for the only Ruteni known to Caesar were those who lived in the interior of southern Gaul far from the English Channel. Geoffrey projected the name Ruteni, who in his day occupied a region of Flanders facing Britain, to the time when other peoples lived there. Holdin, king of the Ruteni came to the plenary court held by King Arthur at the City of the

---

[21]   Caesar, *De bello Gallico*, I.45; VII.5,7,64,75,90; Strabo, 4.2.2.

Legions. The Ruteni fought on Arthur's side in his "war" with the Roman Emperor. These Ruteni are identical with the Flemings.

If one were so inclined one could find more namesakes of the Russians. Let us note briefly that along the coast of the Northern Ocean lived other peoples whose names resemble the Rutuli of Latium, the Ruteni of Gaul and the Rutheni of the Dnieper Valley. For instance, there were the Ruteni of the region of Rostringen in Frisland, while the eastern seacoast of Sweden is called Roslagen, which gave Ruotsi in Finnish.

It is clear that the Ruteni, whose name is almost identical with the name of the Rutuli round Ardea, were the eastern neighbors and perhaps the directional counterparts of the Volcae. There is no evidence in the sources that the Ruteni of Gaul have anything in common with the Rutuli of Latium, other than the similarity of names. As to the Rutheni in the Eastern Carpathians and in the Dnieper Valley, who appeared in the late Middle Ages and called themselves Rusi, Rusini or Rusiči, a connection has recently been proposed.[22] It is suggested here that the only common ground between the names Rutuli, Ruteni, and Rusini is that they all derive from a common Indo-European root designating the color red, and that the peoples who bore these names owed them to their geographical location in relation to their namers, not to their physical appearance, nor to their common descent.

RUSSI OR REDS

Liudprand of Cremona observed that the Rusii were one of the peoples living north of the East Roman Empire. We shall see that this was a common folk's name for the people to whom the learned of Rhomania applied names they took from the writings of the ancient Greeks or from the Bible. The erudite equivalents of the vulgar name Rusii were such ethnonyms as Hyperboreans, Scythians, Northern Scythians, Tauroscythians, Dromitae, Hellenes, etc. These names were used to refer to the medieval Russians in the justified belief that they occupied the same

[22]   Pritsak, *op. cit.*

northern regions once held by these other peoples and that they professed the religion of the ancient Hellenes. The Rusii were called hoi Rhōs because their actions, in the imagination of the Rhomaeans, resembled the role assigned by Yahweh to the leader of Gog and Magog called Rhōs in the Septuagint version of the Book of Ezekiel. The form Rhousioi, in turn, very closely resembles the native Slavic name.

Not knowing the original meaning of the name Rusii Liudprand postulated that it was owed to their red complexion and ruddy hair. Liudprand might have been influenced to give the name this interpretation because the adjective *rhousios* (*russus* in Latin) means "russet" or "red." Also, he may have seen the color red in the name because it reminded him of the Rutuli of Latium or of the Russati of the Roman and New Roman circus factions. Finally, the Russian name may have reminded him of the *rhousia chelandia* "red galleys" in the Rhomaean navy.[23]

We reject Liudprand's explanation of how the Russian name originated. If the Russians had been named "Reds" by the East Romans because of their complexion, this would imply that somehow they stood out among the numerous blond peoples of northern Eurasia. The Romans and the Rhomaeans had intimate contacts with the Nordic type of mankind, yet they had not coined an ethnonym for any of these peoples which could be interpreted as designating the color red. Though they frequently referred to the northerners as the "yellow" peoples, the color associated with their region was mostly black. We suggest that the colloquial East Roman name for the East Slavs reflects some native designation which reminded them of the Rhomaean adjective *rhousios*, perhaps, *rusyj*.[24] We should not be surprised that in the Middle Ages a people appeared whose name derives

---

[23]   These ships were in fact painted red. In Russian epic poetry the fixed color epithet for ships is "red." It is not clear whether the color red of the Rhomaean ships came through Russian influence, or whether it was a native Levantine custom. In the *Iliad* all Greek ships are black, except those which brought Odysseus from Ithaca, "twelve ships with bows red painted." II.637.

[24]   It is commonly accepted that the Greeks had borrowed this adjective from Latin, where *russeus/russus* means "dark red." In the Slavic languages *rusyj* means "yellow, red or ruddy." In the epic poetry of the South Slavs it is used as a fixed epithet with the word *glava*, as in *rusa glava* "ruddy head," or, poetically, a person with golden locks.

from the color red, for we have offered a catalog of ethnonyms associated with this color.

The color attribute in the Russian name may be traced to the ancient division of the Slavic peoples into the Venedae and Antae. It has been suggested here that the name Venedae is a Celtic translation of a Slavic name, possibly, Belcae, which derives from the adjective *bělyj* "white." The Belcae were White or West Slavs, the Antae Red or East Slavs, who also appeared as Russi, "reds."

We shall see that the Arabs learned the native name for the East Slavs from the king of Derbent who in the mid-seventh century guarded the Gate of Gates which Alexander the Great had allegedly built to keep out the northern savages. The Arabic form of the Russian name, *al-Rūs*, reflects both the Slavic designation Rusi and East Roman *hoi Rhōs*.

CHAPTER VII

RHOMANIA AND RUSSIA

THE RHOMAEAN EMPIRE AND SLAVIA

In late antiquity, the Roman rulers of Illyrian origin divided the Empire into the eastern and western halves which were further subdivided into prefectures, dioceses, and provinces.[1] The last legitimate western emperor, Nepos, was assassinated in Diocletian's palace at Split in Croatia on May 9, 480. A good portion of his domain reverted nominally to the East Roman, rather Rhomaean, Empire[2] which tried to assert its authority through its vassals, the Bishops of Rome and the sundry Germanic chieftains. The Diocese of Illyricum, once the heart of the Roman Empire and comprising modern Austria, Slovenia, Cis-Danubian Hungary, Croatia, and Bosnia, came under the control of the native peoples, now called Slavs. The Slavs were establishing their rule in Illyricum while watching several fragments of Germanic peoples wander through on their way from Magna Germania and Sarmatia Europaea to Italy, Gaul, Spain, and Africa. The Goths, Rugi, Heruli, Vandals, and finally

---

[1] Initiated by the Dalmatian Diocletian, continued by theMoesian Constantine and his heirs, the reorganization was finalized by Theodosius, an emperor of Spanish origin, who, like his countryman, Trajan, had earned much martial glory in the Balkans.

[2] Avoiding such insulting terms as "Byzantine, Greek, Graeco-oriental, Greekling, and Schismatic," introduced in the Middle Ages by people who denied the legitimacy to this polity, we follow those fine modern scholars who refer to it by an English rendering of the people's self-designation, which was always and almost exclusively their form of the Roman name, that is, Rhomaean, and to their state as Rhomania.

the Lombards halted for a while in Slavic Illyricum, the last named leaving Pannonia for Italy in 568. Others, like the Gepids and the *Gothi minores* vanished in the strudel of Balkan and Danubian history.

Though we must be grateful for every bit of information recorded and passed down to us by medieval observers, we are disappointed by the paucity of valuable data about their Slavic neighbors provided by the early Rhomaeans. In comparison to the ancient Greeks, Macedonians, and Romans their horizon had shrunk enormously, for it seems that they knew little or nothing about events taking place in the interior of North Central Eurasia. They may have been better informed about developments along the coasts of the Adriatic, Aegean, and Black seas, but the sources that have survived allow us to have only vague ideas. Since "barbarian" territory began almost at the Walls of Constantinople, often the field of vision of early Rhomaean writers also stopped there. They mention rarely the interior of the Balkan Peninsula, while the Danube had become quite a distant stream for them, some identifying it with the Physon of Paradise.

While observing the convulsions of Romania and the agony of Gothia, the Gothic historian Jordanes remarked that the Slavs, Venethi, and Antes (Antae) were carrying out cruel punishments of sinners, that is, were building their own Slavia.[3] At the same time, ancestors of the Russians whom he knew under the name of Antes and Rosomoni, calling the latter "gens infida," were transforming Sarmatia into Russia.[4] In 626, the Slavs and their Balkan and Asian allies laid siege to Constantinople.[5] We shall see that the first Muslim source which mentions the Russians under the year 642 calls them "enemies of the whole world."[6] They and their Slavic cousins continued to hold this position in the imagination of both their Muslim and Christian neighbors throughout the period discussed here.

After the Rhomaean Empire was forced by Slavs to abandon the *limes* on the Danube at the end of the sixth century, its rule

---

[3] *Getica*, 119.
[4] *Getica*, 129.
[5] Bačić, *Emergence*, pp. 291–9.
[6] *See* below, pp. 351–2.

in the Prefecture of Illyricum and the Diocese of Thrace also collapsed. The Emperor Heraclius, the son of a former exarch of Africa, appears to have accepted the *status quo* in the Balkans, concentrating his efforts in Asia and Africa where he was trying to regain territory lost to the Persians and prevent the Muslims from expelling the Rhomaeans from there.

Heraclius' successors divided their state into themata. With Anatolia becoming the Empire's core province, it was there that the new order was introduced.[7] Because the Rhomaeans controlled very little territory in the Balkans, they could not establish any themata there. The imperial possessions in the former Prefecture of Illyricum were reduced to Salonica, Athens, Patras, and Durrës. The former Diocese of Thrace became limited to Constantinople and its environs. The imperial capital, itself, was surrounded by Slavs.[8]

During the period which ran from the siege of Constantinople in 626 to the naval assault on this city by the Russians in 860, the political situation north of the Rhomaean Empire continued to be complex and tense. The Rhomaeans hated the Slavs, for the latter continued to hold onto the territory in the Balkans which they had conquered in the course of the sixth century and which the Rhomaeans believed were theirs by "right." The Slavs were able to challenge the Rhomaeans not only on land but also on the sea and usually cared little for the rights of the imperialists. Refusing to bow to the imperially administered religion, they performed the worship of their ancient gods and Jesus of Nazareth in their own Slavic language. Those Slavs and Antae who settled between the Carpathians and the Caucasus remained adherents of the "Hellenic," that is, pagan, faith until the end of the tenth century.

---

[7] H. Gelzer, *Die Genesis der byzantinischen Themenverfassung* (Leipzig, 1899); Constantine Porphyrogenitus, *De thematibus*, ed. and commented by A. Pertusi (Vatican 1952) (=*Studi e Testi*, 160), pp. 103–111; *see* also, map in *CMH*, IV.1, p. 69. The Cibyrraeot theme is also known as the theme of the Carabisiani.

[8] G. Ostrogorsky, *History of the Byzantine State*, transl. from the German by J. Hussey, rev. ed. (New Brunswick, N.J., 1969); *Miracula sancti Demetrii*, ed. P. Lemerle (Paris, 1979), I: *Le Texte*, miracle 4, 238, p. 210; II: *Commentaire*, pp. 115–16.

Expelled by Muslims from Egypt and the Levant, Christian refugees flooded Anatolia and that narrow strip of land in Europe
which remained under Rhomaean rule. Since the Empire had a
powerful navy and a merchant fleet, the God-protected city of
Constantine dominated the Sea of Marmara, while sharing the
Aegean and Mediterranean with Saracens, Slavs, international
pirates, and the rising Italian merchant republics. The Black Sea
was dominated by Russians.

The situation changed with the arrival of the Carolingian
Franks to the Danube Valley and the Adriatic. With Slavia being
invaded from the west, the Rhomaeans took courage and made
a number of successful sallies into Slavic areas in the southern
Balkans. The turmoil created by the expansionistic wars of the
Rhomaean and the newly revived Roman or Carolingian empires
had a tremendous impact on the peoples of North Central
Eurasia. There was a veritable migration of peoples fleeing
before the advancing imperialists of the west and the east. The
refugees, in turn, exerted pressure and created turmoil among the
peoples of Russia, both those who lived in the nomadic domain
and those who occupied the agricultural zones. The Avars were
utterly destroyed.

Around 830, the Khazar kagan, unable to defend his state,
appealed to the Rhomaean emperor Theophilus for help.
Obliging, Theophilus sent a fleet which included warships from
Rhomaean-held Paphlagonia, the ancient home of the Eneti. The
expeditionary force, commanded by the spatharocandidate
Petronas, landed at Cherson, which was, at that time, a self-
governing city recognizing the Rhomaean emperor. From
Cherson, the Rhomaeans went to the mouth of the Don, where,
in 833, they built a fortress for the Khazars. The local nomads
who spoke a Turkic language called the place *Sarkel*, while
some Rhomaeans used the term *Leukon oikema* (Theophanes),
others *Aspron ospition* (Constantine Porphyrogenitus). The
Rhomaean appellation meaning "white house"[9] may be a translation of the Slavic *Belaja Veža* "white gate," which appears in
Russian sources, where it may have been confused with the
Khazar capital city Itil, *al-Baiḍā*, also called Belaja Veža.[10]

---

[9] *DAI*, ch. 42; *Commentary*, p. 154.
[10] Marquart, *op. cit.*, pp. 1–5.

The Emperor Theophilus devoted considerable attention to the affairs of the Pontic region. In Anatolia he established two new themata, Chaldia and Paphlagonia. In Russia he raised the city of Cherson to the rank of a theme, appointing Petronas its first strategus.[11]

THE RHOS AT INGELHEIM

Such was the situation in and around Russia when a group of men who said they were of Rhos nationality came to Ingelheim. The event, as recorded by Bishop Prudentius in the *Annales Bertiniani* under the year 839, is considered trustworthy. The bishop says:

Venerunt etiam legati Graecorum a Theophilo imperatore directi, Theodosius videlicet, Calcedonensis metropolitanus episcopus, et Theophanius spatharius, ferentes cum donis imperatore dignis epistolam; quos imperator quinto decimo Kalendas Iunii in Ingulenheim honorifice suscepit. Quorum legatio super confirmatione pacti et pacis atque perpetuae inter utrumque imperatorem eique subditos amicitiae et caritatis agebat, necnon de victoriis, quas adversus exteras bellando gentes coelitus fuerat assecutus gratificatio et in Domino exultatio ferebatur; in quibus imperatorem sibique subiectos amicabiliter datori victoriarum omnium gratias referre poposcit. Misit etiam cum eis quosdam, qui se, id est gentem suam, Rhos vocari dicebant, quos rex illorum Chacanus vocabulo, ad se amicitiae, sicut asserebant, causa direxerat, petens per memoratam epistolam, quatenus benignitate imperatoris redeundi facultatem atque auxilium per imperium suum totum habere possent, quoniam itinera per quae ad illum Constantinopolim venerant, inter barbaras et nimiae feritatis gentes immanissimas habuerant, quibus eos, ne forte periculum inciderent, redire noluit. Quorum adventus causam imperator diligentius investigans, comperit eos gentis esse Sueonum, exploratores potius regni illius nostrique quam amicitiae petitores ratus, penes se eo usque retinendos iudicavit, quod veraciter invenire posset, utrum fideliter eo necne pervenerint; idque Theophilo per memoratos legatos suos atque epistolam intimare non distulit, et quod eos illius amore libenter susceperit, ac si fideles invenirentur, et facultas absque

---

illorum periculo in patriam remeandi daretur, cum auxilio remittendos; sin alias, una cum missis nostris ad eius praesentiam dirigendos, ut quid de talibus fieri deberet, ipse decernendo efficeret.[12]

The court at Ingelheim was not only puzzled by the appearance of the Rhos men but was also concerned about security. The Rhos, who turned out to be Swedes, were pagans, enemies of Christendom, and possibly spies. We have no information as to whether clarifications were obtained from Constantinople and what happened to the Rhos men. Under normal circumstances, information of this nature is treated as incidental requiring corroboration. However, in the literature on Russia's origins Prudentius was summoned by Kunik as "an unimpeachable witness" of the Swedish origin of the Russian name, rulers, and state.[13]

Rejecting such hasty conclusions, we offer our own interpretation of the quoted entry. We assume that Prudentius told the truth, because there was no apparent reason why he would not. But, both the Rhos men and the Emperor Theophilus may have had reasons not to be truthful. The Rhomaean Emperor may have used the Rhos men for some, to us, unknown intrigue. The court at Ingelheim became suspicious, detained the Rhos, and asked Theophilus to clarify the matter. Assuming that Theophilus was innocent, we should blame the men for concealing their Swedish nationality. We do not know how the fact that they were Swedes became known. They may have admitted it themselves, or were overheard conversing in Swedish and thus discovered.

The Rhos were either from Sweden or Swedish residents in Russia, more precisely in the domain ruled by the Russian kagan. If they resided in Sweden, they could not be of Rhos nationality and ruled by a kagan, for no people called Rhos ever lived in Sweden and no Swedish ruler ever had the Turkic title kagan. In that case the men said they were Rhos because, for whatever reason, spying being one of them, they wished to conceal their true identity. At the same time, they may have

---

[12]   *Annales Bertiniani*, ed. G.H. Pertz, *MGH SS*, I (1826), p. 434.
[13]   Kunik, *op. cit.*, I, p. 96.

been honest men with nothing to hide, who said they were Rhos at Constantinople because they knew that the Rhomaeans used the name Rhos for a variety of northern peoples, including Swedes. Also, they may have declared themselves as Swedes when they arrived in Constantinople, but the Rhomaeans renamed them Rhos, because to them all peoples of Scythia who were not nomads were Rhos.[14] If we accept the Rhos to be Swedes from Sweden, we must interpret the word *chacanus* not as a title but as a proper name, say, Hakon. With this line of reasoning we would be justified in claiming that the Rhos were some Swedes ruled by a man called Hakon. This could be the end of the discussion.

But we join the majority who believe the Rhos men came from Russia, and the ruler they served bore the title of kagan. Further, we propose that the men had reason to state they were both Rhos and Swedes. There is nothing astonishing in this, for throughout North Central Eurasia lived many native nationalities and countless merchants, mercenaries, and adventurers from other parts of the world, including Scandinavia. The Russian kaganate from which the men came must have also been home to different nationalities and many resident foreigners, just as the Russian kingdom was later. It could not have been otherwise. Few regions in Eurasia have ever been monoethnic and monolingual, least of all Russia. We ought to accept it as quite ordinary that the unnamed Russian kagan had in his service men of Swedish origin who were either natives of Russia or immigrants from Sweden. We should not be surprised that he sent some of them on a mission to Constantinople.

The fact that the envoys of the Russian kagan who came to Ingelheim in 839 were Swedes by language, should not be used as evidence that the kagan, himself, and his entourage were also Swedes. To suggest that he was a Swede because his envoys to Constantinople were Swedes is as wrong as it would be to claim

[14]   Though not a Frank, this writer once told some Anatolian peasants he was one because in their scheme of things the name Frank means European.

that Stalin was a Jew because his foreign minister, Litvinov, was.[15]

The entry in the *Annales Bertiniani* does not offer enough information for us to place the Russian kaganate on the map of ninth-century Eurasia, other than that state was vaguely situated north of the Danube, east of the Carpathians, and north of the Caucasus. It could have been anywhere from Walachia to Lake Ladoga and from the eastern foothills of the Carpathians to the northern foothills of the Caucasus. We have no evidence upon which to restrict this Russian kaganate in the first half of the ninth century to an area around Novgorod or Kiev as the majority of scholars do, nor to the Crimean or Taman peninsulas as do a few isolated dissenters.[16] Nevertheless, we suggest that the ninth-century Russian kaganate was established by descendants of those people whom in the sixth century Jordanes had called "*gens infida*," the same who were known to Syriac Christians as Harūs, and of the same people whom, in 642, the King of Derbent knew as al-Rūs and described to a Muslim general as the "enemies of the whole world."

HOI RHŌS AT CONSTANTINOPLE

Twenty-nine years after the Rhōs men had come to Ingelheim, in 860, Constantinople was attacked by northerners whom most commentators identify with the people called *hoi Rhōs* by the Rhomaeans. This sea and land attack on the center of Rhomania was the subject of two homilies by the Patriarch Photius. The event is also mentioned in the *Chronicle* of George Hamartolos, which was translated into Old Church Slavonic in the tenth cen-

[15]   If readers find similarities between our explanation of Prudentius' information on the Rhos and those of past students of Russia, they should conclude that we have all followed common sense. *See*, S. Gedeonov, *Varjagi i Rus'*, 2 vols. (St. Petersburg, 1876), II, pp. 483–505; and A.V. Riasanovsky, *The Norman Theory of the Origin of the Russian State* (Ann Arbor, Mich. 1960), pp. 176–87.

[16]   *See* for instance, G. Vernadsky, *Ancient Russia*, pp. 278ff.

tury, and from which the Kievan chronicler took his information on the "first" appearance of the Russians in history.[17]

The purpose of Photius' homilies was to urge the people to obey Christian laws, because perdition threatened those who strayed from the true path. Calling Constantinople New Israel, the Patriarch adduces the example of Old Israel to prove his case. The majority of scholars believe that the assailants had come from Kiev, while some allow for the possibility that the Kievans were joined by Crimeans and that their motive was plunder. However, the true reason why its neighbors hated the whore on the Bosporus, to paraphrase Saint John the Divine, is found in the following lines from Photius' homily: "O city reigning over nearly the whole universe. ... O city adorned with the spoil of many nations!"[18] We ought not to exclude the possibility that the Rhōs came to the city to take back something which its subjects had earlier stolen from them.

The name *hoi Rhōs* does not show in the text itself. In some manuscripts it appears in the titles, but others are titled: *Eis tēn tōn barbarōn efodōn* "Attack of the barbarians." The attackers whom we justly identify with the Russians of other sources are called "barbarians," "Hyperboreans," and "Scythians," indicating that Photius was inspired as much by ancient Greek writers as he was by the Bible in naming the peoples settled north of the Rhomaean world.

In the first homily, Photius points to Constantinople's sins as the reason why the "thick, sudden, hailstorm of barbarians," had burst forth against the city. He offers a few glimpses into the possible location of their homeland when he laments the fact that the Christians had no advance warning of their approach, although the invaders "were separated from us by so many lands and kingdoms, by navigable rivers and harborless seas." This may be used as evidence that they had come from Ultima Thule, unless we interpret the plural "seas" as a poetic hyperbole. In

---

[17]   C. Mango, *The Homilies of Photius Patriarch of Constantinople* (Cambridge, Mass., 1958), English translation with commentary; Georgius Monachus, *Chronicon*, ed. E. von Muralt (St. Petersburg, 1859), pp. 726–37; *PVL*, p. 60; A. Vasiliev, *The Russian Attack on Constantinople* (Cambridge, Mass., 1946).

[18]   *The Homilies of Photius*, (Mango's ed.) p. 91.

fact, whether the attackers came from Kiev or only from the
Crimea, there was still only one sea, called the Russian Sea by
the contemporary Muslims, between their homeland and Constantinople.

The second homily was delivered after the barbarians had
lifted the siege. Photius repeats the reasons for their attacks—
sins of the Christians—and reminds his listeners that they were
saved by the intercession of the Virgin Mary and her stole. He
stresses the unusual nature of this barbarian attack because it
was made by a people who used to tremble at the very name
Rome. They were:

> An obscure nation, a nation of no account, a nation ranked among
> slaves, unknown, but one which has won a name from the
> expedition against us, insignificant, but now become famous,
> humble and destitute, but now risen to a splendid height and im-
> mense wealth, a nation dwelling somewhere far from our country,
> barbarous, nomadic, armed with arrogance, unwatched, unchal-
> lenged, leaderless, has so suddenly, in the twinkling of an eye,
> like a wave of the sea poured over our frontiers, and as a wild
> boar has devoured the inhabitants of the land like grass, or straw,
> or a crop (O, the God-sent punishment that befell us!), sparing
> nothing from man to beast, not respecting female weakness, not
> pitying tender infants, nor reverencing the hoary hairs of old men,
> softened by nothing that is wont to move human nature to pity,
> even when it has sunk to that of wild beasts, but boldly thrusting
> their sword through persons of every age and sex.[19]

The atrocities allegedly committed by these people are described
with more detail and gore, but since they were of the kind which
people usually commit against their enemies, we do not need to
dwell on them. An epidemic broke out, and there were many un-
buried bodies. The city lay open to the attackers. Photius urges
his flock to remember the ships of the barbarians that had sailed
threateningly past their city. All the sinners repented on that
night, praying hard and carrying the stole of the Mother of God
along the city walls. The barbarians lifted the siege and retreated. They had come suddenly, they returned unexpectedly.
Then follows a reminder to the people not to forget the promises
they had made on that night, because the deity would deal with

[19]   *Ibid.*, pp. 88–9.

them as it had dealt with the Hebrews. They, being the second Israel, should be warned by the example of the first Israel. The homily ends with an exhortation to the believers to be grateful to the Mother of God for their salvation.

On the basis of these two homilies we can state with certainty that in 860 Constantinople was attacked by sea and land forces of a people settled north of Rhomania. The cause for the attack may have been provided by the Byzantines who perhaps had plundered that people's agricultural produce or cattle, or had taken captives. They are said to be inexperienced in warfare, but this is a topos, for the Rhomaeans believed that they alone knew the art of warfare instilled into them supposedly by the Virgin Mary, who is often lauded in Rhomaean poetry as an accomplished strategist. They were nomads, which may mean that they did not live in stone houses. But they were not steppe nomads, for these as a rule did not take to sea. They were called barbarians, Hyperboreans, Scythians, and *hoi Rhōs*, that is, Russians. The Kievan chronicler knew about the event only so much as he found in the Slavic translation of Georgius Monachus' (Hamartolos) *Chronicle*.

THE RHŌS ACCEPT CHRISTIANITY

Seven years after he had delivered the two homilies just discussed, in 867, Photius reported jubilantly to his Patriarchal colleagues that the Rhōs who used to be a ferocious people "now accepted a bishop and performed Christian rites with great enthusiasm."[20] Were these the same Rhōs who had attacked Constantinople in 860? And if so, where did they live? If, in the language of the Rhomaeans the name *Rhōs* were used to denote one single people, and if this report were truthful, then from the year 867 onward all the Rhōs were Christians. We know that this was not the case with the Rhōs because most of them clung to their "Hellenic" faith till the end of the tenth century.

Scholars who believe that the attackers of Constantinople in 860 came from Kiev, also assume that it was to that city that they took with them the bishop consecrated by Photius. Yet,

---

[20]   Photius, *Epistolae*, in Migne, *PG*, 102, pp. 736ff.

there is no evidence that this was so. Since it is more likely that
the Russian navies came to Constantinople from the Crimea than
from the interior of Russia, we suggest that the Russian bishop
mentioned by the Patriarch Photius also resided in some ancient
coastal city of Russia rather than in the interior.[21]

Of momentous importance for all Slavs was the penetration of
organized Christianity not only in Slavia nova but also in Slavia
antiqua. Around 870 Slavia emerged as an enormous Christian
kingdom. Extending from the Carpathians to the Aegean and the
Adriatic seas, it reached its greatest prestige under King
Svatopluk (871–894).

In Frankish sources Svatopluk's realm was called, not only
Slavia but also Carantania and Moravia. In Byzantine sources
the Transdanubian portion of his kingdom was named White or
Great Croatia and Great Moravia. Muslim writers regarded
Svatopluk as the king of all Slavs. The papal curia called him
officially *Rex Slavorum*. In 869 Pope Hadrian II consecrated St.
Methodius Archbishop of Sirmium, whose legendary founder,
Saint Andronicus, was counted among the seventy Apostles.
Methodius became the head of the Christian church in Svato-
pluk's Slavia.[22] The new Slavic archbishop preferred the Church
Slavonic language written in the Glagolitic script to Hebrew,
Greek, or Latin as the traditional liturgical languages, while
King Svatopluk preferred Latin. Thus Christianity in the heart
of Slavia had an inauspicious beginning, for the Slavic and Latin
parties fought each other bitterly. There was also the question of
the *filioque* to tear the Christian organization apart. Svatopluk
allowed the Latin party to prevail. The followers of Methodius
scattered. Many crossed the Carpathians to Russia to spread the
Gospel in Church Slavonic and the Glagolitic script.[23] After

[21]   This question has been much debated. *See*, V. Mošin, *op. cit.*; *idem*,
"Načalo Rusi: Normany v vostočnoj Evrope," *Byzantinoslavica*, 3 (1931), pp.
35–58, 285–307; A. Vasiliev, *op. cit.*, pp. 169ff; D. Obolensky, *The
Byzantine Commonwealth: Eastern Europe, 500–1453* (New York, 1971),
pp. 182–3.
[22]   F. Dvornik, *Byzantine Missions among the Slavs* (New Brunswick,
N.J., 1970), pp. 149ff.
[23]   It is believed that the dialects spoken at that time by the ancestors of
the Russians, Byelorussians, and Ukrainians differed only slightly from the
first liturgical Slavic language introduced by Methodius' disciples.

Svatopluk's death his sons quarrelled, weakening Slavia's ability to resist outside invaders. There was also a pan-European violent reaction against organized Christianity. At the end of the ninth century, shamanist Hungarians came to settle in the nomadic territory in the heart of Slavia. They helped the "Hellenic" party expel the quarrelsome Christians from Slavia north of the Danube.[24] Also, imperial Christianity, which had made great strides in the Balkans, when, in 855, the khan and the elite of Balkan Bulgaria accepted Christianity from Constantinople, suffered a defeat when Rhomaean clergy were expelled and replaced by Slavs. In the turmoil, the organization headed by Photius' Russian bishop must have also been destroyed. Through the tenth century most Russians kept their ancient "Hellenic" beliefs, which gave license to their Christian enemies to associate them with the awesome Gog and Magog.

RHŌS AND HIS COMPANIONS OG AND MOG

The second documented Russian naval invasion of Rhomania took place in 941.[25] A fleet of 10,000 vessels was led by a king called Ingor in Rhomaean, Ingvar in Latin, and Igor' in Slavic sources. The Rhomaeans were apprised of their coming by the Bulgars, with whom they were temporarily at peace. Crossing the Russian Sea and landing in Bithynia, the Russians ravaged the northern coast of Anatolia between Heraclea and Nicomedia. A Rhomaean chronicler described their atrocities which, as we shall see later, were quite similar to those ascribed to al-Majūs by Muslim writers in the Caspian region and by Muslims and Christians in Spain and along the coasts of the Western Sea.[26]

A powerful imperial force gathered to meet the Russians in battle won the upper hand. The Russians retreated to their boats,

---

[24]   The primary sources on Svatopluk, Cyril and Methodius, and Great Moravia have been published in the collection *Magnae Moraviae Fontes Historici*, Vols. I–VI (Brno–Prague, 1962–74).

[25]   We agree with those who reject the historicity of Oleg's invasion.

[26]   Some scholars are not willing to accept these Russians as Slavs because of the prevailing belief that the Slavs were a peace-loving, musical people, incapable of committing acts of violence.

with the Rhomaeans pursuing and destroying them by Medic fire, called the Greek fire by West Europeans.[27]

We shall see that the descriptions of the Russian invasion of Asia Minor in 941, as presented by Rhomaean writers, suggest that the invaders were the same people whose operations in the Caspian basin were described by Muslim writers. The majority of scholars believe they came from Kiev, though there is no evidence that this was the case. The Rhomaean sources said only that the Russians came from the north and that they returned to their country.[28] It is logical to suppose that the Russians were entrenched on the northern shore of the Black Sea when they launched their invasion of Anatolia. Certainly, it would be difficult for the Muslims to say that the Russians were the dominant people on the Black Sea if they did not settle along its coasts. We know that Igor was king of Russia, and we must assume that his domain verged on the Black Sea, the sea which his Muslim contemporaries called Russian, and on whose shores he assembled his large fleet. Igor appears to have ruled in both Kiev and Novgorod as well as over a wide area of Russia, but to exclude him from the coast of the Black Sea is impermissible.

Igor is the first Russian ruler whose existence and some activities can be documented, but we are still in the dark concerning his origins and early life. He is also the first Russian king who was equated with the Rhōs of Ezekiel. We saw that Photius took passages from Old Testament eschatologists and applied them to the situation of his day.[29] No sermon prompted by Igor's invasion has come down to us. However, his invasion of Asia Minor was woven into a hagiographic work, the *Life of*

---

[27] *PVL*, pp. 71–72; *see* also, p. 237 note 47 for references to the Rhomaean sources.

[28] We shall see later that Leo the Deacon believed Igor's country was at the Cimmerian Bosporus. *See* below, pp. 329, 332.

[29] Once his homilies were written down, future Christian propagandists in Constantinople used them in preaching against and "describing" other enemies of the God-protected city. For instance, in 1422, when Constantinople was under siege by the Ottoman Turks, a bishop updated and delivered Photius' Russian sermon. *See*, X. Loparev, "Cerkovnoe slovo Dorofeja mitropolita Mitilinskogo," *Vizantijskij Vremennik*, XII (1906), pp. 166–71. *See* also, Obolensky, *op. cit.*, p. 183.

Basil the Younger.[30] The work's purpose was to glorify the saint. At a gathering, monks and priests talked about sin generally and specifically about excessive sinning of the Rhomaeans, concluding that pagans would burst into their land anytime as an instrument of divine wrath against sinners. This prompted Basil to say that at that very moment he saw how pagan Hungarians were drowning in the Danube, which they tried to cross in order to go to the Rhomaean land and punish sinners. The deity had decided to spare its chosen that time. Later this vision was confirmed by reports from Macedonia about the drowning of the Magyars. On another occasion Basil predicted the coming of the barbarian peoples named Rhōs, Og, and Mog in four months' time to punish cruelly the Christians of Rhomania. Basil also foresaw that they could not harm Constantinople because the city was protected by the Virgin Mary, though the Rhōs would ravage Bithynia. For the purposes of our topic it is unimportant whether Basil "saw" the Russians before or after their historically documented invasion of Asia Minor, but rather that he described them in words borrowed from Old Testament eschatologists. Igor's armies were perceived by the Christian elite in New Jerusalem as an instrument of divine wrath against sinners.

When medieval Russian patriots read (in South Slavic translations of Rhomaean chronicles) about the defeat of their ancestors in 860 and 941, even though the latter were pagans, they were not pleased at all. So they imagined a revenge and included descriptions of it in their own chronicles. This may be the origin of Oleg's campaign in 904–7, of the second "invasion" of the East Roman Empire by Igor in 944, and of the spurious treaties the two states supposedly signed. The latter documents name quite a few Russians, who, if we judge by their names, were of Scandinavian origin, whether immigrants or born in Russia of Scandinavian parents. They probably were names that were common among the Varangians in Kiev at the time of the composition of the spurious treaties. Of interest for our topic is the fact that the treaties were drawn as if Rhomania and Russia were neighbors. Since the two states neighbored on each

---

[30] *Vita Basilii Junioris*, ed. A.N. Veselovskij, "Razyskanija v oblasti russkogo duxovnago stixa," *Sbornik Otd. Russk. Jazyka i Slov.*, XLVI (1890), Suppl., p. 65ff.

other only in the Crimea which the Russians had held from time immemorial and the Rhomaeans held a slice called the theme of Cherson, the treaties offer oblique evidence of Russian control of that peninsula at the time of the composition of the treaties.[31] Rhomaean sources know nothing of Oleg, nor about Igor's second siege of Constantinople nor of a treaty of peace with him.

OUTER RUSSIA

We are somewhat better informed on the situation in Russia during the second half of the tenth century thanks chiefly to *De administrando imperio* (*DAI*) of Constantine Porphyrogenitus. Passages dealing with Russia and the Russians have been analyzed over and over again. Some have been used as evidence that the early Russians were Scandinavian warriors who collected tribute from Slavs while becoming Slavicized. A few scholars have also adduced evidence from *DAI* that there were two Russias in the middle of the ninth century. Our purpose in discussing *DAI* here at some length is to point out certain aspects of Russia's past which have not been fully appreciated by other commentators.

When Constantine wrote and reigned, the Khazars were in decline, Balkan Bulgaria was an independent Christian khanate, and the Magyars, living in former Great Moravia, were a potential threat to the Rhomaean Empire and to western European states. Most of the Balkan Peninsula, with the exception of narrow strips of coastal territory organized into themata, was ruled by Slavs. The Rhomaeans continued their never-ending battle with the Muslims for control of the eastern Mediterranean, Asia Minor, and the Levant. North of the Danube and in the steppe the dominant nomadic people were the Pečenegs. The

---

[31]   *PVL*, pp. 64–9, 72–8, notes 33, 39 (pp. 235–6), 50 (pp. 237–8). Russia and Rhomania were not neighbors on the Danube at the time when the treaties were supposedly concluded since between them lay Bulgaria. It was only after the empire, with help from Igor's son Svjatoslav, had destroyed Bulgaria and extended its frontiers to the Danube that it became a neighbor of Russia.

Russians and/or Slavs still lived in considerable numbers along the northern coasts of the Black Sea, but their existence there as politically independent people was becoming more and more precarious due to the rising power of the Pečenegs. In fact, based on Porphyrogenitus' work we are able to trace the beginnings of a centuries long process—a northward retreat of Russian Slavs from the Danube and the Black Sea coast.

The first chapter of *DAI*, devoted to the Pečenegs, instructs the heir, for whom the work was intended, on how to take advantage of these nomads. Since the latter were a powerful people, it was useful for the Rhomaean Emperor to be at peace with them, to send gifts to their leaders, etc. The Pečenegs were neighbors of the imperial theme of Cherson and could easily attack it. This means that by the mid-tenth century they occupied the steppe zone on the Crimean Peninsula. These nomads should not be sought in the mountains nor in any parts of the Peninsula that were unsuitable for nomadic pastoralism. We must assume that those regions were still populated by some of the Russians who, in 941, had mustered ten thousand ships.

The next chapter of *DAI*, entitled "Of the Pechenegs and the Russians," shows that the two peoples were neighbors and when they were not at peace the Pečenegs could raid Russia. Like the Rhomaeans, the Russians were also eager to keep peace with the nomads. Porphyrogenitus gives two reasons. First, the Russians buy horned cattle and sheep from the nomads. Second, the Russians could not go to war with other countries unless they were at peace with the Pečenegs, for the latter could easily invade Russia.

Regarding the location of Russia, this passage shows that the Pečenegs and the Russians were neighbors, each occupying a distinct ecological zone. One abounded in horned cattle and sheep, the other could not support these domestic animals. In general horned cattle and sheep were the mainstay of the nomads, while the domain of sedentary people, especially the mountainous coastal strip of the Crimea, could not support large herds of them. Since the previous chapter dealt with Rhomaean Cherson and the Pečenegs on the Crimea, the second chapter may also refer to Russia on the Crimea and Crimean Patsinakia.

As an afterthought, Constantine added a third reason why the Russians were eager to be at peace with the Pečenegs. Unless they were at peace with the nomads the Russians could not come to Constantinople either for war or for trade, because the Pečenegs could attack and kill them at the barrages of the Dnieper. There the Russians could not do two things at the same time, that is, carry ships and fight off the assailants. This passage does not contradict our conclusion that Russia stretched across the Crimea. Here Porphyrogenitus speaks of those Russians who used the Road from the Varangians to the Greeks. Perhaps at that time the name Russia already extended, in Rhomaean imagination, as far as Ultima Thule, but this fact cannot be used as an argument that it did not include the non-nomadic and non-Rhomaean Crimea.

The third chapter states briefly that the Turks (sc. the Magyars) also feared the Pečenegs who had on two occasions almost annihilated them, forcing the survivors twice to seek new homelands. Further, the Pečenegs often attacked the Magyars even in their new homeland in Great Moravia.

Chapter four sums up the usefulness of the Pečenegs for the Empire. When the Rhomaeans were at peace with them and at war with the Russians or with the Magyars, the Pečenegs could easily be won over with money and kindness to attack these two peoples in the rear.

Chapter 5 states that the Pečenegs could be used for the same purpose against the Bulgars, an indication that the Pečenegs controlled the nomadic territory north of the Danube and east of the Carpathians. The Russians, who were called Tivercy and Ugliči, were still the dominant population in the domain of settled agriculturalists between the Danube, the Carpathians, and the Dnieper, although their cities may have, by then, been destroyed by nomads.

Chapter six takes us back to the Crimea. Next to the Rhomaean territory around the city of Cherson lived another Pečeneg people. Trading with the Chersonites, they also "perform[ed] services for the emperor in Russia, Khazaria and Zichia and all the parts beyond." The Chersonites paid for these services with "purple cloths, ribbons, silks, gold brocade, pepper, scarlet or Parthian leather." These Pečenegs were free men and worked only for pay.

In the age when free Pečengs were rendering services to the Empire, Khazaria extended as far as Sarkel on the Don. We are not sure whether at that time it included the Crimean Goths who had earlier been Khazar subjects. Zichia was a Christian principality situated along the coast of the Black Sea between Russian Tmutorokan on the Taman Peninsula and Abkhazia. It is quite possible that Russia, which the free Pečenegs visited to render services for the Empire, included parts of the Crimean and Taman peninsulas. These same nomads may journey inland as far as Kiev and perhaps Novgorod, but we must not exclude them from rendering services to the Empire in that region of Russia which was situated along the coast of the Russian Sea.

Chapter seven offers instructions on how imperial agents should enter Patsinakia from Cherson.

Chapter eight describes the imperial agents' journey in war ships along the coast from Constantinople to Patsinakia. This Patsinakia was situated between the Dnieper and the Danube. In that region, which Porphyrogenitus once called Bulgaria because earlier the Bulgars had roamed there, lived another Pečeneg people who appeared to be independent of and separate from the Crimean Pečenegs.[32] The imperial agent could find these Pečenegs without going to Cherson first, for they roamed in the nomadic zone of this corner of medieval Russia. The Pečenegs had their own set of customary laws called *zakana* by Porphyrogenitus.[33] They may be useful for the Empire because they could readily attack the Russians, the Bulgars, and the Magyars.

As nomads, the Pečenegs had no permanent abodes and no use for cities. Porphyrogenitus says: "When spring is over the Pechenegs cross to the far side of the Dnieper river, and, always pass the summers there." Though the nomads were not numerous enough to occupy the whole region of Russia which ran from the Danube to the Dnieper, they, or the Magyars before them, had destroyed many Slavic cities in this area.

---

[32] In Herodotus' day this region was called Old Scythia. *See* above, p. 108.
[33] The Pečenegs had recently taken this land from the Magyars. The land was still known as Bulgaria after its earlier occupants. The Antae, Tivercy, Ugliči, and other Slavic peoples, known collectively as Russians, were the more ancient settlers of this region which Herodotus had called Old Scythia. The word *zakana* comes from the Old Slavic word *zakon"* "law." *See*, *DAI*, *Commentary*, p. 146.

DAI, Chapter 9

Entitled "Of the coming of the Russians in single-straked ships from Russia to Constantinople," this long chapter is all devoted to Russia. It opens:

> The single-straked ships (*monoxyla*) which come down from Outer Russia (*apo tēs exō Rōsias*) to Constantinople are from Novgorod, where Sviatoslav, son of Igor, prince of Russia, had his seat, and others from the city of Smolensk and from Teliutza and Chernigov and from Busegrad. All these come down the river Dnieper, and are collected together at the city of Kiev, also called Sambatas. Their Slav tributaries (*hoi de Sklaboi, hoi paktiōtai autōn*), the so-called Krivichians and the Lenzanines and the rest of the Slavonic regions, cut the single-strakers on their mountains in time of winter, and when they have fastened them together, as spring approaches, and the ice melts, they bring them on to the neighboring lakes. And since these lakes debouch into the river Dnieper, they enter thence on this same river, and come down to Kiev, and draw the ships along to be fitted out, and sell them to the Russians. The Russians buy these bottoms only, furnishing them with oars and rowlocks and other tackle from their old single-strakers, which they dismantle; and so they fit them out.

Even though there already exists a sizable commentary on the information provided by Porphyrogenitus in this chapter, believing it is useful to look at it afresh, we offer our interpretation in light of our conclusions about the Russians and Russia reached from other Rhomaean sources.

It is important to stress that, seen from Constantinople there were two Russias. The one, nearer to the observer, was unmarked. By naming its more distant counterpart Outer Russia Porphyrogenitus implied its existence and gave us the permission to call it Inner Russia. While the chapters just discussed dealt with the whole of Russia and more specifically with Inner Russia, Chapter 9 deals entirely with Outer Russia, describing in detail the trade route between Outer Russia and Constantinople. The designation "outer" was Rhomaean, while the native peoples may have used other attributes in dividing

Russia.[34] It is clear that Outer Russia was beyond that Russia which was closer to Constantinople and verged on the Black Sea.

Porphyrogenitus starts by describing how Outer Russian merchants journeyed from their various cities to the chief city of that land, Kiev. The land's principal arteries of communication were its rivers. Outer Russian merchants living in Novgorod went in their monoxyla up the Lovat River. Then they portaged them across a relatively short stretch of dry land into the Dnieper. The other Outer Russian cities mentioned in this chapter, Smolensk, Teliutza (which most scholars identify with Ljubeč), and Busegrad (modern Vyšgorod) were all on the Dnieper, while Černigov was situated on the Desna, its navigable tributary. Surely there were other cities in Outer Russia from which merchants used to go down to Constantinople, for Porphyrogenitus did not give us a complete list. Naturally, the majority of Outer Russian merchants originated from Kiev. Just because Porphyrogenitus did not state explicitly in this chapter that Kiev also was a part of Outer Russia, we should not conclude that it belonged to Inner Russia. While recognizing that the passage does not offer incontrovertible evidence, we propose that Kiev be reckoned as the chief city of Outer Russia, or at least as the first place (the second was Vitičev) where merchants from Outer Russia gathered before they set out on an arduous and long journey to Constantinople. Porphyrogenitus did not state specifically how those among the Outer Russian merchants who resided at Kiev came down to Constantinople, because their journey was a part of the common journey of all Outer Russian merchants whose journey to Kiev he had described.

Continuing with our interpretation, we should imagine tenth-century Kiev as an ancient trading center teeming with merchants from the Muslim world, from Western Christendom, from the various Slavic countries, and last but not least from pagan Scandinavia. Anything could be bought and sold at Kiev. The merchants who wished to go to Constantinople by the river could buy monoxyla. Those residents of Kiev could buy them

---

[34] The expression *Verxnjaja zemlja* "upper country" appears in the *PVL*, where it designates Russia north of Kiev.

from established business partners from among the neighboring peoples, the Field-Dwellers and the Forest-Dwellers, while others who came from afar repaired their old monoxyla or bought new ones from the local Slavs, their business partners. The Slavs who sold monoxyla to merchants from Černigov and other cities of Outer Russia were free men and politically independent of the merchants. Regardless of how we interpret Porphyrogenitus' term *hoi de Sklavoi, hoi paktiōtai,* the fact that Outer Russian merchants bought commodities from Slavic peasants and craftsmen does not allow us to interpret their relationship as that of masters and slaves. It rather forces us to consider the producers of the monoxyla merely as suppliers, the Outer Russian merchants as buyers of that product.

In June, the Outer Russian merchants would set out from their gathering place at Kiev on the journey down the Dnieper, stopping at Vitičev, a city which, according to Porphyrogenitus was a tributary of the Russians.[35] At Vitičev, their last stop before they came to the rapids, the Outer Russian merchants from Kiev and other Outer Russian cities "gather during two or three days; and when all the single-strakers are collected together, then they set out, and come down the said Dnieper river." After they set out from Vitičev, the Outer Russian merchants could soon see on their left the open steppe, devoid of villages, trees, and other marks of settled life. They might even notice tents, wagons, herds of cattle, sheep, and some people, because the land on their left was the domain of nomads, which included only pockets of terrain suitable for agriculture. The land on their right, however, was the domain of peasants with pockets of steppe terrain. It belonged to Russia which at that time stretched into the Carpathians.

Once they had passed the rapids,[36] the Outer Russians came to the ford of Krarion, whose modern name is Kačak. At this

---

[35] We must not conclude from this that the city belonged to the merchants from Černigov or Novgorod, but rather that it was subjected to the political control exercised in this part of Russia by the princes of Kiev and their lieutenants.

[36] Most of Chapter 9 is devoted to the names, etymologies and description of the Dnieper River barrages and how the Outer Russians negotiate these. We shall return to this topic later.

point their water route intersected with an overland route used by the Chersonites, Pečenegs, and other people journeying to and from the Crimea. It was also at that crossing that the Pečenegs usually attacked the Russians. After the ford of Krarion there was an island in the river which Constantine calls the Island of St. Gregory. It was situated at the modern city of *Zaporož'e* whose name means "beyond the barrages."[37] The island was an important halting point on the Road from the Varangians to the Greeks. In medieval Russian chronicles it also appears by the name of the Varangian Island. The natives call it Xortica. In the tenth century, the Outer Russian merchants performed their religious rites, thanking their gods for allowing them to come safely through natural and man-made dangers—the barrages and the Pečenegs. Describing the ritual, Constantine states that the voyagers would gather under an oak tree to sacrifice live cocks and offer victuals to the deities.

After the Island of St. Gregory they were free from natural dangers, but not beyond the reach of the Pečenegs. From here the river flowed smoothly, and if the Outer Russian merchants were not massacred by nomads they could reach its estuary in four days. The Dnieper emptied into a large bay, called *liman* in Russian. In the direction of the Bug estuary there was a small island, which the Rhomaeans called the Island of St. Aetherios, the same which the native Slavs have always known as Berezan'. Constantine omitted the Slavic name,[38] just as he failed to give the native name for St. Gregory Island. The Outer Russians stopped at Berezan' for two or three days in order to rest and to prepare for the sea journey. Here they could equip their monoxyla with masts, sails, and rudders which they had brought with them from Kiev.

Their journey from Berezan' to the mouths of the Danube was less dangerous. The Pečenegs, who avoided the sea, could not

---

[37]   After Christianity became the official religion of the Russian kingdom, the island served as a base from which Christians and peasants would launch attacks on their nomadic and shamanist or Muslim neighbors.

[38]   Berezan', though quite small, played an important role in the history of Great Scythia and Russia. It appears to have been the site of a settlement before Olbia was founded. In the tenth century Berezan' was used by fishermen from Rhomaean Cherson.

cause them any harm unless the storm cast their boats ashore.
The merchants would rest at the mouth of the Dniester and again
at the mouth a river which Constantine calls *Aspros* "white."[39]
Once the Outer Russian merchants had passed the Selina River
(identified with a branch of the Danube called Sulina), they were
safe from the Pečenegs whose domain extended only as far as
the left bank of the Danube. From the right bank of the river
stretched Bulgaria.

Their journey along the coast of that Slavicized Christian
khanate was also smooth, provided Bulgaria was at peace with
the Empire and strong enough to prevent the Pečenegs from
crossing the Danube. On Bulgarian territory the Outer Russians
would pass by Konopas, which is the ancient name of one of
several islands in the Danube Delta, perhaps identical with
modern St. George Island, or Dranov Island. Their next stop was
at Constantia in the Dobrudja. Sailing southward, they would
pass by the estuary of the River Varna.[40] From Varna they
would come to the Ditzina River, whose ancient name was
Panysos, the modern is Kamčija. In the tenth century this river
marked the boundary between Bulgaria and Rhomania. Between
that river and the Bosporus was only one important city,
Rhomaean-held Mesembria.[41] Constantine says that at Mesembria the journey of the Russians would end, although at the
beginning he offered to describe how they came to Constantinople. He stopped at Mesembria because their journey from that
city to Constantinople was along a coast controlled by the
Empire and therefore generally well known in Byzantium.

---

[39]   This river has not been identified. From ancient sources we know that
in Old Scythia there was a river called *Axioces* "black river." Constantine
names *Aspron kastron* as one of the several ruined cities in Patsinakia. It is
possible that the city lay on the Aspros River. It is usually identified with
the city called Belgorod in Russian, Akkerman in Turkish and Cetatea Albă
in Rumanian. Porphyrogenitus, gives the Rhomaean translation of the city's
name, saying that the Pečenegs called the place *Aspron kastron* "because its
stones look very white." *DAI*, ch. 37; *Commentary*, p. 57.

[40]   At the mouth of this river, at or near the site of the ancient city of
Ordessos, grew in the Middle Ages the city of Varna. The river which
Constantine calls Varna is now called Provadija.

[41]   Its ancient Thracian name, meaning "mid-day," survives as the modern
Slavic name Nesebŭr.

The Names of the Dnieper Barrages

We saw that two islands on the Road from the Varangians to the Greeks, or as Constantine says from Outer Russia to Constantinople, were named after Christian saints. The native Slavs and other people who used that water route had their own names for these same islands. It is a universally observed phenomenon that places frequented by different ethnic groups bear more than one name. For instance, in the same general area the mouths of the Danube were named by the native Thracians and other peoples, yet these names have come down to us only in later Greek and Latin translations. Further, Constantine is our witness that Kiev was also known as Sambatas. The dual names of the barrages on the Dnieper belong to this category of place names. There is a rich literature about this ordinary phenomenon because some scholars have used it as evidence that the ancient Russians were Swedes rather than Slavs. Constantine is counted by the Normanist school as the crowned witness that the Russians in the tenth century were Swedes by language and nationality.[42] For this reason, it is necessary to *voir dire* him.

From Kiev to Dniepropetrovsk the Dnieper flows in a southeasterly direction. Then it makes a sharp turn due south. To reach the sea it forces its way across granite bedrock which it has not yet dissolved, so that the river cascades over rocks called rapids, barrages, or cataracts in English. The word used by Constantine is *phragmos*. The Church Slavonic equivalent, attested in other Slavic languages, is *prag"*. The East Slavic form is *porog*.[43] In Old Norse the word is *fors*. Constantine names seven or more of the barrages.[44]

The first barrage was called *Essoupi* both *Rhōsisti* "in Russian" and *Sklavēnisti* "in Slavic." Various etymologies for the name have been offered, some from Old Norse, others from Slavic. Since Constantine says that the name means "Do not sleep!," the majority of scholars believe that it derives from the Slavic phrase *Ne spi!*

---

[42] See the Bibliography in *DAI, Commentary*, pp. 16–18.
[43] Vasmer, *REW*, III, pp. 329–30, s.v. "porog."
[44] *See*, map in *Commentary*, p. 39.

Oulvorsi, the Russian name of the second barrage, is clearly Old Norse, its Slavic equivalent being *Ostrovouniprach*. Constantine accurately translated both names as "island of the barrage."

For the third barrage he gives one name only, *Gelandri*, without specifying whether it was Russian or Slavic, stating that the name means, in Slavic, "noise of the barrage." Commentators agree that the name Gelandri is a corrupt form of the Old Norse word *gellandi* or *gjallandi* "loudly sounding." Its modern Ukrainian name *Zvonets* or *Zvonetsky* comes from *zvono* "a bell." As we see both the medieval and modern names of this barrage have the same meaning.

The names of the fourth barrage have caused much difficulty. In Russian it was *Aeifor*, in Slavic *Neasit*, but again Constantine gives for both one etymology, the word "pelican." Although these birds nest at this barrage, philologists have not been able to find words in either Slavic or Old Norse that would explain these names.

The fifth barrage's Russian name, *Varouforos*, is convincingly Old Norse, as is its other name, *Voulniprach*, clearly Slavic, although there is disagreement among the learned about the original words from which the names were formed. Constantine's etymology, which connects the names with the fact that the barrage forms a big lake, is not accepted by all.

The sixth barrage was called in Russian *Leanti*, in Slavic *Veroutzi*. Our author says that the name means "the boiling of the water." The Russian name is interpreted from the present participle of an Old Swedish verb meaning "laughing." Constantine is accurate only in regards to the etymology of the Slavic name, which is recognized as a transcription of the East Slavic participle *viručii* "the boiling, or bubbling."

The names of the seventh and the last barrage were *Stroukoun* in Russian and *Naprezi* in Slavic. Our author's explanation that the names mean "little barrage" is not acceptable to modern scholars, who have offered some etymologies for the Russian and even more for the Slavic name.

Although much still remains unclear regarding the names of the barrages on the Dnieper, there is no doubt that Constantine had before him two sets of names from two different languages. The East Slavic names appear to have reached him through a

South Slavic filter. Constantine knew a Slavic language, so his etymologies, even when they are wrong, were based on his understanding of Slavic, not Old Norse.

Since our author included these names in the chapter dealing with Outer Russia, it is possible that he obtained the Russian names from the merchants whose journey he was describing. When Constantine saw the Slavic names, he recognized them. The other set of names looked foreign to him, as it would to any person who did not know Old Norse. We must exclude the possibility that the Russian names were supplied by a Slav. Slavs may not have even known the Scandinavian names, just as most German-speaking Viennese do not know that their city is called Beč by some Slavs, Dunaj by others. Likewise, the Kievan Slavs may have been ignorant of the fact that their city was also called Sambatas by some foreigners. It is safe to assume that the non-Slavic names of the barrages on the Dnieper were brought to Constantinople by someone speaking a Scandinavian language.

The people who gave Constantine or his source the Scandinavian names of the barrages could have been from Russia or from Scandinavia. If they were from Scandinavia they would call themselves by any of the numerous tribal names attested in that peninsula. We know that there were many Scandinavians in the East Roman Empire at least after 839 when the Rhos men, whom Louis the German found to be Swedes, had first appeared. Yet there is not a trace of any Scandinavian tribal name in Rhomaean sources. Why? Because, regardless of what they called themselves, when they set out on their journey along *Austrvegr* "the eastern way," by the time they reached *Mikligarðr*, their name for Constantinople, the Scandinavians were perceived and named as Russians. They were Russians, because the region which stretched from the Danube and the theme of Cherson across the expanse of Great Scythia to Ultima Thule and which included Scandinavia was called Russia by the Rhomaeans.

Supposing that Constantine's informants were Swedes settled in a land then universally known as Russia, their names for the barrages would certainly be Russian names, for they, too, would be Russians. These Swedes had no problem calling themselves Russians, and Constantine saw no contradiction in this because in his day the ethnonym Rhōs was used generally and specifically. We shall see that the general meaning of the name was known to al-Mas'ūdī, when he said that it designated a multitude of diverse peoples. Here Constantine offers us evidence that it may include Swedes or other Scandinavians, be they residents of Russia or of their mother countries.

The Russian Warriors

Outer Russia, as described by Constantine, was an enormous land inhabited by a variety of peoples. Even though he only mentions Slavs and Russians, we know that it included several Baltic and numerous Finnic peoples. Not all these "Russians" were of Scandinavian origin, although many who resided among the natives or journeyed through their land to Constantinople were.

The first ruler of Russia who is considered historical was Igor. We know about him because the Rhomaeans made note of his attacks on their state. Igor was very active in Inner Russia but lost his life in Outer Russia among the Forest-Dwellers. Olga, his wife, a princess from the Outer Russian city of Polock, ruled in Kiev. Their son Svjatoslav preferred to rule his vast realm from Preslav on the Danube, and was killed in Inner Russia by Pečenegs. Igor, Olga, and Svjatoslav belonged to a class whose function in Russian society was different from that of the merchants—they were the political and military elite, although they also engaged in trade. We propose that in the following passage Constantine is describing them:

> The severe manner of life of these same Russians in winter-time is as follows. When the month of November begins, their chiefs together with all the Russians at once leave Kiev and go off on the 'poludie,' which means "rounds," that is, to the Slavonic regions of the Vervians and Drugovichians and Krivichians and Severians and the rest of the Slavs who are tributaries of the Russians. There they are maintained throughout the winter, but then once more, starting from the month of April, when the ice of the Dnieper river melts, they come back to Kiev. They then pick

up their single-strakers, as has been said above, and fit them out, and come down to Romania. The Uzes can attack the Pechenegs.[45]

At first blush it appears that Constantine here speaks of the same type of Russians, that is, the merchants who, from the various cities of Outer Russia, come to Kiev to buy monoxyla from Slavs. He states that they are the same Russians and that they also come south in monoxyla, so one should conclude that they were the same as the merchants described earlier. In reality, it may have been difficult for Constantine to distinguish these from the other Russians. Nevertheless, we suggest that the Russians whose harsh way of life is the subject of this passage be regarded as the warrior class, who were not strangers to commerce. These Russians would leave Kiev in November for the countryside to be fed by the peasants whom they controlled. They did not have to buy monoxyla from them, for they could get them free, just as they would get food and clothing during the long winter months. Unlike the Russian merchants, these Russians did not have to buy monoxyla from their Slavic subjects, for it is not logical that the peasants would support them all winter long then when spring came they would *sell* them monoxyla. While the warrior elite went around being fed by the peasants, the merchants passed the winter months in the cities, bought food and clothing from the peasants just as they bought their monoxyla. Furthermore, in the cities foreign merchants could keep their language for some time if they congregated with their conationals. The warriors, of whatever ethnic origin, were forced to speak Slavic in the midst of Slavic peasants.

We suggest that the information provided in Chapter 9 allows us to conclude that, in the tenth century, there were two Russias: Inner Russia (or simply Russia) and Outer Russia. Russia, inhabited chiefly by Slavic peasants and Turkic pastoralists, extended along the coast of the Black Sea, while Outer Russia stretched north of the barrages on the Dnieper and had a more heterogenous population. We must further differentiate between several kinds of Outer Russians. The first was the basic population which was all Slavic, as far as Constantine knew, but

---

[45]   *DAI*, ch. 9; *Commentary*, pp. 58–61.

which we know included Balts and Finns, as well as immigrants from Scandinavia. Constantine gives the names of some of the Slavic peoples. Within a short time they would all disappear and take on the Russian name. The second kind of Outer Russians known to Constantine were the merchants who journeyed to Constantinople. There is no doubt that the majority of them were Slavs. Outer Russia was a Slavic land, the barrages had Slavic names and ultimately the Slavic language prevailed in Outer Russia, though it yielded some ground in Inner Russia. As subgroup of this kind of Outer Russians were merchants from overseas, mostly from Sweden, who spoke their own language. They named the barrages in Old Swedish by translating their original Slavic names. En route, they also translated their national names. Whereas in Scandinavia these people referred to themselves as Swedes, Gotlanders and by other names, in Russia they were called Varangians, and beyond the borders of Outer Russia they were known as Russians. The third group of Russians were the warriors, who were Slavs. Later they were joined by priests and monks of Slavic nationality, to protect the peasants and to bring them salvation. Of course not every warrior and every priest and monk was a Slav, for some came to Russia from abroad. But the proof that the majority were Slavs is the Slavic Russian Christian kingdom they established.

THE TAUROSCYTHES, COMMONLY KNOWN AS RUSSIANS

We are fortunate that some major events of the period of Rhomaean history following the death of Constantine VII Porphyrogenitus were recorded by several trustworthy writers, the foremost of whom was Leo the Deacon. His narrative covers the reigns of Nicephorus II Phocas and John I Tzimisces, 963—976. During this time, events important for the formation of Russia also took place, some of which were described by Leo. We discuss them here with the aim of explaining the ethnonym Russi.[46]

---

[46]   Leo the Deacon, *Historiae libri decem*, ed. C.B. Hase (Bonn, 1828). The page numbers refer to this edition. There is a German translation by F. Loretto (Graz—Vienna—Cologne, 1961) (=*Byzantinische Geschichtsschreiber*,

An archaizer, Leo consciously imitated the style of ancient writers, giving the peoples of his day names which the ancients had used for those who had, in antiquity, occupied approximately the same land. Occasionally, he took names out of the Bible and applied them to peoples of his day. For example, for Muslims in general, most of whom were Arabs or Arabized Afroasians, he uses the names Arabs or Saracens, names which go back to ancient authors, as well as the Christian neologism Agarenes. The latter name derives from Hagar, Abraham's concubine who bore Ishmael, the eponymous founder of the Arabs. For the medieval Bulgars he reserved the name of the ancient Mysians who had lived in Homer's time in Anatolia and in the Balkans, although the Bulgars had arrived into their new country around 680 AD. The Bulgars had settled in Scythia Minor as well as in Thrace, but he avoided using the Scythian name specifically for the Bulgars because it was too broad and it included all northern barbarians, while the Thracian name was restricted to the themata of Thracesion in Asia Minor and to Thrace in Europe. The Mysian or Moesian name had not been appropriated by any people, so Leo and other Rhomaean writers used it for the Bulgars who settled among the Vlachs and Slavs of ancient Moesia and Thrace.

The Russians first appeared in Leo's work in a speech delivered by Nicephorus Phocas to the troops at Caesarea in Asia Minor after they had proclaimed him emperor. So far, he said, they had successfully fought the Cretans, Scythians, and Arabs. But an even greater task was before them—the capture of the seat of the Rhomaean Empire.[47] By Cretans Nicephorus meant the reconquest of Crete from Muslims by Byzantine troops under his command.[48] By victories over the Arabs he meant his successful campaigns against the Muslims in Crete, Anatolia, and in Syria. The Scythians were, in fact, those Russians whom Igor had led in 941 in 10,000 ships to the Anatolian coasts of Rhomania.

After he had consolidated his power in Constantinople, Nicephorus believed the time was ripe for the destruction of

---

ed. J. E. v. Ivánka, Vol. X).

[47] *Ibid.*, pp. 42–3.

[48] The imperial forces included a Russian contingent.

Bulgaria. The Rhomaean Empire and its northern Christian neighbor had been at peace with each other since the imperial armies were defeated by Khan Symeon.[49] Symeon's son, Khan Peter (927–969), received a yearly payment as tribute from the Empire to keep the peace. In the fall of 965 he sent envoys to Nicephorus to collect the payment for the current year. Nicephorus flew into a rage, screaming: "Woe to the Rhomaeans who had obtained victory over all their enemies, yet are forced to pay tribute like so many slaves to a poor and dirty Scythian tribe." He went on insulting the Bulgar people and their ruler whom he called a slave, and a beggar wearing a goat skin coat. He ordered the envoys flogged and be sent back to Bulgaria.[50]

The emperor assembled a mighty army and invaded Christian Bulgaria. The terrain was too rough for his soldiers, the resistance of the native Vlachs, Slavs, and Bulgars too stiff for them to accomplish much more than wanton destruction of some frontier posts and adjacent villages. Nicephorus ordered a retreat. Realizing that Bulgaria was too hard for him to conquer he thought of employing the old Byzantine stratagem of using one people to destroy another. So he

> sent Calocyres, an honorable and experienced man, who had the rank of patrician, to the Tauroscythes, who are commonly known as Russians (*es tous Tauroskythas exepempsen, hous hē koinē dialektos Rhōs eiōthen onomazein*). He was given a sum of approximately fifteen hundred pounds of gold and was ordered to distribute it among the Tauroscythes and to lead them into the land of the Mysians that they may occupy it.[51]

Calocyres came to Tauroscythia, where he found the king called Svjatoslav (Sphendoslavos) by his subjects. The Christian gave gifts to the Hellenic prince of the Russians and won him over with nice words.[52] Svjatoslav agreed to follow Calocyres into Bulgaria with a 60,000-strong army. Also, the Russian king promised to help Calocyres ascend the imperial throne.

---

[49]   G. Ostrogorsky, *op. cit.*, pp. 260–9.
[50]   Leo the Deacon, *Historiae*, pp. 61–2.
[51]   *Ibid.*, p. 63.
[52]   *Ibid.*, p. 77. Leo repeats here the cliché about the Scythians being an exceedingly greedy people.

The Russians sailed into the Danube. The Bulgars met them at the river's bank, but were overpowered by the invaders and retreated into their fortress of Durostorum (Silistra). Upon learning that the Bulgars were defeated and that Calocyres was plotting treason, Nicephorus mustered an army and prepared to defend Bulgaria from the Russians. He suddenly remembered that the Bulgars were a Christian people, whereas their Russian enemies were still Hellenes. He sent a delegation which included a bishop. The Bulgar khan was asked to send two princesses so that he could marry them to the sons of the Emperor Romanus to solidify the friendship between the two states. The Bulgars readily agreed to Nicephorus' offer of peace and friendship and begged him to help them against the Russians. As the emperor was preparing to lead an expedition to the north, the news came that his forces had captured Antiochia. At the end of the year 969 Nicephoros Phocas was assassinated by his own wife, the Empress Theophano, and her lover, John Tzimisces. These events caused a postponement of the resolution of the conflict over Bulgaria.

The new emperor was beset by many problems. There had been a famine for three years. Externally, his realm was threatened by invasions of the Carthaginians (Leo's name for North African Fatimids), the Arabs, and the Russians. From the latter, our author says, nothing good could be expected. John Tzimisces decided to negotiate with Svjatoslav whom Leo calls the leader of the Russian army. He sent envoys to urge Svjatoslav to accept the reward which Nicephorus had promised him for his invasion of Mysia, to leave Mysia which belonged to the Rhomaeans anyway, and to return to his homeland on the Cimmerian Bosporus.[53]

The envoys found Svajatoslav allegedly swollen with pride on account of his recent victories over the Bulgars. A cruel man, Leo claims, Svjatoslav had 20,000 citizens of captured Philipopolis (modern Plovdiv) impaled to strike fear into the people and to break their will to resist. He told the Rhomaean envoys he would quit Bulgaria only for a large sum of money. Further, the Russian king said that should the Rhomaeans not agree to this they ought to get ready to return to Asia, for they had no right

---

[53] *Ibid.,* p. 103.

to live in Europe. The Emperor John Tzimisces received this message but he sent a conciliatory reply. Stating that he did not wish to break the treaty of peace concluded between their fathers, he urged the Russians to leave Bulgaria which did not belong to them. He reminded Svjatoslav of the defeat suffered by his father Igor. Igor had come with countless ships against the imperial city, "but returned to the Cimmerian Bosporus with barely ten boats as harbingers of his misfortune."[54] John said he would not recount, then related, nevertheless, how Igor came to a sad end when in his war against the Germans (a corruption of *Drevljane* "forest-dwellers") he was captured by the enemy, tied to two tree branches, and torn in half. The emperor concluded by warning Svjatoslav that he, too, would dare not return to his homeland should he, by provoking the might of the Rhomaeans, lose his entire army.

We should pause now to inquire whether we may use the evidence adduced so far to help us locate Russia at the time these events were taking place. We saw that Leo uses three names for Svjatoslav's people. They were commonly known as Russians, *hoi Rhōs*, a Rhomaean rendering of the Slavic form, which the Russians used as a self-designation. Then he uses the general term Scythes. All northern barbarian peoples since Herodotus may be and frequently were called by this name. The names hoi Rhōs and Scythes do not tell us enough about the ethnicity of the designated people, they only point to the north as the general direction in which their country was located. The third name, *Tauroscythes*, is more specific, because it points to a natural feature—the Tauric Mountain ranges, the abode of the ancient and awesome Tauri. Surely the Russians would not be called Tauri if the Rhomaeans did not believe that they, in fact, occupied those mountains or some areas adjacent to them. This name would not be justified at all if their homeland was limited to Outer Russia. Finally, there is another indication of the location of Russia. John Tzimisces stated explicitly that Svjatoslav's father Igor had returned to the Cimmerian Bosporus after his defeat near the Thracian Bosporus. It is certain that the Rhomaean emperor and Leo the Deacon knew where the Cimmerian Bosporus was.

---

[54]   *Ibid.*, p. 106.

Thus, in the tenth century, the Russians were seen by their Rhomaean neighbors and enemies as a Hellenic (pagan) nation dwelling in several regions of Great Scythia. One of these was the maritime region of the Crimea, where once the Tauri had lived. This is no proof that these Russians did not also control Outer Russia. They did. Igor was killed in a war with the Drevljane, an Outer Russian people. Svjatoslav first ruled from Novgorod, an Outer Russian city, before he transferred the seat of his realm to the Cimmerian Bosporus. According to the Kievan chronicler, he desired to transfer it once more to Pereja-slavec on the Danube.[55]

Returning to Svjatoslav and the envoys of John Tzimisces, when the Russian king heard what the emperor had to say, he grew angry. It was not necessary for the emperor to come to us, said Svjatoslav, for soon we will pitch our tents against the walls of Constantinople. Furthermore, should he at all come out to meet them in battle the Russians would destroy him and "teach him that [the Russians] are no tradesmen who live by the work of their hands, but men of bloody battles who fight against their enemies with weapons."[56] As soon as the emperor received this reply he began to take measures to deal with the Russian threat to the imperial city. He transferred army units from Asia Minor, appointed two of his best commanders, and sent them to the region bordering on Bulgaria to winter there and to train for the impending war. The commanders were instructed to send spies to the areas held by the Scythians (sc. Russians). These spies should be recruited from among the Rhomaeans who were bi-lingual, that is, Rhomaean Slavs who spoke Rhomaean and Slavic and dressed in the Scythian (Slavic) manner.[57] They should discover plans of the Russians and report them to the emperor. When the Tauroscythian king heard that the Rhomaean armies had crossed from Asia into Europe he sent a part of his forces, strengthened by Hunnic (Magyar) and Mysian (Bulgar,

---

[55] *PVL*, p. 86.

[56] Leo the Deacon, pp. 106–7.

[57] *Ibid.*, p. 108. This is one of the numerous indications that the Russians were Slavs, for it is not likely that at that time speakers of Swedish lived in the Balkans. Bi-lingual Rhomaeans were Balkan Slavs who spoke Slavic and Rhomaean and could communicate with the Russians in Slavic, the *lingua franca* of Rhomania, the Balkans, and Russia.

Vlach, and Slav) auxiliaries. Leo described the battle which took place using language and images borrowed from Homer and classical Greek writers. He claims that the Scythian king had fielded 30,000 warriors, the Rhomaean emperor only 10,000. Yet the Rhomaeans were supposedly victorious, killing more than 20,000 Scythians while losing only fifty-five of their own men. Be that as it may, the fact that Svjatoslav and the main body of the Russians did not take part in this battle, which may have been not more than a skirmish, meant that the emperor still felt threatened, so he transferred additional troops from Asia.

As the emperor himself was preparing to take the field, trouble appeared in Asia Minor. The Dux Bardas, a nephew of the murdered emperor Nicephorus, had escaped from Amaseia, the place of his banishment, and had begun to rally supporters around himself to help him seize the imperial power. When he thought he had enough followers he exchanged his black sandals for red ones, signaling his readiness to be proclaimed emperor. He was so proclaimed. But John moved against the usurper, defeated him and forced him to become a monk. Then in the spring of 971 the emperor resumed his war against the Russians. He sent a fleet of 300 ships to the Danube to prevent the Russians from escaping to their homeland, which, Leo states again, was on the Cimmerian Bosporus.[58]

The emperor marched into Bulgaria by land. His aim was the heart of the Bulgar state. The early Bulgar khans had resided at Pliska in the nomadic territory in the Dobrudja. Khan Omurtag (814—829) shifted his residence southward away from the dangers of the open steppe to Great Preslav, a city built and named by Balkan Slavs. John Tzimisces came with a mighty army and siege machines with the intent of taking this city. The Bulgar capital was defended by native Slavs, Vlachs, Turkic Bulgars, and Slavic Russians. The Russian commander, the man who, Leo said, was third in rank after Svjatoslav, was called Sphencelus, presumably a Scandinavian name.[59] Again, Svjato-slav was not at Preslav but was encamped with the main body of the Russian forces at Durostorum (Silistra). The imperial forces took Great Preslav, slaughtering some of the civilians and

[58]   Leo the Deacon, *op. cit.*, p. 129.
[59]   *Ibid.*, p. 135.

soldiers they had caught alive and plundering the city. In the royal fortress they found the treasure of the Bulgar state. Khan Boris was also captured and brought before the emperor. The latter confirmed him as ruler of the Bulgars. He also said that he had come to avenge the Bulgars who had suffered hard at the hands of the Russians. John Tzimisces ordered the city walls to be repaired, the Slavic name abolished, and the city renamed Joanopolis after himself.[60]

After the victory over the Russians and the Bulgars at Great Preslav, John set out to Durostorum to face Svjatoslav. In Svjatoslav's camp there was turmoil. His Bulgar allies were abandoning him and going over to the Rhomaeans. To prevent further defections, he had three hundred Bulgar nobles executed and put many into a dungeon. Then he assembled his forces, which had suffered no casualties so far because they still amounted to sixty thousand men, to face the Rhomaeans.

The Russians, Leo says, fought courageously and desperately, because the very thought that they might be defeated by the Rhomaeans and thus lose their reputation of invincibility was horrible and unbearable for them. The Rhomaeans, on the other hand, would find it shameful to be defeated by a people of foot soldiers, who had no understanding of horse riding.[61] Leo describes the battle at Durostorum in detail most of which appears to be presented more in harmony with some literary conventions than with the reality. He claims that the Scythians came out of the city in the moon-lit night to the field of battle to gather the corpses of their fallen warriors. They took these to the walls of the city and burned them there. As was their custom, they slaughtered many prisoners of war in honor of their dead. They also drowned infants and roosters in the Danube as sacrifices.

---

[60]   *Ibid.*, p. 138.
[61]   *Ibid.*, pp. 140–1. We know from other sources that the Russians won much martial renown in Great Scythia after their victories over the Khazars, the Kashogians and the Jasians. It is at first blush puzzling that Leo thought the Russians only fought on foot. This was true of these Russians who lived in the Tauric Peninsula and other areas of (Inner) Russia, not of the Russians of Outer Russia. Also, as we saw Svjatoslav had brought his troops from the Crimea in ships. This may explain the absence of cavalry.

Our author took the opportunity to tell his readers more about these Scythians:

> It is said that the Scythes preserve faithfully the religious customs (orgies) of the Hellenes in that they offer in their fashion to the deceased bloody victims and drinks. They had been instructed in this either by their wise men Anacharsis or Zalmoxis or by the followers of Achilles. In fact Arrianus claims in his Periplus that Achilles, Peleus' son, was a Scythian from the small town of Myrmecion at Lake Maeotis. Because of his reckless, crude, and arrogant behavior he was expelled from Scythia and settled in Thessaly. As clear proof of the truthfulness of this information is his dress, which was a cloak held by a clasp, his habit of fighting on foot, further his reddish hair, his shiny eyes, and finally his madness, savagery, and cruelty. These character traits were praised by Agamemnon who said: "Forever quarrelling is dear to your heart, and wars and battles." (*Iliad*, I.177) Till this day the Tauroscythes preserve the custom of settling their litigations by murder and blood. The blessed Prophet Ezekiel is one of the many witnesses that these people are bold, warlike, violent, and a threat to all neighboring peoples. He says: 'Behold I will set against thee Gog and Magog, the prince of the Rhōs.'[62]

As we see, Leo made use of the ancient Greek and Hebrew literary traditions in "describing" the Russians of his day. He was not the first to see the Slavs in this manner, for he was preceded by several Christian and Muslim observers.

At day-break Svjatoslav called his leading men to a council which, Leo says, is called *comentus* (a distortion of *conventus*) in their language,[63] to deliberate what course of action to take. Some spoke in favor of a retreat. Sighing, Svjatoslav rose to speak:

> If we were now to yield shamefully before the Rhomaeans, gone would be the glory earned by the Russian arms as we had effortlessly overpowered all the neighboring peoples and had conquered entire countries. Let us therefore take the courage of our ancestors as a model and let us reflect upon the fact that the Russian power has remained invincible until this day and let us carry the fight for our freedom to the end. We are not accustomed to return to our

---

[62]   *Ibid.*, p. 150.
[63]   This Latin word was borrowed by the Russians and other Slavs from their Romance-speaking neighbors, the Vlachs.

homeland as runaways from battle but either to come back as victors or to die a glorious death, after we had shown our heroic courage by deeds.[64]

Of course Leo had no transcript of Svjatoslav's speech to his followers. He put into his mouth such sentiments as seemed to him to correspond best to the reputation the Russians had in the Pontic basin in the tenth century. News of their conquests must have been common knowledge. From Rhomaean, and, we shall see Muslim, sources we may surmise that these conquests were impressive by their geographical scope.

Reportedly, no Russian had yet been captured alive by his enemies, because when all hope of escape is gone they kill themselves, believing that if they were killed by their enemies their souls would have to serve their murderers in Hades. The Scythians abhor such slavery. Imaginative scholars read Valhalla rather than Hades and adduce this alleged Scythian belief as further evidence that the Russians belonged to the Germanic race.[65] Let us remember that knowledge and superstition travel over hill and dale unhindered by ethnic and linguistic boundaries. Of course there were Scandinavians as well as warriors of Germanic, Finnic, Turkic, and possibly Caucasian nationality in Svjatoslav's camp. We must keep in mind that since the Trojan War there had hardly been a major conflict in North Central Eurasia for which we could safely say that it involved only two nationalities. Since most warlike undertakings in Great Scythia had always involved men of different races, nationalities, and languages, let us assume that Svjatoslav's invasion of Bulgaria and his battle with the Rhomaeans, who themselves were of extremely mixed parentage, were no exception.

On July 24, 971, as the sun was about to set, the Russians issued from Durostorum for a final showdown with the Rhomaeans. After he had depicted the battle in language and images borrowed from works of the ancient Greeks, Leo turned to Christian superstition of his time. As the battle was in full

---

[64]   Leo the Deacon, p. 151.
[65]   *Ibid.*, pp. 151–2; for a standard Germanic interpretation, *see*, Kunik, *op. cit.*, pp. 445–96.

swing and the Rhomaeans had begun to slacken, he writes, a storm rose bringing dust and rain over the armies. Then suddenly a rider on a white horse appeared, urging the Rhomaeans to attack the Scythians. The horseman broke the line of the enemy and confounded them totally. Then he vanished without being seen from near by anyone in the army. The emperor sent scouts to look for him, so that he might reward him for his services, but they could not find him. Therefore, it is believed that he was the great martyr Theodorus who had come to help the emperor and his soldiers. On the eve of the battle a young woman of Byzantium had seen in her dream the Mother of God ordering Theodorus to go to Durostorum to help John Tzimisces defeat the Scythians. He obeyed and the young woman awoke.

This is one of the many battles won for the East Roman Empire against its enemies by the Virgin Mary, whom Christian writers often called the Chief strategist. She is said to have acted against the Slavic fleet that besieged Constantinople in 626, then through her stole against the Russian fleet in 860, and finally, she sent Theodorus to Bulgaria to protect her chosen people against the Hellenes from Russia.

The Rhomaeans were encouraged by Theodorus to push for total victory over the Russians. The latter retreated from the field of battle before the Rhomaean cavalry pursuing them to the city's walls. We are told that the Rhomaeans won a complete victory. On the field of battle lay fifteen thousand five hundred dead Russians. Svjatoslav himself was wounded. The Rhomaean losses were only three hundred fifty dead, a high number of Christian casualties, considering that St. Theodorus had fought on their side.

On the next day Svjatoslav sued for peace. He promised to surrender Durostorum to the Rhomaeans, to release the prisoners of war, and to leave Bulgaria. The Rhomaeans should let his forces pass unhindered and not to attack them with Medic fire. They should also give them some food for the road. Trade relations between the two peoples should resume. The emperor agreed to these conditions. Each soldier was given two measures of wheat and the number of men was 22,000. Leo calculated that 38,000 had been killed in Bulgaria, because 60,000 had come from Tauroscythia (the Crimean Peninsula) to Mysia (Bulgaria).

To ratify the agreement the two leaders met at the bank of the Danube. The emperor came on horse, shining with gold and purple, and accompanied by resplendent riders, while Svjatoslav arrived in a Scythian boat, perhaps a monoxylos. Leo was surprised that he rowed along with the other men as if he were one of them. Unfortunately, he describes the Russian king not as he was but in harmony with the image the Rhomaeans had of Achilles as a forefather of the Russians.

After the meeting, Svjatoslav carried out the terms of the agreement and embarked with his army on the homeward journey. But the Pečenegs, whom Leo calls a nomadic lice-eating people,[66] ambushed them and killed them all, including Svjatoslav. From the mighty Russian army only a few survivors reached home, which, according to Leo the Deacon, was on the Crimea.

With the Russians gone, John Tzimisces was free to dispose of Bulgaria as he pleased. He renamed Durostorum Theodoroupolis after the martyr who had helped him to victory, leaving a garrison in the city and returning to Constantinople with booty and captives. Among the objects taken from Bulgaria Leo mentions especially a beautiful icon of the Virgin Mary. The emperor finalized the annexation of Bulgaria by forcing Khan Boris II (962–972) to surrender the symbols of his sovereignty and imperial pretensions. These were a tiara with a purple border and studded with gold and precious stones, a purple cloak, and red shoes.

---

[66] Leo the Deacon, p. 157; our author took the expression *phtheirophagoi* from Herodotus (IV.109) or some other classical source and attached it to the Pečenegs because they lived in the same general region of Scythia once occupied by the original lice-eaters.

CHAPTER VIII

DĀR AL-ISLĀM AND RUSSIA

THE MUSLIM VIEW OF THE NORTHERN QUARTER

Today, Muslim peoples occupy the central belt of the northern hemisphere, from the Tarim Basin in Sinkiang to Morocco. Though numerous Muslim communities are settled outside of this zone (in Southeast Asia, South Asia, Subsaharan Africa, Europe, and the Americas), of interest for our topic are primarily the peoples of North Africa, the Fertile Crescent, Upper Asia, Asia Minor, Iran, and Central Asia, as well as the Muslims who once held Spain, Sicily, southern Italy, and Crete. With these the medieval Slavs and Russians had multifaceted and intimate contacts.

While the Muslims were capturing Persian and Rhomaean provinces in Asia and Africa, the Thracians, Macedonians, and Illyrians, now universally called Slavs, held all of the Balkan Peninsula with the exception of Constantinople and a few other cities. They enjoyed the possession of the Peloponnese and made frequent hostile and friendly excursions to Crete, other Aegean islands, and to Anatolia. They were at home in the Dardanelles, and, at the ancient and famous cities of Sestus and Abydus, they passed freely from Europe to Asia, taking with them, among other "commodities," captive Rhomaeans. Of course, countless Slavs settled on Rhomaean territory and served their emperor. We have no reason to doubt that perhaps the majority of Rhomaean refugees who fled from anti-imperialist Slavs to Anatolia also spoke Slavic either as their native language or as a *lingua franca*. Slavic was the chief language spoken in ancient and medieval North Central Eurasia. Along with medieval

Greek, called Rhomaean, it was the dominant language of the East Roman Empire. This fact is not clearly noted in the Rhomaean sources, which should not surprise us, for it was considered common place and unworthy of note. Also, at that time, Slavic was not a written language, but a speech of barbarians who opposed the Rhomaean state idea, and were considered by Rhomaeans as the enemies of "mankind." To complete the picture we need to adduce those Muslim authorities who clearly noted the equal status of Slavic and Rhomaean in the Rhomaean Empire.[1]

When the Russians entered history under the name which has since then been their national name their land was part of Slavia and they were Slavs. The name *Slav* was a collective designation used at first mostly by outsiders and perhaps by the Slavs living in the valley of the Sala(va) River. The Arabs borrowed this name from their northern neighbors. The Rhomaean form *Sklaboi (Sklabēnoi)* became *ṣaqlab* and *al-Ṣaqāliba* in Arabic, while the expression *Terra Slavorum* had an equivalent in the Arabic expression *Buldān al-Ṣaqālib*.

The East Romans, among whom the majority perhaps belonged to the Mediterranean racial type, saw the Slavs along with other northern peoples as the "yellow or ruddy" races. The Arabs who were even darker than the Romans readily noticed the red complexion of Slavs.

The earliest dated mention of Slavs in the Arabic language is in the *Dīwān* of the poet al-Ahṭal, written between 685 and 705 at Damascus. Al-Ahṭal could have known Slavs personally, for many had settled in Anatolia and some even in the *Dār al-Islām*, in Syria. Like the Achaeans in Homer, who were "golden-haired," the Slavs appeared in this poet's verse with the epithet "fair-haired." In describing a crowd of people he says: "As if you could see them as a throng of fair-haired Slavs." They must have been a common sight for him to use their name as a metaphor. Other Arab writers noticed the light color of the hair and the red skin of the Slavs.[2]

---

[1] Ibn al-Faqīh, *Kitāb al-buldān*, BGA, V, p. 136; ŻADS, II.1, p. 23.

[2] *See*, al-Ahtal, *Dīwān*, ed. by P.A. Salihani (Beirut, 1891), p. 18, for the hair; and for the hair and skin, *see*, Ibn al-Kalbī, quoted by al-Qazwīnī, *Kitāb atār al-bilād*, ed. F. Wüstenfeld as *Kosmographie*, II (Göttingen,

In order to evaluate properly the Muslim sources on Russia, it is necessary to have as clear a picture as possible of how educated Muslims saw the region of the world where the Russians and the Slavs dwelt. The Muslims inherited two great ancient civilizations: 1) Roman Christian, itself a blend of the achievements of the various Afroasian peoples and those of Europe; 2) Persian civilization, shaped in contact and conflict with the peoples of Central Asia, South Asia, West Asia, and North Africa.

When the Koran was revealed many Afroasian peoples had already lived through centuries and millennia of communication with their gods. Muhammad acknowledged several prophets who preceded him in spreading the message of their deities. Elohim, Yahweh, and El had spoken through Adam, Noah, Moses, Abraham, and Jesus, and everything these prophets had originally said was the truth. Since people corrupted the sayings of the prophets, to guide humanity, Allah chose Muhammad as the final deliverer of his law, the seal of the prophets.

To a historian and geographer the Koran is an early medieval document which should be evaluated against the historical and geographical knowledge available to the common people and the learned of Southwest Asia and North Africa at that time. Tough it is replete with allusions to past events, remarkably little of the vast amount of such knowledge is incorporated in the sacred book of the Muslims. Europe and Russia are not mentioned because they lay beyond the field of vision of the conveyor of the divine message and his audience. Nevertheless, the Muslims' attention was drawn to the northern quarter and especially to the dam that is to burst on Judgment Day.

The dam was built by *Dhū 'l-qarnain* "the two-horned" king (identified by all with the Macedonian king Alexander the Great), to keep out *Yājūj wa Mājūj* "Gog and Magog." Gog and Magog had entered the Koran both from Hebrew and Christian

scriptures and from folk legends about the first truly universal
monarch, Alexander the Great. Sura XVIII: 83–101 says:

> They ask thee concerning
> Zul-qarnain. Say,
> "I will rehearse to you
> Something of this story."
>
> .
>
> .
>
> .
>
> Then followed he another way
> Until, when he reached
> (A tract) between the two mountains.
> He found, beneath them, a people
> Who scarcely understood a word.
> They said: "O Zul-qarnain!
> The Gog and Magog (people)
> Do great mischief on earth:
> Shall we then render thee
> Tribute in order that
> Thou mightest erect a barrier
> Between us and them?
> He said: "(The power) in which
> My Lord has established me
> Is better (than tribute):
> Help me therefore with strength
> (And labour): I will
> Erect a strong barrier
> Between you and them:
> "Bring me blocks of iron."
> At length, when he had
> Filled up the space between
> The two steep mountain-sides,
> He said, "Blow (with your bellows)"
> Then, when he had made
> It (red) as fire, he said:
> "Bring me, that I may
> Pour over it, molten lead."
> Thus were they made
> Powerless to scale it
> He said: "This is
> A mercy from my Lord:
> But when the promise
> Of my Lord comes to pass,
> He will make it into dust;
> And the promise of
> My Lord is true."

On that day We shall
Leave them to surge
Like waves on one another:
The trumpet will be blown,
And We shall collect them
All together.
And we shall present
Hell that day for Unbelievers
To see, all spread out,—
(Unbelievers) whose eyes
Had been under a veil
From Remembrance of Me,
And who had been unable
Even to hear.

Gog and Magog appear again in Sura XXI: 94–97:

But there is a ban
On any population which
We have destroyed: that they
Shall not return,
Until the Gog and Magog (people)
Are let through (their barrier),
And they swiftly swarm
From every hill.
Then will the True Promise
Draw nigh (of fulfillment):
Then behold! the eyes
Of the Unbelievers will
Fixedly stare in horror: "Ah!
Woe to us! we were indeed
Heedless of this; and, we
Truly did wrong!"[3]

The need to locate accurately the barrier or the iron gate of Alexander and to be aware of its condition is understandable when one considers that it will remain shut and unscalable until the Day of Judgment. Like their Hebrew cousins, Muslim eschatologists expanded vividly upon the tersely stated purpose of Yājūj wa Mājūj, as Gog and Magog are named in the Koran and in subsequent Muslim writings. Some connect their bursting out of the north with the reappearance of Isa (Jesus). The savage

---

[3] The English is from A. Ali's translation, 2 vols. (Cairo, 1938).

hordes will be so numerous that they will drink up all the water of the Euphrates and Tigris, or just Lake Tiberias. Having killed all the inhabitants of the earth (fortunately only of that portion known to the eschatologists), they will shoot arrows against heaven. Thereupon, Allah will intervene personally by sending worms into their nostrils, necks, and ears which will kill them all in one night. The smell of the putrefying flesh of Yājūj wa Mājūj will fill the earth. Other writers make Allah send birds to pick Yājūj wa Mājūj up and drown them in the sea. Some imagined these people as cannibals. Most believed that they lived someplace in the Caucasus or beyond the mountains of Armenia and Azerbaijan. Like captured criminals, the horrible people work every night to break out of their confinement. They dig a tunnel under the wall and the sound of their tools is heard by the neighboring people. However, every morning Allah repairs the breach they had made in the night.

Local inhabitants near the chief passes from Russia to Southwest Asia, who may have no basis other than their interpretation of the Koran, believe that Alexander had built a dam or gate in this region. Some see it as a 50-mile long 29-foot high wall near Derbent. Others believe it to be near the city of Kars in modern Turkey, still others maintain that it was close to Astrakhan, where the Volga empties into the Caspian Sea.

Regardless of the exact location of the Iron Gate, Gog and Magog, as they were understood by the Muslims, were close neighbors of the Russians.[4]

Like their Afroasian predecessors, from whom they acquired the knowledge of geography,[5] Muslim writers divided the inhabited world into three parts: Europe, Africa, and Asia, while some used a fourfold division. Thus Ibn Khurdādbih, who used the latter, distinguishes: 1) Arūfa (Europe), where he lists al-Andalus (Spain), al-Ṣaqālib (Slavia), al-Rūm (Rhomania), Firanja (the Frankish Empire), and Tanja (North Africa)[6]; 2) Lūbiya (Libya, the Greek name for Africa, which contained

---

[4] Ali, *op. cit.*, I, Appendix VII, pp. 760–5; Anderson, *op. cit.*
[5] Kimble, *op. cit.*, ch. 3.
[6] The name comes from the Roman province of Mauretania Tingitana; Tanja extended as far as Egypt; the name survives as the name of the city of Tangiers.

Egypt), al-Qulzum, al-Habaša (Aethiopia), and the Berber regions which stretched to the South Sea; 3) Ityufiya, comprising Tihāma, Yemen, Sind, India, and China; and 4) Isqūtiyā (Scythia), comprised of Armenia, Khorasan, Turkia, and Khazaria.⁷

The name *Isqūtiyā* "Scythia" comes from ancient geographical works, not from medieval reality. It corresponds to Ptolemy's Scythia Intra Imaum. Another Muslim geographer, al-Khuwārizmī, took from Ptolemy or from other ancient geographers the names Germania and Sarmatia. Germania, he states, "is now [ninth century] called Slavia; Sarmatia [sc. Europaea] is called Burjān [Bulgaria], Sarmatia [sc. Asiatica] is called al-Lān [Alania]."⁸

Of interest for our topic is the fact that educated Muslims who lived during the centuries prior to the emergence of Russia as a Christian polity, believed that the whole northern region of Eurasia which stretched between Khazaria and the Western Sea, including Germany, Scandinavia, and the various real and imaginary islands in that sea, was the domain of the Slavs. The following passage shows that the Muslims thought all northern Europe was part of Slavia and that beyond Slavia there was nothing. Ibn Khurdādbih says:

> Concerning the sea which is beyond the Slavs (al-Saqāliba) the city of Tuliya is located on its shore. Neither ships nor small boats ever cross that sea and nothing ever comes from that sea.⁹

The sea which Ibn Khurdādbih thought washed the northern and western coasts of Slavia was the imaginary northern ocean, called also the Amalchian Sea or the Scythian Ocean by ancient geographers. Tuliya is the fabulous and unidentifiable Thule, which some scholars identify with Denmark.

Slavs and Russians were a common sight in the Umayyad and Abbasid caliphates, both as enemies and trade partners. The

⁷ Ibn Khurdādbih, *Kitāb al-Masālik wa-'l-mamālik*, BGA, VI, p. 155; ŻADS, I, p. 79.

⁸ Al-Khuwārizmī, *Kitāb ṣūrat al-arḍ*, ed. H.v. Mžik (Leipzig, 1926) (=*Bibliothek arabischer Historiker und Geographen*, III), p. 105; ŻADS, I, p. 23.

⁹ *Op. cit.*, BGA, VI, p. 93; ŻADS, I., p. 69.

ethnonym Slav was frequently used as a general designation for Europeans and occasionally synonymously with whites. One of the most productive Arab poets of the ninth century, al-Jāḥiẓ, an African slave, had much to say about the Slavs. In his day in Iraq there were two kinds of slaves, Zanj and Slav, or black and white. It is clear that the term Zanj signified any negroid person, be they from Sudan, Ethiopia, or any other region of Africa, while the term Slav stood for a white person. Even though the Muslims usually distinguished at least three groups among the white race—Rhomaeans, Franks, and Slavs—the Slavic name frequently stood for all Europeans. The following passage shows this:

> Tell me, when did men belong to a single people speaking one language? How many generations after was Zanj made black, Slav white?[10]

Al-Jāḥiẓ made a curious observation about the racial characteristics of white slaves in contrast to black ones, his own group. He states that if one takes two Slav brothers, born of the same mother and father, and if one is castrated, the other not, that the eunuch becomes a better worker, is more inventive, capable to perform varied tasks, and is in general more eloquent and intelligent. On the other hand, his uncastrated brother remains a typical Slav, which is stupid, clumsy, rude, and awkward with the language. Concerning Ethiopian, Nubian, and other black eunuchs it has been observed that they gain nothing through castration, rather their abilities and intellect diminish in relation to their uncastrated brothers. It is clear from al-Jāḥiz' observation that in the Abbasid caliphate the name Slav stood for all white or European eunuchs, and in opposition to the Zanj, black eunuchs.[11] When the poet flourished, the caliphal throne was occupied by al-Mutawakkil (847–61), a son of a Slavic slave woman.

That Muslim writers considered the Slavs a leading European people is also shown by the list of titles of kings of the nations of the world given by Ibn Khurdādbih, where Europe is

---

10   Al-Jāḥiẓ, *Kitāb al-tarbī`*, ŹADS, I, p. 171.
11   *Idem, Kitāb al-Khayāwan*, ŹADS, I., p. 162.

represented by Rhomania, whose king is called Caesar, and by
the Slavs, whose king is called *knāz* (Russian *knjaz*).[12] The same
author says that Rhomania, Bulgaria, and Slavia are situated
north of al-Andalus (Spain). He does not mention any other
European kingdom. This writer also names the countries from
which merchandise is brought to Baghdad, called the navel of
the earth by some Muslim writers. From the Western Sea are
brought eunuchs of Slavic, Rhomaean, Frank, and Lombard
nationality and slave girls of Rhomaean and Andalusian origin.
Furs and other commodities are also listed.

The Muslim geographers inherited from their Afroasian,
Balkan, and Roman predecessors the confusion about the Black
and Caspian seas, their connections with each other and with the
Circumambient Ocean. Since they had no first-hand information
about the northern shores of these seas, they were unable to
improve upon the imperfect knowledge of the ancients. This
contributed much to the vagueness which informs their writings
on North Central Eurasia. Like Herodotus among the ancients,
Ibn Ḥawqal stood out among the medieval geographers who
firmly believed that the Caspian Sea was isolated from other
seas.[13] Although al-Mas'ūdī believed that all the seas
communicated with the Circumamabient Ocean, he argued
against the belief that the Caspian was in contact with the Sea
of Azov and the Black Sea, offering as proof a description of
how the Russians came from the Black Sea by ships to raid the
Muslim peoples along the coasts of the Caspian.[14]

Since the Caspian Sea and its coasts were the theater of early
Russian history, we should try to understand how medieval
Muslim writers saw that body of water. In antiquity it had been

---

[12] Ibn Khurdādbih, *op.cit.*, BGA, VI, p. 5; ŻADS, I, p. 67. We might
consider the Khazars a European people also; their king was called kagan,
as were the kings of other Turkic people and occasionally those of Russian
Slavs.

[13] *Kitāb ṣūrat al-arḍ*, BGA, pp. 386–9; French transl., II, pp. 377–9.

[14] Al-Mas'ūdī, *op. cit.*, *passim*, applies several names for these two seas,
which he saw as one sea and at times uses only one name for both seas. He
and other Muslim writers call them the Roman Sea, *al-Baḥr al-Rūm*. The
Black Sea was also known as the Russian Sea. The more common name for
the Azov Sea is *Māyutis*, which comes from the Maeotis; the Black Sea was
called *Buntus*, from Pontus.

named the Hyrcanian Sea after the Hyrcani and after the Caspii
the Caspian Sea. Al-Mas'ūdī calls the Caspian the Barbarian
Sea, saying that it was also named after the peoples who
inhabited its coasts. In Muslim sources it was most frequently
called *al-Bahr al-Khazar* "Khazar Sea." Al-Mas'ūdī named
specifically the peoples of Gīlān, Daylam, Jurjān, and Tabaristan.[15] Medieval Slavic writers called the same sea *More
Xvalinskoe*, after the land and people called Xvārēzm in middle
Persian.

When al-Mas'ūdī wrote, the Caspian Sea was still in the
imagination of the peoples of West Asia and North Africa a
believable habitat of monsters and of course of Gog and Magog.
Thus, our author reports a belief that this sea gives birth to the
monster called *tinnīn*. He says that the Mediterranean also
produces the same monsters, the Atlantic abounds in them, but
that they are unknown in the Indian Ocean. Some believe the
monster is merely a black wind, which, born at the bottom of the
sea, rises into clouds to cause destruction to humans and nature.
Others believe it to be a serpent-like sea monster, which comes
out of it to cause destruction on land. Carried by clouds to the
land of Gog and Magog it is killed there by hale. Its meat then
serves as food for Gog and Magog. According to still another
opinion, the *tinnīn*, born in the desert, is a serpent, and since
there are white as well as black serpents, there are white and
black *tanānīn*. The monster is called *ajdaha* by the Persians.[16]

Al-Mas'ūdī questioned merchants, sailors, and ship captains
about a connection between the Caspian and the Black seas, but
none could tell anything concerning such connection, affirming
that the sea had been navigated by fishing boats and ships of
commerce until the coming of the Russians. The raiders did not
come to the Caspian by a supposed gulf of the Black Sea, but by
way of the Volga River. The Russian invasion of the Caspian
coasts took place after 300 AH (912–13 AD).[17]

---

[15] *Murūj al-dhahab*, ¶ 281.
[16] *Murūj al-dhahab*, ¶ 281–8. In Slavic folklore the monster called
aždaha, clearly a borrowing from Persian, is a common phenomenon.
[17] For al-Ya'qūbī's view of the Caspian Sea, *see* below, p. 364.

Muslim writers cast the origin of Slavs and Russians within the genealogies derived from the Book of Genesis. The Slavs were the dominant people in the western section of the northern quarter, the domain of Japheth, so most Muslim writers saw them as descendants of one of his sons and grandsons. Al-Mas`ūdī follows other Muslim writers in claiming that the Slavs descended from Japheth's son Gomer, while stating that reportedly the Bulgars (al-Bulghar), the Russians (al-Rūs), and the Slavs (al-Saqaliba) descended from Methuselah, Noah's grandfather, which would make them antediluvian peoples.[18]

Like the ancients, Muslim geographers, too, recognized seven climata, two of which are of interest for Russia. In al-Farghanī's work, beginning in the east, the sixth clime is occupied by the land of Gog (Yajūj), then Khazaria, and the Caspian Sea. This clime continues through Amasia, Heraclea, Constantinople, and, across Bulgaria, to the Western Sea. At the eastern head of the seventh clime was also the land of Gog, which bordered on the Turks. That clime continued along the northern shore of the Caspian to the Roman Sea (here the Black Sea) and across Bulgaria and Slavia to the Western Sea. The land beyond the seventh clime, extending to the end of the earth, was occupied by Gog in the east, then by the Turkic Tughuzoghuz, al-Babr (unidentified, perhaps, Tatars), Bulgars, and by the Slavs whose domain reached to the Western Sea and presumably to the Northern, since the Muslims do not mention any other people north of Slavia.[19] To be noted is the fact that during at least the first five hundred years of Islam, Muslim geographers did not know any Scandinavian peoples by name and were not aware of the existence and of the location of their land.[20] Only Ibn Khurdadbih mentions Tuliya as a place beyond Slavia where nobody lived.

Following the ancient Afroasian geographical convention, al-Mas`ūdī says that six islands, inhabited by a Blessed people (*al-jaza'ir al-khalidat*), floated in the misty waters of the Western

---

[18]   Al-Mas`ūdī, *Muruj al-dhahab*, ¶ 296.
[19]   Al-Farghanī, *Kitab al-harakat al-samawīya wa jawami` `ilm al-nujūm*, ŻADS, I, p. 193.
[20]   A. Seipel, *Rerum Normanicarum Fontes Arabici* (Oslo, 1896—1928).

Sea.[21] In describing the earth, Ibn Hawqal states that on the north it was washed by the ocean whose coast was occupied by Gog and Magog. Going south, their neighbors were Slavs, followed by inland Bulgars, other Slavs, and the Rhomaeans.[22] We see that in the imagination of medieval Muslims the Slavs and the Russians shared the northern quarter not only with real peoples but also with Gog and Magog.

The Medieval Arabs viewed humanity in two main categories: Muslims and non-Muslims. Further, among non-Muslims there were two divisions: 1) peoples of the book, *Ahl al-kitāb*, which included, Jews, Christians, and any other people who claimed to follow a religion revealed through the spoken or the written word; 2) peoples without a book of revealed religion. When Islam appeared most of the northern coast of the Mediterranean Sea was held by Christians. Persia was dominated by Zoroastrians whom the Muslims named *al-Majūs*. Later, this term was applied to all non-Jews, non-Muslims, and non-Christian peoples living in the north and in other parts of the world, the same whom Christian Russians call *jazyčniki*, the English heathens. Since it is often misunderstood, it must be stressed that the term *al-Majūs* says nothing specifically about the ethnicity of the people to whom it was applied other than that they were either Zoroastrians or any of a variety of Eurasian or other peoples who followed neither of the known revealed religions. The designation definitely included the Slavs of Venedia and Antia, some of whom managed to keep their traditional religious beliefs until the twelfth century.

There are two additional reasons why the Arabs may have thought all northern peoples were related: 1) they all looked alike, being mostly blond; 2) they were neighbors and relatives of Yajūj wa Majūj, an unreal people descended, though, along with the real ones, from Noah's son Japheth. The fact that the domain of the Slavs extended from the Laba/Elbe to the Volga prompted the Arabs to tag the Slavic name onto other peoples occupying scattered enclaves within this area. Thus, al-Mas'ūdī calls the Nemčin of Saxony, ruled by King Conrad, thus un-

---

[21] *Murūj al-dhahab,* ¶ 187–8.
[22] Ibn Hawqal, *Kitāb Sūrat al-Ard,* p. 12.

mistakably Germans, a "Slavic" people,[23] while Ibn-Fadlān refers to the Volga Bulgars, a Turkic people, as Slavs.[24] Later, when the Muslims became aware of Scandinavia, they thought it was a region of Slavia. So, since the Slavs were an important group among al-Majūs of North Central Eurasia, their name was often used generally to designate pagans. Within this logic all European peoples, who belonged to no revealed religion, were blond, and lived in the north, could be considered as a kind of Slav, without being necessarily any more Slavic than were the Saxons under Conrad or the Volga Bulgars. We shall see that the Russian name was used by the early Muslims in the same broad sense.

THE RUSSIANS BEYOND THE GATE OF GATES

During the reigns of the four pious caliphs and the Umayyads the Muslims had no occasion to meet Slavs in battle on their own Slavic ground. Though we know generally that Muslims had numerous occasions to meet and battle with Slavic units in the Rhomaean forces in Asia and that they cooperated with free Slavs against the common enemy, the Rhomaean Empire, for lack of sources we ignore the details of this period of Slav–Arab relations.

Coming from the south, the Muslims conquered Iraq, Palestine, and Syria. Against Rhomania they established a *limes* running from Tarsus to Melitene/Malaṭiya. They began raiding Armenia in 640, conquering the country by 652.[25] Like other

---

[23]   *Murūj al-dahab*, ¶ 906.

[24]   Ibn Faḍlān, *Kitāb Aḥmad Ibn-Fadlān rasūl al-Muktadir ali malek al-Ṣakāliba*, transl. into Russian with a commentary by I.J. Kračkovskij (Moscow–Leningrad, 1939).

[25]   The conquered region known by the ancients as Armenia, Colchis, Lazica, Iberia, and Albania, were annexed to the Muslim empire, subdivided and renamed. In general, Muslim administrators did not preserve all ancient names. The names Colchis, Iberia and Albania disappeared, while the Armenian name continued to be applied to a vague area without clear political boundaries. Ancient Media Atropatene came to be known as Azerbaijan. New administrative entities emerged, named after such cities as Tiflis, Bardha, Baku, etc.

conquerors who preceded them in Transcaucasia, the Muslims found the Caucasus Mountains a formidable obstacle. The chief pass in the central Caucasus continued to be known by the Persian name of *Dār-i Alān*, modern Daryal. The Derbent Gate must have impressed the Arabs, for they named it *Bāb al-abwāb* "the gate of gates."

Surely, the Muslims approached the Derbent Gate with a feeling of foreboding. On the one hand it offered easy access to the north, on the other it was dangerous and better left alone, for beyond that gate lived Yājūj wa Mājūj. The Persian empire had been the gate keeper since around the middle of the sixth century. After the Arabs had conquered Iran and especially Armenia and Azerbaijan they came to the Derbent Gate. In Muslim sources the Russians were recorded under the name *al-Rūs*, the Arab version of the name Rhōs.

The Russians are not mentioned by name in the section of al-Ṭabarī's *Ta'rīkh al-rusul wa-'l-muluk* "History of the Prophets and Kings", which deals with Muslim conquests of Armenia and the extension of the *Dār al-Islām* to the Derbent Gate.[26] However, the Persian writer Bal'amī, in his condensed and translated version of Ṭabarī's work, which he completed around the year 963, mentions the Russians under the year 642, on the occasion of the first contact between the Arabs and Šeriar, the king of Derbent. When the commander of the Arab forces in Transcaucasia, 'Abd al-Rahmān ibn Rabī'ah, came to Derbent and asked the king to submit and pay tribute, the latter replied:

> "I am caught between two enemies, the Khazars and the Rus, who are enemies of the whole world and in particular enemies of the Arabs. Since we alone know how to fight them, let us fight the Russians instead of you exacting tribute from us." To this 'Abd

---

[26]   Born in Tabaristan in northern Iran in 839, Abu Ja'far Muhammad ibn Jarīr al-Ṭabarī died in Baghdad in 923. His principal work was the first universal history in Arabic. Organized chronologically, it runs from the creation of the world to AH 302 (915 AD). The original is said to have been ten times as long as the abridged versions. Ṭabarī is regarded as a reliable writer who had at his disposal numerous sources which have not come down to us. Just as Herodotus, the father of history, is the first historian of Russia when it was known as Scythia, so should Ṭabarī, who is esteemed as a Muslim Herodotus, be considered as a source on that land when it was known as Russia.

al-Rahmān replied that he had a commander above him whom he wished to inform regarding this matter. He sent Šeriar, the king of Derbent, with some of his own men, to Surrakh, who in turn promised to speak to the supreme commander, the caliph Omar. Omar approved Šeriar's proposal. It became the law regarding all keepers of narrow passes that they would henceforth pay neither tribute nor taxes, but instead they shall conduct war and keep the infidels away from the *Dār al-Islām*. And after the commander Surrakh himself arrived, all the passes made peace upon the same conditions, so that the Muslims are not required to keep an army in these regions.[27]

Adducing essentially two arguments, modern commentators believe that the king of Derbent could not have had the Russians in mind. Since the Russians in the quoted passage are called "enemies of the whole world," implying that they were a warlike people, they could not have been Russians because the prevailing scholarly opinion is that the Russians, as Slavs, were a musical, peace-loving people who avoided war. *Ergo*, the Russians mentioned by the king of Derbent could not be Slavs, but must belong to some warlike race. Second, because of the prevailing opinion that the Russian name in Russia can be traced only as far back as 862 or perhaps 839, the king of Derbent could not have known any Russians in 642.[28]

Both these objections ought to be rejected as methodologically untenable. We believe we have relegated the story of the supposedly musical talent and avoidance of war by the early Slavs to the realm of fable. If one were pressed to name an especially musical people who at the same time are complete pacifists one might select the Slavs only by denying the truth and suppressing the historical evidence. The argument that Russian history begins with the year 862 has no validity. The Kievan chronicler was able to trace it only that far because he did not have the sources which are available to us. If he had

---

[27]   *Chronique de Tabarī*, translated from various manuscripts by H. Zotenberg (Paris, 1871), III, p. 496. *Cf.*, al-Ṭabarī's version in *The History of al-Ṭabarī*, Vol. XIV: *The Conquest of Iran*, transl. G.R. Smith (Albany, N.Y., 1994), pp. 34–5.

[28]   These arguments, first eloquently expressed by Kunik in his *Die Berufung der swedischen Rodsen durch die Finnen und Slawen*, pp. 84–106, are still accepted by the majority of modern scholars.

access to the *Annales Bertiniani*, for instance, he would readily
extend Russia's past to the year 839 and beyond. If he had
Jordanes' work he would have surely recognized the Russians as
the Rosomoni and would extend Russian history to the fourth
century. If he had read Syriac he might have recognized his
nation under the name Harūs. Finally, had he known Persian he
would have accepted Bal'amī's passage about the Russians
beyond the Derbent Gate in 642 as historical truth. He might
have even derived some pride that his ancestors were considered
"enemies of the whole world," arguing perhaps that the Christian
and Muslim deities had chosen them to punish the sinners both
in Christendom and in the *Dār al-Islām*, just as Hungarian
medieval writers were proud that their ancestors, the Huns, had
been called upon by the Christian deity to perform similar tasks.

Although in Ṭabarī's survived version of the first arrival of
Muslims to the Gate of Gates, the king of Derbent does not
name his enemies, Bel'amī, or even perhaps Ṭabarī, was correct
to put the name al-Rūs into his mouth. It must have been
common knowledge around the Gate of Gates since the sixth
century that the Russians were "enemies of the whole world."
For example, the king might have known that under the names
Slavs and Antae, the Russians, or their close relatives, had
helped the Romans destroy the Goths in Italy and that later they
almost evicted the Romans from Europe. Also, in 642, he could
still have had fresh images in his mind of Slavic assault against
Constantinople which had taken place in 626. Above all the
Russians were an awesome people because they refused to
accept any revealed religion, waiting to lead Gog and Magog
into the final battle.

Other than the mythical peoples, such as Gog and Magog, the
Amazons, and others, the king of Derbent, speaking through
Bel'amī, had an impressive list of real enemies beyond the Gate
of Gates, yet he chose the Khazars and the Russians. The
Khazars were a real people and were actually enemies of the
king of Derbent in 642, so one should not question the
truthfulness of the king's statement concerning them. Therefore,
it is reasonable to suppose that the other people named were

also real.[29] None of the several other nomadic nations beyond the Gate of Gates, most of whom had, by 642 AD, been weakened by the Huns or conquered by the Khazars, such as the Alans, Sabirs, and Bulgars, were of much concern to the king of Derbent. Of the remnants of the Germanic peoples still wandering through Russia, we hardly have a word here and there, since they had been routed by the Huns in the fourth century and most of the survivors had fled into the Roman Empire. The small number of Goths and Heruli who remained in Russia could not be considered "enemies of the whole world." We are not even sure whether there were any pagan Germans in Russia at that time. The Heruli seem to have all vanished, while there were still remnants of those Crimean Goths whom Procopius had called Gothi Tetraxitae in the sixth century. They were Christians and, presumably, not "enemies of the whole world." Therefore, there is no ground upon which we should reject the statement of the king of Derbent, as recorded by Bel'amī, that in 642 the two chief opponents of Christendom and the Chaliphate beyond the Gate of Gates were the Khazars and the Russians.

But since some later translators of Ṭabarī's *History* replaced the name al-Rūs with those of Turks and Tatars, who in their day certainly lived beyond the Gate of Gates and were, in turn, regarded as "enemies of the whole world," some modern scholars, assuming that Tabarī's original version did not name the Russians, concluded that Bal'amī also inserted the name al-Rūs, current in his day, in place of another people who had lived there in 642.[30] During the century which claimed both Tabarī and Bal'amī, the Russians campaigned south and north of the Derbent Gate as well as in Tabaristan. Also, the Muslim world abounded in Russian merchants, mercenaries, and slaves. It is possible that the king of Derbent had used the names Slavs,

---

[29]　No one has argued that the king of Derbent could not have had the Khazars in mind, because, unlike the Slavic Russians, these Turks, are deemed to have possessed those warlike qualities which the Russians as Slavs, supposedly lacked. However, it must be remembered that the allegedly peaceful Slavic Russians in the course of less than a millennium conquered and annexed all the supposedly warlike peoples around them. The first to suffer this fate were the Khazars.

[30]　Kunik, *op. cit.*, p. 105 and note.

Rosomoni, Harūs, or one closely resembling the Slavic form *Rusye*, and that Bal`amī, updating the ethnonymic nomenclature, replaced these ancient names with the Russian name known well to his contemporaries.

Since we know that the people called Harūs lived there in late antiquity as neighbors of the awesome Amazons, that the Rosomoni whom Jordanes had called a "perfidious nation" lived in that region at the same time, that the mighty nation of the Antae also lived there, that they remained pagans until the eleventh century, that the Black Sea became known as the Russian Sea, that the Russians were an energetic people who eventually founded the mighty Rus' beyond the Gate of Gates, and that their descendants are its keepers today, we should believe the king of Derbent. Though Bal`amī does not give an exact location for their country, the Russians must have settled in an area stretching from the northern foothills of the Caucasus toward the Don. They ought to be counted as the ancestors of those Slavs whom the Muslims defeated during their war against the Khazars about a century after they were first mentioned here under the name of al-Rūs.[31]

Though the Muslims may have cooperated with the native peoples to keep control of the passes for them, they also tried to extend the *Dār al-Islām* into the northern quarter. After their first appearance at the Derbent Gate, Arab armies made several sallies through it aimed at conquering Khazaria. In 652, during one such campaign, the Arabs were badly beaten and their commander was killed in battle. Muslim forces retreated in disorder from the north, and for about forty years there was little hostile contact between Arabs and peoples beyond the Gate of Gates. In 722 AD, war broke out again, lasting about ten years with varied luck. In 730, the Khazars invaded Armenia and defeated Arab forces at Ardabīl in Iranian Azerbaijan. In retaliation, the Muslims, commanded by Maslamah ibn `Abd-al-Malik, invaded the north, capturing the Khazar cities Samandar and Balandjar. The next and last Arab invasion of the north was conducted by the commander of the Caucasus frontier, Marwān ibn Muhammad, the future as well as the last Umayyad caliph, Marwān II (744–50). This time the Muslims marched both

---

[31] *See* below, p. 356.

through the Daryal Pass and the Derbent Gate, forcing the Khazar army to retreat as far north as the Volga. Finally, the kagan sued for peace, converted to Islam, and Marwān left him in peace.

This last Arab invasion of Russia is significant for our topic. On their march to the north, the invaders from the south were joined by kings of mountain tribes from the neighborhood of the Derbent Gate, ancestors of the modern peoples of Russian Dagestan. Some of them may have converted to Islam, as did the Khazar elite. However, the Slavs of this region suffered a different fate. Marwān attacked them, defeated them, and transported 20,000 families to the *Dār al-Islām*.[32] Living between the northern foothills of the Caucasus mountains and the lower Volga and the Don, these Slavs were descendants of the Antae, Rosomoni, Harūs, and were identical with al-Rūs mentioned by the king of Derbent. They were the ancestors of the large communities of Russian Slavs whom later sources mention as native inhabitants of Khazaria.

Marwān was unable to annex Russia to the caliphate because the Caliphate itself was in disarray. Six years after his campaign against the Khazars and the Russians Marwān was assassinated, and thus came to a sad end the Umayyad Caliphate and the domination of Damascus and Syria in Muslim affairs.

To conclude, it is methodologically acceptable to treat the Russians mentioned by the king of Derbent, as reported by Bal`amī and perhaps by al-Ṭabari, as a real, historically existing people who in the middle of the seventh century lived north of the Caucasus. If Bal`amī were the only writer to mention them in this region for that period, we might be justified to doubt the truthfulness of his statement. But, as we saw, he was preceded by a number of authors who found there peoples whose names appear to be closely related to the name Russi. It is quite possible that from around the fourth century AD it had become customary to find the Rhōs beyond the Barrier of Gog and

---

[32]   Al-Balādhuri, *Kitāb futūh al-buldān*, ed. de Goeje (Leiden, 1866), p. 208; English transl. P.K. Hitti, *The origins of the Islamic State* (New York, 1916), p. 327. *Cf.*, D.M. Dunlop, *The History of the Jewish Khazars* (Princeton, N.J., 1954; reissued New York, 1967), p. 83; and Vernadsky, *Ancient Russia*, p. 260.

Magog which was usually identified with the Derbent Gate. Furthermore, the biblical Rhōs or Rūs were readily found there because there was a warlike northern people of the same or similar name. This people could only be that branch of the Slavs who were known as Antae by some, as Reds by others. The earliest attested progenitors of the name al-Rūs are the forms Rosomoni and Harūs, which appear to derive from the Slavic adjective *rusyj* "red," a cognate of the Greek *rhousios*. The native form **rusyj* converged with the form Rhōs from the Septuagint, itself a transcription of the Hebrew *rš* "head." In Arabic the name appears as *al-Rūs*.

THE ABBASIDS AND THE RUSSIANS

The forces which brought about the final collapse of the Umayyads were a coalition of Shiites, Iranian nationalists, and descendants of the Prophet's uncle, al-`Abbās. Abū 'l-`Abbās (750−54), the first Abbasid caliph, inaugurated in the Friday Mosque of al-Kufah in Iraq, is better known as *al-Saffāh* "blood-shedder." The white flag of the Umayyads was replaced by the black one of the Abbasids. Al-`Abbās was succeeded by his brother al-Ja'far (754−75) who assumed the title of *al-Manṣūr* "victorious by God's grace." He established the rule of the Abbasid dynasty for his descendants who occupied the throne in lineal succession until the caliphate and Baghdad were destroyed by the Mongols in 1258.

The Slavs appear obliquely in connection with the founding of Baghdad by the caliph al-Manṣūr. According to al-Ya`qūbī, al-Manṣūr remained in his capital city, Hašimīya, until the year 140 (757/8) when he sent his son Muḥammad Mahdī to fight the Slavs. The historian then continues to describe al-Manṣūr's journey to a village called Baghdad which he began to transform into the metropolis that it is today.[33]

Trade between the *Dār al-Islām*, with Baghdad as its capital, and Slavs and Russians continued to be carried on along tradi-

---

[33]   Al-Ya`qūbī, *Kitāb al-Buldān*, BGA, VII, p. 237; French translation by G. Wiet (Cairo, 1937); for a Rhomaean look at the Muslim−Slav conflict, *see*, Theophanes Confessor, *Chronographia*, p. 428.

tional sea and land routes. Especially remarkable were the Slavic communities of settlers, merchants, mercenaries, and slaves in Muslim Sicily and Muslim Spain.[34] Slavic navies and pirates operated throughout the Mediterranean, frequently clashing with Muslim navies and merchant vessels. Except for occasional hostile maneuvers along the coasts of Croatia in the middle of the ninth century and the capture of the Rhomaean-held Salonica in 904, Muslim naval forces stayed away from Slavia's territorial waters. Neither the forces obeying the Abbasid caliphs nor any other Muslim army ventured through the Gate of Gates to wage war on the Russians.

THE PSEUDO-RUSSIANS AT SEVILLE

We saw that in the Muslim imagination North Central Eurasia was the domain of pagans whom they frequently named Slavs and, as we shall see, Russians. Therefore, it is often impossible to interpret accurately such ethnonyms as appear in the texts of medieval Arab and Persian writers. Only when we can compare their information with other sources are we able to establish which people is to be understood by the ethnonyms Slav or Russian. The medieval Muslims used these appellations specifically to designate Slavs as Slavs and Russians as Russians and generally to indicate European pagans, *al-Majūs*. Keeping this fact in mind we readily recognize that the "Russians" who attacked Seville in 843/4 were, in fact, Germanic Men of the North, not Slavs. In order to understand who these attackers were, it is useful to sketch the main developments in the relations between the South and the North in western Europe leading up to the attack on Muslim Seville.

The Franks in Germany and Gaul were the territorial and, to some extent, cultural heirs to the Romans. The defunct empire had bequeathed to its successor state in the west centuries-old hostilities toward the peoples of the North in western Europe. The Franks themselves, along with the Burgundians, Alemanni,

---

[34] Ibn Ḥawqal, *Kitāb Ṣūrat al-arḍ*, pp. 110, 119; *see* further, V. Lamanskij, *O slavjanax v Maloj Azii, v Afrike i v Ispanii* (St. Petersburg, 1859).

and other barbarian invaders of Romania, had participated in the conflict on the side of the North until they conquered their southern opponents. Once they had accepted Christianity, the Franks could not live at peace with their heathen neighbors across the Rhine, becoming determined to visit upon them either death or salvation.

The medieval phase of South–North hostilities between Christendom and heathendom in northwestern Europe began in 521 with an invasion of Gaul from the sea by a fleet of men from the north. Gregory of Tours calls them Danes and their king Chlochilaich.[35] In *Boewulf* this invasion is the only verifiable historical fact, and the king of the invaders is called Hygelac, his people Geats.[36] In the *Book of Monsters*, composed around the eleventh century, the leader of the invading northerners is an unnamed king whose people are called Getae.[37]

After the Franks had brought under their rule their former kinsmen across the Rhine, they became neighbors of the Thuringians, Saxons, and Slavs. The Thuringians were attacked, defeated, and baptized by the Franks in 540. The Saxons resisted successfully as long as the Franks were ruled by the Merovingians. Once Charlemagne became king their fate was sealed, for he was determined to destroy that people.

In 772, the Frankish king marched into the heart of Saxony, aiming at the Irminsal, the chief center of Saxon religious life. The statue of the divinity was destroyed and gold and silver plundered by Christians. For thirty-three years (772–805) the Saxon people fought bravely for their lives and honor but were eventually defeated. Victorious, Charlemagne deported ten thousand Saxon warriors along with their wives and children, dispersing them in small groups through Gaul and Christian Germany. It is estimated that about a half of the Saxon people perished before the wretched remnant submitted to the will of

---

[35] *Historiae Francorum*, III.3.
[36] *Boewulf*, 435, 1202, and *passim*; *see* also, G. Storms, "The Significance of Hygelac's Raid," *Nottingham Medieaeval Studies*, XIV (1970), pp. 3–26.
[37] The Getae originally lived in the Balkan Mountains. Later they moved beyond the Danube into Dacia. Medieval writers did not always distinguish Dacia from Dania.

the Frankish king, accepting baptism and becoming one people in Christ with the Franks.

The Slavs of the Salava/Saale and Laba/Elbe valleys refused the Christian religion well into the eleventh century, long after their eastern neighbors the Czechs, Poles, and the distant Russians had accepted it. Naturally, countless Saxons crossed the two rivers into Slavia as escapees from Christian terror. Also, many took refuge in Denmark, notable among them was the Saxon chieftain Widukind, who, in 777, came to King Sigfrid in Nordmannia (the Frankish name for Denmark). The Franks followed, and, by 785, they reached the Eider River in Schleswig where they established a fortified frontier between Christendom and the free people of the North.

About the year 800, the throne of Nordmannia was occupied by King Godfred, an energetic ruler who tried to roll back Christianity. In 804 he came with a fleet and an army to the frontier of Saxony where Charlemagne was encamped, but the two opponents avoided a showdown. Charlemagne's biographer, Einhard, says that Godfred laid claim to Saxony and Frisia. Failing to recapture these lands for heathendom, Godfred invaded the land of the Obodrites, in 808. These pagan Slavs had sided with Godfred's enemy, Charlemagne, so the Danish king destroyed Reric, their capital city, and captured their king, Drasko. Then he began to build a *limes* to protect Nordmannia from the Christians. Called Danevirke, the defense consisted of a series of ramparts, towers, and other installations along the northern bank of the Eider River.[38]

Around 790, the northern peoples, chief among them ancestors of Danes and Norwegians, aided by refugees from Frisia, Saxony, and Slavia, began to counterattack the Christian lands by sea. In Christian sources the men and women of the North are called pirates, plunderers, etc., though they surely regarded themselves as avengers. The period from 790, when the first sea attacks of the Norsemen began, until the middle of the tenth century is called the Viking age in western Europe. The Viking

---

[38] Einhard, *Vita Caroli*, 6th ed. O. Holder–Egger, *MGH SRGUS* (Hannover/Leipzig, 1907), ch. 14; *idem, Annales Regni Francorum, 741–829*, ed. F. Kurze, *MGH SRGUS* (Hannover, 1895).

warriors came from Denmark and Norway, while Swedes did not take part in any appreciable number.[39]

The northerners who wished to visit the coasts of Britain, Ireland, Gaul, Spain, and Italy took the western way across the Northern Sea, which to them was the Western Sea. Those who desired to seek fortune in the east took the route across the Baltic Sea, which the Danes call Østersalt, the Norwegians Østersø. In Norse sagas this route is called *Austrvegr* "eastern way."

While Irish chroniclers differentiated the raiders of the shores of Ireland who came from the north and east by designating the Danes as *Dubb gaill* "black foreigners," the Norwegians as *Finngaill* "white foreigners," medieval continental Christian writers used the name *Nordmanni* for all pagans from the north who were also called Vikings.[40]

The first Viking raid against Christian Ireland took place in 795. The invaders were White Foreigners, who continued to attack the island. At approximately the same time that some Rhos men appeared at Ingelheim, the Viking leader Turgeis came from Norway to Ireland, where he captured Armagh, the chief center of Irish and western Christianity.[41] Turgeis has earned the reputation as the founder of several seaports, chief among which are Cork, Limerick, and Dublin. Christian England was first attacked by Danes in about 790. The raids continued into the next century, culminating in the establishment of a Danish kingdom in Northumbria. The Norsemen in Ireland and those in Britain tried to form one unified kingdom. Ivar of Limerick, who assumed power in 871, believed he had achieved this goal and styled himself *Rex Nordmannorum Totius Hiberniae et Britanniae*.[42]

The Norsemen, mostly Danes, increased their attacks against the Carolingian empire in 820. In 834–5, taking advantage of dynastic troubles, they intensified these attacks by launching a full-scale invasion of their Christian neighbors and enemies.

[39] G. Jones, *A History of the Vikings* (Oxford, 1968).
[40] *Ibid.*, pp. 75–7.
[41] Did he realize that he had avenged the destruction of the Saxon shrine by Charlemagne?
[42] *Ibid.*, p. 208.

Frankish sources allow us to follow their progress south along the Atlantic coast. In 834 the Norsemen destroyed Dorestad in the Rhine Delta, reaching soon thereafter the mouths of the Seine and Loire. In 841 they burned Rouen; in 845 Hamburg was destroyed and Paris sacked. French chronicles are full of vivid descriptions of atrocities allegedly committed by pagan Norsemen against Christians.[43]

French and Spanish chronicles record, under the years 843–4, a southward journey of a fleet of 150 ships from the North to Seville. The raiders sailed up the Garonne River, plundering its valley, then sailed south and raided the coast of Christian Asturias in northwestern Spain. They were repulsed and forced to continue their journey south to the mouth of the Guadalquivir River. They sailed up this river and took the Muslim city of Seville, save its citadel. After having caused much harm to the citizens, the Norsemen were defeated and forced to retreat.[44]

The next year, 845, the emir of Spain, `Abd al-Rahmān II, sent the poet al-Ghazāl on a peace mission to the king of the raiders of Seville. The Arabic writer, Ibn Dihya, the source on this embassy, says that al-Ghazāl was sent by the emir of Spain to the king of al-Majūs. The king, whose name is not given, reigned on a large island a three days' journey distant from the mainland. It had lovely gardens and was well watered. Near the island were other islands settled by al-Majūs. Ibn Dihya tells us that al-Ghazāl was well received at the court of the Majūs king. The king's wife, by the name of Noud, told the poet that the Madjus were ignorant of the feelings of jealousy and that their women were free to divorce their husbands at will. Nothing more is known about contacts between Muslim Spain and the king of al-Majūs.[45]

It is obvious that the raiders from the North, who are called Nordmanni in the Christian sources, are the same people whom

---

[43]   We should not accept these at face value. The men of the north were perhaps less bloodthirsty than were the Christians. It is known that men are more eager to kill when they believe that their killing serves a higher cause. The Norsemen killed for the earthly reason of revenge and plunder, the Christians for the greater glory of their god.

[44]   *Ibid.*, pp. 213–14.

[45]   *Ibid.*, pp. 214–15.

the Muslim knew as al-Majūs. The question whether they were Danes or Norwegians cannot be answered, for the terms Nordmanni and al-Majūs were applied generally to all peoples from the North who did not accept a revealed religion. Therefore, the raiders of Seville in 844, could have been either Danes or Norwegians or both. Further, they could have come not only from Denmark and Norway, but also from Britain or Ireland. Since Swedes did not participate in Viking raids, they and their country should be excluded from speculation. The fact that the Arabs believed that the al-Majūs kingdom was an island cannot be taken as evidence that it could not be located in Denmark or Norway which are peninsulas. In antiquity and well into the Middle Ages, Mediterranean peoples believed that the Scandinavian Peninsula was an island surrounded by several smaller islands. Besides, in Arabic, the same word is used both for a peninsula and an island.

Unable to answer the question of more specific origin of the raiders of Seville in 844, historians of Muslim Spain and of the Viking age are contented to call them "men of the north" or "fire worshippers." About two centuries ago, historians of Russia joined the debate because two medieval Muslim writers call these men *al-Rūs*. In the section of his work dealing with Spain, the historian al-Ya`qūbī says:

> The city of Seville is west of Algeciras and is situated on the banks of the great river that flows by Cordova. In the year of hegira 229 (844 AD) al-Madjūs called Rūs penetrated to that city, took captives, plundered, burned the city and killed the people.[46]

The quoted passage has been used as the basis for elaborate theories explaining why the attackers who raided Seville in 844, and were known as "the men of the north" by Christian writers were called al-Rūs and al-Majūs by Muslim writers. Some scholars offer this passage as evidence that the Russians were not Slavs but Vikings. Seemingly, the quoted passage appears to lend credence to the theory that in the Middle Ages the Russians were active from the Caucasus to Spain and that they were all of Scandinavian origin. In fact, al-Ya`qūbī's passage is regularly

---

[46]   *Kitāb al-Buldān*, BGA, p. 354.

adduced as evidence that all Russians were Scandinavians. A few dissidents maintain that in 844 Seville was attacked by the Slavic Russians. All scholars appear to hold the view that whenever and wherever the name al-Rūs in Arabic, Rhos in Latin, hoi Rhōs in Rhomaean, or Rus' in Slavic appears that it always designated one and the same people, be they Slavs or Scandinavians. Some see the almost simultaneous appearance of the Russians in different parts of the Mediterranean world as a momentous explosion of the northern seafaring peoples known collectively as Vikings in the west and as al-Rūs in the east. Al-Rūs and the Vikings are supposed to have been the western and eastern branches, respectively, of the same Germanic merchant-warrior-pirate race.[47]

The Men of the North who in the ninth and tenth centuries waged war on western European Christendom and occasionally against the Dār al-Islām were Danes, or Norwegians whom we call Vikings and refer to the centuries of their activities as the Viking age. In Christian propaganda they were demonized as heathens, taking the place of "Them." They were the same people whom al-Ya'qūbī calls al-Majūs. The question to be answered is why did he also call them al-Rūs. We offer our interpretation of al-Ya'qūbī's passage in light of his own information provided in the same book and on the same printed page. Following the passage on which so much scholarly attention has focused over the past two centuries, al-Ya'qūbī states:

> West of Seville is the city of Niebla ... Further west is the city of Beja ... West of Beja one arrives at Lisbon on the Ocean. Such is western Spain, that is, the part verging on the sea which communicates with the Khazar Sea (the Caspian).[48]

The ancient Greeks had such vague notions of North Central Eurasia that they easily imagined their heroes, such as Heracles, Odysseus, the Argonauts, and others, making swift journeys between the Black Sea and the Western Ocean. For instance, in

---

[47]   Kunik, *op. cit.*, II, pp. 285–320; for an analysis of the sources and the literature, *see*, Riasanovsky, pp. 214–25.

[48]   *Op. cit., loc. cit.*

his Scythian logos, Herodotus reports the tale of Heracles going to the Pillars of Heracles (Gibraltar) by way of the Caucasus, from Prometheus to Atlas, and driving back to Scythia the kine of Geryone, who dwelt on the shore of the Ocean near Gadira (Cadiz).[49] Al-Ya`qūbī, and, we shall see, other Muslim writers held beliefs regarding the distances between the Caspian and the Black seas and their connection with southern Spain that were quite similar to those of the ancient Greeks. In their imagination the Majūs whom they encountered beyond the Gate of Gates looked identical to those who came to Muslim Spain. So, they concluded that they must be of the same branch of humanity which they called al-Rūs.

We wish to corroborate this contention with information provided by Ibn Khurdādbih and al-Mas`ūdī. In order to identify the Russians more precisely, we must keep in mind that the name may have been used either specifically or generally. We saw that the name Slav had a general meaning of "European" among Afroasian Muslims. The question to be asked is, Did ninth-tenth century Arabs use the name al-Rūs in the same general sense in which they used the name Slav? We suggest that they did.

At approximately the same time as the "Russian" attack on Seville, Ibn Khurdādbih wrote that a people called al-Rūs were *jins min al-Ṣaqāliba* "a kind of Slavs." They were merchants, he says, and lists their usual merchandise and their customary itineraries:

> From remote regions of Slavia (*Ṣaqlabīya*) they [sc. the Russians] bring otter furs, furs of black foxes, and swords to the Roman Sea (Black Sea) where they pay a tenth to the Roman king. If they so desire they continue along the river Itil, the river of the Slavs (*nahr al-Ṣaqāliba*), and pass through Hamlih, a Khazar city, where the Khazar ruler takes a tenth. From there they proceed along the Jurjān Sea (the Caspian) to their desired destination. ... Some of them bring their merchandise by camel from Jurjan to Baghdad, where Slavic eunuchs serve as their interpreters. They claim to be Christians and pay only a head tax (*al-jizya*).[50]

---

[49] IV.8.
[50] *Op. cit.*, BGA, VI, p. 153; ŹADS, I, p. 77.

Some treat the above as a marginal gloss that insinuated itself
into a much lengthier text describing merchants called al-Rāḍaniya, a Persian term meaning "ones that know the roads." Al-
Rāḍaniya, whom all modern authorities consider Jews, used
three East—West trade routes between Spain and France in the
west and China and India in the east. Two of the trade routes
passed through Muslim and Christian lands. The third ran "behind Byzantium through the region of Slavia, to the Khazar
town of Hamlih" and on to China.[51] The third route seems to
coincide at least partially with that used by Russian merchants.
This coincidence has spawned amusing theories on the origin of
the Russians, the most recent being that the first Russians were
a monstrously large slave-trading company whose tentacles
stretched from Spain via southern France, Frisia, and the Baltic,
to Kiev.[52] Such interpretations must be rejected for they are
based on the apparent identity of pagan (or at most pseudo-
Christian) Russians and the Jewish Rāḍaniya.

The Russian merchants mentioned by Ibn-Khurdāḍbih were
not only a kind of Slav, but they also dwelt in that part of North
Central Eurasia where Slavic was the *lingua franca*. Naturally,
Slavic was one of the languages spoken also by the Rāḍaniya.
Nevertheless, we insist that regardless of whether modern
commentators, unable to tell Russians from Jews, lump together
al-Rūs and al-Rāḍaniya, a medieval Muslim would have to be an
ignoramus to confuse bookless fire-worshippers with a people of
the book *par excellence*.

The "Russian" pirates who attacked Seville were pagans, a
division of humanity to which the Russian merchants and the
Slavs of Venedia and Antia also belonged. We may ask, What
connection was there, other than belonging to the same religious
group, between the Russian merchants and the Russian pirates?
If we did not know that the "Slavs" along the Volga were really
the Turkic Bulgars and that the "Slavs" of Saxony were Germans, we might also wonder whether they were the same people.
We know that they were not and that the name Slav was applied
to them generally and loosely because they were members of the
same blond race as were the Slavs. This realization encourages

[51]   *Ibid.*
[52]   Pritsak, *op. cit.*; Gumilëv, *op. cit.*

us to propose that the Russian name may have been applied loosely and generally by medieval Arabs. That this was the case is demonstrated by al-Mas'ūdī, our second Muslim historian who mentions the "Russians" at Seville.

Referring to the events reported by Christian writers and by al-Ya'qūbī, al-Mas'ūdī states:

> Before the year 300 of the hegira (912/13 AD) ships arrived carrying thousands of men and ravaged the Atlantic coast of Spain. The inhabitants of Andalusia thought that these were al-Majūs who come every two hundred years to attack them and that they approach their country through a channel (*khalīj*) which communicates with the Atlantic Ocean, not through the straits where the copper lighthouses are located. As far as I am concerned, but God knows better, this channel runs into the Sea of Maeotis and the Black Sea and the assailants are the same Russes whom we have mentioned earlier, because these people are the only ones who navigate on these seas which communicate with the Atlantic.[53]

Al-Mas'ūdī was not surprised by the simultaneous appearance in the east and in the west of al-Majūs who looked alike. We saw that al-Ya'qūbī believed erroneously that the Caspian Sea communicated with the Atlantic. Al-Mas'ūdī follows the ancients in their error of imagining a channel connecting the Azov and the Black Sea, by way of the Northern or Scythian Ocean, with the Atlantic. Al-Mas'ūdī knew well that the Russians sailed on the Black Sea, which he called Russian. To reach Seville they would have to pass through the Bosporus, the Dardanelles, and of course the Straits of Gibraltar, sailing by the copper lighthouses that he mentions. Since they did not pass through the Gibraltar, he concluded that they must have reached the Atlantic Ocean from their home bases in the Black Sea and the Sea of Azov by way of what the ancients believed was a channel that connected these two seas with the Circumambient Ocean.

---

[53] *Murūj al-dhahab,* ¶ 404.

However, that al-Mas'ūdī did not believe that one single people occupied the land between Seville and the Black Sea is seen by his next statement:

> The general term Russi designates an infinity of diverse peoples; the most numerous among them, al-Lūdh'āna, come for the purpose of trade to Spain, Rome, Constantinople, and Khazaria.[54]

This statement confirms our thesis that the ethnonym al-Rūs was also used generally by Arab ethnographers. Our Muslim authors who mention the attack of al-Majūs on Seville, in 844, and name the attackers al-Rūs, do not contradict the western writers who said they were "Men of the North," whereby they understood Danes and Norwegians. The correct conclusion to be drawn from this apparent confusion of the Christian name Nordmanni with the Muslim al-Rūs is only that the two were seen as one ethnic monolith united firmly in the Muslim imagination by several common factors. First, both peoples belonged to the blond races; second, both lived in the northern quarter close to the domain of Gog and Magog; and third, both lacked a revealed book and were considered al-Majūs, that is, pagans. We saw that in Byzantium the same northern heathens were also called Rhousioi, hoi Rhōs, and Hellenes.

THE RUSSIANS ON THE RUSSIAN SEA

It remains to discuss to which particular group the name al-Rūs continued to be applied. Or, what was the *specific* application of the Russian name? To answer the question we must leave the west, where the name never became a self-designation of any group, and turn to the east, where it did. Our attention is drawn naturally to Scythia, which had been known for quite some time as Russia, and to the Black Sea, which according to al-Mas'ūdī, was also known as the Russian Sea, "because only they sail on it and they live on one of its shores."[55]

---

[54]   *Ibid.*, ¶ 458.
[55]   *See* below, p. 370.

Al-Mas'ūdī, who died in 956, and who is our witness that the name al-Rūs was used generally, in describing Khazaria, reports that the pagans who lived there belonged to several races, among these were Slavs and Russians. They burn their dead, and along with the deceased they also burn his horse, weapons, and his wife. These burial rites are similar to those which Ibn Fadlān saw on the Volga among the Russians in 921/2, and resemble funerary practices of Serbs, as described by al-Mas'ūdī.[56]

In the tenth century, the Russians also sailed on the Caspian Sea. After 300 AH (912/3 AD), about 500 Russian ships, each carrying 100 men, entered the channel of the Pontus (actually the Sea of Azov) which communicated with the Volga. Coming to the fortress of Sarkel, built by the Emperor Theophilus at the request of the Khazar kagan to control the traffic between the Don and the Volga, they obtained permission to cross Khazaria, promising to give half of their booty to the kagan. From Sarkel on the Don, the Russians, accompanied by cavalry units, portaged their boats to the Volga and continued downstream passing by way of the Khazar capital into the Caspian Sea. They plundered the Muslim peoples living along the coasts of the Caspian in the provinces of Gilan, Dailam, and Tabaristan. They reached as far as the city of Abaskum, on the coast of Jurjan, named so after the ancient Iranian city of Gorgan, near the present border of Iran and Turkmenistan. On their return journey they killed Muslim men, capturing their women and children. Then they retired to some islands off the coast of Baku to rest and enjoy the loot. The king of Shirwān sent a fleet to attack them, but again the Russians scattered it, killing thousands of Muslims. After they had spent three months raiding the domain of Islam, the Russians set upon a homeward journey by way of Itil. They sent word to the Khazar kagan asking him to let them pass, offering, as promised, half of the booty.

At this point the Muslim subjects of the Khazar ruler asked for a permission to attack the Russians to avenge their Muslim brethren. The kagan gave them permission but informed the Russians of it. The Muslim forces, joined by Christians, amounted to 15,000 men. They battled the Russians for three days and came out victorious, having slaughtered 30,000 of the

---

[56] *Murūj al-dhahab*, ¶ 906.

enemy. A remnant of 5,000 Russian men escaped in their boats
to the country of the Burtās where they, too, were massacred.[57]

Al-Mas'ūdī traced the journey of the Russians from the
Black Sea to the Caspian to show that the two seas were
connected only by the Sea of Azov, the Don, and the Volga. If
there were another connection, he argues, the Russians would
not have failed to use it, "because they dominate that sea (both
the Black Sea and the Sea of Azov) without sharing it with any
other people."[58]

Elsewhere al-Mas'ūdī names the various peoples living along
the sea's coasts at the time when his information was gathered.
These were the well known Balkan Bulgars, who were often
confused by Muslim writers with their conationals in the middle
Volga Valley. The Bajna, who cannot be identified, are followed
by the Pečenegs who moved to the Pontic basin in the middle of
the ninth century and finally the Magyars who left the Black Sea
region at the end of the same century. The Bajna, Pečenegs, and
Magyars were all of the Turkic race, says al-Mas'ūdī. They, as
well as the Bulgars, were not seafarers. He continues:

> *Al-Nahr al-Khazar* "Khazar river" [sc. the Volga] communicates
> by one of its branches further upstream with a gulf (*khalīj*) with
> the Sea of Azov (*bahr al-Mayutis* here stands for both the Sea of
> Azov and the Black Sea), called also the Russian Sea because the
> latter people are the only ones to navigate there. They live along
> one of its coasts. They are a populous nation of pagans (*al-Majūs*)
> who acknowledge neither revealed authority nor law. Their
> merchants carry on trade relations with the Bulgars. The Russians
> possess in their country a silver mine comparable to that which is
> in the Mountain of Banjin in Khorasan.[59]

The quoted passage shows that our author clearly saw Russia as
a paramount naval power on the Black Sea, therefore a country
verging toward that sea. When the above information was
obtained the Russian domain extended over a wide territory
needed to sustain a populous nation. On the basis of previously
adduced evidence, we may surmise that the Russians and Slavs

---

[57]   The Russian casualties should be reduced because the Muslim reporter
may have exaggerated them out of hatred of al-Majūs.
[58]   *Murūj al-dhahab*, ¶ 462.
[59]   *Ibid.*, ¶ 455.

dwelt in the Khazar land, both in the capital city and in the provinces. They shared with other peoples a huge area which ran from the lower and middle Volga Valley and from the northern foothills of the Caucasus to the Danube and the eastern foothills of the Carpathians. How far north their domain extended is difficult to ascertain on the basis of the evidence available so far. To exclude the Russians from this region and to settle all of them north of Kiev, as some modern scholar do, is to violate the letter and the spirit of Muslim and, as we saw, Rhomaean sources. At the same time, we must stress the obvious fact that the Slavs and Russians were not the only inhabitants of that land, but rather that they shared it with numerous other peoples, both nomads and settled agriculturalists. However, al-Mas`ūdī's belief that the Russians alone were masters of the Black Sea is not an exaggeration. When he wrote this the Slavs were the dominant seafaring power in the Adriatic; they disputed the Aegean with the Rhomaeans and the Muslims, and their merchant ships were a common sight throughout the Mediterranean from the Phasis to the Pillars of Heracles. In the Black Sea, their Russian cousins had overtaken the Rhomaeans as the chief naval power, and were strong enough to try to take by assault the seat of their empire. Of the other peoples who lived along the shores of the Black Sea in al-Mas`ūdī's day none cared to have anything to do with the sea. Among the notable exceptions we must count the territorial descendants of the ancient Tauri on the Crimea. All agree that the Tauri had vanished by the tenth century. However, their name reappeared as one of the several designations the foreigners used for the Russians.

In addition to Russian and Slavic peasants, merchants, and tradesmen who lived in Khazaria, the Khazar kagan also had mercenaries and slaves of Russian and Slavic origin. Many Russians and Slavs lived in the Khazar capital, which they called *Belaja Veža* "white gate." The city was inhabited by Muslims, Christians, Jews, and pagans. The pagans belonged to several races, including Slavs and Russians who lived in one of the two sections of the city. They burned their dead. When a man died his wife was killed and burned with him. Al-Mas`ūdī says that this was also an Indian custom. Elsewhere he states that the Serbs also followed this custom. Seven judges served at

Belaja Veža. Two for the Muslims, two for the Christians, two for the Jews, all peoples who had their revealed books to serve them in administering justice. The seventh judge served all pagans. He ruled according to *hukm al-jāhilīyya* "pagan law."[60]

[60] *Ibid.*, ¶ 451.

CONCLUSION

We have established that in the Early Middle Ages, the Rhomaeans and Muslims had contacts and conflicts with the Russians whom they saw either as one people, or as a variety of peoples identical or related to the Slavs and confused with the Men of the North, al-Majūs, and with Gog and Magog. None of the writers who dealt with Russia appears to have known the exact location and the extent of the Russian domain. Even the data recorded by the best informed among them, Constantine Porphyrogenitus, are vague and imprecise.

The results of historical processes in Ukraine and Russia, which archaeology can trace to the Stone Age, and history to the middle of the first millennium BC, became clear in mid-eleventh century AD, when the elites ruling the state called Russia by Arabs, Rhomaeans, and Western Christians decided to tell themselves and the world who they were. At that time, both the supreme political and religious authorities resided at Kiev on the Dnieper. The state's population was Slavic, but there were numerous other groups. In the north lived Finnic and Baltic peoples and in the south several peoples of the Turkic language family as well as the slowly disappearing remnants of the ancient populations of Great Scythia. Notable among the latter were the Goths, who survived into the sixteenth century as a separate group in the Crimea. In addition to these native peoples, numerous foreign merchants, mercenaries, and adventurers resided temporarily or permanently within the borders of Russia. Though many languages were spoken in the land, Slavic had been the *lingua franca* in Great Scythia since the seventh century, if not earlier. Church Slavonic, a literary language based on a Macedonian dialect spoken in and around the city of Salonica and written first in the Glagolitic then in the Cyrillic scripts, was the liturgical language of the Russian church and the official language of the state. Thus, regardless of its "original" ethno-linguistic character, Russia entered the Christian community of nations as a Slavic land.

Though the written records examined here provide valuable information on Russia, they are but weak rays of light beamed into the gloom of the northern quarter. We hope that our interpretation of this material has shown that Russia is not a sphinx, not an enigma wrapped in a mystery, to use a trite metaphor for that land and its people, but a natural landscape inhabited by real people, often hidden from outsiders behind the veil of their own ignorance and prejudice.

Even though we have demonstrated here that the ethnonym Russi is a color word and that the red color attribute reflects the people's *positio loci* in relation those who named them, Russia still looks at us as a sphinx from behind a veil. To understand Russia, to unveil the sphinx, we depend on native writers. We have examined these and will publish our findings in the near future, Inshallah.